CHRISTIANITY ENCOUNTERING WORLD RELIGIONS

*The Practice of Mission
in the Twenty-first Century*

TERRY MUCK
FRANCES S. ADENEY

Baker Academic
a division of Baker Publishing Group
Grand Rapids, Michigan

© 2009 by Terry Muck and Frances S. Adeney

Published by Baker Academic
a division of Baker Publishing Group
P.O. Box 6287, Grand Rapids, MI 49516-6287
www.bakeracademic.com

Printed in the United States of America

Library of Congress Cataloging-in-Publication Data
Muck, Terry C., 1947–
     Christianity encountering world religions : the practice of mission in the twenty-first century / Terry Muck, Frances Adeney.
          p.   cm. — (Encountering mission)
     Includes bibliographical references and index.
     ISBN 978-0-8010-2660-7 (pbk.)
     1. Missions—Theory. 2. Christianity and other religions. I. Adeney, Frances S. II. Title.
BV2063.M73 2009
266.001—dc22   2008051072

Contents

Introduction 7

Part 1 Context, Text, and Pre-texts

1 Context: The World of Religion Today 15
2 Text: What the Bible Says 32
3 Pre-texts: Theology and Personality 51

Part 2 Practices: Beyond Competition and Cooperation

4 Universality: Reaching Out to All, Including Christians 79
5 Fellowship: Belonging Precedes Believing 92
6 Localization: Focusing on Questions and Concerns of the Local Community 104
7 Commitment: Holding Ideas with Conviction; Acting Decisively on Those Ideas; Not Letting Those Ideas Be Divisive 115
8 Freedom: Honoring the Principle of Religious Choice 127
9 Effectiveness: Allowing the Context to Determine the Form of Witness 138
10 Consistency: Striving for Consistency between Methods and Goals 150
11 Variety: Communicating the Gospel in Many Forms 162
12 Respect: Not Disparaging Others in Order to Champion Your Own; Not Disparaging Your Own in Order to Respect Others 174
13 Charity: Loving Those to Whom We Witness 185
14 Missional Ecumenicity: Practicing Mission as the Joint Project of the Church 198
15 Jesus, Mission Innovator: Jesus's Model of Giftive Mission 210

Part 3   Method: How Do We Do It?

16   The Spiral of Knowledge Acquisition: Learning about New Cultures and New Religions   221
17   Experiencing: The Influence of Our Personal Histories   230
18   Bracketing: Putting Convictions on Hold   249
19   Encountering: Learning from a New Culture and Religion   263
20   Evaluating: Appraising the New Culture and Religion from a Christian Viewpoint   277
21   Integrating: Reshaping Our Own Views and Mission Practices   290

Part 4   Giftive Mission

22   Metaphors for Mission   303
23   The Four Gifts   329
24   Giftive Mission   353

Appendix: Biblical Interreligious Encounters   379
Bibliography   386
Index   397

Introduction

What is the Christian responsibility to people who already believe in and belong to another religion? How should Christians witness to people who are Buddhist, or Hindu, or Muslim, or members of some other religion?

We believe that Christian responsibility begins with giving witness to what God has done through Jesus Christ to offer us the gift of salvation. We believe that "giftive mission" is the form that witness should take in the twenty-first century. This book is an explanation of and an argument for giftive mission. This approach is necessary because our culture at large gives radically different answers to the question of what the Christian responsibility to people of other religions is.

At one end of the spectrum of these answers is the "do nothing" response. According to this view, Christians should do nothing regarding the spiritual disposition of nonbelievers. If Christians have any responsibility to adherents of non-Christian religions, it begins and ends with concern for the simple requirements of human well-being: food, water, clothing, shelter, peace, and justice.

At the other end of the spectrum of answers is the "wipe them out" response. Christians should spare no energy in eradicating the non-Christian religions of the world. Non-Christian religions and the people who follow them are demonic. We are fully justified in using whatever means necessary to accomplish this goal, including political power and warfare.

Like most end-of-the-spectrum answers to such questions, there is little subtlety to either the "do nothing" or the "wipe them out" responses. Some mission organizations offer more subtle versions of these responses, and many if not most take positions well distanced from either extreme. We will explore many of these positions in this book. But what is surprising, even alarming, in today's climate of tension among religions is that extreme, end-of-the-spectrum answers increasingly seem to be considered plausible by more and more people. Intellectually these positions may seem to be reductive stereotypes. Empirically, however, they are not. People believe them and act on them, to little positive effect and a growing list of negative effects.

We Christians desperately want to think we are still having a positive effect with traditional mission efforts. And it is not hard to produce evidence that seems to support that belief. Never before have more missionaries been sent to "foreign" fields: American missionaries, European missionaries, Korean missionaries, Indian missionaries. Tens of thousands of people convert to Christianity each year as a result of these efforts. Christianity is still the largest religion in the world, with almost two billion members.

But what do these numbers mean? Consider: never before have more Buddhist, Hindu, and Muslim "missionaries" been sent to "foreign" fields. Tens of thousands of people convert to Buddhism and Islam each year as a result of these efforts. Islam grew faster than Christianity in the twentieth century, and Buddhism has become a viable religion in both Europe and North America.

In fact, when Christian growth numbers are considered as a percentage of world population, for the last one hundred years the results of the Christian mission movement have remained stagnant. According to David Barrett and Todd Johnson in *World Christian Trends*, in the year 1900 Christians made up 34.5 percent of the world's population; in the year 2000, Christians made up 33 percent of the world's population (2001, 4).

And what do we do about these realities? We talk about the places Christianity is still growing and ignore those where it is either stagnant or in decline. We wax eloquent about growth that can't be measured or confirmed—house churches in China and background believers in the Muslim world—and pretend we don't notice the closing of national borders to Christian mission workers across the 10/40 window.

The growth of Christianity in the so-called southern world is indeed a wonderful story. But the status quo state of Christianity in the Middle East, North America, and Europe is a scandal. The lack of growth in Asia and South Asia is a nightmare. In those places where people have embraced an enduring world religion other than Christianity, we have had and are having little mission success.

Consider just one aspect of the nightmare: the Buddhist world. The Christian mission movement has failed in cultures with a dominant Buddhist element. Let's generously define failure as at least a century of mission effort that has resulted in less than 25 percent of the people in such cultures coming to know Jesus Christ as their Lord and Savior.

No predominantly Buddhist culture has ever been a Christian mission success, that is, with more than 25 percent of the people in the culture embracing Christianity.

Korea has come the closest. The most recent figures for South
between 25 and 30 percent of the population identifying themselves
tian. But if you add North Korean figures, the figure falls below our
threshold. Other Buddhist countries don't even come close. Consider
other Buddhist countries:

Country	% Buddhists	% Christians
Bhutan	78	1
Cambodia	86	1
Japan	55	3
Laos	43	3
Mongolia	23	1
Myanmar (Burma)	73	8
Sri Lanka	68	9
Thailand	83	2
Vietnam	49	9

Total the figures for these Buddhist countries, and you find that the Christian mission movement has resulted in an average of less than 5 percent of
the population in these countries embracing Christianity, despite almost two
centuries of mission efforts.

Lest we think that this is the norm for Christian mission efforts, compare
it with the results from two other heavily missionized parts of the world,
Oceania and Africa. The first Christian mission workers went to Africa in
the seventeenth century, and by 1900, 10 million Africans knew Christ, that
is, 10 percent of the population. By the year 2000, 360 million Africans had
become Christian, 46 percent of the population.

The first Christian mission workers went to Oceania, the South Sea Islands,
in 1843. By 1900 an astounding 76 percent of the population were Christian
(5 million people), and by the year 2000, 83 percent professed Christ, 25 million people.

A word about what "failure" means when we talk about Christian missions
is in order. To make our point, we have chosen to define success and failure
in terms of the number of people who become Christian. There are other
important ways to talk about the success or failure of Christian mission, ways
that, were we attempting to make other points, we would prefer to embrace.
Those other ways can be handily summarized by the word "faithfulness."
Thousands of Christian mission workers have gone to Buddhist cultures and
"succeeded," if by "success" we mean they were faithful to their calling and
proclaimed the gospel.

9

Korea have
as Chris-
failure
nine

uccess in this book as numerical success, we must
be many reasons why people have not come to
Buddhist cultures. Political conditions may not
in God's good timing that the gospel would
ose are the reasons that mission efforts have
nothing but continue to be faithful.
nsider other ways to present the gospel to Bud-
Hindu peoples and Muslim peoples—that may have a
of numerical success. Perhaps we need a new way, one that will
serve people's physical needs, a clear requirement of the gospel, but
that will also show them the Way taught to us by Jesus Christ.

The idea presented in this book is a simple one: Mission to peoples of
historically resistant religions could be made easier and more productive
with the addition of a biblical metaphor for mission, the metaphor of free
gift. Giftive mission, as we choose to call it, means that we are more than
conquerors of other peoples, more than harvesters of souls, more than win-
ners of metaphysical arguments: we are the bearers of gifts. We bring to the
world the greatest of all gifts, the story of what God has done for the world
through Jesus Christ.

Seeing our mission work through the lens of this metaphor changes more
than one might think. Giving a gift is a different kind of activity. In fact, the
history of Christian mission at its best is better seen through the lens of gift
giving: bringing the gifts of medical care, of education, of Christian community, as tangible expressions of the Gift that is Jesus Christ. And where
missions efforts are achieving success in the most difficult parts of the world
today—China, India, Southeast Asia, the Middle East—it is when, in addition
to medicine, education, and Christian community, they are bringing the gifts
of English-language instruction, business expertise, and fresh water development, among others, again, as tangible expressions of the Gift.

Many good things happen to us when we begin to see our commitment to
building God's kingdom through the lens of gift giving:

- We read the Bible better. Isn't the root metaphor of God's activity among
  us the metaphor of God's grace? We do not earn our salvation through
  fighting the devil or because of good deeds. We are given it by God.
  Grace. It is a gift (see chapter 2).

- We express ourselves better in our own culture and in our relationships
  with other religions when we replace the marketplace metaphor—the
  managerial competition with other religions—with the metaphor of
  bearing and receiving gifts (see chapter 1).

- We develop better theologies that are culturally sensitive but, more importantly, biblically faithful to the commands of witness when we see
  them through the spectacles of gift giving (see chapter 3).

- We do the work of mission better, without succumbing to the temptations of power and manipulation and triumphalism, when we ratchet down our pride and become gift givers and gift receivers rather than mini-saviors of the world. Wherever and whenever faithful mission has been done in the past two thousand years, it has been with a focus on certain gift-giving practices to the exclusion of others (see chapters 4–15).

Conversely, when Christian mission has been done poorly, it is because good practices were ignored in favor of bad ones. To give readers an idea of what we mean by bad practices, each of the practice chapters contains an "antimissionary" sidebar illustrating a bad practice, an example of how not to do mission.

We argue that by the simple emphasis of this biblical metaphor for describing mission we can better see what God expects us to do in today's world. Although giftive mission does not invalidate the other biblical metaphors for mission that have been used in missiological discussions for centuries (see chapters 22–24), global conditions today make it imperative that we bring our understandings and expectations of mission more in line with God's graceful actions toward us. We must become more than imitators of God's actions in developing personal lives of holiness; we need to imitate the way God acts toward the world in our mission activities. Jesus said that as the Father sent him, so he sends us. God sent Jesus as a bearer of the free gift of grace. We are also the bearers of that gift. More precisely, we are the bearers of the news of that gift.

Part 1

Context, Text, and Pre-texts

What resources do we have for answering the fundamental question: What is a Christian's responsibility to people of other religious traditions? We cannot just make up answers that seem to make sense. As Christians, we need to ground our answers in something that goes beyond human opinion.

One of the "givens" of answering this question is the world *context* in which we find ourselves at the beginning of the twenty-first century. Like all historical contexts, our time and place is unique. There has never been—and never will be again—a time exactly like this. Context is so important because any given context determines the problems we face. It would not be hard to make a list of the problems Christians face these days: Muslim jihadists, Asian religious competition from Hindus and Buddhists, the creeping rot of materialism in Western Christianity itself; these issues have become all too familiar, and each of them raises the fundamental question of this book: what should Christians do about other religions?

Of course, our primary resource for answering the questions set by our context is the Bible, a *text* that Christians the world over regard as sacred and holy. The Bible is not exactly an answer book. It was written at a time when the fundamental questions were somewhat different from those we face today, and it is obvious that the answers in the Bible were aimed at slightly different targets—at Osirian mystery religions, at first-century gnosticism, at Roman warlords. That does not mean that the Bible loses its place of primacy for us, however. We must interpret to arrive at longed-for answers, but the biblical text is the final guidance, the first and last resort for the Christian in any context. We go to it first for wisdom, and we go to it last to check our theories and strategies against what the text says.

The development of those theories and strategies depends on how we shape the issues our cultures present to us. They depend on the presuppositions our theologies steer us toward. They depend on very basic things like the personalities of the decision makers and how those subjective elements work together for God's glory. These *pre-texts*, the values and thought forms we bring to our reading of the biblical text, may seem like minor things when compared with the mighty acts of God in history—and in the focus of the big picture, they are. But we don't always see the big picture very clearly, and we have even less chance of seeing it if we neglect to factor in the unique gifts and desires we bring to the table of interpretation and understanding.

So to answer our question, we must begin by understanding the context, text, and pre-texts that inform and influence us all in one way or another. Once we have accomplished that task, we can move on to the work at hand.

Context

The World of Religion Today

Christianity has always been in contact with the world's other religions. The earliest Christians wanted to distinguish their faith from Judaism. Roman Christians in the first century both fought against and borrowed from the mystery religions of the day. Gnosticism of one sort or another seems to have prompted several of the apostle Paul's letters to the young churches he planted in Asia Minor. As Christianity spread throughout the Greek and Roman world, contact with Buddhism in the East, Islam in the Middle East, and indigenous religions such as the Celtic faith and other pagan belief systems in central and western Europe always led to vigorous Christian mission efforts among adherents of these other religions (Neill 1986). In one sense, Christianity has always existed in a religiously plural context.

Yet the religiously plural context in which Christianity exists today differs markedly from that of our forebearers. Radical changes in the political, economic, and cultural configuration of the world's nations make interreligious interchanges today different in both quality and quantity. Christianity engages the world's religions on a playing field leveled by a global economic market, relative religious freedom, and a communications network that makes the whole world a virtual neighborhood. In most places today, Christianity not only confronts the world's religions, but it also coexists with them. Hindus,

15

SIDEBAR 1.1
HOW TO UTILIZE THE CONTEXT IN MISSION

IDENTIFY BOTH THE GOSPEL AND CULTURE.	DETERMINE THE FORM OF MISSION.	ACT, KNOWING THAT MISSION IS ROOTED IN COMMUNITY.
• Giving: Do not take the gospel "out there" but determine how the gospel and culture enter into conversation in our own lives. • Receiving: Hear the gospel in a new way in each culture by asking how the culture can become a mission to us as the church. • Loving: Follow Christ in radical love. • Hearing: See each context as a chance to hear the gospel again for the first time.	• If people are hungry, give bread. • If people are sick, offer healing. • If people are despairing, bring comfort. • If people are confused about the meaning of life, speak words of salvation.	• Needed change can be fostered by allowing a fresh relationship with Christ to show the way in new situations. • Surrendering the old may be necessary to let new life be born in the church. • Find new directions for mission in painful or divisive experiences. • Imagine the Holy Spirit as the presence and power of God in the community.

Buddhists, Muslims, and Confucians are no longer strangers in our midst but residents in our neighborhoods—and, increasingly, we reside in their neighborhoods (Muck 1992).

These changes in the world's religious configuration are the occasion for this book. Both the context and the goal of Christian missions vis-à-vis the world's religions have either changed or been modified in important ways. Three idea clusters define this new mission context: we exist in an increasingly *free marketplace of religious ideas*; we do missions in a nexus of competing evangelisms resulting in what we might call *reflexive evangelism*; and the mode of Christian interchanges with other religions is to both *compete and cooperate* with them.

FREE MARKETPLACE OF RELIGIOUS IDEAS

An extraordinarily powerful and pervasive metaphor consumes our thinking and behaving these days. It is the metaphor of the marketplace. The marketplace is not just a metaphor in a literary sense, a helpful way of describing a complex idea (although it is that). The marketplace metaphor is a reality in every sense of the word and influences human interactions from the macro level of international politics to the micro level of interpersonal relationships. We literally think of the world as a huge shopping bazaar, and we act as if everything in our lives runs according to the "laws" of buying and selling.

So pervasive is the dominance of marketplace thinking that one could say the world is run by an ideology of economism, and the marketplace is the central metaphor of this ideology. Economism influences every aspect of our lives, including the way we look at the interactions among the world's religions. Religions have become commodities like any other, and religious people behave more like consumers than congregants. We buy a religion—and continue to purchase it—if it works for us. If it doesn't meet our expectations, we choose another religious or denominational product.

Marketplace Dynamics

This religious bazaar has been created by three influential dynamics: globalization, freedom of religion, and negative tolerance of religious ideas. Each of these dynamics has important implications for the way the world's religions interact with one another and the way Christian missionaries do their work.

Globalization has many definitions, but it usually refers to the idea that most of the world participates in a global culture (among others) connected by better and better worldwide communications, an increasingly interdependent economic system, a common way of thinking patterned on the scientific method, and a growing championing of democratic pluralisms as the default political form, a politics that relies on some form of capitalism as the economic system.

In the face of these dynamics, religion also becomes globalized. Although the development of a common world religion is unlikely, a common religious form is emerging that makes many aspects of the various religions less distinct. Religions now *look* more alike. As politics and economics become homogenized, the role religion plays in those cultures also becomes homogenized. No matter what the difference in the teachings of religions, people in our globalized culture increasingly look to their religions to be the meaning makers in ever more secularized cultures. Christians in America look to their religion to make sense out of senseless school shootings and other acts of gratuitous violence. Buddhists in Sri Lanka look to their religion to provide some sense of meaning amid a civil unrest that has consumed their country's energies for several decades. Religious people everywhere look to their religions to make sense of dilemmas in their world.

Globalization makes the generic category of "religion" a viable one for the first time in history. In the past, the abstract category of "religion" never made sense to people for whom religion could mean only one thing: Christianity if

17

you lived in the United States or Western Europe, Islam if you lived in most countries of the Middle East, Hinduism if you lived in India, a particular tribal religion if you were a member of a particular tribe, and so forth. With globalization, however, has come a pluralism of religions within each and every culture, and the general category of religion has taken on a descriptive meaning that makes sense. One can be religious, but religious in many ways, even within a single culture.

Freedom of religion is the concept that has made this globalization of religion possible. Without freedom of religion, a free marketplace of religious ideas would not work, and a global category called "religion" would be meaningless. Historically, people have insisted that everyone around them share their religion and have fought to the death to make it so. It has only been

---

SIDEBAR 1.2

FREEDOM OF RELIGION: SOVEREIGNTY OF GOD, SEPARATION OF CHURCH AND STATE, HUMAN RIGHTS

Freedom of religion is mandated by three of the most important documents for American Christians: the Bible, the United States Constitution, and the United Nations Declaration of Human Rights. Each document gives a different rationale for freedom of religion.

Bible: Psalm 2:1–2, 4–5: "Why do the nations conspire and the peoples plot in vain? The kings of the earth take their stand and the rulers gather together against the LORD and against his Anointed One. . . . The One enthroned in heaven laughs; the Lord scoffs at them. Then he rebukes them in his anger and terrifies them in his wrath, saying, 'I have installed my King on Zion, my holy hill.'"

The rationale here is that God is the ultimate power in the universe, not nations, not individuals. Because God is sovereign and made individuals free to choose God (Gen. 1:27), no state power can usurp that freedom by demanding religious uniformity.

United States Constitution: The First Amendment: "Congress shall make no law establishing religion, nor prohibiting the free exercise thereof."

The rationale here is realpolitik. The separation of church power and state power creates a balance of religious interests that makes it impossible for any one religion or religious group to dominate.

United Nations Declaration of Human Rights: Article 18: "Everyone has the right to freedom of thought, conscience and religion; this right includes freedom to change his religion or belief, and freedom either alone or in community with others and in public or private, to manifest his religion or belief in teaching, practice, worship and observance."

The rationale here is that human beings have certain inalienable rights. These universal rights must be protected by all governments of the world.

---

in the past two hundred–plus years that this has changed (except in isolated instances), and it changed with a novel concept promulgated by the framers of the United States Constitution. The authors of the Constitution were fresh from the wars of religion in Europe (intra-Christian wars, actually) and were seeking a way to inoculate their new nation-state against similar interreligious battles. They rightly ascertained that the problem was not with religious belief alone but with the volatile mix of religion and political power: whenever a religion gained political power, it usually used that power to impose its beliefs on others. Separate the passion of religion from the power of politics, and peace would reign—so thought the framers of the Constitution. They acted on this belief by writing the First Amendment to the Constitution, which says, "Congress shall make no law establishing religion, nor prohibiting the free exercise thereof."

This separation of the power of religion from the power of politics has worked reasonably well. Although there have been conflicts over religion in the United States, they have not led to ongoing, violent confrontations, at least compared with religious conflicts in many other parts of the world. The freedom to choose one's own religion as mandated by a strict separation of church and state has proven to be a godsend for religious people in America. And it has been a godsend for the other people throughout the world who have adopted the freedom of religion principle and its corollary, the separation of religion from political power.

Freedom of religion is not universal. Much of the Islamic world still considers Islam not only a religious ideology but also the basis of a political system to be imposed on all citizens. Parts of the socialist world, such as China, still struggle with the concept of religious freedom, as do many smaller totalitarian regimes. But increasingly, religious pluralism and separation of church and state are becoming the approach used throughout the world.

This freedom has many good effects. Religions are thriving. The largest world religions—Buddhism, Christianity, Confucianism, Hinduism, and Islam—are all growing at phenomenal rates (Barrett and Johnson 2001). New religious movements proliferate. When governments endorse religious freedom within their boundaries, there is no shortage of religious innovators who step in with new ideas and new combinations of old ideas. Even indigenous religions normally restricted to a tribe or an ethnic group are experiencing revivals of their old teachings. In one sense, religions have never had it so good.

In another sense, however, globalization and freedom of religion have created a kind of *negative tolerance of all religions* that has the overall effect of minimizing them all. This negative tolerance develops in this way: Religion is a very powerful force, and people tend to be passionately religious. Religious conflict often occurs because people believe their religion is so important and so persuasive that they insist on its truth and uniqueness to everyone around them. If we are to have religious freedom and religious peace, this passionate

---

SIDEBAR 1.3
NEGATIVE AND POSITIVE TOLERANCE

NEGATIVE TOLERANCE: TOLERANCE TO SURVIVE	POSITIVE TOLERANCE: ACCEPT REAL DIFFERENCES
• Trade-off: Tolerate views of others so that your views will be allowed expression	• Appreciation of disagreements • Courage to critique
• Quid pro quo: I'm OK, you're OK	
• Results: Relative truth	• Results: Reflexive evangelism/mission
• Leveling of truth claims: If all views are equally tolerated, no one view can be absolutely correct.	• Mission that respects difference: If real differences are appreciated, mission can happen.

---

character of religious belief must somehow be controlled. Whether intended or not, the free marketplace of religious ideas seems to reduce the overall value level of all religions. If no single religion is the ultimate truth, then all are less important. A relative approach to truth inevitably reduces commitment to a single truth.

The only test of a religion in such a marketplace is its performance. Religions are usually measured not on truth value alone but on their capacity to satisfy individual and social spiritual needs. Global citizens are free to choose whatever religion satisfies their individual needs. Religions are not life-and-death matters that hold sway over us but commodities to be chosen according to their utility. The invisible hand of the marketplace replaces the mysterious hand of God.

Missiological Contexts

What are the missiological implications of the free marketplace of religious ideas with respect to the world's religions? There are many, but let's briefly consider five.

1. *We must recognize the dominance of the marketplace metaphor and use it to our advantage, rather than act as if we can totally rise above it.* Whether Christian, Buddhist, Hindu, Muslim, or whatever, we cannot place ourselves outside culture and escape the thought forms that dominate us. What we can do, however, is clearly identify the common metaphors of the age and by so recognizing them, ensure that the essences of our religious teachings are not lost in the virtual ideas of a complex metaphor. Christian missionaries, for example, would be foolish to think they can avoid the implications of economism in their work. This is how people think. It is how missionaries themselves think. But even as we think in that way, we must show how the essence of the gospel

can both participate in this way of thinking and at the same time supersede it (see, for example, Paul's view of the marketplace, sidebar 1.4).

For example, Christian missionaries from the West have sometimes been accused of attempting to buy converts by providing food and medical services for the disadvantaged. If true, this would surely be an example of economism determining mission strategy. The proper response, however, is not to discontinue providing food and medical services to the disadvantaged in order to

SIDEBAR 1.4
PAUL'S VIEW OF THE MARKETPLACE

In 2 Corinthians 2:12–17, the apostle Paul gives what amounts to a critique of the marketplace as a metaphor for doing mission. He says, "Now when I went to Troas to preach the gospel of Christ and found that the Lord had opened a door for me, I still had no peace of mind, because I did not find my brother Titus there. So I said good-by to them and went on to Macedonia. But thanks be to God, who always leads us in triumphal procession in Christ and through us spreads everywhere the fragrance of the knowledge of him. For we are to God the aroma of Christ among those who are being saved and those who are perishing. To the one we are the smell of death; to the other, the fragrance of life. And who is equal to such a task? Unlike so many, we do not peddle the word of God for profit. On the contrary, in Christ we speak before God with sincerity, like men sent from God."

	SELLERS OF RELIGIOUS GOODS	PAUL'S MESSAGE TO CORINTHIANS
Activities	Aroma of incense sold in markets	Aroma of Christ
	Peddlers of God's word	Paul's evangelism
Attitudes	Desire to profit from sale	Desire that Christ be known
Effects	Sale of religious goods	Aroma of Christ smells of death to some, of life to others
	Sales influence religion of Corinth	Aroma of Christ influences Corinth

APPLICATION OF PAUL'S USE OF THE MARKETPLACE METAPHOR TO TODAY'S CONTEXT

Activities	The Holy Spirit creates around Christians a smell that draws some and repels others.
Attitudes	The influence of rationality and scientific method in our context makes it difficult to accept Paul's aroma theory.
	Yet some are drawn to the beauty of Christ's aroma; some are repelled by its goodness.
Effects	In doubting the influence of Christ's aroma spread through our lives, we fail to see the signs of Christ's influence in our world.

show people who cannot interpret such actions in other than economic terms that their materialistic charges are not true. Rather, we must simply make our motives clearer: we are not attempting to "buy" converts to Christianity, and we are not doing these works because we are a social-service agency. We are doing them because the Bible charges us to show compassion and mercy to the less fortunate.

2. *As mission workers we can no longer count on the help of cultural carriers such as political powers and economic forces to aid us in the task of spreading the good news.* Not only are most of the world's political and economic forces thoroughly secularized but most also espouse values that are thoroughly antireligious. Not only have the powers-that-be opted out of explicitly promoting specifically religious values but most also do not even espouse implied religious values such as peace and justice. For such powers, the separation of church and state has been a license to let their main interests (power for politics and profit for economics) reign unmitigated by any concern for human well-being except that which increases power and profit.

3. *People are much more sophisticated about the world's religions, and this sophistication demands a more nuanced mission approach.* There was a time when one could simply mention other religious systems to people of a certain religion and expect from them very little knowledge of those other religions and thorough approbation of them. Neither expectation can be assumed any longer. Globalization and freedom of religion have resulted in extensive knowledge of other religions for many of the world's religious people and very complex attitudes toward those religions. Increased sophistication on the part of global Christians toward other religions means that increasing sophistication on the part of the missionary is required (Muck 2006).

4. *In an age when religion in general has been devalued to commodity status, the mission task is often twofold: to rearticulate the proper role and status of religion in general and to talk about the teachings of Jesus Christ in particular.* Religion is not psychotherapy or sociology or philosophy, although too often today it is reduced to one or the other—or all three. On the contrary, religion refers to the transcendent dimension of being human. Religion is, of course, vitally interested in human well-being, but it is primarily interested in serving as the human focal point for the interests of the gods. There was a time when all human beings understood this, but today few do. Our first task is to relocate and redefine the role of religion in general. Only then do the teachings of any specific religion, Christianity included, relate to their major focus: the ineffable transcendent.

5. *The current conditions of religious freedom lead to a better understanding of human nature, the* imago Dei, *but also to more competition for the hearts and souls of humankind.* Better understanding of human nature comes from recognizing that true religion prospers only when it is freely chosen by individual human beings and the communities they form. This forces us to be

22

> **SIDEBAR 1.5**
> **MISSIOLOGICAL IMPLICATIONS OF THE TWENTY-FIRST-CENTURY CONTEXT**
>
> 1. We must recognize the dominance of the marketplace metaphor and use it to our advantage, rather than act as if we can rise above it.
> 2. As mission workers we can no longer count on the help of cultural carriers such as political powers and economic forces to aid us in the task of spreading the gospel.
> 3. People have a much more sophisticated understanding of the world's religions, and this sophistication demands a more nuanced mission approach.
> 4. In an age when religion in general has been devalued to commodity status, the mission task is usually twofold: to rearticulate the proper role and status of religion in general and to talk about the teachings of Jesus Christ in particular.
> 5. The current conditions of religious freedom lead to better understandings of human nature, the *imago Dei*, but also to more competition for the hearts and souls of humankind.

content when people make religious choices of which we do not approve. This better anthropology allows us to disagree with other religious teachings but requires us to approve and defend people's freedom to choose any religion they wish. Yet even as we defend as a Christian principle the right of free choice in religious matters, we are implicitly endorsing the right of other religions, of all religions, of our religion, to do mission—or religious self-advocacy. This means that the missionary of today will be faced with stiffer competition than ever before in history.

These are just some of the implications of the free marketplace of religious ideas.

REFLEXIVE EVANGELISM

Anyone involved in Christian work of any kind knows that other religions are forces to be reckoned with. Christian pastors and missionaries are not the only ones attempting to promote a religious idea in this free marketplace of religious ideas. In their own ways, Hindus, Buddhists, Muslims, Confucians, Native Americans, Scientologists, and many others are also promoting their beliefs to cultures that are unusually hungry for spiritual ideas. In the rush hour of the gods, we have the phenomenon of a rush hour of spokespeople for the gods.

This competition takes many forms, but let's look at three.

1. *Competition in the Church-and-State Sphere.* At one time, even though the United States government was not supposed to advance the cause of any single religion, Christianity included, it did support the prevailing Protestant Christian hegemony. The pledge of allegiance to the flag and the Lord's Prayer were used to start the school day. School textbooks, such as the *McGuffey*

Readers, used biblical passages and references to teach reading and comprehension. Teachers assumed their students were Christian and taught about the Christian implications of holidays such as Thanksgiving, Christmas, and Easter. The First Amendment proscription of not supporting any particular religion was interpreted to mean that the government would not endorse any particular Christian denomination at the expense of another.

Demographic changes in the composition of the United States population have altered that interpretation of the First Amendment in dramatic ways. Since 1950 the non-Christian religions in the United States have grown significantly. Today there are more Muslims than Presbyterians in the United States, more Buddhists than Episcopalians, more Hindus than Congregationalists. Remember: Presbyterians, Episcopalians, and Congregationalists were the three dominant religious groups in colonial America. This growth of non-Christian religions has not been lost on lawmakers (senators and members of Congress) and law interpreters (judges and courts). Both groups have reinterpreted the First Amendment to cover all religion, non-Christian groups included. The government is no longer interested in supporting the religious freedom of Christians only but also seeks to ensure fair and equal protection of all religions (Barrett and Johnson 2001).

Some examples: United States military chaplains now include Muslim and Buddhist chaplains as well as Protestant, Catholic, and Jewish ones. Chaplains in prisons now routinely provide Muslim worship services.

On the public school front, several active issues involve religious freedom: the question of whether children should be allowed to begin the day with a prayer of their choice is hotly debated; religious groups are constantly testing the waters regarding whether they can meet on school property; religious holidays and religious dress are issues of importance in public schools.

In terms of governmental policy, Muslims have active lobbying groups in Washington, DC, who argue for foreign policy favorable to nations dominated by Islam, in ways similar to those practiced by Jewish lobbyists for years regarding Israel. The Dalai Lama and his associates have lobbied the government for support of Tibet, often basing those arguments, in part at least, on religious freedom for Buddhists. Native American groups seek rights for Native Americans that often include religious issues such as the location and sacredness of burial sites and holy mountains and other landmarks.

Even though avowed Christians still make up approximately 80 percent of the United States population, promoters of Christianity can no longer assume that the government and public officials will implicitly support their faith as the American civil religion. If the United States government supports a civil religion, it is one based on the teachings of the First Amendment, a two-item creed ("Thou shalt not endorse any specific religion" and "Thou shalt defend all legal religious practices") that is becoming increasingly absolute in American public life.

This development in America is not unique. Because the United States has had a longer history with this particular idea of religious freedom, Americans may be more active in promoting it. But many other countries have embraced some form of the separation of church and state and are also experiencing this form of public religious competition. The issue of proselytizing is a hot political topic in Russia. Public school dress restrictions, particularly the matter of Muslim girls wearing veils in public school classrooms, have reached the French courts for adjudication. Workers' rights in Germany are heavily influenced by religious identity. Religious freedom issues have brought to power, and toppled, several recent governments in India.

2. *Neighborhood Ethics.* A less formal form of competition is taking place in neighborhoods across America and around the world. Indeed, even to call this phenomenon "competition" is perhaps to stretch the meaning of the word too far. More cooperation among the religions of the world exists today than ever before, and much of it is occurring in neighborhoods. These interchanges involve family life, general living conditions, and public school education.

Perhaps the most volatile of these neighborhood ethics issues concerns the various situations that arise when children of different religious backgrounds interact: playing together, going to one another's place of worship for life-transition events, and (as the children grow older) dating and intermarrying. Parents of Christian children today often face questions of how to instruct their children about interacting with Hindu, Buddhist, and Muslim neighbors. Hindu, Buddhist, and Muslim parents, of course, face the same spectrum of issues.

Many public issues that sometimes reach the court system are dealt with and resolved at the neighborhood level. Many neighborhoods, for example, have formed groups of concerned parents that include representatives of the religions to deal with problems such as drugs, religious holidays in the schools, teaching about religions in the schools, coed physical education classes, and religious dress in schools. Some school administrations use these groups as sounding boards for setting school policy regarding matters that have religious implications.

Many workplace issues are dealt with and solved on the neighborhood level. Muslims, for example, often need a place and a time for the prayers they say five times a day, two of which fall during traditional working hours: noon and late afternoon. In many workplaces, a space is provided for these prayers, and Muslims say them during their lunch hour and afternoon break. Religious holidays are another example. Jews sometimes need time off for the High Holy Days in the fall, including Yom Kippur. Businesses often make special provisions for these holiday needs by providing comp time or, if enough workers need them, making them official holidays for the entire company.

So common are these kinds of competition becoming that a pattern can be discerned in their solution. First comes the problem, which often takes the form

25

of a seemingly intractable conflict of interests between members of two different religious groups. Second, a group of people representing all the interested parties is formed to discuss the issues. Third, a compromise solution is often found that satisfies everyone. When these competitions follow this pattern, more is achieved than just the solution to a particular problem (although that would be achievement enough). Often the negotiation itself sets a pattern of interaction that makes future situations much easier to handle.

3. *Competition in Missions Proper.* Some of the competition among religions is mission-and-evangelism competition pure and simple. The religions of the world have adopted increasingly common methodologies for promoting their teachings, which are more frequently taking the form of an economic marketing model. A particular religion identifies its teachings as a product to be sold to a spiritually hungry world. This spiritual product is shaped to conform as much as possible to the perceived and expressed needs of the people of the target culture. Sometimes the service offered to the public is a new one, so a need must be created or brought to consciousness among the people of the culture. After the spiritual product is tested and ready, people must be made aware of it. Ways of publicizing this valuable product are devised: radio, television, newspapers, fliers, and word of mouth are common mediums for this advertisement. Spiritual salespeople, both professional and lay, are trained to sell the product. "Stores" are set up as centers to sell and dispense it. Sometimes comparative advertising is done, extolling the virtue of one spiritual product over against another.

Just as there are many ways of selling secular products, spiritual products are also sold very differently, giving the spiritual marketplace a rich texture. Some see their products as suitable for only a certain segment of the culture, and they adopt very restrained, elitist methodologies; sometimes they do little or no advertising and make the scarcity of the product a major feature of its attraction. Others adopt mass-marketing approaches. Still others segment the market along economic, ethnic, racial, or nationalistic lines.

The bottom line (to continue the metaphor) is that we live in cultures where we see increasing competition for religious market share, and even as some religious groups are becoming more chary of the historical excesses of such missions efforts, more groups are using the powerful marketing tools available (such as the Internet) to market their religions even more aggressively.

In the face of such a situation, how are Christians called to act? In two ways: First, we must recognize that we cannot opt out of the competition. Under current world conditions, one way of opting out of the competition would be opting out of the marketplace. Given the ubiquitous nature of the marketplace described above, this option would require withdrawing from mainstream society. Most religious groups are unwilling to do this because they see public engagement as at least part of their mission. Another way

> ## SIDEBAR 1.6
> ## RELIGIOUS COMPETITION
>
> *Barrett and Johnson (2001, 4)*
>
> Christian denominations are not the only ones seeking converts. Most religions of our market-mad, globalized world are attempting to grow by recruiting people from other religions. From 1990 to 2000, the four largest religious groups grew. Three of the four grew by conversion growth, that is, the number of people who joined the religion minus the number of people who defected to another religion.
>
> | RELIGION | ADHERENTS IN 2000 | CONVERSIONS PER YEAR | RATE |
> | --- | --- | --- | --- |
> | Christianity | 1,999,563,838 | 2,501,396 | 1.36 |
> | Islam | 1,188,242,789 | 865,558 | 2.13 |
> | Hinduism | 811,336,265 | -660,377 | -1.69 |
> | Buddhism | 359,981,757 | 156,609 | 1.09 |

of opting out of the marketplace, however, is to behave as if one has a monopoly on the marketplace. This option also has serious drawbacks because it requires a profoundly revisionist view of the religious demographics of the world. Christians do not have a monopoly on the world's religious scene and, if the parable of the sheep and the goats is to be taken seriously, never will have. There will always, until the end of time, be both Christians and non-Christians in the world.

Thus, given the current world situation, Christians have little choice but to engage in the marketplace of religious ideas. The parable of the talents teaches that Christians are not to bury their talents in the sand and withdraw from engagement but should invest their talents in the world's marketplace. Christians must engage. The only question involves choosing *how* to engage in this religious competition. Two principles seem especially important.

First, Christian love as described in the New Testament demands a powerful, unconditional love for the other. Jesus, John, and Paul all wrote of a radical love for the world's people. Early Christians took a traditional Jewish teaching about hospitality for the stranger in their midst and extended this teaching to include not just hospitality for the stranger but love for everyone. Love your neighbor, they said. Love your enemies, they said. Love your neighbor as yourself, they said. Love of God and neighbor, they said, sums up the whole of the law by which we are to live.

Given this very clear teaching about love, its application to world religion would be something like the following: Love your neighbor; love your non-Christian neighbor; love Hindus, Buddhists, Muslims, and others as yourself, even as you engage them with the gospel of Jesus Christ. In one sense, the marketplace encounter is simply the occasion for this next step of loving everyone even as Jesus loved everyone. One feature of loving one's neighbor is telling him or her about Jesus. But there are many other features, as 1 Corinthians 13 points out, such as being kind, patient, and protecting. It means realizing that our knowledge is imperfect and always will be, but that love endures. Love means we cannot opt out of the competition, but it also means that Christians compete in a very unusual way, at least when measured against the standards of competition set by our business-centered and sports-focused culture. Competition means "playing the game with full gusto" but leaving the winning and losing to God. Given our everyday understandings of what competition means, this is a difficult concept to grasp.

Second, the competition changes not just the person of the other religion; it also changes the Christian. The engagement with the other may change the Christian in many ways. In part 3, we will discuss in more detail how this change takes place. We will call this explanation the hermeneutical circle.

Reflexive evangelism takes into account the marketplace of religious ideas, globalization, freedom of religion, and negative tolerance and carries out the biblical mandates to preach the gospel, but in a way that embraces the great neighborhood that the world has become. It embraces all the people of the world in a way that shows them the unique nature of God's love and the absoluteness of our commitment to the well-being of God's creation.

COOPERATE AND COMPETE

Current world conditions have also given a new nuance to the goal of mission and evangelism. The shorthand way of describing this new goal is to say that it is cooperation and competition instead of conversion. Unfortunately, this shorthand description has a good chance of offending almost everyone interested in Christian missions and evangelism. First, it sounds as if we are doing away with the idea of conversion altogether, and that is not the case. Second, as we showed in the last section, it is jarring to hear competition mentioned as an ongoing goal because many people think that it is precisely the competitive nature of traditional mission and evangelism to the other world religions that is the problem. Third, others hear the word *cooperation* and think it means giving up the traditional goals of mission and evangelism altogether. So the shorthand way of describing the "new" goal needs quite a bit of explanation (Martinson 1999).

Let's start with the conversion issue. Many traditional missionary models begin with the necessity of conversion. William Carey's great call to missionary arms, for example, is titled *An Enquiry into the Obligations of Christians to Use Means for the Conversion of the Heathens* (1988; originally published in 1792). It is clear from these and many other early missionary writings that converting the "heathen" was the singular goal of all Christian missionaries.

In a world built on an economic model, however, beginning with the necessity of conversion may not be best for two reasons. First, the marketplace metaphor tends to reduce conversion to a function of the marketplace, rather than a transcendent, God-initiated act. Conversion becomes equivalent to making a successful sale. We articulated the product, advertised it, made our sales pitch, and the customer bought, that is, was converted. Customers who choose not to buy are not converted. This reduction of conversion to fit the marketplace model is not unavoidably necessary, of course. Indeed, much of what Christian missiologists attempt is to maintain the integrity of conversion as something that the Holy Spirit, not we, accomplishes. But the application is just too easy, and when conversion is seen as the first and last goal of missions, the marketplace metaphor seems to take over.

Second, using conversion as the single, unambiguous goal of missions and evangelism runs the risk of oversimplifying what happens when the gospel is heard by people of other religions. It narrows the vision of what the gospel can do for the world and its people. When the marketplace metaphor dominates, it is difficult to separate Christian conversion from political, economic, and cultural forces. Or, conversely, it is tempting to reduce political, economic, and cultural forces to nothing and consider just the oversimplified spiritual reality. In either case, a disservice is done to the reality and complexity of what becoming a Christian means.

Yet it is too simple to embrace an anticonversionist model. We are not anticonversionist by any means. Conversion happens if and when we understand the complex dynamics of interreligious interaction better, which enables us to get out of the way and see God in action. To do this we need a more complex model.

Thus we offer a model that we think more adequately addresses the complexities of the global context. Call it (for now, at least) the *compete and cooperate model*. We must develop the capacity to both compete and cooperate with the world's religions.

Competition

Why compete? Because it is the very essence of the gospel to announce to the world the good news of what God has done through Jesus Christ. The Bible argues for competition on several different levels. On the emotional level, it is selfish to hide the light that radiates from the hope that is within us. On the theological level, it is disobedient to reject the call to teach and preach to all nations. On the philosophical level, it is arrogant to reduce all religions to a common-denominator rationality that denies equally the reality they all claim. Christian revelation demands competition. Buddhist dharma demands competition. Human rationality demands competition.

Yet this competition demanded by the biblical texts has a distinctive, chastened feel to it. It is hard work divorced from the fruits of its labors. It is playing a game often without the assurance of ever knowing what the outcome will be. It is attempting to succeed with a determination not to let the prospect of either successes or failures sabotage the relationship with the other person.

Further, it is competition that needs a complement. Vegetarians are familiar with incomplete proteins, proteins that need components from two different kinds of food to be fully satisfying nutritionally. Competition by itself is like an incomplete protein in need of something to round it out. Put even more strongly: in the modern context, competition alone, without the complement of cooperation, ceases to live up to the scriptural ideal.

Cooperation

Why cooperation? There are two main reasons, one traditional and one contemporary. The traditional reason is the biblical injunction to love one's neighbor as oneself. This teaching is not a minor or isolated theme but a major motif of biblical teaching. As we noted in the last section, Jesus took the basic law of Middle Eastern hospitality for strangers in our midst and expanded it into a universal ethical injunction. "Love your neighbors," Jesus said. "Love your enemies," Jesus said. "Love your neighbors as much as you love yourself," Jesus said. This is the whole of the law.

The contemporary reason for cooperation is the role religion plays in the world today. Put simply, religion is perhaps our last hope for civilized, humane cooperation among the peoples of the world. If part of the gospel is to support and even create just social systems, then cooperation with other religions to the extent that they contribute to those systems is a gospel requirement.

This is a relatively new phenomenon. There was a time when religions interacted with one another as they were carried by political and economic forces. Religions were coextensive with a tribe or a nation. Americans were Christian; Indians were Hindu; Chinese were Confucian. In such a system of relative religious homogeneity among tribes and nations, the cooperation requirement inherent in all religions could be carried out at the national or tribal level. Justice, although rooted in religious requirements, could be entrusted to politics and institutions of economic betterment.

Of course, governments and merchants carried out these functions very imperfectly. The nation-states' dismal record of colonialism and imperialism is well documented. Religions too often were partners in these imperfect attempts at establishing so-called justice. Still, the idealism of the world's religions managed to impose their requirements on their cultural carriers with enough force that justice to some extent was served.

Conditions have changed. Justice cannot be served through traditional political and economic systems. Change has occurred because tribes and nations are no longer religiously homogeneous, even relatively speaking. In the face of growing religious pluralism within cultures, religions can no longer count on political and economic systems to serve as their conduit for justice, that is, for loving one's neighbor. And for their part, nations, in the face of growing religious pluralism within their constituencies, are increasingly choosing the course of strict separation between political/economic functions and religious ones.

Although this separation has some good features (namely, the reduction of religious conflict within societies and the abuses of colonialism and imperialism), the negative side to the development is that neither governments nor economic systems are leavened by religious values. Governments operate according to the rules of power, and economic systems operate according to the rules of profit. The requirement of justice, that is, the promotion of human rights regardless of power or profit, is thrown back directly on religion.

In such a climate, to love one's neighbor as oneself when that neighbor is not of one's own religion takes on new, more radical meaning. Religions are the primary agents in the world that are still committed to human well-being as a part of their agenda. Realpolitik and transnational corporate greed have made justice almost purely a religious matter.

Without doubt this complicates the missiologist's task when it comes to relating to other religions. Many people of other religious persuasions have effectively addressed issues of peace and justice on a global scale—and continue to do so. They are good people, concerned with human well-being in ways compatible with similar Christian concerns. The question for Christians is how to relate to these people of other religions and their civilizing activities. The answer to this question (that is, learning to both compete and cooperate) is the subject matter of this book: how Christians must engage world religions in the twenty-first century.

2

Text

What the Bible Says

I f we wish to make the gospel story meaningful to adherents of other religions, we must acknowledge, use, and augment the context in which we find ourselves in the twenty-first century, especially that part of the context that makes the marketplace metaphor the dominant way of looking at interreligious interchange. But this realization still leaves unexplored the methods of contact we might use in different settings and, of course, what we are going to say. For both of these issues, we must turn from a study of our context and move to a study of the Bible. What does the Bible say about our responsibility toward people of other religions?

Why the Bible? Because the Bible communicates the story we are to tell. Mission and evangelism mean nothing less than telling the world the story of Jesus in thought, word, and deed. The Bible tells us what to say and gives us ideas about how to say it. This is simply said but not always simply done.

The story of Jesus is at once simple in its expression yet complex in its implications for specific cultures. And if the examples provided for us in the Bible are any indication, telling the story in thought (that is, the witness of who we are), word (the witness of what we say), and deed (the witness of what we do) can mean literally hundreds of different ways of "doing" evangelism among people of other religious traditions and cultures.

SIDEBAR 2.1

WHAT THE BIBLE SAYS ABOUT OTHER RELIGIONS

The appendix lists 239 biblical incidents or teachings about what happens or should happen when the people of God (patriarchs, Israelites, New Testament followers of Jesus) come into contact with people of other religious traditions. Based on these 239 examples we have drawn some general conclusions:

- Three-fourths of the references are from the Old Testament.
- The five most frequently occurring nonbiblical religions are
    Egyptian religion (5%)
    Nabatean religion (10%)
    Canaanite religion (25%)
    Mesopotamian religion (10%)
    Greek/Roman religion (30%)
- About 140 actual clashes with other religions take place in these references.
- It is twice as likely that the clash was conflictual rather than cooperative.
- Roughly 100 teachings about other religions are represented in the 239 references.
- God, Jesus, and Paul are the three major teachers.

The Bible records at least 239 occasions when the people of God—patriarchs, Israelites, New Testament followers of Jesus—come in contact with people of other religious traditions or leaders give lessons regarding such contacts. The appendix lists these contacts and lessons with a short annotation of each. That makes over 239 models of how the people of God creatively witnessed to or told the story, over 239 lessons to teach us how we can responsibly interact with Hindus, Buddhists, Muslims, and others. It takes only a quick perusal of those passages to see that the missional intent of Scripture is clear (Bosch 1991). The story we read in the Bible and, eventually, the story of Jesus are explicitly intended to bring hope to the world.

Yet in spite of the clear missional intent of all 239 examples, it is equally clear that there is no single prescription of how witness should be done. After reading the stories and digesting the teachings, one is left with a cornucopia of methods and results and words of wisdom. Reading through these biblical texts is like reading a collection of the best short stories of English literature. Great plots, all of them. All stories that convey a truth. But all different. Interesting characters, all of them. But all unique. Surprising endings, many of them. But no formula writing here. What becomes clear is that witnessing, like all human relationships, is a complicated affair.

These examples demonstrate that there are many different occasions for the people of God to have contact with the religious other: war (aggressive and defensive), friendship, community projects, economic trade, marriage, travel. The contacts may result in conflict or cooperation, condemnation or conversion. The political systems in which the contacts take place range all the way from monarchies with "established" religions to feudal conglomerates with scores of tribal beliefs.

The variety makes for interesting reading. That same variety, however, makes it difficult to discern *the* biblical approach to people of other religions. Quickly it becomes evident that interpretation is needed if we are to distill some principles of biblical witness. Yet the discerning reader sees the danger of this. If the principles become too far distanced from the practices, they lose their validity. What worked well in one context fails famously in another. Part of the genius of sixty-six different books in different settings written in different literary genres is that it shows that everything except the gospel story is open-ended. And every time the gospel engages a cultural setting it does so in a unique way (Scherer 1987).

This complexity makes discerning biblical truth regarding other religions high adventure indeed. It puts biblical exegesis on the same plane as skydiving, on the same steep slopes as mountain climbing, in the same ballpark as the World Series. It is risky business, taking our gospel talents and investing them in the quixotic world of the everyday. It would be safer to tend the ninety and nine than to search for the lost one.

Thus it is understandable that in the face of such heart-stopping risk and mind-stretching complexity, we would search for safer ground. Often we seek safer ground in methodology. We decide, together, to approach the text asking certain questions. We delimit acceptable answers to those questions. We do this not just to be safe (although biblical exegetes will never be mistaken for big-game hunters) but also to enable discussion among us. If we are all asking similar questions, we can compare answers more easily.

But we must not lose sight of the fact that often a new question begs to be answered, a question we had not thought of before, a question that turns everything on its head. Perhaps that is the source of the different methodologies biblical exegetes have developed to explore the far country of scriptural texts: different questioners, different delimiters, by faithful people interested in Christian conversation.

Thus we find ourselves in need of suggestions on how to use what the Bible says in our witness to Hindus, Buddhists, Muslims, and others. In the following discussion we offer a simple way to think about this issue, a way we call the three spheres of biblical interpretation. The three spheres are the data sphere, the question sphere, and the theme sphere. Each sphere can be explained by a question:

Data sphere: What does the Bible say about people of other religions?

Question sphere: What is my specific question regarding this relationship?

SIDEBAR 2.2
THE THREE SPHERES OF BIBLICAL INTERPRETATION

Data Sphere: What does the Bible say?

The Bible is a resource book for finding data we need to address our issues. When faced with our core question—what is the Christian's responsibility to people of non-Christian religious traditions?—we need to determine what the Bible says about it.

Question Sphere: Does the Bible answer my question?

The most specific question to ask of the biblical texts is whether I can find an answer to my specific question or the question of my group. Sometimes this question is very specific, sometimes more general. But it is shaped by my understanding and experience of the world. It depends on who I am (soldier, sailor, tinker, spy), my gifts and personal qualities (intellectual, practical, community-oriented), and the quality of my experience of the world (great, good, average, bad).

Theme Sphere: How can we fit together what the Bible says in different places?

Evaluating data from the Bible usually starts with organizing it under a general theme or themes. For Christian exegetes, it is axiomatic that there is a general theme, that all the biblical data is somehow consistent with everything else.

Theme sphere: What lens or hermeneutical principle should I use to understand my question in light of what the Bible says?

DATA SPHERE: WHAT DOES THE BIBLE SAY?

In one sense, the Bible is a resource book for finding the data we need to address issues (McQuilkin 1984). When faced with such a question—for example, what is the Christian's responsibility to people of non-Christian religious traditions?—we need to determine what the Bible says about it. This discovery process can be broken down into five steps:

1. Identify all the passages.
2. Collect and group the passages.
3. Find the "gold nuggets," important information or distinctive truths in each passage.
4. Search for the most important or dominant nuggets in each group of passages.
5. Apply the distinct truths discovered to particular contexts.

An especially clear example of this approach is the book *Christianity and the Religions: A Biblical Theology of World Religions* (1995). Edward Rommen and Harold Netland, the volume editors, describe their work as an

---

SIDEBAR 2.3
A MASTER LIST OF BIBLICAL DATA

Rommen and Netland (1995)

• Pentateuch: Yahweh's characteristics
• Wisdom literature: Arrows pointing to God
• Prophets: Exclusive worship of God
• Gospels and Acts: Gospel in context of religious pluralism
• Paul: Contextual theology
• Epistles and Revelation: Uniqueness and supremacy of Jesus Christ

---

"attempt to address the contemporary questions raised by religious pluralism by looking again in a fresh manner at the biblical data" (5). They and the other authors of the essays collected in this volume proceed as miners to dig out the ore of biblical data in order to refine it into the pure metal of biblical truth. They then apply that truth to the missiological situation of the modern world. It will be helpful to examine their argument under the above headings.

First, they identify the passages. In doing this, they seem to err on the side of collecting even low-grade ore to avoid missing something of importance. The collection is thus a large and inclusive one.

Second, they collect and group the passages into readily identifiable clusters. The organizing principles vary, but in this book the clusters begin with the traditional divisions of Scripture: the Pentateuch, Wisdom literature, the Prophets, the Gospels and Acts, the Pauline letters, and the general Epistles and Revelation.

From the Pentateuch, Ed Mathews identifies the incomparability of Yahweh, the jealousy of Yahweh regarding other gods, the oneness of Yahweh, the prohibitions against idolatry, and the exclusivity of Yahweh as themes important for this subject (Rommen and Netland 1995, 30–44).

In the Wisdom literature, Michael Pocock sees little condemnation of religions; rather, these books focus on the positive, "the single arrow pointing to the one North Pole (Yahweh)" (Rommen and Netland 1995, 54).

In the Prophets, says Robert Chisholm, the great issue is the polemic against Baal worship. In this polemic Yahweh is shown to demand exclusive worship and hold unrivaled power (Rommen and Netland 1995, 56–71).

William Larkin discovers that the Gospels and Acts "give us an understanding of the gospel in the context of religious pluralism—the gospel is unique and its reception is indispensable for salvation" (Rommen and Netland 1995, 73). Acts, especially, gives us an evangelistic strategy for dealing with non-Christian religions.

Paul, observes Don Howell, confronted Greek, Roman, Egyptian, and mystery religions with a theocentric Christology. Paul also used pagan religious terminology in his attempts to communicate the gospel message. He attacked idolatry and syncretism in particular (Rommen and Netland 1995, 92–112).

Finally, Andreas Köstenberger mines the general Epistles, discovering along the way that they argue for the supremacy of Jesus, the uniqueness of Jesus as the suffering savior, and the way non-Christian religions "distort the purity of the Christian faith" (Rommen and Netland 1995, 136).

QUESTION SPHERE: DOES THE BIBLE ANSWER MY QUESTION?

The most specific question to ask of the biblical texts is not, can I find an answer to some general query or develop some universal theory? but rather, can I find an answer to *my* specific question or the question of my group? Sometimes this question is very specific, sometimes more general. But it is shaped by my understanding and experience of the world.

A particularly clear and instructive example of this method is found in *Christianity and Plurality: Classic and Contemporary Readings* (1999). Richard Plantinga, the editor, offers us a collection of works from throughout the history of the Christian tradition that deal with the questions raised by the plurality of religions in our world. What interests us here, however, is the way he deals with the biblical data in the introduction and part 1 of the text.

Plantinga begins by analyzing why the problem of religious plurality is unique in the present-day context. He concludes that it is not because the fact of religious pluralism per se is new. There has always been a plurality of religions in the world. By the first century (the beginning of Christianity's historical presence), all the world's major religions existed (except for Islam).

What is new, however, is our understanding of this situation. Modern conditions have brought religious plurality into our consciousness in a vivid way (Hastings 1999). This increased, subjective awareness of the situation results from several historical factors: the discovery and exploration of the world, the Reformation, the Enlightenment, the scientific study of religion, the renewal of Asian religions, and globalization. Together these developments have raised in the Christian community the question of Christianity's uniqueness vis-à-vis the world's other religions. Several different theological answers to that question have been proposed: exclusivism, inclusivism, pluralism, and universalism.

Plantinga presents an examination of selected raw data pertaining to the problem. He gives us a brief guided reading tour of the original texts, thirty-seven Old Testament passages and thirty-nine New Testament passages. Plantinga justifies this examination in general by noting that "all Christian traditions recognize the authority of the Bible, as well as the necessity of biblical interpretation, in order to know and understand God, the world, and humanity" (1999, 12).

Because he is a philosopher, Plantinga presents the question as he understands it in philosophical terms. He states it in the form of a question to be kept in mind as we read through the texts: "Given a particular divine revelation which makes possible a special kind of divine-human relationship culminating in salvation, how are Christians to think about the existence of a seemingly universal religiosity which takes a multiplicity of forms and which often comes to expression in seeming oblivion of the particular divine revelation recorded in the Bible?" (1999, 12).

This statement of the problem is particularly useful for Western readers, who are heirs to the Western philosophical tradition rooted in the Greek philosophers Plato and Aristotle. Each of these philosophers dealt at some length with the problem of the universal and the particular, especially how they relate to each other. Plato and his heirs (often called idealists) considered the universal to be separate and distinct in essence from the particular. Aristotle and his heirs (often called realists) considered the universal to be a human experience of similarities in material objects; the universal idea is real but not separate from the objects of study. This formulation of the problem is reflected in several important Christian doctrinal issues, including the transcendence and immanence of God, and the incarnation, Jesus Christ. Plantinga thinks it is also a useful way of looking at the phenomenon of one God and many religious expressions seeking to find that God.

To illustrate this approach, Plantinga systematically examines the seventy-six biblical texts he has chosen and identifies the way they relate to both the problem of pluralism and the problem of the universal and the particular. In the creation story, for example, we see the transcendent God creating ex nihilo the world and human beings, who are to be in relation to God. This is a good example of the universal God's creative act relating to the many. Another example is God's decision to elect one particular nation, Israel, to witness God's universal creative intentions to all the nations. After examining all the sections of the texts in this way, Plantinga reaches a conclusion about the problem of the universal and the particular as they relate to the Christian view of religious plurality: "The universal divine concern for creation comes to expression in the dramatic measure of the particular, Christological revelation; and the particular, atoning revelation of God in Christ is of universal consequence, making possible the salvation of all the world" (1999, 24).

The result of Plantinga's methodology is a sense of discovery, of having a powerful explanatory tool to use in analyzing a body of data that at first glance seems dauntingly complex and even confusing. The universal-particular distinction helps us manage and limit the implications of the data in a very helpful way.

One wonders, however, how useful the tool would be to readers of the biblical text who are not heirs to the Western philosophical tradition. For some people the problem of how the universal relates to the particular has little if any value as an analytical tool. To be sure, they might welcome such a tool to help them in their reading. But a different tool might be more useful, depending on their philosophical tradition.

It is unlikely that Plantinga's choice of the problem of the universal and the particular as his tool to organize this material is the only tool that could be used for Western readers either. Others could be used, with different results.

THEME SPHERE: HOW CAN WE FIT TOGETHER WHAT THE BIBLE SAYS?

Another way of evaluating data from the Bible is to organize it under a general theme. For many people, it is axiomatic that a general theme exists—that all these findings are somehow consistent with everything else. The organizing work in Edward Rommen and Harold Netland's book is found in Rommen's essay called, appropriately, "Synthesis." Rommen does his synthesizing work by creating a "systematic statement of an evangelical theology of non-Christian religions" (Rommen and Netland 1995, 241). He defines theology as "a human activity resulting in the formulation of summary statements that capture the essence of revelation and help guide our application of that teaching" (241). To accomplish this task, Rommen builds a system of definitions, axioms, and propositions that account for all the material mined from the biblical texts. The first two—definitions and axioms—are provided by the Bible; the last—propositions—is deduced by the reader from the definitions and axioms. Rommen deduces three propositions:

Proposition 1: Christianity must acknowledge the existence of other religions.

Proposition 2: Christianity's evaluation of other religions will be primarily negative but must be highly differentiated.

Proposition 3: Christianity's mode of engaging other religions depends on the intentional context.

Finally, the propositions are applied to our context. In this text, Harold Netland applies the findings to the task of mission in a pluralistic world. After discussing the new pluralistic, global context, he gives six guidelines for the practice of mission: understand other religions, evangelize through Christian mission, engage the plausibility structures of modernity and pluralism, adopt appropriate forms of dialogue in mission, live consistently as disciples of Jesus Christ, and immerse the encounter with other religions in prayer.

INTEGRATING THE ANSWERS TO THE THREE QUESTIONS

Of course, all three questions have value. Of course, we need the answers to all three questions in order to grapple with what our responsibility to people of other religious traditions is. The question is how to fit them together. Questions 1 and 2 seem to fit together. Questions 1 and 3 also seem to fit together. But questions 2 and 3 seem to be at odds with each other. And can all three fit together at once? How might we do that?

Figure 2.1, depicting the three spheres of biblical interpretation, illustrates an integrative approach to understanding what the Bible says about religious pluralism. To explain this approach, we will discuss the diagram in relationship to five theses.

Thesis 1

To understand a biblical passage about other religions, one must examine relevant biblical passages (circle 1), identify the biblical hermeneutical principle that applies to the passages (circle 2), and relate the passage to a relevant, specific question confronting us today (circle 3).

FIGURE 2.1
THE THREE SPHERES OF BIBLICAL INTERPRETATION INTEGRATED

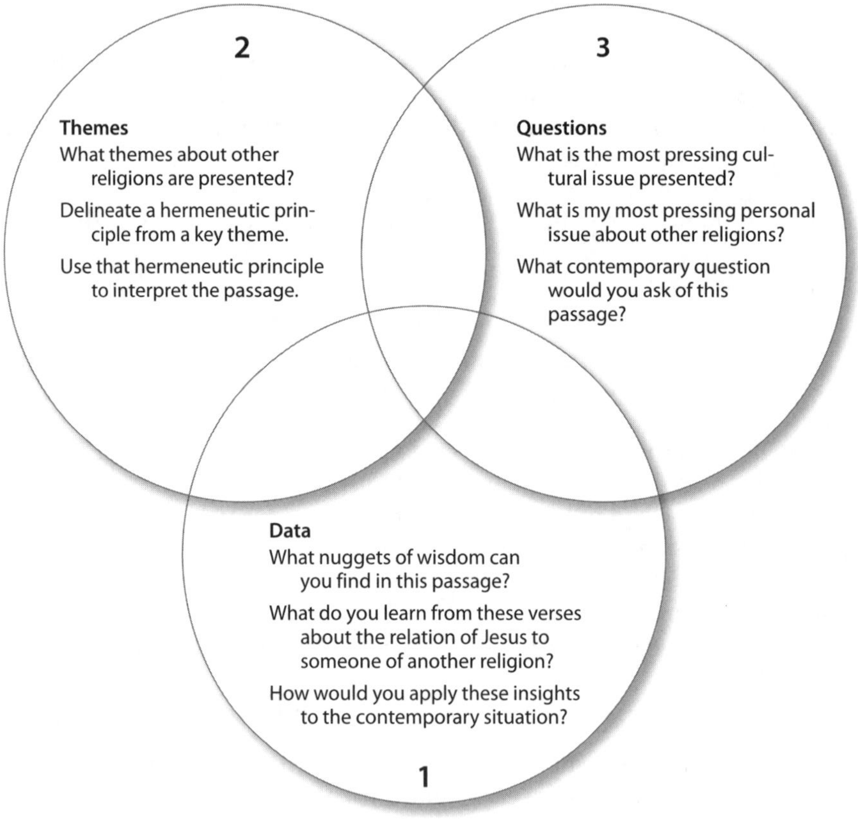

2

Themes
What themes about other religions are presented?

Delineate a hermeneutic principle from a key theme.

Use that hermeneutic principle to interpret the passage.

3

Questions
What is the most pressing cultural issue presented?

What is my most pressing personal issue about other religions?

What contemporary question would you ask of this passage?

Data
What nuggets of wisdom can you find in this passage?

What do you learn from these verses about the relation of Jesus to someone of another religion?

How would you apply these insights to the contemporary situation?

1

This thesis teaches us that all three circles must be represented in any valid application of biblical wisdom. Using data only from circle 1 results in proof texting; using data only from circle 2 results in scholasticism, an untrue abstracting of biblical wisdom; using data only from circle 3 results in cultural or religious relativism.

Thesis 2

Choosing one aspect (text, principle, question) from each circle as appropriate to the situation in question does not vitiate all the other texts, principles, and questions in the rest of the three circles.

Let us say, for example, that we choose to examine Matthew 5:43 about Jesus's command to love not only one's neighbor but also one's enemies for possible application to the way Christians should relate to people of other religions. Each of the three circles makes a contribution. Choosing Matthew 5:43 from circle 1 does not thereby relegate all the other 238 possible sources of data to the dustbin. Each of those passages also has potential worth for other possible situations. Choosing conflict reduction (peace) as the biblical hermeneutical principle from circle 2 does not mean that all other biblical principles are, as a result, deemed wrong. And choosing a question such as, how should I interact with Muslims in my neighborhood? does not mean that other valid contexts cannot be brought to bear with this text and this principle, such as, what about Muslims who belong to al-Qaeda?

This second thesis acknowledges two important yet almost commonsensical points. The first is that we always come to the Bible with a certain perspective. Depending on what is happening in our lives at a certain moment, we see the Bible in a particular way. We can read the same biblical passage over and over and get something new from it each time. Thus, one passage or theme or question may be more important to us at a particular moment, but that does not mean that other passages or themes or questions are less important. Second, not all aspects of each circle can be expressed in a single moment. Our minds are finite. We are limited in what we can process. Even if we are perfectly open to all passages and all faithful themes and all questions, we can only process them one by one. When we look at the material through one lens, other information is temporarily obscured, which anticipates the danger inherent in the next thesis.

Thesis 3

Choosing one aspect to study or use as our hermeneutical focus may blind us to the logic and meaning of other aspects.

This danger is understandable. It usually derives from the very positive facts of our intense commitments to our faith. God calls us to act on behalf of his kingdom. We act in ways that seem fit and proper. We probably base the action we take on a certain passage of Scripture. Many of us have life verses that for one reason or another stimulate us to action. We also probably base the action we take on our community of faith's understanding of the biblical requirements of faithful service. Further, we probably base our actions on the needs of the world that we see before us.

So intent do we become on our particular actions and ways of doing things that we lose sight of the value and faithfulness of other ways of doing things. In *Biography as Theology* (2002), James McClendon shows how people's life experiences affect the way they understand and act on their Christian faith. Martin Luther King Jr., for example, grew up in a situation of racial conflict and suffered the degradation of discrimination. In his reading of the Bible, the Old Testament prophets and their commitment to seeing God's justice implemented in their own political world impressed him. His life verse, and many of the verses he used in his preaching and speeches, came from the prophets: "But let justice roll on like a river, righteousness like a never-failing stream" (Amos 5:24).

Thesis 4

There is a contribution for every moment from all three circles.

This is a statement about the sufficiency of Scripture. Although the Scriptures are old texts by some chronological measures, there is a word of the Lord to be derived from the text for every single moment of every single day. Sometimes the Bible speaks explicitly to the moments of today. The Sermon on the Mount, for example, could have been written yesterday, so clear is its guidance on interpersonal relationships and respect for God's created order. Sometimes the Bible speaks implicitly to the moments of today. The word of the Lord on stem cell research and human cloning does not appear to be so clear. But with prayer and study, a message for these moments emerges also. As one can see from the diagram in figure 2.1, the word of the Lord emerges from the intersection and overlap of the three spheres—where what the Bible says intersects with a question of the day as understood through a universal theme of Scripture.

Consider an example. Suppose in our morning devotions we read the parable of the sheep and the goats in Matthew 25. It is clear from a reading of the text that one of the points of the parable, the disposition of people at the end of human time, intersects with a major question of the day vis-à-vis people of non-Christian religions: who is saved? More precisely it intersects with a subquestion of that question: is everyone saved? It also intersects with a major theme of all biblical writing, the theme of God's gracious provision for humanity through various covenants and then through Jesus Christ, God's Son.

Notice that one normally starts with an element from one of the three circles: a text or a question or a biblical theme. But then in order to do justice to that text, or that question, or that theme, one must look for the elements from the other two spheres. Given the current world situation, where people of non-Christian religions are moving into neighborhoods here and abroad that used to be almost 100 percent Christian, it would have been just as natural to begin with the question, is everyone saved? The question would have then led to the data (the parable of the sheep and the goats) and to an examination of the overall biblical theme that would enable us to bring other texts to bear in our search for the word of the Lord.

Finally, one can easily imagine the study beginning with that theme rather than with a specific text or a question drawn from the context of our everyday life. The theme of this particular example—God's gracious provision for humanity through various covenants and through Jesus Christ—has interested Christian theologians, pastors, and laypersons for the entire two-thousand-year history of the church.

Thesis 5

Proper understanding of what the Bible says requires the Spirit of God, that is, putting on the mind of Christ.

Bible study is successful to the extent that it is faith seeking understanding. Faith is expressed in an attitude of humility before the revealed word of God, regular times of prayer during which we ask God for guidance through the Holy Spirit, and an acknowledgment that the good we seek must also be the good God seeks. With this faith, we will find understanding. Without it our efforts at understanding will be incomplete at best.

It is both interesting and instructive to see how Paul uses the idea of "putting on the mind of Christ," in 1 Corinthians 2. Paul was writing to a divided church, a contentious group of young Christians. They couldn't agree on proper Christian behavior, and they couldn't agree on how to agree what was proper Christian behavior. Paul's recommendation on how to begin to solve these enormous differences is to rely on the Spirit of God. Using his own approach to and experience of ministry as a model, he recommends preaching Christ, not human wisdom, to minister in weakness and trembling rather than arrogance, using the mysterious wisdom of God, not the wisdom of this age. We would do well, both as communities of believers and as individuals, to approach the text in the same way and with the same reliance on the Spirit of God.

> **SIDEBAR 2.4**
> **FIVE THESES OF INTERPRETING THE SPHERES**
>
> Thesis 1: To understand a biblical passage about other religions, one must examine relevant biblical passages (circle 1), identify the biblical hermeneutical principle that applies to the passages (circle 2), and relate the passage to a relevant, specific question confronting us today (circle 3).
>
> Thesis 2: Choosing one aspect (text, principle, question) from each circle as appropriate to the situation in question does not vitiate all the other texts, principles, and questions in the rest of the three circles.
>
> Thesis 3: Choosing one aspect to study or use as our hermeneutical focus may blind us to the logic and meaning of other aspects.
>
> Thesis 4: There is a contribution for every moment from all three circles.
>
> Thesis 5: Proper understanding of what the Bible says requires the Spirit of God, that is, putting on the mind of Christ.

SPHERE OF QUESTIONS

Questions change as cultural conditions change. Put another way, one can tell a lot about a culture by examining the questions it asks. Further, it doesn't take long for cultural fashion to generate new questions and relegate others to the question trash heap. Consider, for example, a list of questions regarding people of other religions written by British missiologist Stephen Neill in 1970 (see sidebar 2.5).

An informal survey of more recent books (post-1995) on the questions surrounding the Christian's responsibility to people with other religious traditions reveals that some of Neill's questions are still regularly being asked (particularly 1, 7, 8, 9), while two-thirds of them are rarely if ever mentioned. This is less than forty years after Neill composed his list. And some new questions have emerged. A representative list of questions being asked today would include:

1. Truth: Is there truth in non-Christian religions?
2. Salvation: Can adherents of non-Christian religions be saved?
3. Cooperation: How much cooperation should we have with people of non-Christian religions?
4. Dialogue: Should we have dialogue with or evangelize people of other religions?
5. Practices: Do spiritual practices (meditation, yoga, etc.) from other religions work for Christians?
6. God: Is the Christian God the god of all religions?
7. Religion: Where do non-Christian religions come from?

SIDEBAR 2.5
STEPHEN NEILL'S QUESTIONS ABOUT OTHER RELIGIONS

Neill (1970)

1. Are non-Christian religions to be treated as wholly false and wherever possible to be destroyed or do all non-Christian religions have in them much of truth?
2. Do Christian faith and Western culture go together and should the convert as far as possible be Europeanized or should old customs not be disturbed unless they are clearly irreconcilable with the Christian gospel?
3. Should education be supplied without discrimination to all who are desirous of receiving it or should education be reserved for Christians?
4. When political circumstances permit should a measure of pressure be exercised on non-Christians to become Christians or should the decision to follow Christ be left entirely to the individual conscience?
5. Must everything be directed to the baptism of those who are willing to receive it or is faith in Christ more important than baptism?
6. When dealing with poor and oppressed people, should improvement in social conditions precede the preaching of the gospel or should direct preaching of the gospel come first?
7. Should the whole faith as understood by the older churches be transmitted to the peoples who have not yet received it or does it suffice to communicate the essentials of the gospel, leaving the converts to make their own discoveries as to the full meaning of the faith?
8. Is the goal of missions the establishment of living churches or is the church a secondary matter when it comes to more essential gathering of believers in whatever cultural form is appropriate?
9. Is conversion the aim of all Christian preaching or should the idea of conversion be excluded from the start, with the aim being the creation of a climate of mutual understanding?
10. Is the aim of mission the formation of living Christian cells within a non-Christian culture or is the aim the penetration of a non-Christian culture by Christian ideas so that the culture is transformed from within?
11. Must Christians be a "garden enclosed" as far as possible separated from the corrupting influences of the world or should Christians be fully in the world, influencing it on every level by their presence?
12. Should Christians have nothing to do with politics or should Christians be prepared to play a leading part in the social and political revolutions of our time?

How might we go about answering each of these seven questions? We don't have the time or space to give fully supported answers to each. And be warned. There is no consensus on how to answer any of them. We know responsible Christians who answer them differently. Biblical evidence can be brought to bear on both sides of the issue raised by each question; for some of them there are more than two sides to the issue.

But since they are crucial questions for our time, let us consider how the discussion might develop around each question. We consider most of them to be still in play, so the answers are evolving as world conditions change and evolve. But we will conclude by stating our position on each one as of this moment.

Truth: Is There Truth in Non-Christian Religions?

This question has become extremely important because most Christians' knowledge of non-Christian religions has increased exponentially in the last century. This makes the easy answer—no—much more difficult. It was easy to say no when non-Christian religions were the largely unknown religions of Sunday-evening missionary presentations showing strange people "over there." It is much harder when they are the religions of those very nice and moral people who live next door. Still, the answer to the question must come from the Bible. Those who argue that the Bible teaches that there may be truth in other religions argue from the classical texts used in defense of natural revelation: Genesis 1:27, which tells us we are all made in the image of God; Psalm 22:27, which finds the glory of God everywhere in the created world; Romans 1:19–20, which assures us that no one anywhere has been left without a knowledge of God; Romans 2:15, which tells us that even our flawed human consciences remind us of God's law; Acts 17:22–34, in which Paul sermonizes about the unknown god the Athenians seemed to be aware existed; and Revelation 21:24–26, which indicates that representatives from every culture will worship God around the throne. Those who argue that there is no truth in other religions usually define truth in a much more limited way, as knowledge that leads to salvation only, and use passages such as John 14:6, where Jesus says no one comes to the Father except through him; Acts 4:12, which says that salvation comes by no other name; Ephesians 2:8, which locates salvation in grace, not works; 1 Timothy 2:5, which talks of only one God and one mediator; and 1 John 5:11, which reminds us that life is found in the Son only.

We believe there is truth, a great deal of truth, actually, in other religions.

Salvation: Can Adherents of Non-Christian Religions Be Saved?

This question has become prominent for some of the same existential reasons we noted in response to the first question. When we discover that our neighbors, whom we like very much, belong to a non-Christian religion, the question of their eternal destiny becomes personified and more difficult to answer. Those who argue that people from other religions are not saved by their religious beliefs or practices use New Testament texts such as John 3:16, the classic description of salvation; Acts 4:12, which says that salvation comes by no other name than that of Jesus; Romans 10:9, which equates verbal confession with salvation; and 2 Timothy 1:10, which describes the work of Jesus. Those who argue that people from other religions can be saved usually begin with Old Testament texts that speak of the tradition of "holy pagans" such as Melchizedek (Gen. 14:17–20) and Job. Also cited are the Magi in Matthew 2:1–12 and the Roman centurion Cornelius (Acts 10); Romans 5:18, which assures us that Christ died for everyone; and an analogy from Acts 15: if Gentiles do not have to take on Jewish culture to be Christian, should non-Christians have to take on Christian culture to be saved?

We take a third position, a "maybe" position based on passages such as Isaiah 55:8–9, where God reminds us that we are not privy to his thoughts, and Matthew 7:1–5, which cautions us against judgments regarding other people's eternal destinies. The "maybe" position takes very seriously God's desire that everyone be saved, as expressed in passages such as 1 Timothy 2:4. We are especially careful not to conflate it with the truth question above.

Cooperation: Should We Cooperate with People from Non-Christian Religions?

Some Christians say no. When the Israelites entered Canaan, God warned them against comingling for fear of endangering religious purity (e.g., Gen. 28:1); Proverbs (e.g., 1:10–15) warns that bad company corrupts good character; 2 Corinthians 6:14 warns against unequal yoking; Hebrews 10 talks about assembling with believers but does not mention unbelievers; and 2 John 10–11 warns against associating with false teachers. Some Christians say yes. Leviticus 19:18 makes it a requirement of the law to provide hospitality to strangers and enemies. Jesus ate with publicans and sinners (Matt. 9:10–13). Jesus told a parable of an unwise person who refused to invest his talents in the world (Matt. 25:15). First Corinthians 10:27 recommends eating with unbelievers. In Galatians 2:11–13, Paul considers calls for separation from unbelievers hypocrisy. Finally, 1 John 1:8 warns us against thinking too highly of ourselves at the expense of our view of others.

We favor cooperation on this one. Our position is based largely on two teachings. One is a commitment to solidarity with other human beings since we are all made by God in God's image. The other is borne of a commitment to witness, a commitment that takes a backseat to little else. Witness done from a stance of antagonism or separation will fail in today's world. We do not want it to fail. Successful witness is based on relationships, and relationships are built in part by regular fellowship and, yes, cooperation.

Dialogue: Should We Have Dialogue with or Evangelize People of Other Religious Traditions?

Some Christians argue for dialogue. Jesus's ministry with the Samaritan woman was very nonjudgmental and dialogical (John 4). In Acts 17:16–34,

Paul is shown dialoguing with the Athenians in their religious temple. First Peter 3:15 tells us to always be ready to give an accounting for the hope that is within us. Other Christians stress evangelism. Elijah on Mount Carmel insisted on a choice between Yahweh and Baal (1 Kings 18:16–46). Matthew 28:18–20 emphasizes teaching and preaching. Paul's charge to Timothy is clearly evangelistic (1 Tim. 2:4). Some take the view that neither dialogue nor evangelism will change things. Mark 10:40 reminds us that those who are listed in the book of life are already determined and the sovereignty of God cannot be gainsaid. Romans 8:29–30 tells us of God's predestined will.

We take a fourth position, that both dialogue and evangelism are required of Christians in their relationships with people of other religious traditions. The variety of witness methodologies in thought, word, and deed indicates that many modes of interaction with non-Christians are called for. Philip's interaction with the Ethiopian eunuch (Acts 8), Peter's interaction with Cornelius (Acts 10), and Paul's interaction with the Athenians (Acts 17) are just three examples.

Practices: Do Spiritual Practices (Meditation, Yoga, Etc.) from Other Religions Work for Christians?

Those who argue that other religious practices, such as Buddhist meditation and Hindu yoga, can be used by Christians often cite the passage in Matthew 7:15–20 that argues that a good tree is judged by its fruit. The implication is that practices that produce good Christian virtues (Gal. 5:22–26) are acceptable. A further argument in favor is that in practices such as social services (food for the hungry, clothes for the cold, shelter for the homeless) all religions can join together to help (Matt. 25:31–40). Those who argue the contrary cite reasons of purity, association, and witness. Old Testament passages that recommend distance from all aspects of other religions (e.g., Asherah poles in Exod. 34:13) abound. Second Corinthians 6:14 warns that mere association with the things of false gods is dangerous. Paul cautions against eating otherwise nutritious food offered to idols because it might be a bad witness, raising needless questions in people's minds about one's ultimate allegiances (1 Cor. 10:14–22).

We take an "it depends" position on this issue. Since witness is risky anyway (putting the ninety and nine sheep at risk to find the one lost one; Luke 15), perhaps it is best to err on the side of embracing the wideness of God's mercy when it comes to finding ways to worship and honor him. That should be the criterion: does a practice have the prospect of honoring God, both in our own devotional life and in our public witness? Practices are, after all, just practices. The same practice can be used to dishonor God and to honor God—see the Pharisees' mistakes with prayer (Matt. 6:5).

God: Is the Christian God the God of All Religions?

Those who answer yes note that God created the whole world and everyone in it. God created us all in his image. God created us to want to know him (Gen. 1:27). Thus, when human beings, no matter when or where, reach out to something beyond space and time, they are, whether they know it or not, reaching out to *the* God. Those who answer no argue that when the non-Christian religions describe their transcendent principle, whether Brahma, dharma, Allah, or whatever, the differences between that principle and the God of the Christian Bible are so distinct that to say they are the same is to play fast and loose with language. And God is a jealous God when it comes to other gods (Exod. 34:13).

We agree with both the yes and the no. If we were philosophers, we would say that if you answered this question ontologically, according to the way things are, you would answer yes. There is only one true God, so anyone describing the ultimate principle of the universe, no matter what the quality of the description, is referring to the biblical God. But if you answered the question epistemologically, according to what we as human beings know and how we perceive the world, you would begin to make distinctions according to the way the ultimate principle is described.

Religion: Where Do Non-Christian Religions Come From?

Some say that non-Christian religions come from the devil, the father of all lies (Matt. 13). And the devil does try to deceive us (Job 1:9–11). Others emphasize that since God is the creator of everything (Gen. 1:1), all religions, as creations of his creation (us), come from God. God gave us the freedom to choose our own destinies, thus our own religions (Ps. 119:45). Therefore, non-Christian religions at their best are the well-intentioned but in many ways mistaken creations of human beings instinctively reaching out to God. The resulting religions are thus imperfect mixtures of truth and error, good and evil (2 Cor. 11:13–15).

We think the religions of the world are human creations.

SPHERE OF HERMENEUTICAL THEMES

Even after we have limited the biblical data by choosing a specific question to ask of it, most of us still find ourselves longing for some overarching way of looking at the bigger question, how should we as Christians relate to people of other religious traditions? Most of us long for a simpler statement of what it means to be Christian in such contexts.

This was the longing of the rich young ruler when he came to Jesus asking what he lacked in living a godly life. Jesus answered by identifying one thing that the rich ruler needed: "If you want to be perfect, go sell your possessions

---

SIDEBAR 2.6
THE EIGHT THEMES

It is probably wrong to say that there are an unlimited number of hermeneutical themes. It might be better to consider themes we actually find in the Bible. But it is probably also true to say that what really makes the task come alive for you may not do the same for your best friend. Prayerfully consider each of the following as themes that make the gospel an operational reality for you:

1. Great Commission: Preach the gospel.
2. Great Commandment: Love your neighbor as yourself.
3. Golden Rule: Do unto others as you would have them do unto you.
4. Great Model: What would Jesus do?
5. Great Transformation: Kingdom of God.
6. Eschatology: Spiritual warfare.
7. Human Well-Being: God's preferential option for the poor.
8. Judgment: Reward and punishment.

---

and give to the poor" (Matt. 19:21). It was also the longing of the teachers of the law when they asked Jesus which commandment was the most important: "Love your neighbor as yourself" was Jesus's answer. Jesus also gave a similarly comprehensive summary of what we are to do when he was about to leave his disciples to return to the Father: "Go and make disciples of all nations," he said.

One of the first things we notice is that these are different summary statements. One is to give to the poor, one is to love your neighbor, and a third is to make disciples. What do we do when we are looking for a similar overarching summary statement under which to organize all our activities in relation to people of other religions? We instinctively know it would be a mistake to put all these statements in competition with one another, trying to decide which one is the right one for everyone for all time. After all, Jesus said them all. We presume he meant them all, that he wasn't just willy-nilly suggesting something to satisfy a nagging questioner.

Perhaps the answer, then, lies in recognizing that all these themes are true and good, and that knowing which one organizes our attempts to live out the gospel lies more in first deciding the nature of our call and our gifts. Evidence suggests that this was what Jesus was doing: the organizing principle for the rich man was to serve the poor, for the lawyers to follow a summary law, and for the disciples to make more disciples. Perhaps Jesus was discerning what would best make the gospel come alive for each of these groups of people.

Pre-texts

Theology and Personality

I t would be idealistic, of course, to think that we can approach the Scriptures with our minds a blank slate. Try as we might to empty ourselves of certain preconceived notions and ideas, we still bring many of them to the reading of the text. These notions and ideas are the grid through which we interpret the text, and for heuristic purposes they can be divided into two categories: theological and personal.

Together these two categories become a person's unique theological fingerprint. They determine how a person interprets the text, at least for the first reading or two. Categories of thought, ways of learning, and personal idiosyncrasies all influence the way we read the biblical record and attempt to discover the word of the Lord.

So important are theology and personality that with regard to people of other religions, we need to bring a different understanding to bear on what we are undertaking. We need to see ourselves as bearers of God's gift of grace. The questions we must ask concern how we can give this gift in the most appropriate way. Giftive mission is the way forward with the difficult-to-reach populations of other religions.

To see the value of making this metaphor of witness the central one, it helps to identify some alternative metaphors rooted in other theologies that most often determine how we approach the reality of other religions. Following is a brief summary of the most common possibilities, categorized according to traditional sectors of the church, the most commonly embraced theological and missiological positions, and different geographical regions of the world. See where you find yourself agreeing. Don't be worried if you agree with more than one.

THEOLOGY

Before we can begin to see how theology influences the way we answer our key question—what is the Christian responsibility to people who believe in and belong to another religion?—we must know what theology is: *Theology is the way a community of believers constructs the world so that members can begin to see the world through God's eyes and can communicate with one another, acting accordingly.*

To see how this definition functions, let's look at the four key ideas it contains. The first idea is *community*. Theology is in the end a group, not an individual, endeavor. Communities develop, believe, and act according to the theologies they develop together, not as individuals. This may seem like an odd statement given that most of our Christian theologies bear the name of an author: Augustine, Aquinas, Luther, Calvin, Simons, Wesley, Edwards, Barth, Tillich, and hundreds more. But unless the theologies these men developed influenced communities—Roman Catholic, Lutheran, Reformed, Free Church, Methodist—to act in accordance with their teachings, these theologies would have died soon after they were written.

Second, theology is a *constructive* exercise. That is, theologies are human creations, not divine ones. God revealed the Bible, not Calvinism. Theologies are human attempts—constructions—to give immediate meaning to God's revelation in a particular setting. God intended his revelation—the Bible—to

---

SIDEBAR 3.1
DEFINITION OF THEOLOGY

Theology is the way a community of believers constructs the world so that members can begin to see the world through God's eyes and can communicate with one another, acting accordingly.

Communal: Theology at its best is a group, not an individual, endeavor.

Constructive: Theologies are human creations. The Bible is revelation; theology is reason.

Sui generis: Theology is a unique way of conceiving the world, not to be confused with philosophy, ideology, or piety.

Communicative: Theology is a way of communicating with one another so that we know how to act.

speak to all generations, to all times and places. Because of differences in language, culture, history, philosophical worldviews, and so on, however, God's meaning must be constantly contextualized, that is, put into forms that have meaning for different groups of people. God's revelation is the same yesterday, today, and forever, but theologies change.

In practical terms, this means that we have quite a bit of choice in which theology we choose to serve as our vehicle of meaning. We can choose to be a Wesleyan one day, a Calvinist the next. Most of us, however, are not quite so cavalier about our theologies as that notion might imply. We choose a theological point of view because we believe it to be the truest representation of God's revelation possible in our respective context—our time, this place. We believe our theologies are true, and therefore, we do not change them lightly even though in theory we believe that "doing theology" is an ongoing exercise.

Third, theology is a special way of *conceiving* the world. That is, it is not just any old construction that could be mistaken for philosophy or ideology or advertising. In doing theology we are attempting to see the world in a different way. Christians believe that at the heart of faith is a reorientation of our perspective. Whereas once we were lost and saw the world through the eyes of our passions and our lusts and our desires, now we are found and see the needs of the world through a different set of values. We see the world through God's eyes, measuring the needs using God's values, not ours, as our standard. We desire that our hearts be broken with the same things that break the heart of God (Graham 1984).

It is this goal, this attitude, that prevents our constructive exercises in theology from becoming either our or our community's exercises in self-aggrandizement. We are, in a sense, constructing theological buildings meant for God's habitation, not ours. Theology as seen through God's eyes may surprise us: it may—indeed it should—challenge us. Even though we in a sense create our theologies, if conceived in this way our theologies immediately assume a life of their own. They become vehicles of judgment. They become reservoirs of mercy. They become storehouses of tradition. They become these things because we give them up, even as we write them, to glorify God (Newbigin 1995).

Finally, theology eventuates in *communication*. Theology is all about communication. Good theology creates thought forms and ideas and terminology and expectations that enable us to live and act together so that we are "made complete in the same mind and in the same judgment" (1 Cor. 1:10 NASB).

Most of us during our lifetimes have two theologies. The first, call it Theology I, is the one we inherit from our parents and our church. It is most often not an explicit theology. Rather, it is a way of looking at the biblical text that results from the questions we were taught to ask in Sunday school, the answers we were given in sermons, the emphases put on certain biblical texts and not others because of the way our pastors, priests, and teachers were taught

53

themselves to view people of other religions. Some of us go on to develop a more explicit theology, call it Theology II, which is a result of specific study as we grow older and mature in our faith. Often it does not differ a great deal from our Theology I. Sometimes it does, however, because we choose to look at the questions in different ways or to ask a new set of questions.

Let's take a look at some emphases of a few of these theologies, especially as they relate to mission to people of other religions. Most of us grow up being heavily influenced by one or more of the following ways of looking at mission to non-Christians.

Roman Catholic

In a sense, the community of theologians, missionaries, and missiologists in the Roman Catholic Church have the longest tradition of thinking together about people of other religious traditions. They trace their history as a community back to Jesus's words to Peter in Matthew 16:18–19: "And I tell you that you are Peter, and on this rock I will build my church, and the gates of Hades will not overcome it. I will give you the keys of the kingdom of heaven; whatever you bind on earth will be bound in heaven, and whatever you loose on earth will be loosed in heaven." From one perspective, then, Roman Catholic approaches to mission flow from the emphases of this key biblical passage (Schmidlin 1933).

Two emphases seem especially important for mission: the building of a church and the importance of the church hierarchy as God's representatives on earth. Given these priorities, it makes sense that the goal of mission for Roman Catholics has focused on planting churches and establishing leaders of those churches who are duly ordained in the apostolic line. This focus led to a key phrase that has characterized this mission approach: "Outside the church there is no salvation" (*extra ecclesium nulla salus*). This approach has been widened among some Roman Catholic missiologists in recent years, but the key elements have not changed: the planting of a church complete with apostolic leadership (Abbott 1966).

The modern missionary movement in this tradition can be coordinated with the colonial expansions of two Roman Catholic countries, Spain and Portugal. Missionaries hitched rides on merchant ships and accompanied military forays generated by the respective kings of those two countries. To avoid conflict among the missionaries of the two countries, a fifteenth-century accommodation between the two kings and the church leaders divided the incipient colonial regions between the two countries, giving appointment power to the kings, an arrangement called *patronato real*.

The growth of the colonial ventures created a need for large numbers of missionaries. This need led to the establishment of missionary orders, congregations, and societies within the Roman Catholic Church in the sixteenth

SIDEBAR 3.2
ROMAN CATHOLIC MISSIONS

Mark of mission	Establish churches and the church tradition
Origins	First century
Locus classicus	"You are Peter and on this rock I will build my church" (Matt. 16:18).
Mission heroes	Bartolomé de Las Casas in Latin America, Ignatius Loyola in Rome, Francis Xavier in Japan, Matteo Ricci in China, Roberto de Nobili in India, Junípero Serra in North America
Demographics	Over one billion Roman Catholics, 100,000 foreign mission workers

century. Differences of opinion about how mission should be done could be accommodated by allowing the different orders to focus on their respective methodologies. The founding of a large number of these groups in a short period of time led to the formation in 1622 of a mission administration body within the church called the Congregation for the Propagation of the Faith. This congregation still administers Roman Catholic missions from its office in the Vatican. Since not all Roman Catholics who are called to missions work are also called to take holy orders, lay missions organizations have proliferated. The Society for the Propagation of the Faith, established in 1817, acts as an umbrella organization for many of these lay missions groups.

The geographical sweep of Roman Catholic missions has been worldwide. Naturally, great heroes of missions emerged from these efforts: Francis Xavier (1506–52 in India, Japan); Ignatius Loyola (1491–1556 in Rome); Matteo Ricci (1552–1610 in China); Junípero Serra (1713–84 in California); Bartolomé de Las Casas (1484–1566 in Latin America); and Roberto de Nobili (1577–1656 in India), to name a few. The man sometimes considered the father of Roman Catholic mission studies, Josef Schmidlin, wrote his treatises in Munster from 1876 to 1944 (Dries 1998). Today there are just over one billion Roman Catholics in the world, and they are represented by approximately one hundred thousand foreign missionaries (John Paul II 1990).

Orthodox

Some people would consider the phrase "Orthodox missions" an oxymoron. Yet the history of the Orthodox Church (the so-called Eastern church) would belie that perception. Constantine himself was given honorific titles by the early church that expressed their mission expectations: "Equal to the Apostles" and "Overseer of the People Outside." It is clear from these titles and from the deeds of the early Eastern church that mission was important.

The Orthodox were mission-minded before the rest of the church had even identified the concept (Ware 1963).

We read much about the spread of the church to the West following the conquests of the Roman imperial army. The church also moved east, yet without benefit of an empire to follow.

The Doctrine of Addai tells how the missionary Addai (second century) took the gospel to Syria, the first missionary to cross the Roman border into the East. Ulfilas (311–83) triumphantly spread the gospel among the Teutonic tribes, earning him the title "Apostle to the Goths." Alopen, "a highly virtuous man," carried the gospel to China along the Old Silk Road in 635–49, attracting the attention of Emperor T'ai Tsung (Moffett 1992).

Of course, calling Addai, Ulfilas, and Alopen Orthodox missionaries is to commit an anachronistic error since the history of the Orthodox Church is usually dated to the Great Schism of 1054. Even the great missionaries to the Slavs, Cyril and Methodius, who are most closely identified with the Orthodox Church, did their work a century or two before the Great Schism.

From the West's traditional point of view, Orthodox missions don't register as emphatically on our radar screens because they don't entirely fit our traditional concept of missions. The Orthodox Church fully embraced the concept of indigenization long before it was called that. The signature verses of Orthodox missions might be Acts 2:9–11: "Parthians and Medes and Elamites, and residents of Mesopotamia, Judea and Cappadocia, Pontus and Asia, Phrygia and Pamphylia, Egypt and the districts of Libya around Cyrene, and visitors from Rome, both Jews and proselytes, Cretans and Arabs—we hear them in our own tongues speaking of the mighty deeds of God" (NASB).

SIDEBAR 3.3
ORTHODOX MISSIONS

Mark of mission	Create national/regional churches
Origins	The Great Schism, tenth century
Locus classicus	"Parthians and Medes and Elamites, and residents of Mesopotamia, Judea and Cappadocia, Pontus and Asia, Phrygia and Pamphylia, Egypt and the districts of Libya around Cyrene, and visitors from Rome, both Jews and proselytes, Cretans and Arabs—we hear them in our own tongues speaking of the mighty deeds of God" (Acts 2:9–11 NASB).
Mission heroes	Addai in Syria, Ulfilas to the Goths, Alopen to China, Cyril and Methodius in Monrovia
Demographics	250 million Orthodox with 2,500 cross-cultural mission workers

Orthodox missionaries believed in doing missions in the vernacular, in the languages spoken by the peoples they sought to reach. They translated the Scriptures into the vernacular. They translated the liturgy into the vernacular. And they straightaway insisted that the church be run by indigenous leaders. The goal was to plant the church, but a "national" church, essentially running on its own, tied only loosely to the patriarch at Constantinople: "The goal is a national church that embodies the particular characteristics of that people" (Stamoolis 1986, 53).

Practically speaking, this means that missions in the Orthodox Church are local affairs, administered for the most part by national churches. Missions in the Orthodox Church, it might be said, are as much a matter of liturgy as of street preaching, as much a matter of reaching people here as of reaching people over there. Today there are approximately 250 million people who belong to Orthodox Churches. About 2,500 of them might be considered cross-cultural missionaries.

Anglicanism

When Queen Elizabeth I finished in 1558 what Henry the VIII had begun, she laid the groundwork for a church that was to grow far beyond the borders of England. When she established the Church of England, she assured its success in the home country. But it was up to the church to be the church, that is, to reach beyond its borders as a mission church.

It took a while. As Stephen Neill observes, "The missionary efforts of the Anglican Church had been few, weak, and intermittent" before the eighteenth century (1986, 286). But in 1699 and 1701 two events accentuated the church's commitment to mission. In 1699 the Society for Promoting Christian Knowledge (SPCK) was founded to publish and disseminate books, tracts, and other information about the Christian faith. And in 1701 the Society for the Propagation of the Gospel in Foreign Parts was established and began its mission campaign by sending the first church missionaries to America. In 1799 a third group was formed, the Church Missionary Society (CMS), to create a triumvirate of mission-minded agencies.

It may seem a bit odd that in a church of episcopal structure, two of the three (SPCK and CMS) were essentially parachurch agencies serving the church structure proper. But maybe it is not so odd in a church called together out of one part Catholic sacramentary, one part Protestant theology, and one part episcopate.

The goal of Anglican missions is to transform the world and everything in it. This transformation includes individual souls to be sure. But it also includes social structures such as political process, economic functions, arts, and science. There is a striking parallel not only between the spread of the British Empire and the spread of the Anglican Church but also between the methods used by each. Indigeneity came late to both.

But come it did. Anglican churches have become models of indigenization and local participation. The Anglican Church enjoys this advantage because it can incorporate a variety of culturally appropriate theologies. Centered as it is in liturgy, in the Book of Common Prayer, the Anglican Church has produced its share of heroes of the faith. They include Henry Martyn (1781–1812) in India, who in his thirty-one short years translated the Bible into Arabic, Hindustani, and Persian; James Legge in China (1815–97), who translated the Confucian classics into English; Robert Codrington (1830–1922) in Melanesia, who led the way for the nearly total conversion of Oceania; and of course Roland Allen (1868–1947), who wrote one of the most influential missiology books of the twentieth century, *Missionary Methods: St. Paul's or Ours?* (1962).

Anglican missionaries have not penetrated the world with the gospel like "the thief who comes only to steal and kill and destroy." They "came that they may have life, and have it abundantly" (John 10:10 NASB). Through both official church boards in local communions and voluntary societies, the word has been spread. Today approximately four thousand foreign missionaries represent approximately eighty million members of the worldwide Anglican communion.

Mainline Churches

The Protestant Reformation produced the mainline churches, the Lutherans and the Reformed churches. A later reformation in England led by John Wesley produced the Methodist churches. In the twentieth century these three church groups developed an approach to missions that remains distinctive to the theologies of Martin Luther, John Calvin, and John Wesley, yet they also have certain common characteristics that have led them often to be grouped together as mainline churches.

First, the distinctives: For Luther, mission meant reestablishing the church on its true evangelical foundation in Jesus Christ and the gospel. The goal is universal proclamation although not universal conversion. Gustav Warnack (1834–1910),

---

SIDEBAR 3.4
ANGLICAN MISSIONS

Mark of mission	Celebrate worship together using the Book of Common Prayer
Origins	Sixteenth-century England
Locus classicus	Book of Common Prayer
Mission heroes	Henry Martyn in India, James Legge in China, Robert Codrington in Oceania
Demographics	80 million Anglicans with 4,000 cross-cultural mission workers

SIDEBAR 3.5
MAINLINE MISSIONS

Mark of mission	Establish partnerships with indigenous churches
Origins	Twentieth century
Locus classicus	"Do nothing out of selfish ambition or vain conceit, but in humility consider others better than yourselves" (Phil. 2:3).
Mission heroes	Gustav Warnack, Bartholomaeus Ziegenbalg in India, Nikolaus von Zinzendorf in Moravia, John Wesley in North America

the father of Protestant missiology, systematized this approach. Bartholomaeus Ziegenbalg in India (1682–1719) and Nikolaus Ludwig von Zinzendorf in Moravia (1700–1760) were prime exemplars of Lutheran missions.

John Calvin taught that the goal of mission is to glorify God. Jesus summed up his work in John 17:4: "I have brought you [Father] glory on earth by completing the work you gave me to do." Mission succeeds because of faithfulness, not results. Since nothing exists outside of God's kingdom and God is sovereign over all, in one sense everything we do to further God's kingdom is mission.

John Wesley himself was a missionary for a time to the American colonies. As a result of his experience, Wesley always saw himself as what we today call a global Christian. Wesley was fond of saying, "The whole world is my parish." As a result, Methodists of all sorts have always had a passion for mission. For United Methodists this passion is institutionalized in the Board of Global Ministries.

A significant recent emphasis of mainline mission efforts has been the partnership concept. As the sharp demarcation between "sending" churches and "receiving" churches continues to blur, the idea of mission as a joint effort between two or more partners has grown. In such relationships, each partner church has a higher regard for its partner than for itself, following Philippians 2:3 and Romans 12:10. Partnership means full equality and freedom in decision making (Hutchison 1987).

Free Church

One outcome of the Protestant Reformation in the sixteenth century was the flowering of so-called free churches. Free churches are "free" of two things: restrictive denominational structures and establishment as national churches. Ironically, what associative structures these free churches do develop tend to arise from a commitment to missions (Latourette 1941).

Originally the term "free church" referred to three dissenting churches in England: the Baptists, the Congregationalists, and the Methodists. Since then the term has come to mean any church that distinguishes itself intentionally from the Roman Catholic, Orthodox, or mainline church structures. Such churches usually consider the primitive church normative because of its lack of structures and connections. Thus, free churches today include Baptists, Mennonites, and Brethren, among others. Although each of these denominations has distinctive approaches to mission, the Baptist mission story is an illustrative example of how free church mission functions.

It was an English Baptist pastor, William Carey, who earned the title "Father of Modern Protestant Missions." Carey and his English Baptist brethren were separatists who because of their Calvinist understandings didn't participate in missions. Predestination, or at least their understanding of predestination, made missions redundant. Carey, after studying Scripture—particularly Isaiah 54:2–3—demurred and began a call to cross-cultural missions. He wrote a call to missions: *An Enquiry into the Obligations of Christians to Use Means for the Conversion of the Heathen* (1792). He then was instrumental in forming the Baptist Missionary Society, which raised money to send him and his family to India in 1793. The trend caught on. Congregationalists formed the London Missionary Society (1794) and the American Board of Commissioners for Foreign Missions (1810). Baptists in America formed the General Missionary Convention of the Baptist Denomination in the United States (1814), whose first missionary was Adoniram Judson to Burma (Myanmar). The Southern Baptist Convention formed its mission board in 1845.

Free church missions are influenced in the scope and nature of their work by their congregational polity and their advocacy of the separation of church and state. Planting local, largely self-governing churches that attend to the spiritual needs of their members is the goal of free church missions. Although this does not necessarily translate into a split between the proclamation and social action aspects of mission, it does lead to a relatively low public profile of free church missionaries in most missionary contexts. Mennonites, for example, are often referred to as the "quiet ones in the land."

That does not mean that the free churches have not produced their fair share of missionaries; notable free church missionaries include George Whitefield

SIDEBAR 3.6
FREE CHURCH MISSIONS

Mark of mission	Use means to convert the lost
Origins	Eighteenth century
Locus classicus	"Enlarge the place of your tent" (Isa. 54:2).
Mission heroes	William Carey, George Whitefield, Adoniram Judson, Thomas Coke

(1714–70), William Carey (1761–1834), Samuel Mills (1783–1818), Adoniram Judson (1788–1850), and Thomas Coke (1747–1814), among others.

As one might surmise, free churches tend to do missions through independent mission boards and agencies, although increasingly the larger denominations have formed their own mission boards. Because of the difficulty of clearly labeling some denominations as free churches, only very rough estimates of their numbers can be assigned.

Pentecostal/Charismatic

The Pentecostal/charismatic movement began in the twentieth century with four revivals that spanned the globe: the revival in Topeka, Kansas, in 1901; the Welsh revival in 1904–5; the Azusa Street revival in 1906; and the India revival in 1906. Almost from the beginning the movement was missionary. Because Pentecostals and charismatics believe that miracles of the Holy Spirit will accompany the preaching of the gospel, missions are not so much planned presentations of the gospel as they are extemporaneous witnesses to the power of the Spirit in one's life (Wacker 2001).

The goal of these spontaneous witnesses is the filling and fullness of the Holy Spirit. These witnesses anticipate Joel's expectation set forth in 2:28–29:

> "It will come about after this
>> That I will pour out My Spirit on all mankind;
>> And your sons and daughters will prophesy,
>> Your old men will dream dreams,
>> Your young men will see visions.
> Even on the male and female servants
>> I will pour out My Spirit in those days." (NASB)

This theological expectation led to mission efforts that emphasized Spirit baptism, miracles in preaching, indigenous church principles, and church growth. Because these methods didn't always coexist well with those of existing mission agencies, early Pentecostals formed their own mission institutions such as the Assemblies of God in 1914, Pentecostal Assemblies of Canada in 1922, Pentecostal Holiness Church in 1911, and Church of God Cleveland Tennessee in 1902.

Recognition of Holy Spirit power for missions soon became more acceptable in mainline denominations, and many charismatic renewal movements within the denominations produced a second wave of missionaries. A third wave was created by the signs and wonders movement of the 1960s.

Pentecostal/charismatic missions have been enormously influential, especially in so-called third world countries. Because of their focus on the work of the Spirit, they readily relate to cultures for which spirit power, especially demonic power, are realities. This gives Pentecostal/charismatic missionaries

---

SIDEBAR 3.7
PENTECOSTAL/CHARISMATIC MISSIONS

Mark of mission	Enable the filling and fullness of the Holy Spirit
Origins	Twentieth century
Locus classicus	"It will come about after this that I will pour out My Spirit on all mankind" (Joel 2:28 NASB).
Mission heroes	A. B. Simpson, A. J. Gordon, David Yonggi Cho, Rick Seward, Loren Cunningham, David DuPlessis
Demographics	Nearly 600 million Pentecostals, 85,000 cross-cultural mission workers

---

access to indigenous forms of spirituality that more rationalized theologies do not have.

The recently formed Association of International Missions Agencies (1985) has over two hundred member organizations of Spirit-led missionaries, including Youth With A Mission (YWAM) and Christ for the Nations. Notable missionaries and mission leaders in the movement have included A. J. Gordon, David Yonggi Cho, Rick Seward, Loren Cunningham, and Gordon Lindsay. David DuPlessis has been one of the key theorists of the movement.

Evangelism and missions and theology flow together naturally in the Pentecostal/charismatic movement and eventuate in expected church growth. A sure sign of the filling (and then fullness) of the Spirit is an enthusiasm to witness, whether at home or abroad. Connections with the Spirit/spirits in others create a bridge to the gospel that makes church growth inevitable. Of the approximately 585 million Pentecostal/charismatic Christians in the world, over 85,000 identify themselves as full-time, cross-cultural missionaries.

Evangelical

More than any other, perhaps, evangelical approaches to missions are both old and new. Evangelical missiologists assume the best of the modern missionary movement since William Carey, even as they readily acknowledge their own recent arrival on the mission scene.

The modern evangelical movement in the West can be traced to two roots, one secular, one religious. At the end of the nineteenth century, Darwinism, biblical criticism, and Marxism replaced what until then had been the dominant theistic worldview. Theists found themselves on the defensive. Some in the church, modernists, set about reconciling theology to this new, materialistic worldview. Others in the church, fundamentalists, decided to fight for supernaturalism. In the early twentieth century, this led to the second root of evangelicalism, an interchurch fight known as the fundamentalist-modernist

SIDEBAR 3.8
EVANGELICAL MISSIONS

Mark of mission	Conversion through Bible translation, medical work
Origins	Twentieth century
Locus classicus	"Go and make disciples of all nations" (Matt. 28:19).
Mission heroes	Billy Graham, Jim Elliot, Bruce Olson
Demographics	210 million evangelicals, 56,000 cross-cultural mission workers

controversy. This controversy swept through the major denominations, Baptist and Presbyterian especially. Fundamentalists lost the church fights and left the denominations to set up their own parallel church worlds, including mission agencies (Marsden 2006).

Although evangelicals identified with the fundamentalist separatists until the 1940s, they often sided with the anonymous middle in this controversy. Taking the best of Reformed theology, German pietism, and Wesleyan experientialism, evangelicals led by theologian Carl Henry and a young evangelist named Billy Graham carved out a theological and ecclesiological position that made unique contributions to mission theory.

Perhaps the most significant contribution is the unswerving commitment to missions as a central, not peripheral, dimension of the church. Mission is not an add-on for evangelicals. A second feature is the goal of evangelical missions, which is consistently stated as individual conversion or the born-again experience. Third is the vehicle of evangelism and missions, the voluntary agency, or as it is called in the United States, the parachurch.

These three contributions reveal why Matthew 28:19–20 has been the locus classicus of what is sometimes called Great Commission missions: "Therefore go and make disciples of all nations, baptizing them in the name of the Father and of the Son and of the Holy Spirit, and teaching them to obey everything I have commanded you."

This passage of Scripture can be read as the marching orders for all Christians to make mission central. If each of us is called to missions of some sort, then it makes sense to have a variety of mission institutions, in addition to denominations, in order to provide a wide variety of opportunities for mission—thus the large parachurch mission structure.

Heroes of evangelical missions tend to be those who made the most radical commitment to this central feature of Christian life, sometimes creating their own extrachurch structures to support their mission efforts: Jim Elliot (1927–56), who attempted to initiate a mission effort among a dangerous tribe in South America and died for his efforts; and Bruce Olson who simply caught a plane to South America and began mission work among the Motilone

(1978). Great Commission missions highly value this type of entrepreneurial mission, both individual and corporate. There are approximately 210 million evangelical Christians worldwide represented by approximately 56,000 missionaries (Nichols 1989).

Ecumenical

It is arguable whether a section should be devoted to the ecumenical missions movement. Three important considerations would seem to argue against it. First, the ecumenical movement is new, a twentieth-century phenomenon. In its institutional form as represented by the World Council of Churches (WCC), it is only a half century old. Second, it is not a church, not a mission-sending agency on its own. It is an association of 340 member churches whose first priority is church unity. Third, the WCC has been anything but traditional in its approach to missions. No church group has been clearer in its condemnation of traditional Western mission practices whenever those practices have slipped over into colonialism and Western imperialism (Beaver 1962).

Still, one might argue that this gadfly approach to traditional missions has been the strength of the WCC's contribution. It has nurtured one of the most important and influential approaches to mission today, and through its journal, the *International Review of Missions*, has widely influenced modern mission theology (Thomas 1995).

The mission theology the WCC advocates is a form of the theology called *missio Dei*. This approach teaches that mission is first and foremost God's mission. The churches of the world, far from being the sole institutional representations of God's mission on earth, are one of many institutional participants in God's mission. Political and economic institutions are also participants in God's mission, at least to the extent that they act on and embody gospel truths. Wherever you find good in the world, you are experiencing the *missio Dei* (Vicedom 1965).

The goal of this type of missions takes seriously the very nature of goals as future prospects rather than present reality. *Missio Dei* is rooted very much in

---

SIDEBAR 3.9
ECUMENICAL MISSIONS

Mark of mission	Enable participation in God's universal mission (*missio Dei*)
Origins	Twentieth century
Locus classicus	"The time is coming to gather all nations and tongues. And they shall come and see My glory" (Isa. 66:18 NASB).
Mission heroes	Aloysius Pieris, M. M. Thomas, Lesslie Newbigin, Kōsuke Koyama

eschatological hope. The goal of this approach to missions is the building of the kingdom of God in the world among all its peoples: "The time is coming to gather all nations and tongues. And they shall come and see My glory" (Isa. 66:18 NASB). All peoples will "no longer [be] strangers and aliens," but "fellow citizens with the saints, and are of God's household" (Eph. 2:19 NASB).

Mission in this understanding is a matter not of mere talk but of encountering, sharing, dialoguing. This conversation has produced one of the finest missiologists of the twentieth century, Lesslie Newbigin, who wrote some of his best work in response to WCC activities. Member constituencies of the WCC account for approximately 550 million Christians. The WCC does not officially send out foreign missionaries.

Asia

We usually think of the Asian church as the product of mission efforts, not as a producer of new churches. That thinking must change. The Asian church is developing its own theology, which gives its approach to mission a distinctive flavor, and has produced thousands of cross-cultural missionaries (Ramachandra 1996).

Some of the so-called theologies of Asia are imitations of Western theologies. Traditional mission theologies simply transposed Augustine, Aquinas, Luther, Calvin, Wesley, Tillich, or Barth into an Eastern context. More recently Asians such as Aloysius Pieris of Sri Lanka and the Minjung theologians of Korea have written Asian versions of Latin American liberation theologies. Raymundo Panikkar, M. M. Thomas, and Stanley Samartha, all in India, have attempted to show the applicability of Western pluralist theologies to India's Hindu (Panikkar and Samartha) and secular (Thomas) settings. Evangelicals like Vinjay Samuel and Ken Gnanakan have made attempts at transposing evangelicalism to Asia. A minority, including Japanese scholar Kazoh Kitamore (pain of God theology) and Kōsuke Koyama (water buffalo theology), have attempted truly Asian theologies that focus on shame rather than guilt, the community rather than the individual, the spirits, the interconnectedness of reality, contemplation instead of action, and becoming as opposed to being (Fernando 2001).

These themes are producing distinctive approaches to missions that attempt to reveal the gospel in both method and substance. Naturally, those approaches are as varied as the cultures of Asia's thirty-plus nations are varied. And they depend on recent trends such as economic globalization, scientism, and secularization, and more regional histories of colonialism and communism and the resurgence of Hinduism, Buddhism, and Islam. Since at present only 3 percent of Asia's three billion people are Christian, the missionizing of Asia is a future task, not a past history.

That is not to say the past has been insignificant. Thomas brought the gospel to India in the first century, Alopen to China in the seventh, Francis

> ### SIDEBAR 3.10
> ### ASIAN MISSIONS
>
> | | |
> |---|---|
> | Mark of mission | Use of Asian thought forms |
> | Origins | Nineteenth century |
> | Locus classicus | "What you worship in ignorance, this I proclaim to you" (Acts 17:23 NASB). |
> | Mission heroes | Watchman Nee, John Sung, Vinay Samuel |
> | Demographics | 30,000 Asian mission workers |

Xavier to China in the sixteenth, and Adoniram Judson to Burma (Myanmar) in the nineteenth.

But the future lies with the Asian churches themselves. In 1973 the Asia Missions Association was formed to coordinate mission agencies throughout Asia. In 1990 the First Asian Mission Congress was held in Seoul, Korea, with 1,200 participants. A second, held in Pattaya, Thailand, in 1997 had 300 participants. Over 30,000 Asian missionaries are currently sent out by Asian countries, with India (20,000) and Korea (20,000) leading the way.

Asian missions are characterized by the absolute necessity of positively engaging the worldviews underlying the world religions of Hinduism, Buddhism, and Islam. The signature verses of Asian missions come from Acts 17:23, Paul's acknowledgment of the world's religions at Athens: "While I was passing through and examining the objects of your worship, I found an altar with this inscription, 'TO AN UNKNOWN GOD.' Therefore what you worship in ignorance, this I proclaim to you" (NASB).

It has become almost commonplace these days, with the economic growth of both China and India, to say that Asia, with 60 percent of the world's population, most of whom are unreached for Christ, holds the key to the church's mission of the future.

Africa

Africa today is the best example of an indigenous church mission movement. A joint product of early Western missions efforts and what is sometimes called the African Initiated Church movement, the African church's mission efforts have led to one of the fastest growing churches in the world (Mugambe 1989).

Interestingly, the theologies that underlie the vast majority of these mission efforts have given pause to many in non-African churches. On one hand, the theologies prevalent in many of the mainline and free churches of Africa are mostly Western imports overlaid with African themes: liberation theologies

---

SIDEBAR 3.11
AFRICAN MISSIONS

Mark of mission	Use of African thought forms
Origins	Eighteenth century
Locus classicus	"The Spirit gives life" (John 6:63).
Mission heroes	David Livingstone, Isaiah Shembe

imported from Latin America, pluralist theologies manufactured in academia, and evangelical theologies modeled after capitalist economics. On the other hand, the theology underlying the African Initiated Church movement includes so many elements of African traditional religion that the World Council of Churches balked at admitting these churches as members because of fears of syncretism. (They were recently admitted as associate members.)

In many ways, the African continent has had a Christian presence longer than any geographical area save the Middle East. Mark brought the gospel to Egypt in the first century. It spread across the northern coast until the Muslim presence halted missions until modern times. Then, during the sixteenth through nineteenth centuries, Portuguese (Roman Catholic), Dutch (Reformed), British (Anglican), and other European (free church) merchants and traders brought with them all imaginable varieties of Christianity. The twentieth century has seen the development of the African Initiated Church movement, which has created a vital church with mission distinctives of its own (Irvin and Sundquist 2001).

Two distinctives of indigenous African missions seem most important. First is their radical *indigeneity*. The African Initiated Churches have produced congregations that have seriously included African worldviews on subjects such as the ancestors, time, tribalism, God, and sin. At its best this theology is both African and Christian. Second is the *incidental* nature of African missions. This distinctive concerns more the method of mission than its theology, or one might more accurately say lack of method. The African church has spread because of social urbanization, geographical relocation, and political turmoil, not necessarily because of planned mission campaigns. (However, there have been numerous such campaigns in postcolonial Africa, and many Africans—Kenyans and Nigerians especially—are involved in cross-cultural mission across denominational stripes.) Looking at the way the church has spread in Africa due to migration and immigration forces one to reexamine how the church has spread in the rest of the world and consider whether we have, in our analyses, emphasized too much human agency and planning and not enough the serendipitous working of the Spirit through nonreligious factors (Hiebert, Shaw, and Tienou 1999).

Perhaps the signature verse of African mission could be that "the Spirit gives life" (John 6:63). The goal of this kind of mission is to be open to the working of the Spirit as churches based on existing tribal and social structures become a reality.

PERSONALITY

Of course, theology is not the only grid through which budding missiologists view biblical revelation and empirical data as we seek the word of the Lord for today. There is also the matter of personality, that is, the matter of what each of us individually brings to the text and context as we seek answers to our question, what is the Christian responsibility to people who believe in and belong to another religion? We each have a multifaceted personality, unique in many respects, common in others, that we bring to the task.

What is personality? A personality is the pattern of dispositions to behave in certain ways that characterizes an individual. This pattern of dispositions includes habits, thoughts, feelings, and values, all of which come into play when we interact with and adapt to what is going on around us, especially when we interact with people of other religions. Each of us has a distinctive pattern of these elements. That is, we are all unique.

If our uniqueness were the end of the story, then it probably would be useless to continue this discussion. Each individual person would become a totally new object of study. In our discussion of how personality affects a Christian's answers to missiological questions, we would be left with saying, "Well, we can discuss how John Smith or Jane Doe (individuals) responded to the question when asked, but we can make no generalizations from that." We could make the point about the importance of the role of personality in the quest for biblical truth but do nothing further.

But we can do more because observations have taught us that there are common elements to human personalities that can be defined and measured. These common elements include observable behaviors, patterns of thinking, feeling and value structures, and overall approaches that structure the way we see the world. Observation has taught us that in each of these four areas, human beings tend to behave, think, value, and structure life in a finite number of ways. We share most of our traits and dispositions with other human beings (Hiebert 1985).

So how does personality affect mission? Our position is that the work we do as missiologists is neither totally free of our personalities nor totally dependent on them. That is, total objectivity is a chimera, yet it is a mistake to think that our work is totally dependent on our personalities and our personal circumstances.

Can knowing that our personalities are, to some extent, a factor in our missiological witness to people of other religions help us in that work? The

---

SIDEBAR 3.12
ELEMENTS OF THE THEOLOGICAL PERSONALITY

Behaving: self-directing or collaborative or deferring
Theologizing: comic or romantic or tragic or ironic
Feeling/Valuing: sacred rite or right action or devotion or shamanic mediation or
    mystical quest or reasoned inquiry
Knowing: assimilators, convergers, accommodators, divergers

---

simple answer is that knowing something about our personalities and our gifts does help. Our personal approach is an additional piece of data to be factored into our attempt to discover the word of the Lord. We then have three very different kinds of "knowledge" contributing to our exegesis: revelation, contextual knowledge, and personal knowledge.

Personal knowledge—that is, the knowing that results from the mixture of our unique personality with the text and context—is not simple to analyze. It does not qualify as data that can be publicly verified. By definition it is subjective. Perhaps it is easier to speak of it instrumentally. Personal knowledge is the way we know something, not the knowledge itself. Personal knowledge is the perspective we bring to a subject. Personal knowledge involves what happens to the text and context when (and because) we engage it (Polanyi 1964).

Although personal knowledge has as many dimensions as there are different persons, for illustrative purposes let's look at four dimensions of personal knowledge: ways of behaving, ways of theologizing, ways of feeling/valuing, and ways of knowing. Actually, these are not randomly selected aspects of personal knowledge. We picked these four for two reasons: First, they correspond to a reasonable consensus among personality theorists that there are four well-defined levels of personality, moving from the public, observable, and conscious (behavior) to the private, implicit, and unconscious (knowing). Second, measurement tools exist for each of the four. After briefly describing each level, focusing especially on its religious manifestations, we have selected a measurement tool (from among hundreds in each category) that again focuses on the religious dimension of the category.

Behaving

The first level is *behavioral*. There are many ways of analyzing religious behavior, from the overt measures of church attendance to tithing habits to Bible reading, and so on. Some behaviors are more specific, however. One such set of behaviors might be called problem solving. To measure the extent to which people use their religion and religious beliefs to solve problems, Kenneth Pargament and his colleagues developed a test called the Religious

Problem-Solving Scale (Pargament et al. 1988). When faced with a problem, we tend to take one of three approaches to solving it, using our religion as a resource. The *self-directing* approach is basically a self-help approach that calls on ourselves as religious resources to solve the problem—the pray-to-God-but-row-to-shore-yourself approach. The *collaborative* approach is based on the notion of people seeing themselves as copartners with God to solve their problems. The *deferring* approach is derived from Eric Fromm's concept of an authoritarian religion that stresses passive submission to an omnipotent, sovereign God when we are faced with problems (1998). Most of us tend toward one or another of these basic orientations when faced with life's issues.

Theologizing

The second level is *theologizing*. The more general category here might be called thinking. The kind of theologizing or thinking we are identifying here is distinct from the theological positions one chooses to take, which we discussed in the first half of this chapter. The two are not unrelated, of course. But the one discussed earlier concerns theology, the actual positions one takes on the issues. The one we will examine now concerns theologizing or the way one does theology and the overall theological outlook one brings to the task.

Many tests are used to measure this factor. We have chosen to call your attention to one developed by James Hopewell (1987), who says that there are four theologizing styles or worldviews. The first he calls the *comic*. Those with a comic worldview are sure that everything will work out in the end, that the great forces in this world will be harmonized. Comics learn things by a kind of gnostic intuition and are convinced that our current difficulties are illusory, that underneath lies a fundamental harmony we cannot yet see. Life is the story of the discovery of that harmony. You can hear these essential assumptions in phrases like "go with the flow" or "it all adds up." A religious leader like Robert Schuller might exemplify this type.

Romantics see life as a quest guided by knowledge that comes from a charismatic (inspired) spirit. Life's complications are the result of the adventure and risk of pitting protagonist—often a heroic figure—against antagonist. The result is a priceless reward: a great love, a holy object, a boon for the world. The story moves from tranquility to crisis to fulfillment. You can hear this worldview in phrases like "expect a miracle" or in accounts of transforming encounters with God's Spirit. Someone like Oral Roberts might fall into this category.

Tragedy, like romance, involves a hero or a heroine whose vicissitudes force his or her decline. The opposite of romance, the story begins with apparent—but mistaken—fulfillment and moves through crisis to decline. Here there is a great power to which one can only submit, a transcendent will against which struggle is futile. The sacred canonic texts that reveal this divine will are the only sure source of knowledge. You can hear this worldview in calls for "dying to self" and "submitting to God's will." Jerry Falwell might fit with this style.

An *ironic* view of the world simply takes life on its own terms—no heroes or intuition or transcendent wills here, just the empirical facts, please. What seems to be an uncommon blessing or strange uncertainty proves to be naturally explainable. The reward in an ironic story is not the resolution of some grand dilemma but the camaraderie of the all-too-human actors who face it. You can hear this worldview in emphases on "relevance" and "fellowship." Walter Cronkite's famous closing line, "And that's the way it is," exemplifies the ironic worldview.

Note that this way of measuring theological personality divides things differently than our ten theological positions did. One can theologize as a comic and be Roman Catholic, Orthodox, Anglican, mainline, free church, Pentecostal, Evangelical, ecumenical, Asian, or African. In other words, each of the ten theological loci includes people who do theology from each of the four theologizing positions: comic, romantic, tragic, and ironic. What we are measuring here is not a person's theological position but their way of doing theology.

Feeling/Valuing

The third level of a person's theological personality involves their feelings about religion—more specifically, how individuals value certain aspects of the religious life. The test we offer for measuring this aspect of personality is derived from Dale Cannon's *Six Ways of Being Religious* (1996). Cannon argues that there are six primary ways of being religious:

1. *Sacred Rite.* For people who embrace this way the most important aspect of their religious life is the rituals they perform, both alone and in community. These include both regular worship and ongoing sacraments, such as communion, and one-time rituals such as baptism, marriage, church membership, and so on. This way of being religious values ritual the most highly.

2. *Right Action.* People who favor this way value correct behavior the most. Correct behavior is defined by religious teaching and is taught/encouraged by called prophets. Right action people most admire people who live everyday lives and do right by their friends. They aspire to be like those people in everything they do.

3. *Devotion.* For some people the most important way to be religious is to show devotion to key figures in the tradition, particularly God and Jesus Christ. Religious life for these people can best be described as emotional nurture. A successful day is one begun by some devotional practice that reveals an attitude of dedication to God.

71

4. *Shamanic Mediation.* The fourth way of being religious may seem the most strange. Cannon calls it shamanic, but it is actually a quite common concern with finding spiritual resources and power to help with the mundane, everyday events of life. In this understanding the most important function of religion is to help with personal crises.

5. *Mystical Quest.* The fifth way of being religious is the path of the spiritual journey. Life is best seen as an ongoing process, not a fait accompli. What is most important is growing, moving ahead. The religious life is best seen as a series of unfolding events and experiences. One can "fail" at these experiences only by not persevering in them or not pursuing them in the first place.

6. *Reasoned Inquiry.* For some people the most important part of the religious life is the intellectual. Thinking about God and believing the right things about God and God's gracious activity toward us is the sine qua non of religion for the reasoned inquiry way.

In describing the six ways of being religious, Cannon cautions against making too sharp the distinctions among them. The paradigm is a teaching device meant to illumine, not pigeonhole, us. The six ways become important only in the context and content of someone's religion—more specifically, the theological content of a person's religion. The ways of being religious have no content of their own.

Knowing

The fourth and deepest level of one's theological personality involves one's overall way of knowing. Again, many measures of this capacity have been developed. But one of the more useful is the Learning Style Inventory, developed and tested by David Kolb (1993). The test identifies four types of learners:

1. *Assimilators.* Assimilators score high in observation (as opposed to action) and high in thinking (as opposed to feeling). Thus, assimilators tend to be the theory makers of the thinking world.

2. *Convergers.* Convergers also score high in thinking but lean toward taking action rather than observing. They look for win-win situations that can pull people together.

3. *Accommodators.* Accommodators score high in feeling and acting. They are the peacemakers whose feelings encourage actions that will create harmony.

4. *Divergers.* Divergers are observers who feel strongly. They are very principled people who both see and feel the problems of the world. Calling attention to those problems often constitutes their life's focus.

USING KNOWLEDGE OF YOUR THEOLOGICAL PERSONALITY

Needless to say, knowing how one knows, that is, how one approaches problems in terms of these four categories—behaving, theologizing, feeling/valuing, knowing—can be a great aid in predicting and anticipating how one's interaction with people of other religions might go. It is important to realize that none of these four approaches to the world are necessarily either good or bad. There are perhaps three specific values of knowing one's general theological personality:

1. It helps us factor in the influences of our own theological personality on our thinking about people of other religions.
2. It helps us find our missiological niche, what God is calling us to do in terms of people of other religions.
3. It helps us relate in effective ways to people of other religions, who also tend to have their own specific "theological" personalities.

Theological personality influences the way we do theology, the way we read the Bible. Theological personality influences our missiology and how we witness to people of other religions.

This influence is both obvious, on the one hand, and difficult to analyze, on the other. The difficulty derives from the complexity of human nature. Dividing the so-called theological personality into four parts—behaving, thinking, valuing, knowing—helps somewhat but in the end is itself artificial. And the problem of verification is bothersome. Still, the very obviousness of the influence means we must try to understand it.

Consider an example: Paul's sermon to the Athenians in Acts 17, the unknown god sermon. Paul sees the religiously plural Athenians cover their spiritual bases by dedicating a statue "To An Unknown God," in case they have missed one. Paul identifies the unknown god as the God of the Bible. It is a masterful example of contextualized witness.

Yet the sermon itself is complex and subtle. Paul's contextualization is also subtle. His methodology reveals much, and the sermon must be read carefully. The more one reads here, the more one learns. And the more Spirit-led the readers, the greater the insights discovered. For example, consider two different theological personalities reading the same text. One reader has a theological personality identified by the following four characteristics derived from the four elements of the theological personality:

Behaving: Collaborative. Partners with God to address presenting issue.

Theologizing: The comic outlook. Optimistic, sure everything will work together for good due to the underlying unity of God's creation.

SIDEBAR 3.13
INTERRELIGIOUS ENCOUNTER

When a Christian meets someone who belongs to a non-Christian religious tradition, we call that an interreligious encounter. All such meetings have certain things in common:

1. An encounter is a process that reflects both opposing wants and coinciding wills.
2. An encounter is a state produced by energy and interests that demand a solution.
3. Encounters, whether positive or negative, should lead toward the following eight goals:

    i. Clarification of issues, both primary and secondary
    ii. Understanding of persons
    iii. Acknowledgment of differences
    iv. Channeling of aggression into constructive methods of expression
    v. Encouragement of everyone to participate in decision-making process
    vi. Establishment of agreed-upon procedures for problem solving
    vii. Improvement of decision-making process
    viii. Reconciliation when conflict is present

Valuing: The mystical quest. Considers most important the spiritual journey of life that leads us closer and closer in our relationship with God.

Knowing: Assimilator. Looks for the overarching meaning of all experience, a theory builder, observing reflectively from the sidelines.

What does such a person see in Paul's sermon to the Athenians? He or she is likely to emphasize certain of Paul's themes and methodologies. Verse 22—"Men of Athens! I see that in every way you are very religious"—would appeal to the assimilationist tendencies of Paul's understanding of general revelation (Rom. 1:19) and his method of calling people of other religions' attention to the ways God may already be at work in another religious system. Verse 23—"Now what you worship as something unknown I am going to proclaim to you"—would appeal to the comic outlook that sees the underlying harmony of various points of view when they exist. Verse 28—"For in him we live and move and have our being"—would appeal to the value this person places on the mystical-quest nature of the religious life.

Now consider a second theological personality:

Behaving: Deferring. Willing to allow God's sovereignty to take its course.

Theologizing: The tragic outlook. A great power exists to which one can only submit, a transcendent will against which struggle is futile. The sacred canonic texts that reveal this divine will are the only sure source of knowledge.

Valuing: Reasoned inquiry. Thinking about God and believing the right things about God and God's gracious activity toward us is the sine qua non of religion for the reasoned inquiry way.

Knowing: Diverger. A principled person who both sees and feels the problems of the world. Calling attention to those problems often constitutes her or his life's calling.

What might this person see in Paul's sermon to the Athenians? He or she might focus on verse 31—"He has given proof of this to all men by raising him from the dead"—a verse that presents a warrant for a certain belief and would appeal to the value this person places on reasoned inquiry. Verse 29—"We should not think that the divine being is like gold or silver or stone"—calls into question the Athenians' practice of worshiping images of gold, silver, and stone and would probably be something a diverger interested in the problems of the world would note. And this person would probably read verse 28—"For in him we live and move and have our being"—not in a mystical-quest way but with the tragic outlook that sees the world in terms of an inexorable divine will.

These two readings are both faithful renderings of Paul's sermon and its meaning for us today, but each has different emphases due in large measure to the theological personalities of the readers.

PART 2

Practices

Beyond Competition and Cooperation

Let's complicate what we said in chapter 2 about context with one more factor. Remember, we said that our current world religious context is unique. We then went on to describe the most important distinguishing features of today's world religious context. Seemingly simple so far.

But the complicating factor is that in addition to the global factors affecting our context in general, there are features to every local context that influence the form of the global factors. Put simply, there is no single context but rather many local contexts across the globe. The answer to our question—what is the Christian's responsibility to people of other religions?—will be a little different in each of the many local contexts we might face.

Does that mean that it is impossible to draw general conclusions or find universal answers to our question that will apply everywhere? Not exactly. We believe that a study of Christian mission history shows that faithful, successful Christian mission to people of other religions follows universal practices that can be distilled for our benefit. We will identify eleven Christian mission practices that seem to be present in all faithful, successful Christian mission efforts to people of other religions. Together these eleven practices constitute the how-to of giftive mission.

These eleven practices take different forms in different contexts. But if we look hard enough, they are there. They are like the unseen structural supports that hold up a well-built building. They are not reducible to simple bromides about mission as a competitive exercise, or mission as a cooperative exercise, or mission as proclamation, or mission as service. They are deeper than theories, deeper than methods, deeper than strategies.

And because they are deeper than theories, methods, and strategies, it would be easy to talk about them in abstract ways. To avoid that, we have identified a Christian mission hero whose approach seems to typify a specific practice. In some cases, it is almost as if that person discovered it; it seems as if that mission hero were the first to make a particular practice a linchpin of mission strategy.

We believe, though, that the following eleven mission practices are present in every faithful, giftive mission. We believe that properly understood and applied to each unique context, they are what makes Christian mission Christian. They are both models and standards of what Christian mission to people of other religions should be today.

As proof of that view, we have intentionally selected mission heroes from across the world, from across the Christian denominational spectrum, and from across the religious audiences they chose as their field of labor. Good mission is no respecter of denomination, geography, or religious context. Good mission practice is such because it is faithful to biblical warrants and is astutely applied in different contexts around the world according to the leading of the Holy Spirit.

Universality

Reaching Out to All, Including Christians

Mission Exemplar: Paul
Location: Asia Minor, Rome
Audience: Gentiles
Time: First century

Timeline
- Saul the persecutor of Christians (Acts 8)
- Saul's conversion: Damascus road experience (Acts 9)
- God's call to Paul (Acts 9:15)
- Peter's vision (Acts 10)
- The Antioch church's commitment (Acts 13)
- The focusing of the call (Acts 13:46–52; 18:6)
- The Gentile controversy (Acts 15)
- 46–57, 57–67 Paul's missionary journeys
- 67–68 The mature mission (letters to the churches)
- 67–68 Paul's imprisonment and death in Rome

Resources to Consult on Paul's Mission

Roland Allen, *Missionary Methods: St. Paul's or Ours?* (Grand Rapids: Eerdmans, 1962).
Robert Banks, *Paul's Idea of Community*, rev. ed. (Peabody, MA: Hendrickson, 1994).

Dieter Georgi, *The Opponents of Paul in Second Corinthians* (Philadelphia: Fortress, 1986).

Dean Gilliland, *Pauline Theology and Mission Practice* (Grand Rapids: Baker Academic, 1983).

Martin Goodman, *Mission and Conversion: Proselytizing in the Religious History of the Roman Empire* (New York: Oxford University Press, 1996).

Michael Green, *Evangelism in the Early Church*, rev. ed. (Grand Rapids: Eerdmans, 2004).

L. J. Lietaert Peerbolte, *Paul the Missionary* (Leuven: Peeters, 2003).

Wayne Meeks, *The First Urban Christians: The Social World of the Apostle Paul*, 2nd ed. (New Haven: Yale University Press, 2003).

Johannes Munck, *Paul and the Salvation of Mankind* (Richmond: John Knox, 1959).

Rodney Stark, *The Rise of Christianity: How the Obscure, Marginal Jesus Movement Became the Dominant Religious Force in the Western World in a Few Centuries* (San Francisco: HarperOne, 1997).

I t would be hard to argue that Paul was the Christian church's first mission worker. You could make that case for any one of several of the apostles: Peter, James, John, Thomas, or even others.

Paul was first, though, in a much wider sense. He was first in that he saw the task in a much wider frame of reference than anyone before him. It is that wider frame of reference that really captures Paul's mission innovation, his practice, from which all mission workers everywhere benefit.

Paul's frame of reference was the whole world. To be sure, Jews like Paul saw God as universal in that God created the whole world and all its people in the beginning and provided for that world and its people to the end. But for Paul, that sense of universal was not enough. Jesus came that the whole world might be saved. This was a sense of universal that surely would have struck first-century hearers as almost incomprehensible. The God of one "tribe" was interested in the people of all "tribes."

Such a radical innovation presented Paul with two problems. They are the same problems that face all innovators. One was the problem of how to actually carry out the innovation—in Paul's case, preach the gospel story to the whole world and everyone in it. This included all Gentiles, which was Paul's term for non-Jews. The second problem was as difficult—how to convince his colleagues in the church that this was actually what Jesus commanded. Paul, in effect, was fighting two battles, a frontline battle with the Gentiles and a rearguard action with his own constituency.

Radical innovations call for radical methodologies, or what appear to be radical methodologies to the people involved. Paul had a radical story of God's universal love and a radical idea that all people, even Gentiles, needed to hear this story because it was for them. Paul's sermons in Acts and in his letters to the new churches he founded exemplify his radical new approach. And they also begin to tell the story of who responded first to this new kind of universalism—and who resisted it.

For some people such a story was liberating. It freed them from the prisons of poverty and class and race and religion. For others such a story was a threat to power and privilege. Paul's universalism was presented as a gift to Jew and Gentile alike, but it was a gift with strings attached.

As a gift, the story of Jesus was readily available. The challenge was to find ways to give it, and that meant finding people with skills to spread the word. Paul needed people with storytelling skills. He needed helpers and coworkers.

Make no mistake. Paul was the innovator here. His idea was not just an abstraction; it was also a way of doing mission that has motivated all mission workers in the two thousand years of Christian mission history. His universalism—that all people benefited from the story of Jesus and needed to hear it—became paradigmatic for all mission workers.

The story of Paul's innovation, his novel missionary practice, makes for fascinating reading. His idea changed the world. It was the initial step in Christianity's long journey to becoming the world's largest religion. Where did this idea come from? Why did it strike everyone as being so new?

PAUL'S IDEA

It is clear that Paul and others since him have seen that the ultimate source of the innovation was God (Acts 9:15). And with regard to the development of the idea in practice, we must recognize that Peter laid an important piece of groundwork when he had a decisive vision before visiting Cornelius, the Roman centurion, a vision that did not just blur the distinction between clean and unclean but obliterated it (Acts 10). Even the early church at Antioch must be given some credit for having the courage to send Paul to the field, providing him with missionary authorization and support (Thomas 2004). Many people in the Jerusalem church did not agree with this decision.

Still, that doesn't do full justice to the newness of Paul's idea that the gospel was for Jew and Gentile alike. We still must ask how new this understanding of universalism was in Paul's day. How did it compare with what passed for universalism in the general cultural milieu in which Paul lived? Not all the "universalisms" of the first-century Middle East were the same, of course. In Paul's day, three universal "ranges" dominated: geographical, ethnic, and utilitarian.

No one, not even Paul, had a grasp of the full geographical scope of the world. Paul's conception, trained as he was with a Hellenistic education in Tarsus, surely had a wider conception than most. His geographical scope probably extended just beyond the borders of the Roman Empire and the

---

SIDEBAR 4.1
THE MANY MEANINGS OF UNIVERSAL

1. Sociological: Religion as a single universal culture; "we are the best, the one and only."
2. Philosophical: Religion as a universal message; "the one, true philosophy."
3. Religious: Religion as universal salvation for everyone; "everyone will be saved."
4. Christian: Religion as a universal offer of eternal salvation; "everyone who accepts God's gift of grace will be saved."

---

lands formerly conquered by Alexander the Great. Perhaps he had even studied Strabo's geography. But his concept of the "whole world" did not approach ours geographically.

For the people of Paul's day, the concept of universal was limited not just by geography but also by class and function. According to their understanding, "my" god(s) acted on behalf of "all people," but "all people" referred only to people like me. Other people had their own gods. Further, the measure of my gods' universality was taken by evaluating their power, not their geographical or ethnic scope, not their divine intentions. Gods were as gods did. Their universality was inextricably tied to the political and military reach of the people who worshiped them.

Enter into this henotheistic climate the Jewish idea of universality introduced by Abraham. El Shaddai was a universal God in principle but was still tied to a single people, the Israelites. God had created all people and cared for all people but had a special relationship with Abraham's extended family and their descendents. This was a two-tiered universality. There was only one God to be sure, but that one God could not break totally free of the tribal structure of the day.

Into this climate Paul introduced a new understanding, one with five main features. The first feature was its *compatibility* with the Jewish understanding of El Shaddai. Yahweh's creation was an intentional one, with humankind created in God's own image so that relationship with Yahweh was not only possible but desirable. In this early Jewish understanding of universality, Yahweh's special provision for Israel was a necessary step in reconciling all people to God and to one another. This step was made necessary only because the original Edenic universality had been ruptured by the fall.

Paul's *universality*, then, had as its context the Jewish story. It would have seemed new to his Jewish hearers but not totally foreign. And since the Jewish story posited a radical Edenic universality, it could be made compatible also with the worldview of Paul's Hellenistic listeners. In explaining his new understanding of universality, Paul could either root it in the current Jewish experience of history (which he always did when his sermons were addressing primarily Jewish audiences), or he could appeal to Hellenistic understandings of universality (see Acts 17). Either way, his innovation had a quality demanded of all successful new ideas, a "newness" still rooted in the common experience of his listeners.

Still, it was a new idea, and Paul had to show that it was better than the old ideas. And its advantages were obvious. Paul's idea did away with the three prerequisites of the old universality. Most of the existing versions of universality based inclusion on birth: one had to be born to a Jewish mother, born to a Roman father, born into a proper Greek family. In Paul's version this was no longer required. Many of the existing versions of universality also required one to do something to earn inclusion. Proper birth was necessary but not enough. Worship rites of some kind were also required. And for some versions of universality, extensive initiation rites were a prerequisite.

Paul's universality had none of these requirements. He was fond of calling his version a gift. A gift, he implied, is freely given. Nothing is required of the receiver except acceptance: no special birth, religious deeds, extensive learning, or skill acquisition. All the cultures with which Paul came into contact had gift rituals, of course. But Paul was the first to apply these understandings to religion. His new idea was better, because it really was free, a gift of grace.

Perhaps it is too much to draw from this advantage a third feature of Paul's universality, its *simplicity*. But perhaps not. The way Paul explained the gospel put it within reach of everyone he met. Everyone understood what a gift was. Ever since they were children, they had been taught the implicit cultural rules related to how one gave and received gifts. All that was required was to apply these understandings to a new cultural sphere, that of religion.

The fourth feature of Paul's innovation was its *trialability* (Rogers 1983, 231). All one had to do was receive this gift and try it on for size. See if it doesn't make a big difference in your life. Full commitment and public declaration could come later if you liked. For now, "try it, you'll like it" was enough.

This feature was important for a fledgling radical movement such as the way of Jesus. The Hebrew tax collector Nicodemus was a case in point. That he came by night to explore this new idea symbolized the social danger of public declaration. Although for some—the poor and already dispossessed—the danger was nil, for those with social standing the freedom to try the new religion and see how it affected their lives was an extremely attractive feature. The gospel was free, available to all, and, for the moment at least, risk free.

The power of the Holy Spirit to change lives, to make things better, enhanced tremendously Paul's notion of the gospel story. Thus, the fifth feature, the fact that the gift of grace *made a difference* in the lives of those who tried it, set this new idea apart from the secret faiths of the mystery religions. It was one thing to feel the difference in one's own life because of the power of God's grace; it was quite another to be able to observe it in the lives of others who had also embarked on the experiment/way.

SIDEBAR 4.2
PAUL'S SERMONS ON UNIVERSAL MISSION

SERMON	AUDIENCE	PLACE	CONTACT POINT
Acts 13:16–41	Jews/God-fearers	Antioch (synagogue)	People who worship God
Acts 14:15–17	Unbelievers	Lystra	A common humanity
Acts 17:22–34	Greek philosophers	Athens (temple)	Unknown God
Acts 20:18–35	Church elders	Ephesus	Our shared community
Acts 22	Jewish mob	Jerusalem	Personal testimony
Acts 26:2–23	King Agrippa	Caesarea	Religious rights

Early Christians became known as the ones who cared for one another: who buried the unwanted dead of others; who were peaceful and faithful subjects of the ruling authorities (within limits); who gladly suffered persecution and even death for their new way of life; who rejected certain lifestyles and dark practices because they were incompatible with their faith in the story of Jesus.

HOW PAUL SPREAD HIS NEW IDEA

There can be little doubt that the content of Paul's message—the gospel is for Jew and Gentile alike—was innovative. There is less agreement, however, about the novelty of his method. Some scholars insist that Paul did little more than adopt and slightly adapt the methods already in use by the Jews, mystery religionists, and Hellenistic philosophers of his day.

Scholars generally agree that there was no shortage of Jewish proselytizers, cultic recruiters, and philosophical apologists walking the streets of almost any first-century Mediterranean city. Factor in freelance teachers ("false teachers," the biblical texts sometimes call them) and spiritual opportunists (sorcerers, witches, etc.), and one quickly gets the picture: Paul started out as little more than a bit player in a cornucopia of available religious ideas offered to the faithful, the jaded, and the naive.

The agreement ends, however, once the de facto scene is described. Paul, some contend, did much more than other self-advocating religionists of his day. Paul had not just a novel message but a distinctive method. Some argue that whereas the teachers of Judaism, mystery religions, and Greek philosophy taught for basically informational purposes only (and accepted conversions to their way of looking at things almost reluctantly), Paul's method aimed at and was based on actively seeking converts.

Of course, all of Paul's competitors wanted converts too. "It is natural for people to expand the realm of their environment through aggressive, peaceful, subtle, or understated ways so that other people might become participants in it. . . . It is natural for people to be offended when people from some other environment compel them to change or successfully win members of their community over to a new and different environment. These processes will continue as long as there is human society" (Borgen, Robbins, and Bowler 1998, 13).

Yet it may be that even though Paul seemed to be doing what scores of others were doing at the same time and in the same places with similar goals, his approach did indeed have some distinctive features. To explore this notion, let's sample the evidence of self-advocating activity among Paul's three main competitors: Jews, mystery religionists, and Hellenistic teachers.

Jewish Proselytizers

There is evidence that Jews of the New Testament world spent time in what they described as proselytizing activity (Georgi 1986, 7–8). Matthew, for example, makes a disparaging reference to scribes and Pharisees who "cross sea and land to make a single convert" (23:15 NRSV), and Paul in Romans 2:17–24 describes four ways Jews relate to non-Jews: as guides to the blind, as lights to those who are in darkness, as correctors of the foolish, and as teachers of children. It appears that at least one of the reasons Jews were twice expelled from Rome was their proselytizing activity. Several Greek authors reference this activity (Origen, Josephus, Juvenal, Tacitus, Horace). Finally, a large body of Jewish literature written in Greek seems to have at least in part a powerful apologetic intent to Greek readers.

Mystery Religion Recruiters

The evidence for mystery religion recruiters is as strong as for Jewish proselytizers. It is a bit harder to characterize these particular attempts at gaining new members because of the diversity of cults. The cult of Mithras, for example, was spread by the Roman military. Immigration to the city of Rome was one of the primary ways of spreading the Egyptian story of Isis and Osiris, the basis of a couple of other powerful cultic groups. Traders and merchants always brought with them new religious movements: political cults such as Roman emperor worship, more traditional religious cults such as the worship of Asclepius, and philosophies such as the teachings of Dionysius. The claims of other groups ranged in purpose from apologetic to propagandistic to proselytic. Plutarch, Apuleius, Livy, and others clearly attest to the self-advocacy of the many diverse religions of Paul's day (Georgi 1986, 9).

85

Hellenistic Philosophy Teachers

Livy, in particular, offers detailed descriptions of traveling Greek philosophers who would enter a town, set up shop in the public square, and use this first-century "speaker's corner" as a venue for seeking adherents. He tells the story of how the worship of Bacchus "was introduced by a single Greek who . . . found success in seeking fellow worshippers" (Lietaert Peerbolte 2003, 70). The list of the traveling philosophical teachers includes Apollonius of Tyana, who advocated the teachings of Pythagoras; Alexander of Abonouteichos, who advocated the teachings of Apollonius; and Diogenes of Sinope, who taught Cynic philosophy, as did Alcidamas. From the letters of Paul, we learn that he was especially influenced by this last group of Cynic and Stoic philosophers. Paul both countered their teachings (i.e., in the Corinthian correspondence) and copied their methods (i.e., in his frequent use of diatribe form) (Hengel 1989, 11–12).

It seems incontrovertible that Paul was engaged in a work of persuasion and that, other than a few strategic differences involving matters of time and place, he was no less nor more persuasive than his competitors. As a persuader he was asking people to change, and in doing this he was in good, even multitudinous, company.

This is not to say, however, that there were no differences among the four groups we have chosen to examine. But the differences had little to do with the persuasive methods their representatives used and relatively little to do with the fact that change was being sought; they differed most regarding the kind of change being advocated.

Jewish proselytizers in their travels over sea and land to find converts were asking for a change that involved becoming a member of a culture defined by a set of clearly prescribed cultural norms. Beliefs were secondary and worship flexible, but becoming part of a people and doing what others want us to do (following Torah, practicing circumcision, keeping kosher, etc.) were paramount.

Mystery religion recruiters wanted people to join their *cultus*, which was defined as a set of worship practices. These worship practices were central to

SIDEBAR 4.3
PAUL'S COMPETITION

COMPETITION	ADVOCATES	CHANGE SOUGHT	METHOD USED
Jews	Proselytizers	New culture/religion	Lifestyle training
Mystery religionists	Recruiters	New worship practices	Secret teachings
Greek philosophers	Teachers	New way of thinking	Apologetics

the religion. So important were they that they were often kept secret, revealed to initiates in a series of staged levels of knowledge. Recruits were asked to learn and faithfully practice these rites.

Hellenistic teachers wanted their pupils to adopt a new way of thinking. The meaning of life became clear only to those who asked the right questions in the right way. Clarity and precision of thought—wisdom—superseded lifestyle and worship (if any worship was a part of it). To think right would lead to right living no matter what the cultural conditions.

Paul wanted change too, but not a change in culture, nor a change in worship practices, nor a change in thinking. Although these things might change over time (indeed, probably would), the primary change he sought involved the way people saw meaning in their lives. "Jews demand miraculous signs and Greeks look for wisdom, but we preach Christ crucified: a stumbling block to Jews and foolishness to Gentiles" (1 Cor. 1:22). Paul's primary request was that people accept an invitation to become part of a story that included their story but then superseded it. He was inviting people to become part of an all-encompassing gospel story, God's story. In this Paul differed from Jews, mystery religionists, and Greek philosophers. The innovation gave people a reason for living rooted in a new way of life.

THE RESPONSE TO PAUL'S INNOVATION

As we have noted, an innovation, any innovation, must succeed on two fronts. One is the community from which the innovation comes. In the case of the early Christian church, this is sometimes called the *missio interna*. For Paul this was the fledgling church, headquartered in Jerusalem. The second is made up of new "customers," in Paul's case the Gentiles of Asia Minor hearing the gospel story for the first time. This is sometimes called the *missio externa*.

Groundwork for acceptance of the universality of the gospel story had been well laid. Peter, after his vision dispelling the uncleanness of all Gentiles before his visit to Cornelius's house, had introduced the idea through his bold luncheon with Cornelius. And even though Peter may have backslid on the issue (Gal. 2), many Jewish Christians were exposed to this idea. It is probable that many accepted it. Further, many Gentiles in Antioch had become Christians without the interim step of becoming God-fearers, that is, proselytes of Judaism. They were models of what could be—Gentiles could become Christians.

The argument that they could become Christian without becoming full Jewish proselytes—that is, undergoing the rite of circumcision—was fairly easily won, with Barnabas and Paul telling a Jerusalem council meeting of their successes on their first missionary trip (Acts 15). Feeling the need, however, to establish some kind of criteria for membership, the church leaders mandated four seemingly unrelated criteria (vv. 28–29; a face-saving action?) and in effect gave Paul permission to follow his God-given calling.

The church at Antioch was given the task of staging the mission as part of its overall ministry portfolio. It selected Paul, Barnabas, and John Mark as the first missioners. On subsequent trips Paul teamed with Silas, and Barnabas teamed with John Mark.

The Gentile mission controversy did not simply disappear. Indeed, Acts 21–23 describes the Jewish community of Jerusalem having Paul arrested for teaching "against our people and our law and this place. And besides, he has brought Greeks into the temple" (Acts 21:28). This arrest ended with Paul being sent to Rome for trial. Before these developments, however, Paul firmly established the idea in the central towns of Asia Minor, where new churches were planted and grew.

And this, after all, was the second selling of the innovation. It was the heart of the matter, the *missio externa*. It would be easy to say that the selling was a success. Paul's letters to young churches form an impressive body of evidence that the universality of the gospel was an idea whose time had come. In addition to Paul's letters, we have a third-person account (the Acts of the Apostles) written by Paul's sometime companion, Luke, that corroborates the story distilled from Paul's letters.

As might be expected, the majority of the instances mentioned in Acts and Paul's letters involve Gentiles who heard Paul's invitation, evaluated his witness, and accepted the gift. A little over ninety names are mentioned in these sources, and eighty are mentioned positively as accepters of the gift, many of whom (thirty-five) became coworkers with Paul in the further spread of the gospel. (The line between accepter and coworker is often difficult to draw; we rely on what Paul or Luke says about the person, incomplete as that may be.)

Consider the story of Sergius Paulus, the proconsul of Paphos, an island in the Mediterranean Sea. A proconsul was a Roman political official charged with keeping in line the people in Rome's empire. Luke describes Sergius Paulus as an intelligent man who listened to Paul tell his story and, despite opposition from a skeptic also present, believed Paul's account of things and became a follower of the Way (Acts 13:6–12).

Some were healed through Paul's invocation of the Holy Spirit and became believers as a result. A good example is the story of an unnamed cripple in Acts 14:8–18.

Paul's ministry lasted long enough for some young people to become followers of Jesus because their parents had. One of Paul's ministerial protégés, Timothy, became a Christian because his Jewish mother was a believer, as well as perhaps his Greek father (Acts 16).

Some of the most instructive stories are of people who listen to Paul's presentation and decide for one reason or another not to accept the gift. Paul's response to these rejections is often as instructive as the refusals themselves. Consider a few of these stories:

1. Bar-Jesus (Elymas) was a sorcerer who not only rejected Paul's gift personally but attempted to subvert Paul's ministry to others (see Acts 13:6–12). Continuing a tradition established by Jesus, Paul responded vociferously and temporarily struck this seller of religious services blind.
2. At Athens Paul dialogued with Stoic and Epicurean Greek philosophers (see Acts 17:18–31). Although skeptical of Paul's claims, the philosophers invited him to make his case. Paul complied. Some accepted Paul's offer of the gift; others rejected it. Paul seemed to have felt he had been fairly heard, and he departed.
3. There is explicit and implied evidence that some people, seeing the healing power of the Holy Spirit evident in Paul's work, tried to use the power for their own ends without making the necessary commitments. The seven sons of Sceva mentioned in Acts 19:14–17 are the most explicit of the counterfeiters. No response from Paul was necessary.
4. Jews who rejected Paul's claims about Jesus were often the most threatening. Acts 23 tells the story of forty of these rejecters who took strict vows of abstinence until they had killed Paul. Paul's response was to seek protection and flee.
5. Some rejecters, such as the silver worker Demetrius (Acts 19), found Paul's message threatening to their business. Demetrius crafted silver images of the goddess Diana. Naturally if people quit worshiping Diana, his business would dry up. Paul, in this case of rejection, let the laws of commerce run their course.
6. Alexander the coppersmith apparently made personal attacks on Paul. "[He] did me much harm," Paul reports in 2 Timothy 4:14 (NASB). Paul supposed that this was a personal attack, and his response was distinctive. He simply turned revenge over to God: "The Lord will repay him for what he has done."

It is evident that Paul's response to rejection of his universal invitation was contextual. It depended on the nature of the rejection. It ranged from denouncement to silence, from gracious withdrawal to flight for his life. Saying something is contextual, however, doesn't mean that no underlying principle guided his response.

In his responses, Paul was both an idealist and a pragmatist. His responses are summed up in what might be called Paul's evangelistic principle: "I have become all things to all men so that by all possible means I might save some" (1 Cor. 9:22). Paul responded to rejection in whatever way would enhance future understanding and acceptance of the gospel story.

SIDEBAR 4.4
ANTIMISSIONARY: JONAH

Practice: Universality—Reaching out to everyone, including Christians

The hard work of mission can itself become an impediment to Paul's practice of universality. Mission is difficult. It takes our full energies. It becomes much more than a job or a vocation; it becomes a way of life. And when that happens, each of us naturally focuses more on the task at hand, sometimes becoming, in the process, blind to the bigger mission task in which others are engaged.

We hesitated to name Jonah, of Jonah-and-the-whale fame, as an antimissionary but in the end decided to do so with the caveat that we are talking about Jonah before his about-face.

You remember the story. God asked Jonah to "go to the great city of Nineveh and preach against it, because its wickedness has come up before me" (Jonah 1:2). But Jonah refused to go. He "ran away from the Lord and headed for Tarshish . . . found a ship bound for that port" (v. 3), and set sail. A great storm came up, and the panicked sailors threw Jonah overboard, where he was swallowed by a whale. He survived, however, and decided after all to do what God had asked of him.

This reluctance over his call is not why we are calling Jonah an antimissionary. Many of us run away from our call at first, and it usually doesn't take something as dramatic as being swallowed by a big fish to change our minds.

No, Jonah is an antimissionary because when God decided to forgive the Ninevites, even after Jonah had told them of their doom, Jonah's pride was hurt. He was angry with God for, well, being God. It is God's nature to extend the gift of grace to everyone and to forgive any and all who will accept the gift.

If we want to be God's missionaries, that universal sense of gift has to become our nature also. We are the messengers, not the setters of the conditions for forgiveness. God has already done that. We simply tell the story and to the best of our capacity model what God has done.

When Jonah got angry at God for being God, God said to him, "Nineveh has more than a hundred and twenty thousand people who cannot tell their right hand from their left, and many cattle as well. Should I not be concerned about that great city?" (Jonah 4:11). Shouldn't Jonah be concerned also? Shouldn't we?

REFLECTION AND DISCUSSION

1. Reflect on an experience when you became angry with God for being more forgiving than you wanted to be toward some individual or group.

2. Identify three practices that could help you learn to be more graceful in your attitude toward God's boundless grace toward others. Support your answer with scriptural references.

3. How can we extend God's gift of grace to people who "cannot tell their right hand from their left" and to animals (Jonah 4:11)?

One further type of rejection deserves mention. It might better be called desertion or abandonment. A few people apparently accepted Paul's innovative message and then after a period abandoned it. Several of these are mentioned in 1 and 2 Timothy: Archippus, Hymenaeus, Alexander, Philetus, Jannes, and Jambres. Paul's response to these backsliders might be characterized as a warning to those who remained faithful. These rejecters were perhaps teaching false versions of the gospel, and the faithful needed to be protected.

THE EFFECTS OF PAUL'S INNOVATION

The effect of Paul's mission work is, as they say, history. The church grew from its original group of Jesus and twelve disciples to become the largest religion in the world, with over 2 billion adherents today. Of the 6.5 billion people living on planet Earth today, one-third of them identify themselves as Christian.

And Paul's mission innovation, that the gospel is for everyone, is even more ubiquitous. That the gospel is a universal message is never debated (Meeks 2003, 107). We simply don't hear arguments that the gospel should be only for Americans or only for Africans or only for Asians. Only a radical, heretical fringe might make such arguments.

Even non-Christians in the world today acknowledge the universal intentions of the Jesus story. Of course, they don't always acknowledge it admiringly. Often they even argue that no religion should be a universal faith, or more likely, they want their own religion, be it Hinduism, Buddhism, Islam, or whatever, to be the universal religion. These critics often borrow Christian methods of mission and Christian arguments for the universality of Jesus's message as rationales and methods for their own religious tradition.

Paul changed the world and the world of religion because he dug deeply into the meaning of what Jesus did in first-century Palestine. He understood the message, and he understood what Jesus wanted us to do with it. The rest is indeed history.

5

Fellowship

Belonging Precedes Believing

Mission Exemplar: Patrick
Location: Europe, Great Britain, Ireland
Audience: Indigenous Celts
Time: Fifth century

Timeline
(All events occur in the late fourth and early fifth centuries.)

- Born in Britain
- Is kidnapped to Ireland (at age fifteen)
- Escapes back to Britain (after six years in slavery)
- Training for mission
- Returns to Ireland as missionary
- Establishes faith communities in different locations
- Is accused in ecclesiastical court by colleagues
- Dies

Resources to Consult on Patrick's Mission

Bede, *The Ecclesiastical History of the English People*, ed. and trans. Judith McClure (Oxford: Oxford University Press, 1994).

John B. Bury, *The Life of St. Patrick and His Place in History* (New York: Dover, 1998).

Alexander Carmichael, *Carmina Gadelica* (Edinburgh: Floris, 1992).

Douglas Dale, *Light to the Isles: Missionary Theology in Celtic and Anglo-Saxon Britain* (Cambridge: Lutterworth, 1997).

Liam De Paor, *Saint Patrick's World* (Notre Dame, IN: University of Notre Dame Press, 1993).

Máire B. De Paor, *Patrick: The Pilgrim Apostle of Ireland* (New York: HarperCollins, 1998).

Esther DeWaal, *Celtic Light: A Tradition Rediscovered* (London: HarperCollins, 1997).

Joseph Duffy, *Patrick in His Own Words* (*The Confession and the Letter to the Soldiers of Coroticus*) (Dublin: Veritas, 2000).

John Finney, *Recovering the Past: Celtic and Roman Mission* (London: Darton, Longman and Todd, 1996).

George Hunter, *The Celtic Way of Evangelism* (Nashville: Abingdon, 2000).

At sixty years of age, fifteen years after Patrick had been appointed a bishop in the Christian church of Ireland, he was brought to trial by his fellow bishops in Britain. For Patrick—who had been kidnapped, enslaved, and threatened with violent death at least twelve times in his mission to Christianize Ireland—this ecclesiastical trial on trumped-up charges was the low point of his life. "On that day I was powerfully tempted and might have fallen, now and in eternity" (M. De Paor 1998, 26).

As Máire B. De Paor relates in her masterful biography, *Patrick: The Pilgrim Apostle of Ireland*, "it is impossible to exaggerate the anguish Patrick endured on this occasion. . . . So soul-shattering were the allegations made, that he was stunned by the verdict to a point verging on despair" (147). Why was this sham trial so devastating? For a person who had suffered far worse in terms of physical danger, why was this petty betrayal by his peers Patrick's worst experience? The answer to that question reveals much about Patrick and his mission innovation.

The charges against Patrick were brought forward and evidence given to support them by one of Patrick's closest friends, a bishop who had recommended him to be a bishop in the first place. Patrick was stunned: "To him I had confided my very soul. . . . He it was who had said to me in person, 'Look, you are going to be raised to the rank of bishop.' How then did it occur to him afterwards to let me down publicly before all, good and bad, over something that he had previously granted me freely and gladly?" (M. De Paor 1998, 32).

The official charges against Patrick were two:

1. He had committed an unnamed indiscretion as an adolescent.
2. He had mismanaged the funds of his bishopric.

In the inquiry and subsequent trial, neither charge was found to have merit. Patrick survived the inquiry with his holy orders and his ecclesiastical appointment intact. It did not hinder his mission work, his reputation emerged as good as ever, and his orthodoxy was publicly approved. So why was this the worst experience for Patrick? Because it seemed to challenge the whole basis of his mission to the Irish.

Patrick believed that true mission was created in community. He believed that the church began by creating living communities of people trying to discover what it meant to be part of God's great story. For Patrick, belonging to such a community was the first step in discovering what it means to behave as a Christian and, finally, what to believe about God. Patrick's mission innovation might be summarized this way: "Belonging precedes believing." And the betrayal that led to his trial threatened that fundamental principle of witness.

What was threatened was the "belonging." As we have seen, Patrick became a bishop because of the support of his "dearest friend." Patrick owed this man much because it is likely that Patrick's qualifications, compared with those of other bishops, were lacking in areas they deemed important:

- Patrick had less official British church education. While his playmates were being educated in the "system," the British Patrick was kidnapped by Irish slavers and taken to Ireland for forced labor;
- Patrick had held fewer traditional church appointments leading to the bishopric. He had an odd career path. He chose what we would today call "frontier missions" as his calling instead of climbing the traditional ecclesiastical vocational ladder at home; and
- Patrick relied less on advice from his superiors in executing his mission and was more dedicated to contextualized mission methods to the decentralized, tribal Irish.

Yet in spite of these "shortcomings," Patrick's friend insisted that he would become a bishop. And he made good on his promise. So it was natural for Patrick to expect, when his trial came, for his friend to stand up for him. When the friend did not, when for some reason he not only did not defend him but joined in the accusations, Patrick felt deep betrayal. Wasn't "belonging" the basic thing, the most important thing, the nonnegotiable thing? Didn't members of the body of Christ, in spite of differences in worship, in belief, and in polity have an indissolvable unity in Christ?

Community is what made Patrick's mission to the Irish people work: a team of workers; an open invitation to join at any time; and an extension of the basic tribal nature of the Irish to the tribal nature of a Christian church, of *the* Christian church. The breaking of community because of false charges and personal betrayal challenged more than Patrick's title and reputation. It must have made him look long and hard at the basic principle of his life's work.

PATRICK'S IDEA

So what was this innovation of belonging preceding believing? For one, Patrick's mission innovation turned the current practice of the church on its head. The church as organized under the influence of the Roman Empire proclaimed, "If you believe properly we will let you belong." When Christian faith is approached from an institutional point of view (and building organizations and institutions is the Roman métier), this approach is understandable. It is the institution that represents the faith. The health of the institution becomes the most accurate reflection of the health of the faith. Thus, the church must be kept pure.

The theological justification for this position came from Augustine, who in the Donatist controversy was forced by circumstances to conclude that improper belief, heresy, and apostasy were grounds for dismissal from clerical status. The purity of the church was paramount, and purity as measured by belief became the standard.

Patrick had no shortage of belief. His credo shows theological acumen and sophistication. He often begins sections of his *Confession* with language about belief. For example, the second section of the *Confession* begins, "The Lord there made me aware of my unbelief that I might at last advert to my sins and turn whole-heartedly to the Lord my God." The fourth section of the *Confession* is Patrick's statement of faith in the Trinity:

> There is no other God,
> there never was and there never will be,
> than God the Father
> unbegotten and without beginning,
> from whom is all beginning,
> holding all things as we have learned;
> and his son Jesus Christ
> whom we declare
> to have been always with the Father
> and to have been begotten spiritually by the Father
> in a way that baffles description,
> before the beginning of the world,
> before all beginning;
> and through him are made all things, visible and invisible.
> He was made man,
> defeated death
> and was received into heaven by the Father,
> who has given him all power over all names
> in heaven, on earth, and under the earth;
> and every tongue should acknowledge to him
> that Jesus Christ is the Lord God.
> We believe in him

> **SIDEBAR 5.1**
> **PATRICK'S BREASTPLATE**
>
> *Carmichael (1992, 79)*
>
> *(Patrick may not have written this classic prayer to the Christian Trinity, but it fully captures what we know of his theology and has come to be associated with his name, that is, with what he did in Ireland. The prayer is also sometimes called "The Deer's Cry" or "The Lorica.")*
>
> I arise today
> Through a mighty strength, the invocation of the Trinity
> Through the belief in the threeness,
> Through the confession of the oneness
> Of the Creator of Creation.
>
> I arise today
> Through the strength of Christ's birth with his baptism,
> Through the strength of his crucifixion with his burial,
> Through the strength of his resurrection with his ascension,
> Through the strength of his descent for the judgment of Doom.
>
> I arise today
> Through the strength of the love of Cherubim,
> In obedience of angels
> In the service of archangels,
>
> In hope of resurrection to meet with reward,
> In prayers of patriarchs,
> In predictions of prophets,
> In preaching of apostles,
> In faith of confessors,
> In innocence of holy virgins,
> In deeds of righteous men.
>
> I arise today
> Through the strength of heaven:
> Light of sun,
> Radiance of moon,
> Splendor of fire
> Speed of lightning,
> Swiftness of wind,
> Depth of sea,
> Stability of earth,
> Firmness of rock.
>
> I arise today
> Through God's strength to pilot me:
> God's might to uphold me,
> God's wisdom to guide me,
> God's eye to look before me,
> God's ear to hear me,
> God's word to speak for me,
> God's hand to guard me,
> God's way to lie before me,

and we look for his coming soon
as judge of the living and of the dead,
who will treat every man according to his deeds.
He has poured out the Holy Spirit on us in abundance,
the gift and guarantee of eternal life,
who makes those who believe and obey
sons of God and joint heirs with Christ.
We acknowledge and adore him
as one God in the Trinity of the holy name.

(Duffy 2000)

God's shield to protect me,
God's host to save me
From snares of devils,
From temptations of vices,
From everyone who shall wish me ill,
Afar and anear,
Alone and in multitude.
I summon today all these powers between me and those evils,
Against every cruel, merciless power that may oppose my body and soul,
Against incantations of false prophets,
Against black laws of pagandom,
Against false laws of heretics,
Against craft of idolatry,
Against spells of witches and smiths and wizards,
Against every knowledge that corrupts man's body and soul.
Christ to shield me today
Against poison, against burning,
Against drowning, against wounding,
So that there may come to me abundance of reward.

Christ with me, Christ before me, Christ behind me,
Christ in me, Christ beneath me, Christ above me,
Christ on my right, Christ on my left,
Christ when I lie down, Christ when I sit down, Christ when I arise,
Christ in the heart of every man who thinks of me,
Christ in the mouth of everyone who speaks of me,
Christ in every eye that sees me,
Christ in every ear that hears me.

I arise today
Through a mighty strength, the invocation of the Trinity,
Through belief in the threeness,
Through confession of the oneness,
Of the Creator of Creation.

These five sentences are a brilliant summary of the Christian faith, of what we believe, couched in the characteristic Trinitarian form that became the essence of Celtic Christianity as it developed after Patrick. Anyone who reads these sentences and grasps what they stand for could never question the importance of belief in Patrick's understanding of what Christian faith is.

Yet when it came to communicating the gospel story to people who knew little or nothing about it, Patrick felt strongly that an invitation to join, to belong to the community of the faithful, should precede a demand for doctrinal allegiance. Mission was not enhanced by an approach that made such demands. It excluded instead of invited. It was a defensive approach to the religious tradition that betrayed a distinct lack of faith in the ability of God's people to absorb the hoi polloi without polluting the purity of the faithful—as if such purity really existed. In Britain of the fourth and fifth centuries, the doctrine-as-gatekeeper approach led to growth only if enforced by the political and military power of the Roman Empire. In short, Patrick recognized that in most situations in the world, and especially in wild and woolly Ireland, the doctrine approach did not work. Something else was needed.

The something else was the idea that the gospel invitation to accept the free gift of grace offered by God was not an invitation to perfect belief as a prerequisite for membership. Instead it was a no-strings-attached invitation to join the community, even if one did not yet know all the subtleties of systematic theology, even if a person's intellectual capacities did not predict that he or she would ever be able to grasp the theological nuances of Christianity. One could belong and that would lead to believing at whatever level one could manage and also to behaving as a Christian who lives by the fruits of the Spirit. This was Patrick's idea.

HOW DID PATRICK IMPLEMENT HIS INNOVATION?

We don't have enough information about Patrick's time to help us see clearly how he actually put his innovation to work. Compared with the extensive biblical record we have of Paul implementing his innovation, written records from fifth-century Ireland are few.

We do know that Patrick could not have picked a better time for his innovation. When one considers what was happening to the Roman Empire, to Britain, and to Ireland in the fourth and fifth centuries, it becomes clear that profound upheavals had created enough social uncertainty so that changes in church structure and practice must have seemed to be just a part of much wider social turmoil and therefore somewhat more acceptable.

Consider Rome, for example. The Roman Empire, so carefully organized into provinces and cities (*civitas*) and their cantons, was crumbling. The empire was under attack almost everywhere from tribal groups intent on gaining some sort of independence (in the case of tribes within the empire) or rich plunder (in the case of tribes outside the empire). Also, the tribes themselves were attacking not just Roman garrisons but one another, upsetting the internal peace of which Rome was so proud.

Not all the disorder was military and political. The Pelagian heresy was being fought by the church, and this conflict was especially important for Britain and Ireland since the monk who taught it, Pelagius, was originally from Britain. Churches everywhere found themselves forced to take sides in this dispute regarding grace and free will.

For Patrick, this general, empirewide disorder was important because the imperial order—so carefully imposed—was essentially the same order the church followed. Christianity, because of imperial Rome, had been to this point largely a hierarchical, top-down, urban movement, organized along the same lines as the empire. For reasons we shall see, this organization did not work well in Ireland.

Britain offers another example. The church in Britain had organized itself along the same lines as the Roman model, with centralized cities and bishops as administrative officers in those cities. Constant invasions from tribes—the Celts, the Picts, the Anglo-Saxons, and others—had thrown the situation into disarray. Patrick himself, son of a well-to-do merchant, was captured in one of these tribal raids and taken to Ireland as a slave.

Finally, Ireland itself was a rural country with no cities. The wildness of the countryside and its swamps and bogs made centralized control extraordinarily difficult. Attempts to establish the Roman system were tried and, when Patrick arrived, were de rigueur. Because of local conditions, however, this system was not working well. Patrick's genius lay in recognizing this, in seeing that the Irish Christian church would have to be organized differently if it were to succeed. It must be, for one thing, a rural church. Instead of large provinces with defined boundaries, the Irish church would consist of regional church centers that radiated their influence outward, instead of using rigid boundaries to keep its influence within.

In such a setting, Patrick saw that membership should be based not on where one lived (as in the Roman canton system) but on a choice to join. Membership was not assumed as a feature of where one lived, with participation level the aspect involving choice; membership was all there was, initially, and it had to be made attractive enough so that people would want to join.

We might say that Patrick implemented his innovation by seeing that it was the one most congenial to the conditions in Ireland at the time. His major battle was to convince his superiors, the church hierarchy in Britain, that this was the way to proceed. His major battle was the *missio interna*, the internal mission to convince his apostolic colleagues that under such conditions at least, belonging must precede believing.

WHAT WAS THE IRISH RESPONSE TO BELONGING?

Two modern writers, John Finney (*Recovering the Past: Celtic and Roman Mission*, 1996) and George Hunter (*The Celtic Way of Evangelism*, 2000), have described Patrick's approach in some detail. Both Finney and Hunter contrast the Celtic approach with the Roman approach. The Roman approach was to present the Christian message to a non-Christian person, ask if he or she was ready to make a decision based on this message, and, if the person responded positively, invite him or her to activate church membership and experience fellowship. Hunter asks if this doesn't sound very familiar: "Most American evangelicals are scripted by it" (53). He calls it the presentation, decision, assimilation model.

Hunter then presents the contrasting Celtic model of evangelism: "(1) You first establish community with people, or bring them into the fellowship of your community of faith. (2) Within fellowship, you engage in conversation, ministry, prayer, and worship. (3) In time, as they discover that they now believe, you invite them to commit" (Hunter 2000, 53).

Both Finney and Hunter quote Robin Gill, who says that for most people today, "belonging comes before believing. For this reason, evangelism is now about helping people to belong so that they can believe" (Finney 1996, 46; Hunter 2000, 54).

When Jesus invited the fishermen to pick up their nets and follow him, he was inviting them to become part of an apostolic community. Other than the enigmatic reference to becoming fishers of men, which did indeed communicate something to these men of the Sea of Galilee, they really didn't understand all that well what they were being called to and by whom. They knew they wanted to be part of a fellowship with this man, but fuller realization of what that meant came only slowly. They watched Jesus work. They watched him relate to people, heal the sick, and cast out demons. They listened to him tell mysterious-sounding parables, and when they asked Jesus what these very engaging stories meant, his answers tended to be almost as mysterious as the stories themselves.

Over time, however, they learned enough. They began to understand, and after Jesus's death they became the heart and soul of the new church. Their Christian commitment stood the tests of persecution and failure and great success. Most died in the cause. Their dedication to the cause began not with commitment to a creed but with acceptance of an invitation to fellowship.

BELONGING PRECEDES BEHAVING PRECEDES BELIEVING

There can be little question that Patrick's innovation had significant effects in Ireland (see next section). But if we want to place it in the larger context of Christian mission and Christian mission history, it might be worthwhile to dig a little deeper into the idea. We might start by inserting the qualifying word *usually*: Belonging *usually* precedes believing. Intellectual competence in Christian theology is, of course, not a disqualifier for membership in the church, and some people do become Christians because of it.

We also suggest that one could add a third element to the practice: belonging precedes *behaving* precedes believing. An important part of becoming a Christian is that we learn to behave like a Christian. In his letter to the Galatians, Paul summarizes this lifestyle by identifying nine fruits of the Spirit: love, joy, peace, patience, kindness, goodness, faithfulness, gentleness, self-control (Gal. 5:22). In Christian mission history, some have advocated an approach that asks potential converts to begin by acting like Christians: by following the Ten Commandments or a monastic rule or canon law; or simply by displaying the fruits of the Spirit, that is, by doing things (like burying the unwanted dead of poor people) that are obviously done because of one of these motivating fruits. Out of that initial experience of adopting a formatted lifestyle comes a sense of fellowship and a set of beliefs that more precisely define what it means to be Christian.

The apostle Paul, in fact, did not seem averse to this approach. When speaking to Jewish audiences especially, he seemed inclined toward it, prob-

SIDEBAR 5.2
CELTIC EVANGELISM, ROMAN EVANGELISM, JEWISH EVANGELISM

CELTIC EVANGELISM (PATRICK)	ROMAN EVANGELISM	JEWISH EVANGELISM (PAUL)
Establish community	Present the gospel	Practice lifestyle
Engage in conversation	Invite commitment	Remind of community
Invite commitment	Establish community	Invite to new understanding

ably because he was talking to people for whom the law or Torah was central to the way they viewed religion. The first questions people in such a religion would ask about another religion would be about the practice of the religion, the behaviors one would be required to follow. Do I have to be circumcised? Are there any restrictions on food consumption? What principles determine what I do each day of the week? To be a Christian, one might argue, you must start by acting like a Christian. One might call this Paul's Jewish approach to evangelism.

We now have three approaches to mission: the Jewish way of mission, which focuses on a lifestyle; the Roman way of mission, which focuses on a set of beliefs; and the Celtic way of mission, which focuses on fellowship. All seem to have a strong biblical warrant. How do we choose between them? Must we choose between them? Some points to consider:

1. These are methods of witnessing and as such have little to do with salvation. Put another way, one can believe all of orthodox Christian theology and still not be saved. One can live exactly like a Christian lives and still not be saved. One can belong to a Christian church or fellowship and still not be saved. Salvation is a free gift of God. Salvation is not earned by deeds, beliefs, or membership.
2. As methods of witnessing, the aim of each is to put non-Christians in the frame of mind, the physical context, the habits of life that have the best chance of leading them to fully experience the power of the Holy Spirit in their lives so that salvation becomes a reality for them. Salvation is indeed the goal, but no method of witness can guarantee salvation.
3. There is no single right order in which belonging, behaving, and believing must occur in a person's salvific process. It may be true that in certain contexts, because of psychological, social, or philosophical conditions, one of the three might indeed precede the others in order for the mission to be most effective. Patrick's genius was discovering the order that worked best in Ireland. And it may be that that order is best for our context today. But in another context, another order might be best.

SIDEBAR 5.3
ANTIMISSIONARY: JUAN GINÉS DE SEPÚLVEDA

Practice: Fellowship—Belonging precedes believing

A too-energetic insistence on correct belief can obscure a whole range of behaviors, both psychological and social, that are as important to conversion as understanding and acceding to church doctrine.

In July 1550, Charles V, Holy Roman Emperor and ruler of Spain, called for a halt to all Spanish conquests in the New World until a debate could be held over the moral legitimacy of those conquests. The debate was to be held in Valladolid, and the two main debaters were Bartolomé de Las Casas and Juan Ginés de Sepúlveda.

Charles V's expressed question was quickly agreed upon by the two disputants. Both Sepúlveda and Las Casas agreed that Spain had a moral right to conquer the New World. And they both agreed that the purpose of such conquest was Christian conversion; the preaching of the faith was necessary and proper.

They disagreed, however, over the methods proper to such conquest and such conversion. The real question of the debate quickly became "to discuss and determine the best form of government and the best laws which will permit the most favorable preaching and extension of the Holy Catholic faith in the New World" (Hanke 1974, 67).

Las Casas argued that the draconian practices currently being used to spread the gospel—torture, murder, rape, and slavery—were not acceptable Christian evangelistic techniques.

Sepúlveda, a Christian theologian, argued that they were. His argument had four main points:

1. The spread of the gospel by God's chosen instrument, Spain, was of paramount concern, and all questions of methods were subservient to this divine calling.
2. The Native Americans were naturally inferior beings—homunculi or semihumans—evidenced by their practices of cannibalism, human sacrifice, and idolatry.
3. Following Aristotle, he argued that because of this natural inferiority, the Indians were natural slaves.
4. Following Augustine, he argued that the Indians' slavery was a logical consequence, punishment, for the sins of cannibalism, human sacrifice, and idolatry.

The Disputation of 1550–51, as it came to be called, never reached a conclusion. Both sides claimed victory, of course, but the Spanish practice of *encomienda*—the allotting of Indian slaves and their former land to selected Spanish colonists—continued apace. Meanwhile, the population of Native Americans was decimated, by as much as 90 percent in many places.

REFLECTION AND DISCUSSION

1. How would you refute the argument that Spain was God's instrument of conversion of the American Indians, and therefore any methods the Spanish used were justifiable?
2. Use passages from the Bible to show that "natural inferiority" of some groups of humans cannot be supported by biblical standards.
3. Outline a way for giftive mission to be used in this debate.

4. All three—believing, behaving, belonging—are important to a mature Christian life. As a person grows in faith, all three areas will grow. One way to measure the depth of a person's Christian walk is to look for growth in all three areas.

5. Mature Christian evangelists should have in their repertoire the capacity to do Roman evangelism, Celtic evangelism, and Jewish evangelism. The context should determine which one is used.

EFFECTS

What, precisely, were the effects of Patrick's innovation, as influenced by monasticism, especially in comparison to the prevailing approaches to mission? The most obvious, of course, is that it worked. Ireland became a Christian nation. Not just a nominal Christian nation, but one that has ever since been in the vanguard of Christian mission work. It is a remote corner of the world indeed that has not seen and felt the presence of Irish mission workers in the centuries since Patrick.

Two other effects seem to have come directly from the monastic influence. First is transparency. The public effects of Patrick's innovation must have been like an advertisement to join: "Join us. We take everyone. You don't have to be Roman to join us. You don't have to give up being Irish to join a Christian community."

Second is simplicity. Patrick's approach was utterly simple. It did not require detailed patterns of argumentation and persuasion. It was a simple invitation to join. Whatever additional witness that was needed was supplied by the members of the community doing what they did every day anyway, living together in peace and meeting the needs of people around them as they became known to the community.

6

Localization

Focusing on Questions and Concerns of the Local Community

Mission Exemplars: Cyril and Methodius
Location: Constantinople, Byzantium, Russia
Audience: Slavic peoples
Time: Ninth century

Timeline
- 815 Methodius born
- 826 Cyril born
- 837 Methodius is appointed administrator of Slavic province.
- 842 Cyril studies at emperor's court in Constantinople.
- Cyril librarian of the patriarch at Church of St. Sophia
- Cyril at monastery and as philosophy teacher
- Methodius at Mount Olympus
- Cyril debates Icons (vs. Patriarch Anis) and the Trinity (vs. Jews); joins Methodius at Mount Olympus.
- 860 Harazan Mission
- 861 Methodius abbot at Polichon monastery
- 862 Moravian mission
- 869 Cyril dies at age forty-two.
- 870 Methodius bishop to Slavs
- 871 Methodius in prison
- 879 Methodius in Rome

- 881 Methodius in Constantinople
- 885 Methodius dies at age seventy.

Resources to Consult on Cyril and Methodius's Mission

I. Boba, *Moravia's History Reconsidered: A Reinterpretation of Medieval Sources* (The Hague: Springer, 1971).

Ivan Duichev, ed., *Kiril and Methodius: Founders of Slavonic Writing* (New York: Columbia University Press, 1985).

F. Dvornik, *Byzantine Missions among the Slavs* (New Brunswick, NJ: Rutgers University Press, 1970).

Edward G. Farrugia, Robert F. Taft, and Gino K. Piovesana, eds. *Christianity among the Slavs: The Heritage of Saints Cyril and Methodius; Acts of the International Congress Held on the Eleventh Centenary of the Death of St. Methodius, Rome, October 8–11, 1985, under the Direction of the Pontifical Oriental Institute* (Rome: Pontifical Institutum Studiorum Orientalium, 1988).

Kliment Ohridski, "Life and Acts of Our Blessed Teacher Konstantin the Philosopher," in *Kiril and Methodius*, ed. Ivan Duichev (New York: Columbia University Press, 1985), 49–80.

Kliment Ohridski, "Memory and Life of Our Blessed Father and Teacher Methodius," in *Kiril and Methodius*, ed. Ivan Duichev (New York: Columbia University Press, 1985), 81–92.

Michael Lacko, *Saints Cyril and Methodius* (Rome: Slovak, 1969).

Anthony-Emil N. Tachiaos, *Cyril and Methodius of Thessalonica: The Acculturation of the Slavs* (Crestwood, NY: St. Vladimir's Seminary, 2001).

A. D. Vlasto, *The Entry of the Slavs into Christendom* (Cambridge: Cambridge University Press, 1970).

Cyril and his older brother Methodius created an alphabet for the Slavs, who had none; translated the Scriptures into the resulting written language; created a liturgy in Slavic; and tirelessly translated classic Greek texts into Slavic. For his trouble Cyril was accused of heresy and brought before bishops, priests, and monks who "fell upon him like crows on a falcon" in Venice in 865: "Tell us, man," they hissed, "how is it that you now invent books for the Slavs, and teach them? None has so far invented such books—neither the apostles, nor the Pope in Rome, nor Gregory the Theologian, nor Jeromine of Augustine. We only know of three languages in which it is becoming to praise God with books: Hebrew, Greek, and Latin" (Kliment Ohridski 1985a). Cyril's answer typified his mission approach:

Does not God send rain on the just and the unjust alike? And does not the sun rise on the evil and on the good? Do not we all breathe the air equally? How come you are not ashamed to single out only three tongues, leaving all other tribes and peoples deaf and blind? Tell me, do you think God powerless to give them this, or do you think him envious and loathe to give it? We on our part know of many peoples who have books and

105

give praise to God each in its own tongue. Such peoples, it is known, are the Armenians, the Persians, the Abzags, the Ivers, the Sugds, the Goths, the Tirsians, the Hazaras, the Arabs, the Egyptians, the Syrians, and many more. (Kliment Ohridski 1985b)

The Venetians were championing a doctrine called trilingualism, which taught that the Scriptures and official church liturgy could be translated only into Hebrew, Greek, and Latin. Very soon, however, they were hoisted on their own petard. Instead of being heresy accusers, they were themselves accused of heresy. Over time, trilingualism itself came to be considered a heresy, and the translation of both Scriptures and liturgies into indigenous languages was accepted. But the story of how this came about can only be told by telling the story of Cyril and Methodius, apostles to the Slavs, teachers of the Slavs, enlighteners of the Slavs.

CYRIL AND METHODIUS

Cyril and Methodius were born to a well-respected family in Thessalonica. Two of seven brothers, Methodius was born in 815 and Cyril in 826 or 827. They were both prodigies, Cyril known for his studies and Methodius for his all-around competence. Their studies in Thessalonica, the second most important city in Byzantium after the capital, Constantinople, would have focused on classical Greek texts. The curriculum would have included grammar, poetics, and rhetoric.

Cyril excelled in scholarship. He became known as an excellent poet and seemed to master whatever his tutors put before him (there were no schools as such; education was done by private tutors). Cyril was so accomplished that when he finished his school-boy days, the Byzantine emperor heard about his accomplishments and invited him to come to Constantinople and study in the court, with his *logothete* (a court philosopher) as his tutor. The *logothete*'s name was Theoctistus. Cyril did so well as a student at court that the *logothete* wanted him to marry his niece and take a governorship of a province of the Byzantine Empire.

Cyril demurred and chose to follow the celibate life of a scholar in pursuit of wisdom. He spent time in a monastery, as a philosophy teacher in Constantinople, debating for the emperor and the patriarch the theological issues of the day, and finally as a missionary to the Slavs, the call for which he and his brother are remembered. Cyril worked so hard, so purposefully, that he died at the young age of forty-two, consumed by his call to scholarship dedicated to the task of Christian mission.

Methodius also excelled as a scholar, but his skills extended even further. His biographer tells us that

from his tenderest youth he was beloved by the notables, who honored him by discoursing with him, until eventually the Emperor himself came to hear of his astute intellect and charged him with the governorship of a Slavic province, as though foreseeing that he would one day send him to be the teacher and first archbishop of the Slavs. He was therefore to learn all their Slavic customs and gradually habituate himself to them. (Kliment Ohridski 1985a)

By all accounts, Methodius excelled in this first administrative charge even though it came at a very young age. But like his younger brother, Methodius heard a higher call. He quit his job as a governor and joined a monastery. Chapter 3 of his biography describes his call:

Spending many years in this princedom and seeing the turmoil, sins and crimes in this earthly life, he replaced his aspirations for bleak earthly things with celestial thoughts. He did not wish to trouble his noble soul with things that are not ever-lasting. And finding the proper moment, he got rid of his governorship and went to Olympus, where all holy fathers live. There he donned black cloth and obediently subjected himself to monastic rule, performing every duty and assiduously applying himself to the books. (Kliment Ohridski 1985a)

When Cyril was called on two missions to Slavic peoples, Methodius went along as his assistant. After Cyril died, Methodius assumed responsibility for the mission, eventually being appointed archbishop to the Slavic territories by the pope. Although the missions were originally conceived and supported by the Byzantine emperor and the patriarch, Moravia was technically in Rome's jurisdiction. Methodius excelled in a very difficult situation created by both Rome and Constantinople's desire to control this area. He finished translating the Scriptures into Slavic, a task begun by Cyril. He encouraged the produc-tion of other ecclesiastical texts, either writing them himself or having them written by one of many protégés. He died at the age of seventy.

THE SOURCE OF THE PRACTICE

Neither Cyril nor Methodius became known for their ministry to Thessalo-nians, or Constantinopolitans, or even Byzantians, but to Slavs. And their dedication to the Slavs seems to be not a matter of chance but the working out of a lifetime call for which they were uniquely prepared, not just by time and circumstance but by personal intention. It is very helpful to trace both the intentions and the influences that led to this mission and the innovations it required in order to be done successfully.

In one sense, it was natural that the two brothers would show interest in the Slavic people. The Slavs were part of the culture of Thessalonica. The Slavs were actually several wandering tribes that were tied together mainly by their language, a simple language of warfare and trading and daily life. It was an unwritten language with no alphabet. Thus the tribes had no philosophy or literature in common. What they did share in addition to their language was an aggressiveness that led them to seek to expand and control new territory. For a couple of hundred years, they attacked Thessalonica itself in an attempt to subdue it but were never successful. By the time of Cyril and Methodius, the Slavs had begun to settle almost peacefully in areas adjacent to the territory of the Thessalonians, and the Thessalonians for their part encouraged trade with them, even allowing them inside the city gates during the day so that they could engage in mercantile activities. On a certain level, then, the brothers grew up with Slavs in their midst.

Cyril and Methodius also had an interesting model of how to relate to this outside ethnic group, a model that uncannily presages the kind of mission they eventually established in Moravia. Anthony-Emil Tachiaos, in his fine book *Cyril and Methodius of Thessalonica: The Acculturation of the Slavs* (2001), notes a special feature common to merchants of the Thessalonian marketplace:

> Each morning, when the great gates in the city walls opened—the Golden Gate, the Letaea Gate, the Cassandria Gate—groups of Slavs would enter the city and pursue their affairs there; and since the Slavs were uncultured and unable to communicate with the Greek inhabitants, the latter were obliged to learn their language. For centuries this was a feature of Thessalonica's lively market—and indeed it continues even today: the merchants learn the language of their foreign customers in order to sell them their wares.

It seems likely that Cyril and Methodius heard the Slavic language spoken in the streets of such a city. Given their unusual interest in learning and new ideas, it surely would have piqued their interest to know more about this language, perhaps even to begin to pick up some words and phrases in Slavic. Tachiaos thinks that here the brothers naturally acquired their interest in the Slavs. Once their supernatural calls to ministry came, leading both to give up lucrative secular political careers in favor of spiritual scholarship, they possibly had already begun Slavic studies. Perhaps it was at Mount Olympus for Methodius, where the monastics likely included Slavs.

The biographies of both Cyril and Methodius leave the impression that the call to the Slavs came from the interest of the emperor Michael, who, for political reasons, trained, appointed, and supported the missions to the Slavs. This, of course, would have been the logical and politically prudent way to write the story. But it is likely that the emperor's political interests dovetailed nicely with a long-standing desire on the part of the brothers to do mission work among the Slavs. It was convenient that the Byzantine way of doing mission made this possible. And it was fortuitous that the models of interaction the brothers had learned in the Thessalonian marketplace taught them a way of interacting that was probably the only possible way the Slavs could be brought into the Christian fold: by taking the local interests of the Slavic people into consideration and making the enculturated shape of the gospel fit their needs rather than insisting that they learn Greek and give up their indigenous culture.

THE MORAVIAN MISSION

The mission to greater Moravia began with a call from the princes of that territory, Rastislav and Svetopolk, to the emperor Michael:

> We are here by the grace of God. Many teachers of Christianity have come to us from Italy, from Greece, and from the German parts and they all teach differently. But we Slavs are a simple people and do not have among us a man to instruct us in the ways of truth and to explain to us the meaning of the Scriptures. Therefore, good master, send hither such a man capable of guiding us in the ways of every truth. (Kliment Ohridski 1985a)

The Moravians had already been missionized, but it seems the mission hadn't been particularly effective. We might speculate on why by taking the case of the German mission. The Germans were the people group closest to Moravia, and we know the most about the kind of mission they did because of their ongoing attempts to dominate the church in Moravia.

Two things are worth noting here. First, the Germans had as much political interest in the area as did the Byzantines. Greater Moravia was geographically in the orbit of Rome, and since the Germans were part of the Roman church, the bishops there were interested in the Slavs as both spiritual children and potential citizens of the Roman Empire. Since the political princes of the area, Rastislav and Svetopolk, appealed to the Byzantine emperor for aid, we can deduce that they were not finding the political machinations of Rome and the Germans all that comfortable and were indirectly seeking political relief as well as spiritual aid. Thus, we would be remiss not to recognize the realpolitik dimension of this call.

Second, regarding the spiritual side of the call, we know from later events that the Germans insisted that Latin be the language of religion. The Bible needed to be read in Latin. The Mass needed to be intoned in Latin. Real theological discourse needed to be carried out in Latin. Theoretically, the Germans would have acknowledged that the Scriptures, liturgy, and theology could also be faithfully carried out in either Hebrew or Greek, the biblical languages. But practically, they required that the Slavs learn Latin in order to be good Christians.

Is it too much of a conjecture to say that this is why the German mission had failed to produce a satisfactory level of Christianity among the Slavs? Possibly the Slavs sensed that in the case of the Germans, the requirement for becoming Christian went far beyond acknowledging Jesus as Lord but included also the learning of a new language, the adoption of a new culture (whether Latin or German), and the continued stunting of their own culture, their Slavic way of looking at things.

We do know that Cyril and Methodius did not have these expectations. Among Cyril's first acts was the creation of an alphabet for the Slavic language, an alphabet that came to be known as the Glagolitic alphabet. Over time he and Methodius created a vocabulary of abstract nouns and verbs and a theological vocabulary that had been missing from the Slavic language. Then they began to translate the Scriptures into Slavic, a task that Methodius and his assistants finished after Cyril's death. While Cyril was still alive, however, he and his brother created a Slavic liturgy so that the Slavs could celebrate Mass in a language they understood. And they both encouraged a cadre of specially identified young theological students to begin producing theological and literary works in Slavic, in effect filling a large cultural gap that had always existed among the Slavic tribes. Over time this put Slavic culture on a much higher footing in its interaction with the other more traditional cultures of Eastern Europe and Asia.

To be fair and accurate, we must note the strong Greek bias to all of this. Cyril's alphabet had Byzantine elements; the Greek classics of literature and philosophy were the ones translated into Slavic (not Latin ones). But the goal was not to create a vassal culture to the Latin and German cultures, or even to Byzantine culture, but to eventually foster an independent Slavic culture that could stand on its own. In this the brothers more than succeeded.

The story of the Moravian mission is fascinating. The Slavs, as one might imagine, accepted Cyril and Methodius with enthusiasm and a growing respect that culminated in their canonization not long after each died and an acknowledgment that they were the fathers of Slavic culture today. Despite the enthusiastic reception from the Slavs themselves, however, the German clergy, whom the brothers were slowly but surely supplanting, reacted negatively. The Germans complained to Rome of the brothers' incursions. They complained about the use of Slavic in the liturgy, claiming this was theologically unsound. Despite some occasional vacillations, the popes consistently decided theological issues in the Slavs' favor.

Politically things were a bit tougher. Rome needed to exert control over this area, and the Byzantine-oriented brothers had to acknowledge Rome's control. They did so. Methodius eventually became the Roman-appointed bishop to the Slavs. But that meant he and Cyril had to play the Germans' political game, and occasionally they lost. Methodius, for example, was arrested and spent two and a half years in a German prison until the pope came to his rescue.

The long-term political results were that Rome never lost geographical control of this area, and eventually it reverted to Latin-dominated Christianity. The Slavic people's growth took place far from Moravia. It was first championed in Bulgaria under Boris the Great and then in Russia when Vladimir was converted to Christianity in the tenth century. Even Cyril's alphabet was

SIDEBAR 6.1
THE SLAVIC ALPHABETS

Cyril is rightly given credit for developing an alphabet for the Slavic peoples. But the current alphabet in use by Slavic peoples from Eastern Europe to Russia, although named after Cyril, is actually a later development:

Glagolitic alphabet: created by Cyril the Philosopher
Cyrillic I: created by Constantine, bishop of Preslav
Cyrillic II: created by Patriarch Euthymius of Bulgaria

replaced by one named after him, the Cyrillic alphabet, but which he did not write.

Still, the Slavs recognize that these developments came about because of what Cyril and Methodius did, because of their mission strategy and their practice of considering the local needs of the indigenous country more important than the empire-building of a centralized church. This is their great contribution to the history of mission practice.

THE EFFECTS OF THE PRACTICE

One way to measure the contributions of Cyril and Methodius is to consider the immense respect both receive in the Eastern church of today. It is no exaggeration to speak of the respective cults of the two brothers, using that word in its best sense. Each have familiar icons, and it is a rare Orthodox church that does not honor them in its iconography. Yet both brothers would surely want this section to be devoted to the effect their mission practice had on the church's ongoing mission, rather than to their respective personality cults. Thus, one might specify four areas where the contributions of Cyril and Methodius have been most significant.

Orthodoxy

Although it must be acknowledged that Slavic contributions to theology are firmly in the Greek/Byzantine mode of thought, Slavic culture has made original contributions that would not have occurred in the church unless poured through the Slavic sieve. One must begin with the brothers' own writings. Each contributed important texts to the Slavic tradition. Cyril, for example, was an outstanding poet, and his poetic works in Slavic became an important contribution to Slavic and Byzantine hymnody. Methodius contributed much. Ironically, he had a much better command of the Slavic language than his brother. His writings focus a great deal on questions concerning church organization and administration.

The Slavs did not accept all Byzantine texts equally, and the way they chose texts influenced the nature of Slavic Byzantinism. They seem to have favored three authors: Basil the Great, John Chrysostom, and Gregory the Theologian. Perhaps the most significant contributions to Orthodox theology had to wait until the Russian church matured. After it did, the Russian theological contribution became central.

Translation

The decision to translate the Bible and liturgy into Slavic was a decision of immense importance. It was one of those decisions that is so large and so pivotal, we can hardly imagine it being otherwise. One of the first instincts of missionaries after Cyril and Methodius has been to determine as soon as possible how to render the Scriptures into a language the people can understand on their own. This thinking has become so central to missions, it is hard to imagine a time when this impulse was not the instinct of all missionaries.

Contextualization

More subtle, perhaps, has been the brothers' contribution to what we now call the contextualization debate. It was not just Bible translation that made Cyril and Methodius's contribution so important. And it was not even Cyril's philological contributions through the creation of a written alphabet that changed the face of mission. Rather, their larger insight, sometimes only implicitly, revealed that people view the world through a cultural lens unique to them—this is the contribution that is stunning in its perceptiveness and world-changing in its implementation.

Cyril and Methodius possibly never realized the long-term significance of what they were doing. They certainly didn't have the hindsight we have today of watching the transformation of adaptation into acculturation into accommodation into contextualization in mission history. They certainly did not have the language of the debate we have today. In that sense it may well be that we are ascribing to them an anachronistic contribution that they themselves would not have recognized. It is certainly possible that they only saw these practices as a mission technique that would work with the Slavs, where the Germans, Italians, and Greeks had failed. What they certainly did have was an instinct that once the gospel story was poured through the Slavic mind-set, it would be a contribution of importance to the whole church.

National Churches

Cyril and Methodius's work raised an issue that is still unresolved in the way the twenty-first century sees the global church. We have come to assume that the church has both global and local expressions, and that both are neces-

SIDEBAR 6.2
ANTIMISSIONARY: BISHOP WICHING

Practice: Localization—Focusing on questions and concerns of the local community

Localization can cut two ways. It can be used as a way of opening up the gospel story to people by presenting it in their own language and by facilitating worship in a language they can understand. Cyril and Methodius used it this way.

Localization can, however, be put in the service of ethnocentrism of one sort or another. The human proclivity to self-centeredness can be applied not just to individual wants and desires but to the elevation of whole cultures and languages to premier status. Localization, because of pride, can quickly become the rationale for denigrating other cultures and languages in favor of one's own. The Frankish cleric Wiching, bishop of Nitra and one of the most outspoken leaders of the Bavarian German church, used it this way.

He was opposed to Cyril and Methodius's translation program from the start, primarily because it threatened his ecclesiastical jurisdiction over the Slavic churches. The brothers were from the Eastern church, sent by Constantinople. Bishop Wiching was appointed by the Roman church. Even after Methodius was officially appointed bishop of the Slavic regions, Wiching opposed him, at one point having him imprisoned in a German castle for almost two years.

Wiching argued that the gospel could not be adequately translated into Slavic but could only be expressed in Hebrew, Greek, and Latin. This position even became a proposed theological doctrine, called trilingualism. Fortunately it was eventually denounced by church authorities as heresy.

Trilingualism was advanced based on an argument that turns localization on its head. Only our "local way" is the allowable one. Only the gospel in our language qualifies as acceptable. This position allows "us" to reap the fruits of having the gospel and worship in a language we can understand but does not extend the fruits to other groups of people.

Bishop Wiching is an antimissionary because he championed this perverted notion of localism, turning the gospel God meant for everyone into a gospel for a privileged few. Methodius held Wiching at bay during his lifetime, but after Methodius died, Wiching banned and persecuted Methodius's disciples in the areas where he held political power.

REFLECTION AND DISCUSSION

1. Are there ways in which Bishop Wiching's inverted concept of localization characterizes the church today? If so, in what way(s)?
2. Explain how the concept of giftive mission works to prevent an inversion of localization.
3. Describe two practices that your own congregation uses (or could use) to support localization and that reflect the concerns of your local community without placing them above the concerns of other communities.

sary for us as humans trying to understand the work of God. Various sectors of the church, however, have different understandings of how the global and the local fit together. Cyril and Methodius had something different to offer than the prevailing Roman church of the day. The Church of Rome, even in the ninth century, continued to operate in the "the church is all there is" mode of Christendom. Cyril and Methodius were pioneers in the Orthodox model: national churches. This model suggests that the local expression of the church should be tied to nation-states or at least to geographical areas.

The question we still struggle with is what should be the ideal expression of the local church? Protestants have worked with a denominational model for four hundred years or so, but that model seems to be less and less effective. What might be the most effective and faithful expression of the local church in our century? Individual, independent, autonomous megachurches and clusters of churches? Cyril and Methodius had their answer. What they did for us is focus the question. Finding the answer is up to us.

7

Commitment

*Holding Ideas with Conviction; Acting Decisively
on Those Ideas; Not Letting Those Ideas Be Divisive*

Mission Exemplar: Thomas Aquinas
Location: Europe, North Africa
Audience: Muslims
Time: Thirteenth century

Timeline
- 1225 Born
- 1239–44 Studies at University of Naples
- 1244 Joins Dominican order
- 1245–48 Studies at University of Paris
- 1248–52 Studies at Cologne
- 1258–60 Writes *Summa Contra Gentiles*
- 1259–68 Teaches in Italy
- 1267–73 Writes *Summa Theologiae*
- 1268–72 Teaches in Paris
- 1272–74 Teaches in Naples
- 1274 Dies
- 1323 Is canonized
- 1879 *Summa Theologiae* is declared official teaching of the
  Roman Catholic Church by Pope Leo XIII.

Resources to Consult on Thomas Aquinas's Mission

Curtis Chang, *Engaging Unbelief: A Captivating Strategy from
  Augustine to Aquinas* (Downers Grove, IL: InterVarsity, 2000).
Marie-Dominique Chenu, *Aquinas and His Role in Theology*
  (Collegeville, MN: Liturgical Press, 2002).

G. K. Chesterton, *Saint Thomas Aquinas* (Garden City, NY: Doubleday, 1956).

Jacques Maritain, *St. Thomas Aquinas* (New York: Meridian Books, 1958).

Josef Pieper, *Guide to Thomas Aquinas* (New York: Random House, 1962).

Thomas Aquinas, *Summa Contra Gentiles*, trans. Anton C. Pegis (Notre Dame, IN: University of Notre Dame Press, 1975).

Three things dominate Thomas Aquinas's life: studying, writing, and teaching. He studied to be a master of theology at Naples, Paris, and Cologne. He wrote much, his two dominating works being the multivolume *Summa Contra Gentiles* and the *Summa Theologiae*. He taught in Italy and France.

Aquinas joined a religious order, the Dominicans. His parents opposed this decision and made it difficult for him to pursue his calling, but he persevered. He also fought numerous heresies in scholarly confrontations. Aquinas lived what seems a peaceful, stolid life of scholarship. And by most measures it was: a life of studying, writing, and teaching.

But when measured by missiological standards, Thomas's life looks different. Underlying everything he did, one soon detects not stolid passivity but the apostolic impatience of the gospel. Thomas was a master of theology, which meant he was expert at reading biblical texts, arguing the issues and problems that emerged from those texts, and preaching the results of his scholarship to the church. Thomas understood better than almost anyone that the theology mined from the Bible is complete only when it has been transmitted to someone—particularly to those whom we now call the unchurched.

Thomas Aquinas was committed to the mission of the church in a way few mega-theologians have been. That and what he wrote about mission in the *Summa Contra Gentiles* are sufficient to merit his inclusion among the principal innovators of the practices of faithful mission. But he modeled the practice of commitment in such a way that it becomes a lesson for us all in how to be fully committed to the gospel of Jesus Christ and at the same time fully open to devising myriad ways to communicate that gospel to those who need it. He lived a life that modeled a willingness to become all things to all people in order to save some.

WHO WAS AQUINAS?

The events of Thomas Aquinas's life have been well documented and thoroughly analyzed, as befits the work of a man considered the most important theologian of the largest sector of the Christian church, the Roman Catholic

Church. Although it wasn't until 1879 that Pope Leo XIII declared him to be the principal theologian of the Roman Catholic Church, his work had played that role almost from the time Aquinas first committed his thoughts to paper.

What hasn't been quite as thoroughly examined is Aquinas's contributions as a missionary or, perhaps better, mission theorist. One writer who has explored in some depth his missiological contributions is Curtis Chang (2000). Chang takes Aquinas's disputation model of writing and teaching (explored in more depth in the next section) and shows how this is a uniquely effective and appropriate mission practice for our time. Chang uses the language of story to describe the *disputatio* model and simplifies it into three steps: entering the story, retelling the story, and capturing the story.

By *entering the story*, Chang means fully engaging the other person's story in an attempt to understand it on its own terms. In the *Summa Contra Gentiles*, for example, Aquinas masterfully enters into the Arabian intellectual's story of God. He succeeded in understanding the Muslim conceptions of God in Muslim terms and thought forms, using the same sources that the Muslim theologians use.

Aquinas used only Aristotle and reason to describe God as Muslims described God. In this case, actually, these are two of the same primary sources that Aquinas used in developing his theology, so it wasn't really difficult to enter the Muslim story at this point. Remember Aquinas's comment: "My God is the God of reason." He makes sure that his Muslim interlocutors feel at home with his understanding and, to this point, his agreement with them.

Notice what he does *not* do. He does not bring to bear the primary sources that he and other Christian theologians use in their attempts to understand God—the Old and New Testaments. At this step of entering the story, Aquinas restricts himself to using only the sources that Muslims use. This method allows plenty of time for that later, when further discussions take place.

Aquinas also enters the Muslim story by looking at what Muslims believe about God. Muslims believe that God exists (is for real, not a human projection) and that God is one. Aquinas is clear that he agrees with both of these Muslim beliefs about God. Aquinas believed that any mission interaction with a person of another religion was successful to the extent that the Christian made clear where he or she agreed with the other person's belief system.

Aquinas then enters the story by acknowledging a belief that Muslims have about God with which he disagrees. Muslims believe that creation, God's creative actions, are out of time, timeless. Aquinas states that he and other Christians believe that God created the world and human beings in time. But Aquinas is quick to note that he does not believe either side can prove this point and that it is not central. Thus, why argue about it? This kind of vulnerability creates trust for the discussion ahead. Aquinas does not simply overlook the Christian position but acknowledges that it is a peripheral one and that either side might be right.

The first step, entering the story, is an attempt to remain fully on the Muslim's turf and to understand the dynamics of Islamic theology, using Islamic terms, sources, and thought forms. The second step is to show that the first step has taken place. Chang calls this second step *retelling the story*. The Christian shows that she has so mastered the other person's argument or story that she can retell it in such a way that the Muslim can say, "Yes, you have fully understood our story." In the course of this retelling, the storyteller indicates and recapitulates her agreements with and respect for the story, but also at the end of the telling begins to prepare the way for the third step by indicating where the story differs from the Christian understanding.

It is important that this step be done well, Aquinas claims. He did not believe that it was especially fruitful to argue against errors in the other person's religion. Call them to attention, yes. Tell why we disagree with them, yes. But try to refute them, no.

Instead, give the positive Christian argument in favor of the expanded Christian version. Chang calls this third step *capturing the story*. Aquinas, Chang argues, was a master at presenting his disagreements in language that told the Christian story as a larger one that captured most of the opponent's story within it. It was as if to say, "Yes, but have you thought of this additional piece of the puzzle that we Christians believe? How does your story look in the light of what God did in creation from the Christian point of view?" With Muslims, it is at this point that the Christian brings to bear the transcendent point of view as revealed in the Christian texts. Hopefully the Christian dialoguer shows the Christian story to be a wider, more compelling, more true-to-human-experience tale. The Christian does not totally discount the beliefs and experiences of the Muslim story but shows it in the wider, more comprehensive context of the larger gospel story.

The apostolic impatience that is evident in all of Thomas Aquinas's works reveals a central interest in missions. But it wasn't until he wrote the six-volume *Summa Contra Gentiles* that Aquinas as missiologist fully emerged on paper. He undertook this great work after receiving a letter from a confrere, Ramon of Pennyaforte, in Spain asking for an evangelism primer for Dominican missionaries to Muslims. Aquinas didn't write primers, or if he did, he defined the word *primer* much more elaborately than most of us. Chang has performed a real service by presenting this work in such a practical, missiological form.

DISPUTATION AS A MISSION METHOD

One does not have to read much of Thomas Aquinas's writings to begin to recognize a common form that characterizes all his works to one degree or another. It is the method of disputation that Aquinas used not only in his writing but, by all accounts, also in his teaching. Disputation was not Thomas's creation; it was commonly used by thinkers and theologians of the Scholastic period of the church. But as with everything else Aquinas did, he modified and improved the form.

Josef Pieper performs the great service of summarizing this method of argumentation in his *Guide to Thomas Aquinas* (1962). In the following discussion, we rely heavily on his summary but add our own thoughts on how Aquinas used disputation in such a way that made it a particularly effective mission method.

Disputatio can be divided into two sections. First are the actual steps of the method of argumentation; second (which Thomas considered just as important) is the spirit of *disputatio*, the way one relates to the person whose ideas are being considered as part of the discussion.

Disputatio consists of five steps: question, opposing arguments, agreement with opposing arguments, disagreement with opposing arguments, and answer. Anyone who has read portions of Aquinas's most famous and influential work, the *Summa Theologiae*, will recognize immediately the five steps from the form that his systematic discussion in each section takes. Pieper illustrates the five steps by taking one of the questions of the *Summa Theologiae* and working through the steps.

Question

The question Pieper chooses as an illustration concerns "whether the degree of passion of an action increases or decreases the moral value of that action" (Pieper 1962, 80). Like all great thinkers, Aquinas was expert at determining the question in the most logical and parsimonious way. The questions in the *Summa Theologiae*, for example, were devised to achieve one of Aquinas's main goals: comprehensiveness. He wanted to raise and answer every possible question about all the issues the systematic theology of his time would ask. In the case of the *Summa Theologiae*, that would include everything about God, creation, providence, and salvation, the subjects of the four main sections of this work.

Opponent's Answers

Following the statement of the question, Aquinas would give in summary form the answers his opponents had given to the question. Sometimes this would be only one answer, but more often three, four, or five. In the case of this question on the effect of passion on the moral component of an action, he identified and summarized three answers: (1) Passion clouds rational judgment; therefore it diminishes the moral value of an action. (2) God and pure spirits know no passions; therefore, passionlessness adds to moral value. (3) To do wrong out of passion is less bad than to do wrong with clear intent; conversely, to do right out

119

of passion subtracts from the moral value of the action. Aquinas did not make judgments at this point on the positions of his interlocutors. His goal was to state them as clearly and generously as possible. Given his gifts, he succeeded at this greatly: "Thomas succeeds not only in presenting the opponent's divergent or flatly opposed opinion, together with the underlying line of reasoning, but also, many times, in presenting it better, more clearly, and more convincingly than the opponent himself might be able to do" (Pieper 1962, 73).

Agreements

Aquinas further betrayed his interest in truth by generously giving credit for the parts of his opponents' answers that are correct. This was a way not just of being fair but of recognizing a central truth about human existence: that truth and error rarely exist in pure form, but that every action and thought and feeling are almost always, because they are human, admixtures of both truth and error. For Aquinas, one of the theologian's tasks was to sort these out in each question and each answer.

This particular approach to debating an opponent is an enormously important missiological principle. The great theologians of the church all took note of Genesis 1 and Romans 1 and in some way acknowledged that God is everywhere, at all times, active in the world. For Calvin it was his recognition of the *sensus divinitatus*, the sense of the divine we all possess (and all creation possesses), which means that our best efforts will somehow reflect the goodness of God, even when we don't realize it. For Wesley the optimism of grace suggested that God had worked and was working everywhere to give good things to his creatures. As mission workers we should expect to find evidences of that goodness no matter how far from the Christian community we find ourselves.

Aquinas taught that the *imago Dei*, the image of God, is a factor in us all, despite the reality of our fallen, sinful nature. In clear, rational, human thinking, one sees residual evidences of that imaging. Thus, one should expect to find it even in opponents with whom one disagrees overall—and one should acknowledge that truth when it appears.

Disagreements

Of course, at some point we must point out the differences between our partner's answer to the question and our own answer. Thus, the next part of the *disputatio* involved demonstrating why the other answers did not quite measure up.

Answer

Finally, it was time for Aquinas to sum up the discussion with his answer to the question. In the case mentioned above, his answer was that "to act *out of* passion" diminishes both the value and the unworthiness of an action; on the other hand, "to act *with* passion" increases both the value and the unworthiness of an action.

For Aquinas, however, the formal part of the *disputatio* approach was not complete unless one also took into account and followed the spirit of *disputatio* or disciplined opposition. He summed up this "spirit" in five reminders:

1. *Understanding the Interlocutor.* Aquinas taught that in order to have a faithful discussion of an issue, one must understand the argument of the interlocutor as well as, if not better than, one understands his or her own argument. According to Aquinas's rule, one could not respond critically to an opponent's argument until one had successfully restated that argument so that the opponent, upon hearing the restatement, could acknowledge the argument as his or her own. This was not for the purposes of decency, of some ideal of being nice. And it was certainly not a form of personal modesty about one's own argument. Aquinas advocated this approach because it was necessary to understand the real strength of an opponent's argument, so that one could both acknowledge that strength and whatever truth might reside in it—and then go on to critique it. As Pieper notes, Aquinas thought that "there is always something right and truthful in [one's opponent's words], and although this may be minimal, the refutation must begin there if it is to be convincing" (1962, 78).

This would apply not just to Christian theological opponents but also to people of other religions. Aquinas made this point repeatedly in the context of the *Summa Contra Gentiles*, a book written to correct Muslim thought. But he would have made the same point also in relation to Hindus and Buddhists had they been within his geographical view in thirteenth-century Europe.

2. *Respecting Both Argument and Person.* Understanding the other person's argument is itself a form of respect, of course. But Aquinas's version went beyond "mere respect." Aquinas's respect took the form of real gratitude for the time and trouble that it took to formulate a clear and cogent argument, even if he felt it was wrong. Aquinas put it this way: "We must love them both, those whose opinions we share and those whose opinions we reject. For both have labored in the search for truth and both have helped us in the finding of it" (Pieper 1962, 78).

Aquinas was in good company in demanding this kind of respect. All the great theologians of the Christian church demand it. Although Aquinas had major disagreements with Augustine, on this point they were in harmony, as evidenced by Augustine's comment in an essay against his old foes, the Manichaeans: "Let those rage against you who do not know with what toil truth is found . . . ; let those rage against you who do not know with what difficulty the inner man's eye becomes sound; . . . let those rage against you who do not know how many groans and sighs accompany the winning of even a tiny morsel

---

SIDEBAR 7.1
DISPUTATION AS A MISSION METHOD

THE STEPS OF *DISPUTATIO*	THE SPIRIT OF *DISPUTATIO*
Question	Understanding the interlocutor
Opponent's answers	Respecting both argument and person
Agreements	Revealing oneself to him or her
Disagreements	Refraining from arbitrary jargon
Answer	Seeking clarity with charity

---

of divine insight" (Pieper 1962, 79). One of Aquinas's contemporaries made the comment that Aquinas treated his opponents as if they were his pupils, with the same care and concern that they grow in truth together.

3. *Addressing Oneself to Him or Her.* A requirement of theological and interreligious discourse for Aquinas was that both participants in a conversation, by agreeing to participate, were implicitly agreeing to reveal themselves as clearly as possible to the other side. Misdirection as a debating tactic achieved nothing for either side. Silence was not an option. Each conversant was expected to give as clear and honest an accounting of his position as possible. Of course, there is some danger in being clear and honest and open. One lays oneself open to correction. But for Aquinas that was a part of the disputation.

4. *Refraining from Arbitrary Jargon.* Part of this openness is an avoidance of using language that has become meaningless because of overuse, oversimplification, or even malice. Such language is often called jargon. One thinks, for example, of a contemporary illustration. Beginning one's remarks by calling the opponent's position "an obviously liberal view" or "an obviously fundamentalist view" is to resort to the use of language that has become so generalized as to be meaningless and doesn't really deal with the substance of a person's argument. It is dismissed with no consideration simply by associating it with a stereotyped position.

5. *Seeking Clarity, Not Sensationalism.* Aquinas was an idealist with regard to scholarly conversation. He truly believed that it helped all parties come to a clearer understanding of truth. Proverbs 27:17 could have been on his heraldic shield: "As iron sharpens iron, so one man sharpens another." And by one man, Aquinas meant all people, no matter what their theological position, no matter what their religion. But this could only happen if clarity and charity were the hallmarks of a disputation.

COMMITMENT

Aquinas's great contribution to mission practice was to show us the way to hold firm theological positions without creating the conditions in which we actually become alienated from people who do not have Christian beliefs—people who may be as committed to their belief structure (Hindu, Buddhist, Muslim, or whatever) as we are to ours. This may seem merely a matter of common sense. Or it may be that you have never put the question that way. But doing theological apologetics in a respectful way—that is, a way congenial to doing mission—is easier said than done.

We have decided to call this mission practice *commitment*. We believe that Christian mission loses its way when it loses theological commitments. The best mission is based on clearly articulated theological commitments. When mission practice is divorced from theological commitments, it becomes indistinguishable from social service, political justice, friendship, fellowship, and human solidarity. These are all very good things, but they are not Christian mission—at least not when unaccompanied by clearly articulated theological commitments. Christian theological commitments are the salt that gives mission its distinctive flavor.

AQUINAS TODAY

Today, when mission involves presenting the gospel to people who already have a firmly held set of religious beliefs, particularly those in the civilizational religions of Hinduism, Buddhism, and Islam, Aquinas has much to offer. He was far ahead of his time in many regards. Consider two of his contributions.

First, in the much-discussed area of how to converse with people of other religions, Aquinas continually offered practical suggestions on how a Christian can do this and juggle three somewhat competing goals: be firm in our Christian commitments, act on those commitments missionally, but do not let them separate us from two-thirds of the human race.

For example, he recounted how difficult it was to attempt to refute the errors of other religions. His approach, as we have seen, was to call attention to areas where Christians disagree with other religions but then go on to state the Christian position positively. Aquinas also related the futility of arguing from sources that people of other religions do not find authoritative. When we have human reason (created by God), the natural creation (created by God), and some commonly agreed-upon sources (Aristotle in the case of Muslims and Christians) as common authorities, why not use those to make our Christian positions clear? Finally, when it comes to God's revelatory truths, particularly those related to the supernatural, such as miracles and other signs, don't try to prove them rationally. Since they cannot be satisfactorily proved through reason, use experiential witnesses of various sorts (see sidebar 7.2).

123

SIDEBAR 7.2
AQUINAS ON WITNESSING TO UNBELIEVERS

Thomas Aquinas, Summa Contra Gentiles 1.2 and 9

It is difficult to argue against errors. First of all, we know too little about the troubling ideas of different opponents, so we can't begin our argument (as we should) by examining what they really feel in order to critically rejoin their false conclusions. The doctors of the early times knew the doctrines of the pagans, since they had once themselves been pagans (or had at least lived among them) and were acquainted with how they thought.

Further, we can't have recourse in dialogue with the Muslims or pagans to the same authorities to support our arguments. With the Jews, we can bring the Old Testament to bear; with heretics, the New Testament. But unbelievers do not accept these books. So with unbelievers we are obliged to have recourse to pure reasoning, to which everyone can give their assent. But reason is feeble in treating of divine matters.

In dealing with reasonable truths, we can convince our opponent through rational arguments; but in treating of God's revelation, our investigations have to go beyond the toil of reasoning. We should not seek to convince others concerning revelation by reasonable arguments, but reason only to resolve objections to the faith by showing that they do not contradict the faith.

The methodology of theological discussion implies the authority of God's word confirmed by miracles, since it is exclusively upon this word that we build our faith in the supernatural truths about God. In dialogue with believers, we can certainly have recourse to arguments of convenience (persuasion) to expand and strengthen their already existing faith. But we can't do this with unbelievers; otherwise the inadequacy of our rational arguments might confirm them in their denial of the faith and lead them to imagine that our own assent in faith is based upon only the poor reasoning we come up with.

Second, he was ahead of his time in the less discussed but equally important area of finding some kind of agreement on what the goal of religion should be. Most people who have found themselves in discussions with adherents of other religions know that it is enormously useful to find some points of common experience that can serve as starting points for discussions. One of the most important is to agree that human beings lack something and have goals, religious goals, that they believe will satisfy that lack.

Aquinas helps here by suggesting that the common goal of all religions is to find happiness in God. In part IIb of the *Summa Contra Gentiles*, called "The Divine Life of Man," in the chapter "Religion: Happiness in the Service of God," Aquinas posits that human beings are happiest when they are serving God. He believed that this was the case because

SIDEBAR 7.3
ANTIMISSIONARY: POPE INNOCENT IV

Practice: Commitment—Holding ideas with conviction; acting decisively on those ideas; not letting those ideas be divisive

Commitment to truth contributes to good mission. But when used to separate us from other Christians and those in need of the gospel, it contributes to bad mission.

Pope Innocent IV did not have a bad papal record as papal records go. But in two instances we would have to say that he qualifies as an antimissionary.

The first was a papal bull he authored, *Ad exstirpanda*, one provision of which acknowledged the right of the state to punish heretics after they were convicted of heresy. This was an implicit endorsement not only of the Inquisition but also of whatever punitive actions the political powers that be might take against heterodoxy.

The second instance was a face-to-face missionary action. In 1246 Innocent sent an emissary, sixty-five-year-old cleric Friar Giovanni (John) of Plano Carpini, to a parlay with Genghis Khan's grandson, Güyük Khan. Even though Güyük's mother was a Christian, and Güyük himself probably was as well, the message was not one of welcome to a brother in Christ but a pedantic synopsis of the life of Jesus and the main tenets of Christianity. It was a thirteenth-century model of an attempt at ecclesial sheep-stealing: if you don't believe exactly as we do, you don't believe.

Whereas Aquinas was always looking for what might be included from other Christian sources in his attempt to articulate orthodox Christian teaching, Innocent was obviously rejecting out of hand anything that might be considered different.

In his biography of Genghis Khan, Jack Weatherford summarizes well the results of this kind of mission practice:

> Despite the extensive spiritual beliefs that the Mongols and Europeans shared in common, the opening relationship had been so negative and misguided that in future years, the entire base of shared religion would eventually erode. The Mongols continued for another generation to foster closer relations with Christian Europe, but in the end, they would have to abandon all such hope, and with it they would, in time, abandon Christianity entirely in favor of Buddhism and Islam. (2005, 125)

REFLECTION AND DISCUSSION

1. List two advantages of the modern separation of church and state based on this thirteenth-century example of possible consequences of a too-close relationship between the two.
2. Evaluate Friar Giovanni's interaction with Güyük Khan. How did Giovanni's presentation of Christianity become divisive?
3. Imagine a situation in which you are beginning a friendship with the parents of one of your friends. One parent is a Christian and the other a Muslim. How would you interact with them on issues of faith?

125

- It is a sign of recognition that God has created human beings, not vice versa. "God has created man. He is therefore man's beginning."
- It is a sign of recognition that God has created human beings for himself. "God created man for himself. He is therefore man's final goal."
- These two recognitions mean that what human beings do in the religious realm is for their own welfare. "Men pay honor to God not for God's sake, but for their own sake."

Thus, religion is a human thing. According to Aquinas's definition, "religion is the virtue by which man gives to God the service and the honor which are due to God."

Of the hundreds of definitions of religion that one might find in the pages of religious studies textbooks, this is one of the most fruitful in terms of producing positive interreligious discussion and furthering productive Christian witness. Aquinas's definition is surely a Christian theological one, but it does not dismiss other religious endeavors as totally useless. Rather, it makes room for them—at least the possibility of them.

As we might imagine, knowing Aquinas's context, it is most useful with Muslims, who would find nothing to argue with in it. But for those of us who have some experience of Asian religions and their adherents, it strikes a chord there also. It recognizes the universal root of religion as identifying some kind of lack, a need that we all as human beings have. It acknowledges that we are all looking for a way to satisfy that lack, which is the common drive of all religions. And happiness is something all human beings can relate to in one form or another. Thus, it is an intriguing starting point for discussion.

It leaves open, of course, the question of whether religion is a virtue—or even what a virtue is. It leaves open the question of who or what God is and is not. And, of course, the concept of service is universal, but the actual forms religious service takes and the motivations for those services vary widely.

Aquinas again shows himself to be the master teacher, the master theologian, the master mission theologian. His contributions continue to enrich the Christian church.

8

Freedom

Honoring the Principle of Religious Choice

Mission Exemplar: Bartolomé de Las Casas
Location: South America, Latin America
Audience: Indigenous peoples
Time: Sixteenth century

Timeline

- 1484 Born in Seville
- 1498 Receives slave from father's expedition with Columbus
- 1502 Leaves Spain for the New World
- 1510 Is ordained as lay priest
- 1514 Receives *encomienda* after helping to conquer Cuba
- 1515 Renounces benefits of *encomienda* and returns to Spain
  to inform king and queen of abuses
- 1522 Enters Dominican order
- 1531 Letter to Council of the Indies arguing for peaceful
  persuasion of Indians
- 1532 Writes *The Only Way*
- 1533 Refuses absolution to *encomenderos*
- 1537 Treatise *De Unico Vocationes Modo* and Pope Paul III's
  bull *Sublimis Deus*
- 1542 New laws are passed to protect Indians and favor
  colonists.
- 1550 Defense against Sepúlveda
- 1576 Dies

> ### Resources to Consult on Bartolomé de Las Casas's Mission
>
> Lewis Hanke, *All Mankind Is One: A Study of the Disputation between Bartolomé de Las Casas and Juan Ginés de Sepúlveda on the Religious and Intellectual Capacity of the American Indians* (DeKalb: Northern Illinois University Press, 1974).
>
> Bartolomé de Las Casas, *In Defense of the Indians*, trans. Stafford Poole (DeKalb: Northern Illinois University Press, 1992).
>
> Bartolomé de Las Casas, *The Devastation of the Indies: A Brief Account,* trans. Herma Briffault (Baltimore: Johns Hopkins University Press, 1992).
>
> Bartolomé de Las Casas, *A Short Account of the Destruction of the Indies*, trans. Nigel Griffin (New York: Penguin Putnam, 1992).
>
> Bartolomé de Las Casas, *Witness: Writings of Bartolomé de Las Casas*, trans. George Sanderlin (Maryknoll, NY: Orbis, 1971).
>
> Paul S. Vickery, *Bartolomé de Las Casas: Great Prophet of the Americas* (New York: Paulist Press, 2006).

When he was fourteen years old, Bartolomé de Las Casas received a gift from his father. The gift was a boy about his own age, an American Indian slave whom his father had received from Columbus upon his return from a voyage to the New World in 1498. Juanico became a companion to Bartolomé, an amazing gift that taught him at an early age not the virtues of slavery but the humanity of the Indians. The boy was intelligent and companionable. He and Las Casas became fast friends. After a few years, Queen Isabella ordered that all three hundred of Columbus's captured slaves be returned to the New World, declaring, "What right does the admiral have to give anyone my vassals?" Bartolomé and his new companion vowed eternal friendship to each other and made plans to meet again when Bartolomé traveled to the New World himself (Vickery 2006, 32).

Bartolomé de Las Casas lived during an era of increasing European expansion. Born in Seville, Spain, in 1484, he grew up in a merchant's family, hearing tales of New World exploits by merchants and missionaries. This latest journey by his father was Columbus's second voyage, a trip to secure for Spain the new colonies. At age eighteen Bartolomé himself left for the New World; he arrived in what is now Haiti on April 15, 1502. As part of the colonialist world, he served the Crown and the church.

At first he did not question the subjugation of the indigenous peoples. Ordained as a lay priest in 1510, he helped conquer Cuba for Spain and was granted an *encomienda* by the pope in 1515. The *encomienda* system, set up by Queen Isabella to protect and convert the indigenous peoples, also benefited the Spanish conquerors. In fact, the *encomienda* received by Las Casas entitled him to the income produced by a number of slaves.

A Change of Heart for Las Casas

Las Casas, however, became increasingly uncomfortable with the *encomienda* system. Although created to protect the indigenous peoples and teach them Christianity, it also effectively relegated them to slave status. The Spanish controlled where they lived, what they did, and how the fruits of their labor were used. Las Casas's Christian conscience began to bother him as the double standard of using people for economic gain, while stripping them of human agency, came into conflict with his belief in the free gift of God's grace to all. In 1511 he heard or read a sermon by the Dominican Antonio Montesinos against keeping the American Indians in servitude, insisting that Indians were rational humans and that Christians were obliged to love them as they loved themselves (Las Casas 1992d, xx).

This tension came to a head in 1514, when Las Casas had a "Damascus Road" experience. While studying in preparation for his Easter sermon, he was struck by the words, "He that takes away his neighbor's living slays him" (Ecclus. 34:26 NRSV). Las Casas was thrown into a turmoil that, after many agonizing days, led to his conclusion that "everything which had been done to the Indians in the Indies was unjust and tyrannical" (1992d, xxii). One could not be a Christian and participate in the *encomienda* system, which exploited the indigenous peoples and relegated them to less than human status. Las Casas took a radical step. He gave up the privileges of his *encomienda* and set off with Montesinos to declare the injustices of the system to the king of Spain.

After his enlightenment on this issue, Las Casas never looked back. He spent the remainder of his life arguing for the full humanity of the Indians as rational beings who should have the freedom to choose their religion.

Spanish Conquerors in the New World

Las Casas's conversion to the notion that all humans could freely choose the gospel may sound prosaic to modern ears. But in the context of the conquering European powers, it sounded incredible. Spain's military expansion in the New World was based on conquering and using indigenous populations to garner wealth. Gold and silver were obtained from local kings, and Indians were forced to work in the mines. Indigenous peoples were used to dive for pearls, grow crops for the Spaniards, and serve them in every way. Slave trading was established and Indians transported by boat to other islands where they were sold. To argue that Indians were human beings, entitled to human rights and fair treatment, went against every tactic the Spaniards used to gain control of these colonies.

The fervor of the Spaniards as military conquerors was matched by the economic gain they brought to Spain. Some new territories were settled by Spaniards, but the emphasis was on bringing treasures back to the mother country. Farming was neglected in favor of putting American Indians to work

129

in the gold mines. Widespread starvation resulted. What little food there was went to Spanish settlers. Disease became rampant, wiping out thousands or perhaps even millions of American Indians. The devastation of lands and their inhabitants did not account for much since wealth, not settling the territories, was the major priority.

Of course, the Spanish settlers themselves, many of whom were farmers, also benefited from discounting the humanity of the indigenous peoples. Using them as servants to clear the land and help with farm labor was economically advantageous for the settlers. And according to Las Casas, the settlers were among the cruelest overlords. Spain sent convicts to the New World, promising them release from their prison sentences if they worked a mere one or two years in the colonies. Many were hardened criminals, even murderers, who became free settlers and hard taskmasters.

Not that the more "civilized" of the Europeans would have been much better. Socially, the European cultures had not had much positive interaction with other cultures. The Arab conquests of a few centuries earlier had taught them to fear and even abhor Muslims. The notion of the civilized world being limited to Europe made it difficult for Spaniards to see the good in another culture. Strange religious practices were considered idolatrous, and unfamiliar customs were deemed demonic. The idea that difference could be neutral or even good seemed inconceivable to those without firsthand experience. Las Casas wanted to witness to the goodness of the indigenous peoples. He stressed their innocence and purity. He lauded their gentleness and simplicity. Somehow, he thought, Europeans could learn to appreciate vicariously what he had learned firsthand: that New World indigenous peoples were full human beings, entitled to freely choose their culture and religion.

But political, economic, and social pressures against considering the indigenous peoples as fully entitled to choose their religion were complicated further by philosophical considerations. Influenced by Greek philosophy, Europeans followed Aristotle in believing that people were born to a certain social class and function. Aristotle argued that a slave could be a highly skilled doctor or silversmith, but a slave's purpose in life was to fulfill that role for the good of the larger community. Slaves had no status as citizens. The same was true for women, who, according to Aristotle, did not possess the capacity for moral reasoning. Those arguments were brought into play as priests and government officials argued for the exploitation of indigenous peoples as slaves and the childlike incapacity of the Indians to reason about morality. According to many, they could not embrace Christianity without first being conquered and subdued.

THE TIME WAS RIGHT

But the context also included elements that aided Las Casas's cause. First, the Spanish Crown had, since the twelfth century, consulted jurists and theologians to help it govern well. Christian values influenced the theologians who advised the Crown about treatment of people during and after military conquests. Humanitarian considerations and the morality of military ventures began to be considered important factors in decision making and colonial expansion. Those discussions had resulted in an uneasy conscience among many Europeans. Las Casas fostered and helped develop that conscience among Spanish rulers as he argued the immorality of Spanish activities in the Americas.

Another positive factor was Las Casas's views on other issues, views that supported the Crown and gave him credibility as a critic. Las Casas actually remained conservative politically and religiously all of his life. He believed that the Spanish Crown *should* rule over the colonies. He supported *obedience* to the church. The desire to spread Christianity also spawned a mission movement at this time. Columbus himself was sent by Queen Isabella to convert the indigenous peoples. Her concern that people in the New World learn about Christianity was, in fact, the motivation behind the *encomienda* system. Queen Isabella established the system as a benevolent patronage. Spanish settlers and leaders would take care of the indigenous peoples, civilizing them and educating them in the Christian faith.

The Christian intent, the desire to save the Indians for Christ, was not a supplemental rider of Spain's work in the New World. In fact, it was the primary goal, according to Queen Isabella. Missionaries, as carriers of the morals of the faith, were open to Las Casas's message of freedom of choice for Indians. As missionaries traveled to the Americas, they encountered generous hospitality from the indigenous peoples, an intelligent consideration of the gospel message, and earnest changes of lifestyle by Indians studying the Christian faith. Convincing missionaries that the indigenous peoples did not need to be subdued militarily in order to receive Christianity was easier than convincing settlers or treasure seekers for the Crown.

Finally, a couple of printers in Seville were important to the dissemination of Las Casas's ideas. Seville was a major trading port, a meeting place for Europeans who engaged in commerce with the colonies. In a single year, 1552, one printer put out nine of Las Casas's statements about the devastation of the Indies. Those "tracts" contained vivid descriptions of atrocities perpetrated by Spanish conquerors in the New World. Drawings were added, and specific numbers of those tortured, enslaved, and killed were noted. Whether or not those figures were accurate, the point was made, and the tracts received wide attention. The debate with a high-ranking priest, Juan Gínes de Sepúlveda, was also circulated, adding Christian and philosophical arguments to the "scandal success" of the tracts. News of Spanish atrocities spread throughout Europe.

Those mitigating factors gave Las Casas a hearing from the international community, and the conscience of European colonizers was awakened. Over the course of nearly forty years, from his own conversion in 1514 to well into the 1550s, Las Casas put forth his arguments on many fronts.

HOW HE DID IT

To make his case, Las Casas had to show that the Indians were fully human in the first place. That was the center of the debate in the sixteenth century. Las Casas's strategy included four main components: the authority of his own life experience, the authority of Scripture, the centrality of evangelism, and a wise choice of audiences.

The Authority of Experience

In all his arguments and witness, Las Casas boldly presented his own experience as a central authority. He recalled his early experience of receiving an American Indian slave from his father. At that formative time of his life, Las Casas learned that his slave companion was intelligent, caring, and fully human. His later experiences—participating in the *encomienda* system, documenting the maltreatment of Indians, and encountering biblical passages that convicted his spirit—all became central to his message and the force with which he proclaimed it.

Much like Augustine in his *Confessions*, Las Casas repeatedly referred to his sinful actions—his military involvement in conquering Cuba, his personal gain from the *encomienda* system, his inability to perceive the wrong of his actions. Then he described his conversion from that unrepentant state to a totally new apprehension of the wrongness of everything the Spaniards had done in the New World. He repeatedly explained how that total transformation revolutionized his actions. He gave up his privileges of *encomienda*; he established colonies such as Tierra Firma in Venezuela that practiced equality with American Indians; he spoke and wrote about what he had seen and learned from those experiences.

Las Casas was convinced of the Crown's good intentions and remained a lifelong admirer of Columbus. He felt certain that if Queen Isabella and King Ferdinand were informed of the atrocities being committed by their conquistadors, they would change their tactics in the New World. He was the one to inform them; he had seen those atrocities firsthand.

The Authority of Scripture

The influence of Aristotle on the European intelligentsia also needed to be addressed. The Crown set up a "debate" between Sepúlveda and Las Casas. Each wrote treatises refuting the other's arguments. The issue at stake was the humanity of the indigenous peoples. Sepúlveda argued with Aristotle that some people were born to be slaves (Aristotle, *Politics* 1.1). Those people could not reason morally but must be directed in their work and moral behavior by free citizens. Sepúlveda believed that the indigenous peoples had displayed an immorality of conduct that put them forever in this category.

Las Casas strongly objected not only to this classification but to Aristotle's very idea. He cited the Scriptures, claiming that every person was fully human and capable of reasoning about morality. All were created in God's image. All could choose the good. After all, he argued, God would have failed in his project of good creation if so many—indeed all the people in a particular region—were not fully human. Also, freedom of choice was proclaimed by the apostle Paul. Scripture, then, disagrees with Aristotle. So, "Good-bye, Aristotle!" he said. "From Christ, the eternal truth, we have the command 'You must love your neighbor as yourself'" (Las Casas 1992a, 40).

The Centrality of Evangelism

After his conversion experience, Las Casas traveled back to Spain with Montesinos to personally present to the Crown his information about the devastating events taking place in Spain's new territories. He saw himself as a witness, bringing firsthand knowledge to those who could not travel themselves. Las Casas was familiar with the queen's goal of evangelizing the New World, and he admired Columbus's efforts to fulfill that goal. Now he traveled home to report the failures. He described the abuses of the *encomienda* system and documented the torture of indigenous peoples by the military. He argued that subduing the Indians for the purpose of converting them was ineffective.

Evangelism was at the heart of that message. Las Casas understood that Spain's involvement with the New World must display Christ's love in word and deed. King Ferdinand and Queen Isabella had clearly established conversion of the indigenous peoples to Christ as the major goal of their expeditions. Las Casas further insisted that evangelism was necessary not only for the indigenous peoples but for the Spaniards—for those within the church as well as for those without. He believed that all people had the capacity to understand and accept the good gift of salvation. Anything that stood in the way of proclaiming God's grace needed to be moved aside so that God's love could reach every person. He vigorously opposed those who thought that Spain must conquer first; then when the indigenous peoples were humbled, they could be converted to the gospel.

The Wise Choice of Audiences

Las Casas was quick to identify his enemies and gravitate to those who would hear his message. In 1532 he brought his case to the Council of the Indies, the governing body that handled the new territories. After his letter of appeal to the council was rejected, he spoke instead to the church, to the Spanish Crown, and to the international community.

In 1534 he finished his treatise *The Only Way*, which showed the weaknesses of forced contact as a method of evangelization. "Win the mind with reasons and win the will with motives, gently, graciously," he said (Vickery 2006, 27–28). Forcing Indians into communities of Spaniards to do their work did not foster the free gift of grace that God had to offer. This was a message

---

SIDEBAR 8.1
THE LAS CASAS MISSION METHOD

Las Casas, "The Only Method of Converting the Indians" (1971a, 137–42; 1992c)

THE ONLY METHOD SUMMARIZED

"The one and only method of teaching the true religion was established by Divine Providence for the whole world, and for all times, that is, by persuading the understanding through reason, and by gently attracting or exhorting the will."

PREACHING ACCORDING TO THE ONLY METHOD

• Preachers should make clear to hearers that they have no intention of acquiring power over them through their preaching.

• Preachers should make clear to hearers that they have no desire for riches.

• Preachers should be mild, humble, courteous, and goodwilled.

• Preachers should display love of all men in the world, that they might be saved.

• Preachers must be holy, just, and blameless.

WHY CONQUEST IS THE WRONG METHOD OF CONVERSION

• A rational creature has a natural capacity for being moved, directed, and drawn to any good gently because of his freedom of choice.

• If men are forced to listen, they will not want to give assent to what they have heard.

• Conquest is not Christlike, right, or effective.

REFLECTION AND DISCUSSION

1. Describe the sixteenth-century context in which Las Casas worked. What were the two opposing views of American Indians, and around what circumstances and interests did they revolve?

2. How did Las Casas's experiences influence his change of heart toward the oppression of the indigenous peoples of the New World? How did he use those experiences to argue for the freedom of the Indians and their right to choose their religion?

3. What was the most basic assumption of Las Casas's argument, the foundation upon which everything else was built? How did he use it to argue for employing only peaceful means to present the gospel to the American Indians?

4. How do you argue for freedom of choice in matters of religion? What authorities do you invoke? What experiences do you recall that influence your view?

5. How does freedom in the choice of religion influence your views of the following?
   • Human rights and responsibilities
   • Evangelism
   • Individualism
   • Community responsibility

addressed to those truly interested in God's work in the New World, rather than an appeal to those who wished to amass wealth through their contact with indigenous peoples.

Las Casas formed coalitions with other people of the same persuasion. He aligned himself with Montesinos and others who espoused the cause of the freedom of the Indians. He quoted province leaders such as the bishop of the province of Santa Marta when they recommended solutions to the Crown (Las Casas 1992d, 81–82). He worked with those of like mind to establish communities, one of which he located in Venezuela—which was considered one of the most barbaric regions. In that place, "fear of God, duty to the Crown and respect for their fellow-men were all discarded in [the conquerors'] blind and obsessive greed, and they went further than any of the predecessors in devising new and ever more refined methods of cruelty and duplicity to obtain the gold and silver they craved, behaving as absolute dictators of the territory and without a thought for their own souls" (1992d, 96).

WHO LISTENED? LAS CASAS'S INFLUENCE

Las Casas influenced the church, especially after entering the Dominican order in 1522. After his years of novitiate training and study, he spoke persuasively to the Dominicans, and to the Franciscans as well, about the matter of freedom for the Indians. Although he was not the first to pick up this torch nor the last to carry it, he later declared in writing that he did influence those Catholic orders to adopt this way of life themselves. Perhaps more importantly, his treatise *De Unico Vocationis Modo* influenced Pope Paul III's bull *Sublimis Deus*, which advocated conversion of the Indians by peaceful means alone (Hanke 1974, 17).

Las Casas influenced the debate between European philosophy and Christianity. In tempering the use of Aristotle's view of function, he prepared the way for a more person-centered approach to societal life, a view that was more compatible with New Testament teachings. The individualism of the Enlightenment and the Reformers' ideas of the importance of personal response to God followed this trend from determined function to free choices in individual life.

Las Casas also influenced the Spanish Crown, presenting his case with Montesinos in 1515 and on subsequent occasions. Queen Isabella listened. And although she was unable to stop the atrocities of her conquistadors, she continued to support peaceful means for converting the indigenous peoples. As part of her last will and testament, she admonished King Ferdinand and Prince Phillip to continue her evangelizing work without hurting the indigenous peoples.

Las Casas influenced the colonies. Although his two experiments in living on an equal basis with the Indians ultimately failed, the communities had an effect on those in the colonies. Missionaries and settlers who affirmed values of

SIDEBAR 8.2
ANTIMISSIONARY: LOUIS IX

Practice: Freedom—Honoring the principle of religious choice

Mission is more effective when people are given a chance to freely choose (or reject) the gospel. Mission is unfaithful to God's commands when people are manipulated to believe or forced to believe by political fiat or military might.

There have been many King Louis of France far worse than Louis IX (1215–70, reigned 1226–70). One thinks, for example, of Louis XIV, who made Protestantism illegal in France. Or of Louis XVI, who was unfit by temperament and education for kingship. In fact, Louis IX was known for his religious piety. He was called Louis the Pious. He was canonized in 1297, the only French monarch to be so honored. The Americans named a city after him—St. Louis. Can he possibly have been an antimissionary?

We think three of his acts more than qualify him. First, he led not one but two Crusades against the infidel Muslims in the Middle East, the Seventh Crusade in 1248 and the Eighth Crusade in 1270. Of course, in Louis' day this made him seem more religious than ever. But the long-term effects of these Crusades against Muslims have been disastrous. These attempts at Christian conversion by the sword have closed most Muslim nations today to free expressions of the Christian gospel. These two Crusades alone qualify Louis IX as an antimissionary.

But there is more. In 1243 he expelled all Jews from France. He confiscated their property (in order to finance his first Crusade). And then he staged a book burning. He collected all the copies of the Talmud that he and his henchmen could find (at least twelve thousand according to some sources) and burned them in the public squares of France.

Is there a possible connection between these acts and the fact that France today almost always leads other Western nations in the number of anti-Semitic acts? Although it is probably impossible to assign full credit to Louis IX for these modern acts of inhumanity, it certainly cannot have helped that a few short centuries ago the most powerful politician and the most saintly Christian in all of France treated Jews and their religion with such disdain.

Christianity has often found itself in its two-thousand-year history with enough secular power at its disposal to force groups of people to accede to Christian faith. Whenever it has used the slightest bit of this power for manipulative mission, the results have been disastrous.

REFLECTION AND DISCUSSION

1. Give two reasons why Louis IX's Crusades may have added to his image as a pious king.
2. Why do you think the "different-ness" of the Jews inspired crimes against them in thirteenth-century France?
3. What kinds of differences among groups of people today do you find disconcerting?

136

equality and freedom could take heart from Las Casas's example. They could see that forced labor was not needed to effectively reach the Indians with the Christian gospel. The peaceful example of godly love, treating every person as a human being endowed with reason, made a statement in the concrete realm of everyday life.

Las Casas influenced the legal system. His arguments for freedom of choice as a natural right followed the reasoning of Francisco de Vitoria, a legal adviser to the Crown, and were incorporated into legal reasoning as the Enlightenment progressed. Las Casas stands forcefully in the line of thought from Aquinas to the Dutch jurist Grotius, who used the notion of natural law, *jus naturae*, to unravel ethical dilemmas (Vickery 2006, 15–16).

Las Casas was far ahead of his time in applying that notion to people of another race and culture. He became one of the first of his era to speak out against slavery. Although for some years he favored bringing African slaves to Hispaniola to relieve oppression of the indigenous peoples, his study of Ecclesiasticus changed his mind. He became fervent in his opposition to slavery in all forms. In the ensuing centuries, the recognition of the full humanity of all people and the responsibility to treat them as such has become part of international law, documented in the United Nations Declaration of Human Rights in 1948.

In the contemporary world, freedom of religion is honored by the constitutions of the very nations that objected to it in the sixteenth century. It is honored as well in the New World nations that were subjected to the misguided methods of "evangelism" used by the Spanish and other European conquerors. Leaders of world religions exalt this practice in the Declaration of Human Rights by the World's Religions (Adeney and Sharma 2007). And it has become a normative practice in the mission world, whether Catholic, Orthodox, Anglican, or Protestant. Freedom to choose one's religion is now considered to be at the center of the gospel message. It is the heart of giftive mission.

Effectiveness

Allowing the Context to Determine the Form of Witness

Mission Exemplar: Matteo Ricci
Location: Asia, China
Audience: Confucians, Taoists, Buddhists
Time: Sixteenth century

Timeline
- 1552 Born in Macerata, Italy
- 1571 Joins Society of Jesus (Jesuits)
- 1578 First assignment: Goa, India
- 1583 Chao-ch'ing (Zhaoqing), China
- 1595 Nanking, China
- 1601 Peking (Beijing), China
- 1602 Publication of *The True Meaning of the Lord of Heaven*
- 1610 Dies in Peking, China

Resources to Consult on Matteo Ricci's Mission

William Theodore De Bary, Wing-tsit Chan, and Burton Watson, eds., *Sources of the Chinese Tradition* (New York: Columbia University Press, 1960).

Kenneth Latourette, *A History of Christian Missions in China* (New York: Macmillan, 1929).

Samuel Moffett, *A History of Christianity in Asia*, vol. 1 (San Francisco: HarperCollins, 1992).

Matteo Ricci, *China in the Sixteenth Century: The Journals of Matteo Ricci, 1583–1610*, trans. Louis Gallagher (New York: Random House, 1953).

Matteo Ricci, *The True Meaning of the Lord of Heaven*, trans. Douglas Lancashire and Peter Hu Kuo-chen, ed. Edward J. Malatesta (St. Louis: Institute of Jesuit Sources, 1985).

Arnold Rowbotham, *Missionary and Mandarin: The Jesuits at the Court of China* (Berkeley: University of California Press, 1942).

Christopher Spalatin, *Matteo Ricci's Use of Epictetus* (Taegu, Korea: Waegwan, 1975).

Jonathan Spence, *The Memory Palace of Matteo Ricci* (New York: Penguin, 1984).

C. K. Yang, *Religion in Chinese Society* (Berkeley: University of California Press, 1961).

Of all the pagan sects known to Europe, I know of no people who fell into fewer errors in the early ages of their antiquity than did the Chinese. From the very beginning of their history it is recorded in their writings that they recognized and worshipped one supreme being whom they called the King of Heaven, or designated by some other name indicating his rule over heaven and earth. . . . Nowhere do we read that the Chinese created monsters of vice out of this supreme being or from his ministering deities, such as the Romans, the Greeks, and the Egyptians evolved into gods or patrons of the vices. (Ricci 1953)

This passage is from the journal of Matteo Ricci, sixteenth-century missionary to China. Ricci was a very special missionary. Many have seen in his work a willingness to grapple with the difficulties that currently face mission workers in Asia, particularly regarding questions of how to incorporate the rich cultures of ancient Asia into the telling of the gospel story. Gone are the days when the easy road of complete rejection of the "darkness and satanic influences of the East" made the approach seem clear: condemn, condemn, condemn, and then, into the vacuum, insert the gospel story.

This attitude made the method of telling the gospel story easy, to be sure. But it didn't work. Not one Asian country has responded to this telling of the gospel in any significant numbers. No Buddhist or Hindu culture of any size, for example, has become more than 5 percent Christian despite five hundred years of concentrated mission work to China, Japan, India, and other South and Southeast Asian countries (representing almost half the world's population). Korea may be an exception to these statistics; with almost 20 percent of Koreans now Christian, it is nonetheless still far short of even a simple majority.

Matteo Ricci was the first missionary to realize that condemnation of indigenous religion and culture would not work in Asia. Ricci saw the inherent difficulties in attempting to replace Asian Confucian culture with Western

139

Christian culture. He struck on what was then the novel idea of not attempting to replace Asian culture with Western culture. Instead, he thought, why not begin the process of developing an Asian Christianity, one that would be compatible with Asian culture? Both his successes and failures in this attempt make him one of the most significant innovators of mission practice in the history of Christian mission.

WHO WAS MATTEO RICCI?

Ricci was born on October 16, 1552, in Macerata, Italy. His family sent him to Rome when he was eighteen to study law. He did not want to study law, however, and instead joined a religious society, the Sodality of the Blessed Virgin, and lived by their rules. Following the lure of the church, he studied theology, and through that study the call of missions became increasingly clear.

Ricci heard about a new order that only recently had been given formal recognition (in 1540) by Pope Paul III to do mission work in the most untouched, difficult parts of the world. It was called the Society of Jesus and had been established in 1534 by Ignatius Loyola. Popularly called the Jesuits, the order declared as its aims "to strive especially for the defense and propagation of the faith and for the progress of souls in Christian life and doctrine" and also "to go . . . to whatsoever provinces [the popes] may choose to send us—whether they are pleased to send us among the Turks or any other infidels, even those who live in the region called the Indies" (Papasogli 1959, 198). Already by Ricci's time, Jesuits had begun work in the Americas, India, and East Asia.

The more Ricci learned about this type of mission work, the more intrigued he became. He joined the Jesuits in 1571 and continued his education under their auspices. By the time he finished his studies in Rome, he had volunteered for work in India—and the attraction to Asia grew. He was given permission by the Society to join the India mission and arrived in Goa, India, in 1578. The Jesuits' mission philosophy emphasized education and language preparation. For four years, Ricci continued his studies in India and began an intensive study of Chinese.

In 1583 he finally received permission from the Chinese government to take up residence in China. He moved to Chao-ch'ing, China, in 1583. In 1595 he transferred his work to Nanking, because it was closer to Peking, his eventual goal. Finally in 1601 he obtained permission to set up a mission station in the capital city, Peking, where he worked for ten years until his death in 1610. Altogether Ricci spent twenty-seven years in China developing the mission approach for which he was to become known.

Ricci recorded all his experiences and ideas. He was a faithful journal writer, and his journals have been collected, edited, translated from the Latin, and published in 1953 by Louis Gallagher in *China in the Sixteenth Century: The Journals of Matteo Ricci, 1583–1610*. Ricci was also a prolific correspondent, and we can learn much from his letters. Finally, Ricci published a book in 1601, *The True Meaning of the Lord of Heaven*, cast in the form of a dialogue between Ricci and a Confucian scholar about the similarities and differences between Christianity and Confucianism.

THE CHINA CHALLENGE

From the beginning, mission work in China was difficult. The Chinese, like the Japanese, were wary of Western influences, and even when they began trade with the colonial powers, they tried to restrict the interactions to economics only. One way they did this was to set up entrepôts where the Portuguese (and then the Italians and eventually the British) could mix with Chinese merchants; often these restricted zones were on offshore islands.

The Chinese were not worried about the Christian religion itself. They are pluralists with regard to religion and open to religious discussions from all corners. As early as 635, Nestorian Christians had come to China from Persia and successfully engaged the Chinese, particularly the Mahayana Buddhists, in interreligious dialogues that led to the establishment of a Christian church near the modern province of Xi'an. For various reasons probably having more to do with dwindling support and theological controversy back home than with events in China, the Nestorian mission withered away.

Rather, the Chinese, often known as the people of three religions at once—Confucianism, Taoism, and Buddhism—are more chary of what foreign religion might bring politically than they are afraid of foreign religious ideas themselves. As long as they are convinced that a religion brings no political—that is, colonizing—danger, the Chinese are quite open to new religious ideas. And the best way to reassure the Chinese in this regard is for the religion to show how compatible it can be with the Chinese way of life. In the case of Christianity this means that the Chinese were and always will be wary of Western Christianity but have been and will continue to be quite open to a Chinese Christianity.

The Jesuits knew this. This was the great insight of Francis Xavier and other Jesuit officials such as Alessandro Valignano and Michele Ruggieri. It was the insight that Ricci brought with him and built a mission strategy upon as no one before him—and perhaps since—had done. Due to conditions we will discuss in more detail later, Ricci's insights and mission innovations did not last much beyond his lifetime. His mission approach did not flourish as perhaps it might have had he enjoyed more support from his superiors back home and had a stronger successor to carry on the work.

RICCI'S MISSION PRINCIPLE

In developing and establishing his mission strategy, Ricci wanted to avoid the experience of the Portuguese. The Portuguese, of course, took mission workers with them on their merchant ships. The primary mission converts of the sixteenth century were made by these Portuguese missionaries. They were Chinese who for one reason or another came in contact with the Portuguese traders on Macao. The Portuguese began by teaching them the Portuguese language; they gave them Portuguese names and instructed them on how to live as the Portuguese did. These Chinese became Christians certainly, but Portuguese Christians.

Although Ricci did not want to belittle the quality of the conversion of these few Chinese, he saw that this approach could not be replicated in any significant way in the whole of China. There was no chance that China would become a Portuguese colony, which would be necessary to create Portuguese Christians on a large scale. And it was highly unlikely China would become anyone else's colony, for that matter. In order for the mission to work in China, Christianity had to be poured through the Chinese cultural sieve.

The question for Ricci was how to do that without jeopardizing his commitment to the truth of Christianity. He started with the idea that the best approach would be through Buddhism, a religion that came to China from India in the third century but had changed form in major ways to become indigenized to the Chinese worldview. Why he chose Buddhism as his vehicle of entrée is unclear. Perhaps he had familiarized himself with the partially successful Nestorian mission, which had used Mahayana Buddhism in this way. Thus when he and Michele Ruggieri finally received permission to enter China, to make themselves more acceptable, they thought, they shaved off their hair and beards and dressed themselves in the gray cloaks worn by Buddhist monks of that time.

But cultural conditions were quite different during the time of the Nestorian missionaries and that of Ricci's party. Buddhism's fortunes in China rose and fell with the level of imperial support it received and was most influential during the time of the Nestorians. It was not influential during Ricci's century. He quickly discovered that Buddhist monks were not respected by the higher classes of Chinese society; they considered the monks lazy noncontributors to the cultural and economic scene. If Ricci wanted to impress the Chinese with the value of Christianity to the Chinese way of life, it was counterproductive to associate the religion with Buddhism.

Ricci quickly modified his strategy and goals. He decided that the way to reach the higher classes, who tended to be Confucian, was to show how compatible Christianity was with some of the principles of Confucius's teaching. He set about becoming a Confucian intellectual. This meant studying the Confucian classics. By 1591 Ricci had become fluent enough in Chinese to begin translating these important books (the Confucian *Analects*, the *Book of Mencius*, the *Great Learning*, and the *Doctrine of the Mean*) into Latin. He also began to dress and behave as one of the Confucian literati would.

This adaptation also meant assuming some negative behaviors. To be a Confucian during this period meant becoming an enemy of both Buddhism and Taoism. Ricci joined in the polemics against these two religious systems to show his solidarity with the Confucian worldview.

Thus, his main operating strategy and principle became presenting Christianity as the fulfillment of primitive Confucian teaching while joining in the condemnation of both Buddhist and Taoist religious teachings. In Chinese, the phrase, "Draw close to Confucianism and repudiate Buddhism," became Ricci's watchword.

RICCI'S APPROACH TO CONFUCIANISM

Ricci's approach to Confucians was the opposite of his approach to Buddhists and Taoists. Here we find most clearly illustrated Ricci's innovation of allowing the context of mission to determine the form that mission would take. Ricci was convinced that in the ancient Confucian texts lay the seeds of the gospel. They were monotheistic according to his reading of those texts, and they were interested in ethical self-cultivation. Although both their monotheistic belief in the Lord of Heaven and their ethical approach to divine and human relationships needed quite a bit of tweaking to conform with biblical Christianity, by Ricci's reckoning they were not incompatible. Confucianism, therefore, did not need to be replaced by Christianity but rather augmented by it.

Ricci came by this understanding honestly. He did not make it up *de novae*. It was part of the Jesuit tradition; in regard to China, it was first expressed in an interesting form by Francis Xavier, one of the founding members of the Society of Jesus. Xavier became interested in China while planting churches in Japan. The Japanese frequently referred to Chinese wisdom when making philosophical and religious arguments and told Xavier that if Christianity were really the one true religion, then the Chinese intellectuals would surely know about it. Xavier and his successors (Xavier did not reach China before he died) fully expected to find evidence of Christianity in Chinese thought.

Ricci inherited this expectation, not directly from Xavier but from Alessandro Valignano, Xavier's successor as director of Jesuit missions in Asia. Earlier we noted that Valignano was the Society's novice master when Ricci joined the order and had great influence on the development of Ricci's thought and his eventual mission practices. Ricci's approach was based on this understanding and consisted of at least five elements.

Chinese Language

Valignano firmly believed "that if missionaries were to have any chance of success among the Chinese they would have to do what, heretofore, none had done: they would have to master the Chinese language" (Ricci 1985, 5). Ricci spent four years in Goa, India, learning Chinese and never stopped improving his knowledge of the language after he arrived in China in 1583.

Confucian Cultural Gaps

In the process of learning Chinese and interacting with the Confucian classics, Ricci became well acquainted with Chinese culture and the interests of the Chinese. Geography, astronomy, and music were strong interests, but the Chinese knowledge of them was quite parochial. They were interested in European approaches to these subjects. Ricci became famous for his maps, clocks, stargazing, mathematical insights, and music that he created for the Chinese.

Confucian Points of Contact

Ricci mined the Confucian classics for evidence of the Chinese people's already-existing belief in a supreme being and their total dedication to moral

---

SIDEBAR 9.1
ISSUES OF TERMINOLOGY

Matteo Ricci was determined to make key Christian terms as user-friendly to the Confucian intelligentsia as possible. The following is a summary of his thinking on three key terms:

TERM	PROBLEM	SOLUTION
God	The Chinese moved from a more personal reference to deity, *shang-ti*, to an impersonal force ruling the universe, *tien*. Choosing *shang-ti* would not have been in keeping with current Chinese thought; choosing *tien* would have made God seem impersonal.	He created the phrase *tien-chu*, which means Lord of Heaven.
Soul	Ricci wanted to use Thomas Aquinas's idea of three souls: vegetative, sensitive, intellective. The Chinese had no terminology for this.	He chose as a base word *hun*, which for the Chinese meant the spirit of a person capable of existing apart from the body, and prefixed Chinese terms for plant (*chih-hun*), feeling (*chueh-hun*), and intelligent (*ling-hun*) to the basic word.
Holy, Sacred, Saint	The Confucian term was *sheng*, which meant the ideal person; however, the negative to *sheng* (sage, saint) was not sin and sinner but ignorance and ignorant.	He used *sheng* but added an additional word meaning spiritual (*shen*), thus the word *sheng-shen*.

---

living. He spent a great deal of time talking with Confucian scholars about terminological equivalences for Christian beliefs, such as words and concepts for heaven, hell, the devil, angels, soul, holy, sacred, saint, and more.

Publications

Confucians were literate. Ricci and his colleagues quickly realized that if something wasn't written and published, it didn't have much meaning for the literati. So he determined to focus on publications. Most of what Ricci published were translations into Chinese of material he thought they would find important and interesting. He began with very simple translations of things such as the Ten Commandments, the Lord's Prayer, and the Apostles' Creed. Then he moved to simple texts such as beginning catechisms. As noted previously, in 1601 he published an apologetic book in the form of a dialogue with a Confucian scholar, called *The True Meaning of the Lord of Heaven*.

Pre-evangelical Dialogue

Ricci was a realist. He realized that learning the Chinese language, the Confucian classics, and Chinese culture and then relating them to the gospel story was the work of a lifetime. And since he also believed that short-circuiting this process by bypassing these steps and presenting the unvarnished gospel in Western thought forms was likely to alienate the Chinese—they were uncomprehending of the suffering and death of Jesus, Christianity's primary personage, for example—he considered his work to be pre-evangelical dialogue. He saw himself as preparing the way for future mission workers who would continue his work and provide more of the gospel's supernatural requirements. One can see the influence of Aquinas's thought here. Ricci's work treated every topic that could be approached from the standpoint of reason alone (using philosophical consideration, explanation, and proof). But he placed much less emphasis on those things that Aquinas thought could be known only through God's supernatural revelation. Ricci saw his task as presenting an exposition of Christian thought with the aid of China's cultural heritage.

Clearly, Ricci's approach to the religions of China was contextual, not ideological. For Ricci, there was no one right way to deal with a non-Christian religious thought form. One's approach was determined by whatever would help the target audience understand the gospel the best in the long term. In his context in sixteenth-century China, this meant apologetically attacking Buddhism and Taoism and sympathetically appropriating Confucian philosophy in the service of the gospel.

THE RITES CONTROVERSY

Did Ricci's approach work? It depends on who you ask. According to the Jesuits and many modern missiologists—and us—the answer is yes. Douglas

Lancashire notes that "from the compilation of the first draft of *The True Meaning of the Lord of Heaven* and its subsequent circulation in manuscript form, the work had an incomparable effect on the propagation of the Christian faith" (Ricci 1985, 39). Ricci had some promising success during his own time in China. He gained the trust of the Chinese leadership and was eventually allowed to move to Peking, the capital, and live close to the emperor. And although he never met the emperor—one of his goals—the emperor, through his proxies, endorsed the pre-evangelical dialogue approach of Ricci. When Ricci died, the emperor allowed him to be buried in a special place and permitted the continuation of Ricci's work. And it is said that a later emperor, K'ang-hsi (1662–1723), based his decision to issue an edict of toleration of Christians in 1692 in part on a thorough reading of Ricci's work.

That is not to say that Ricci's acceptance was universal in China. Certainly the Buddhists and the Taoists reacted negatively. After all, Ricci reserved his strongest negative language for them and what he understood (wrongly as it turned out) to be the inadequacies of their religious traditions. They attacked Ricci's flawed understandings of their traditions with justifiable dismay. And the Chinese in general objected to Ricci's implications that their culture was scientifically backward. The government, although generally favorable, never lost the fear of the political consequences of allowing Christianity to gain a foothold in China. The Buddhists were trying to gain a rapprochement with the Confucians so that they could find a place in Chinese culture, and Ricci's strategy, "draw close to Confucianism and repudiate Buddhism," threatened that attempt.

Not even all Confucians accepted him. Perhaps the strongest objections to Ricci's work came from neo-Confucianists, who were displeased with

SIDEBAR 9.2 CHINESE RITES CONTROVERSY	
The Issue	Whether to accommodate Christian terminology and behavior to more satisfactorily connect with Confucian terminology and behavior
Ricci's Accommodations	Examples include the following: Using *tien* (heaven) as a term for God Calling Confucius *sheng*, or "holy" Dressing as a Confucian intellectual
Complainants	The Dominicans and the Franciscans objected to Ricci's methods.
Resolution	Pope Clement XI decided against Ricci's accommodationism in 1704 and 1710 and ordered a return to Latin ways.

their religion being regarded as a preparatory stage for the higher religion of Christianity. The Confucian scholar Hsu Chang-chih collected a large number of articles critical of Ricci's work and published them in 1640 in a work titled *Collection of Writings of the Sacred Dynasty for the Countering of Heterodoxy*. Many neo-Confucianists were either explicitly or implicitly attempting to draw attractive Buddhist teachings into what became the three religions of China, and Ricci's strategy interfered with that goal. For these writers, the official stance was that Confucianism (with certain implicit adjustments from Taoism and Buddhism) was complete in itself and needed no fulfillment from Christianity.

Some of the strongest objections to Ricci's work, however, came from inside the church. This is a theme we have seen repeatedly with our mission innovators. The *missio externa* is difficult simply because of the nature of mission work, whether the geographical or philosophical landscape is friendly or not. But the *missio interna* is even more difficult because the very success that the new mission practice generates threatens either the theological sensibilities of the current mission theorists (who have usually said "it can't be done that way") or the power balance of the church (church groups often compete for scarce mission resources) or arouses personal jealousies within the church.

In Ricci's case these criticisms focused on three elements: the equation of the Christian God with the Chinese *shang-ti*; the use of other Chinese terminology for key Christian concepts (such as the use of *tien* for heaven); and the fact that little of what traditional mission workers considered to be the gospel appeared in Ricci's work. It mattered little that Ricci agreed with the last. He always considered his work to be pre-evangelistic, gaining a foothold in Chinese culture that would be built on by others who came after him. From this point of view, what some considered a criticism, Ricci saw as a strength.

This internal criticism generated what has become known as the rites controversy. Other mission orders, especially the Dominicans and the Franciscans, objected to Ricci's methods and made them an ongoing issue in Rome. The controversy was brought before the papal court, and long after Ricci died his methods were disavowed by Pope Clement XI in both 1704 and 1710. The Jesuits in China, who were still following Ricci's mission template, were ordered to resume imposing Roman ways on the Chinese Christians. Clement's decision stood until the twentieth century, when Roman Catholics began to accept the principles of what they called enculturation and what Protestants eventually began calling contextualization.

From a twenty-first-century mission perspective, many missiologists criticize Ricci not for going too far down this road but for not going far enough. Ricci's practices have been labeled accommodationism. According to this view, missionaries still practice "accommodations," such as Ricci's use of *tien* for heaven and *shang-ti* for God, instead of letting the indigenous Chinese find their own ways of expressing the gospel story. Ricci is also criticized for

SIDEBAR 9.3
ANTIMISSIONARY: PIERRE-JEAN DE SMET

Practice: Effectiveness—Allowing the context to determine the form of witness

Mission works best when one does the hard work of understanding the target culture and then teaching the Jesus story in a way that connects. Mission is easiest when one brings a "set-piece" understanding of the gospel from one's own culture and simply imposes it on other cultures. Would you rather your mission be easy or effective?

It is difficult to find any writings about Pierre-Jean De Smet (1801–73), a Belgian Jesuit missionary to Native Americans, that are less than adulatory. He started his ministry in Council Bluffs, Iowa, and from there worked his way west to Missoula, Montana, and finally the Willamette River region of Oregon. By all accounts, he was hardworking. Although foreign born, he gained the trust of the United States government, so much so that it frequently used him as a peace negotiator with Indian peoples when the government was concluding treaties with them.

That was one of the issues that qualifies him as an antimissionary. The so-called peace treaties that resulted from these discussions were almost always not advantageous to the Native Americans. For example, he helped negotiate the early treaty with Sitting Bull of the Lakota Sioux, the Sioux Tribe Treaty of 1868. It was so unfair that Sitting Bull, who had advocated living in peace with the white people up to that point, decided fighting for Sioux rights was the only way

forward. The result was the Battle of the Little Bighorn in 1876.

Eventually Sitting Bull was captured, then released. He spent the last years of his life working in Buffalo Bill Cody's Wild West Show as a showpiece Native American warrior. At the appropriate time in the program, he would ride out in his Indian regalia, salute the crowd, and say a few words in his native tongue. The people would cheer wildly. Little did they know that he was cursing them, their government, and their Christian religion.

Native American author George Tinker traces De Smet's weaknesses to his total belief in his rationalistic Catholic theology and his contempt for Native American beliefs. He would regularly "imitate in mocking fashion the rituals and practices of the indigenous peoples" in his ultimately failed attempts to plant the Christian faith among them.

REFLECTION AND DISCUSSION

1. How did the idea of peace as the absence of overt conflict work against effective gospel-oriented mission for De Smet?
2. What kind of mission work with Native Americans might have been more beneficial to them than De Smet's method of working to achieve the goals of the US government?
3. How can we avoid the pitfall of mocking the practices of non-Christian religions?

focusing more on externals, such as rituals and worship practices, than on deeper religious structures.

The contextualizers of today nonetheless see in Ricci a mission worker who started us on the right road. So perhaps it is fair to say that Ricci's greatest successes came long after he died. Perhaps his most significant successes are the ones we are experiencing right now: the focus on letting the contexts determine the forms mission takes.

Whether he knew it or not, Ricci raised a theological issue of monumental importance for twenty-first-century missions. The question is whether it is possible to pour the gospel story through the worldview of Asian—and Latin American and African—worldviews. Or does it require the worldview of Western theologians and theorists in order to be expressed correctly?

It seems likely that were Ricci alive today, he would say that what he attempted in the sixteenth century—to demonstrate some of the deep structural compatibilities of these religious worldviews with the larger Christian story—is still what must be done today.

10

Consistency

Striving for Consistency between Methods and Goals

Mission Exemplar: William Carey
Location: Asia, India
Audience: Hindus
Time: Eighteenth century

Timeline
- 1761 Born at Paulerspury, England
- 1781 Marries Dorothy Plackett
- 1785 Pastorate at Moulton
- 1789 Pastorate at Leicester
- 1792 Deathless Sermon
        Publishes the *Enquiry*
- 1793 Founds the Baptist Missionary Society
        Is appointed to India
- 1801 Moves to Serampore
- 1834 Dies

Resources to Consult on William Carey's Mission

Eustace Carey, *Memoir of William Carey, D.D.* (Hartford, CT: Canfield and Robins, 1837).

Pearce S. Carey, *William Carey* (New York: George H. Doran, 1923).

William Carey, *An Enquiry into the Obligations to Use Means for the Conversion of the Heathens* (Dallas: Criswell, 1988).

Mary Drewery, *William Carey: A Biography* (Grand Rapids: Zondervan, 1979).

Timothy George, *Faithful Witness: The Life and Mission of William Carey* (Birmingham, AL: New Hope, 1991).

John C. Marshman, *Life and Times of Carey, Marshman and Ward: Embracing the History of the Serampore Mission* (London: Longman, 1859).

George Smith, *The Life of William Carey, D.D.* (London: John Murray, 1885).

Saying that William Carey is a man for our time, the twenty-first century, requires explanation because in many ways he wasn't a man for our time. He was a man of the eighteenth century.

Consider his monumental provincialism, seen, for example, in the language he used to describe non-Christians and those who disagreed with him. In his principal work, *An Enquiry into the Obligations to Use Means for the Conversion of the Heathen*, we find the following vocabulary: "uncivilized barbarians," "South Sea savages," "grossest ignorance," "daring infidelity," "heathenism," "idolatry," "darkness," "pagans," "popish missionaries," "uncultivated tribes," "barbarous clans," "heathens or Jews," "hypocrites," "imposters," "naked pagans," "cannibals," "popish cruelty," "Episcopal tyranny," "gross superstition"—all of these and more in a short work of sixty-five pages.

One can make the case that this kind of language revealed a deep-seated hostility toward other cultures and people of those cultures that contributed in no small measure to the political and cultural excesses that often accompanied missions, seen in colonialism and cultural imperialism. Carey definitely exemplified what twenty-first-century missiologists call the Christianity-plus-Western-civilization syndrome. Christian mission workers were bringing not just the gospel but a superior civilization as well.

Carey's disdain was not reserved only for non-Christians but also extended to Christians who did not measure up. Roman Catholics did mission with "popish cruelty." Episcopalians displayed "Episcopal tyranny" to any who opposed them. And Jews were "enemies of the church." Carey dismisses most of the first fifteen hundred years of Christian mission with this remark: "Blind zeal, gross superstition, and infamous cruelties, so marked the appearances of religion all this time, that the professors of Christianity needed conversion as much as the heathen world" (W. Carey 1988, 22).

Yet he was a man for our time because our time struggles with a version of the very issue with which Carey saw his ecclesial community struggle: whether it is appropriate to do mission, that is, to attempt to create the conditions under which the Holy Spirit can work in non-Christians' lives so that they come to know Jesus Christ as Lord and Savior.

In Carey's day, as we shall see, this theological reservation toward mission resulted from a certain kind of Calvinism. In our day this antimissionary position has been generated as much by cultural factors as theological ones. Perhaps it can best be illustrated by a popular television series, *Star Trek*, whose intrepid space explorers would only engage other cultures when they had been invited by the aliens (yes, we have our own version of Carey's language) to come and help them with some problem. Otherwise, they stayed away. Compare that with the scriptural missionary charge that Carey made central to the modern Protestant mission effort, the Great Commission, from Matthew 28:19: "Therefore go and make disciples of all nations, baptizing them in the name of the Father and of the Son and of the Holy Spirit, and teaching them to obey everything I have commanded you."

It is the conviction embedded in this charge that makes William Carey a man for our time. He insisted that mission was theologically central to being a Christian. More specifically, he insisted that God expected human beings to help in the mission effort, to "use means" for doing the work of God's mission. He undertook developing the theological goals that would be consistent with the strategic means of doing mission.

Carey had yet more to offer. He provided important guidance to those who agreed with him that God expects human beings to help in the mission effort but may have gone a bit overboard in what "means" one might use. All means? All means regardless of their ethical integrity? All means that work? Perhaps Carey's greatest contribution to Christian missions in the twenty-first century is his answer to that question: "all means that are consistent with the gospel message." Every "lawful method" was to be used.

WHO WAS WILLIAM CAREY?

William Carey was born in the village of Paulerspury in Northamptonshire, England, in 1761. His father was a weaver of cloth. In that day that meant he had a small loom in his home, where he did his work. It would have been normal for Carey to follow in his father's footsteps, but with the Industrial Revolution on the horizon, most of the small home weaving operations were being replaced by factories, and Carey began to look elsewhere for a career. He had a strong interest in gardening, which presumably could have led to some kind of pastoral, nursery, or agricultural work, but severe allergies made such work impossible for him. Carey needed to pursue indoor work.

He chose shoemaking. Carey took an apprenticeship as a shoemaker and began learning a trade that provided an income to help his family. His apprenticeship also fired his interest in religion. His master, Clarke Nichols, was a churchman; another apprentice in the household, John Warr, was a Dissenter. Many a shoemaking session was likely filled with discussion of the religious issues of the day. Even during his teenage years, Carey showed a strong interest in the Bible and biblical literature. He spent hours studying the Bible and was devoted to his local church. He had a facility for languages, teaching himself both Latin and Greek.

In 1781 Carey married Dolly Plackett, and they had six children, four boys and two girls, both of whom died in infancy. The realities of life struck Carey after he married; now he had a family to support. And when his sister-in-law's husband died, Carey found himself with two families dependent on him.

To make ends meet, he took a job as a bivocational pastor of a small Particular Baptist church. Particular Baptists, in contrast to the more common Arminian approach of other Baptists, held to a Calvinist theology. A larger Particular Baptist church in Leicester soon called Carey. Despite the additional source of income, he still could not pay his bills and was forced to add a third job as a teacher in a small grammar school. Pastor-shoemaker-teacher—but none of these careers, or all three together, could deflect Carey from his true life's calling. His biblical study and pastoring soon convinced him that the church was derelict with regard to mission. The lost were dying all over the world, and the church was doing nothing about it. And whatever the church was doing, its methods were not fulfilling the goal of the Great Commission.

This personal crisis of conviction seemed to come to a head in 1792, when Carey preached a sermon on a text in Isaiah 54:2–3: "Enlarge the place of your tent, stretch your tent curtains wide, do not hold back; lengthen your cords, strengthen your stakes. For you will spread out to the right and to the left; your descendants will dispossess nations and settle in their desolate cities." Such texts were made for Carey's increasingly focused missiological convictions. In the course of the sermon, which has come to be called the Deathless Sermon, he uttered a phrase for which he has become famous as he challenged his audience: "Expect great things from God; attempt great things for God!" By this time the die was cast for Carey. He was to devote the rest of his life to encouraging others to do mission and to use his own life as a model for what a life devoted to mission should be.

Carey wasn't just preaching on the obligation for all Christians to do mission. He was writing about it also, and in that same year, 1792, he published the pamphlet that made him the pivotal figure in Christian mission history. He titled the book *An Enquiry into the Obligations to Use Means for the Conversion of the Heathens*, a title whose chief advantage is its clear statement of the basic thesis of his thinking: Christians, all Christians, are obligated to preach the gospel to non-Christians and to use means consistent with that goal.

This obligation was a hard sell to the denominations of the day. The Church of England, which Carey had left to become a Particular Baptist, was not interested. And the Particular Baptists were not organized for mission activity. So Carey decided to act on his own. Together with Andrew Fuller, John Ryland, and John Sutcliff, Carey founded the Particular Baptist Society for Propagating the Gospel among the Heathen (soon shortened to the Baptist

Missionary Society) in October 1792. Their goal was to raise money and send missionaries to the lost. Their first act through this organization was to decide to help support a medical missionary to India, John Thomas, who was home on furlough. When they learned he wanted a co-missionary, Carey himself volunteered and was appointed to the position.

Carey sailed for India in April 1793 and arrived in Calcutta in November. One of Carey's mission principles was that mission workers should, as much as possible, be self-supporting. To that end, he found a job managing an indigo plant. During the six years that Carey managed the plant, he translated the New Testament into Bengali. His facility with languages served a second of his principles well, that one of the first tasks of a missionary is to provide the Scriptures in the indigenous language.

During this first Indian period, a son, Peter, was born to the Careys and died of dysentery. The experience probably contributed to his wife's nervous breakdown. Dolly Carey had been a reluctant participant in the mission venture, and she found life in India hard. She never recovered her health and died in 1807 at the age of fifty-two. Carey, who was only fifty-three at the time of her death, married twice more, in 1808 and 1823.

The Baptist Missionary Society decided to send more missionaries to India. The missionaries all moved to Serampore in 1800, bought a large house, and lived in common. They established a school (led by Joshua Marshman) and a printing house (led by William Ward). During their thirty-four years there, an estimated six hundred Indians came to know Christ. Carey continued his translation work and became known as a scholar. He was offered the position of professor of Bengali at a newly founded college intended to educate civil servants, Fort William College. In Carey's lifetime, the mission printed and distributed the Bible in whole or part in forty-four languages and dialects, with most of the production work done by Carey. He also began translating Hindu Sanskrit works into English.

In 1818 the missionaries founded Serampore College to train indigenous ministers for the church, another of Carey's mission principles. As part of their mission, they addressed certain social issues, such as the injustices of caste distinctions, infanticide, and widow burning, achieving an impressive number of laws banning the excesses. Carey died in Serampore on June 9, 1834, at the age of seventy-three.

THE *ENQUIRY*

The Serampore Mission is one of the great success stories of Protestant mission history. All three of the principal workers—Carey, Ward, and Marshman—deserve biographies of their own. But Carey stood out, not only because of his role as the driving force in the founding of the Baptist Missionary Society but also because of his literary output. And perhaps the most important product of his pen was his original manifesto, *An Enquiry into the Obligations of Christians to Use Means for the Conversion of the Heathens*. Because it is so important, it is worth examining in greater detail.

The *Enquiry* has six parts. The first is a short introduction, which presents his thesis that we should "use every lawful method to spread the knowledge of his name" to all non-Christians. In general terms we need to do this because of our sin, but we don't do it precisely because of our sin. Yet it is God's intention that we do it in order to overcome our sin.

In the second part, Carey discusses whether the Great Commission, Matthew 28:19, is still binding on us. That is, are we still enjoined to go and preach the gospel as Jesus and his immediate apostles did? It *is* a biblical obligation, Carey says, but he acknowledges that biblical injunctions are sometimes repealed (e.g., Jewish law), repudiated (e.g., Paul told not to go to Bythinia), made moot by circumstances (e.g., places where everyone has become a Christian), or for some reason become impossible. Sometimes the time is not right; God's timing for a place has not yet come. Yet Carey argues that none of these factors apply to the obligation to use means to preach the gospel.

In the third part, Carey uses the history of Christian mission to clinch his point: that we still have an obligation to use means to convert. He divides Christian history into eight periods—pre-Christian, Pentecost, Stephen/Philip/Peter, Paul, early Church, Roman Empire, Christendom, and the present—and shows the mission activity in each era. He questions the thoroughness of mission in all the other eras save the present, his own, which he calls the "seeds of the church." His point is that the church has always acknowledged the obligation to preach, even though it has not always done so as faithfully as possible.

In the fourth part, he provides the reader with a survey of the world and its mission needs. He divides the world into four geographical areas: Europe, Asia, Africa, America. Similarly, he parses the world into four religious groups: Jews, Christians, Muslims (Mahometans), and pagans. He subdivides the geographical areas into regions and countries and gives the number of adherents to each of the four religious groups in each region or country. Carey also sometimes divides Christianity into smaller segments and provides statistics for those subdivisions (see sidebar 10.1).

In the fifth part, Carey returns to the question of using lawful means. If the Bible says we should do it and if the history of Christian mission shows a trajectory that indicates a positive course for Christian mission, then why don't people do mission? Carey lists five practical reasons that keep people from mission. The first is simply the distance it takes to travel to some of the remote places. The second is the difficulty of living in some places, which have what he calls barbarous lifestyles. Third is the danger that accompanies being a foreigner in many places. Fourth is the difficulty of obtaining the necessities of life, of getting travel money to reach the remotest areas, and then of

---

SIDEBAR 10.1
CAREY'S STATISTICS VERSUS CURRENT STATISTICS

Barrett and Johnson (2001, 4)

RELIGIONS	ADHERENTS IN CAREY'S DAY	ADHERENTS TODAY (2000)
Jews	7 million (1%)	13 million (.002%)
Christians	174 million (24%)	2 billion (33%)
Muslims	130 million (18%)	1.2 billion (20%)
Pagans*	420 million (57%)	2.8 billion (46%)
Totals	731 million	6 billion

*Includes Hindus, Buddhists, Confucians, adherents of indigenous and other religions, secularists

---

having enough income to live there. And fifth is the necessity and difficulty of learning a new language. For some people, like Carey himself, learning another language is second nature. For others, however, it is very difficult, a lifetime task of learning to communicate in indigenous tongues. Although Carey acknowledges the reality of each of these impediments, he insists that none of them is so difficult that it cannot be overcome. We must systematically overcome these obstacles.

The sixth and final section is a kind of summary and a call to arms. Carey says that we should all, every one of us, become pray-ers for the mission of God in the world:

> One of the first and most important of those duties which are incumbent upon us is fervent and united prayer. However the influence of the Holy Spirit may be set to nought and run down by many, it will be found upon trial that all means which we can use will be ineffectual without it. (W. Carey 1988, 59)

But we cannot stop with prayer. We must act on God's behalf. Carey uses the illustration of a retail or wholesale business. Such businesses do not form themselves into companies and then do nothing. They go out and try to earn a profit. Similarly, the nature of a Christian church is to do God's business, which is to spread the gospel. Gospel "profit" is people coming to know Christ. Thus, we should form societies for this purpose. Carey says: "Suppose a company of serious Christians, ministers and private persons, were to form themselves into a society, and make a number of rules respecting the regulation of the plan, and the persons who are to be employed as missionaries, the means of defraying the expense, etc." (W. Carey 1988, 62).

SIDEBAR 10.2

CAREY'S FIVE REASONS WHY PEOPLE DON'T DO MISSION

W. Carey (1988, 52–58)

1. *Distance*: Mission fields are too distant and too hard to reach.
2. *Difficult lifestyles*: Living conditions are primitive at best on most mission fields.
3. *Danger*: One can get sick or die doing foreign missions.
4. *Resources*: It is difficult to secure travel money and monthly support money for an ongoing mission.
5. *Language*: Learning a foreign language well enough to preach and teach is very hard.

Because of the divided nature of the church, Carey recommends that these societies be formed by each denomination. He proposes that he begin one for the Particular Baptist denomination: "There is room enough for all [these societies] without interfering with each other; and if no unfriendly interference took place, each denomination would bear good will to the other, and wish and pray for its success" (W. Carey 1988, 64). Finally, the local churches should financially support these societies.

Such is Carey's *Enquiry*. It is a short work, about fourteen thousand words, not counting the twenty-four pages of charts. In its most recent published form, it consists of only sixty-five pages. Its tone is primarily that of a manifesto, a call to action for the Christian church to get involved in mission work through prayer, the sending of missionaries, and financial support. Three features of the *Enquiry* are worth exploring.

First is the nature of its argument. Carey surely intended it to be a theological argument. It is and it isn't. He chooses not to take on the Dordtian Calvinists directly, at least those who argue that because of God's sovereignty, if God wants people saved, God will do it; God has already determined who will be saved. Rather than explicitly address this issue or make a counterargument to predestination, Carey presents a very positive theological argument by referencing the biblical calls to mission, particularly Matthew 28:19. And in a sense he employs historical theology by using the church's commitment to mission throughout history as an indicator that we must continue this commitment.

Second, Carey's main metaphor for mission is warfare. We have already seen the language he uses both for those who oppose Christian mission and for those who are the subjects of Christian mission. They are enemies and combatants. Every chapter of the *Enquiry* contains warfare language. God's intention is to "prevail finally over the power of the Devil and to destroy all his works" (W. Carey 1988, 2). "Uncivilized barbarians yielded to the cross" (2). The evil "witnesses must be slain" (7). "Before the coming of our Lord Jesus Christ, the whole world were either heathens, or Jews; and both, as to

157

the body of them, were enemies to the gospel" (9). Paul and Barnabas made the "first attack on the heathen world" (13). In the history of mission, the church has "conquered pagan nations by force of arms and then oblige[d] them to submit to Christianity" (21).

Third, although Carey explicitly states that all lawful means are to be used to promote the gospel, his understanding of what is lawful is only implied. It may be that Carey thought that deciding on strategies of mission would be lawful simply because good Particular Baptists were making the decision. Unfortunately, history has not supported his confidence that lawful means would always be chosen. Various segments of the church, for instance, have chosen at times to coerce, buy, or manipulate conversions. In light of some of the excesses of mission employed by the movement Carey began, it is worth teasing out of the *Enquiry* a more specific understanding of what Carey considered lawful means.

It is clear that in his own deliberations on what is lawful, Carey uses three authorities: the Bible, the history of the church, and the leading of the Holy Spirit. He ignores the religious authorities and pundits of his day and makes his case straight from Scripture and his own experience of God's calling.

God's role in choosing lawful means is also clear: God puts only certain means within our power. It is almost as if Carey believes that if God wants us to do something, it will be obvious to us because God makes it possible. God calls us to mission, but God calls different people to different missions. Clearly, Carey has a great belief in the power of the Holy Spirit to empower us, once we discern the call of God. He almost seems to consider the question of which means are lawful an easy one. It is deciding to use means that he considers the watershed decision.

Judging from the history of Protestant missions after Carey, we might question whether lawful means are that obvious to those of us who are called. Perhaps Carey should have made more explicit his reliance on the direction of the Holy Spirit of God.

THE STATE OF MISSION: THEN AND NOW

There are many reasons why William Carey is a paradigmatic missioner for our day. First, he did not just talk about mission; he took action consistent with his understanding of God's call and goals. He believed in the mission of the church. Second, he acted on his beliefs in the most practical ways. This practice is so important because it is precisely the one under attack today. The attack, however, is the same as in Carey's time. It is an attack that advocates the do-no-mission approach to Christian service. It is not just the Hippocratic do-no-harm approach to mission, a kind of selective action that we are sure does good rather than harm to non-Christians; such caution would probably be good. What we are fighting against now, and probably in the future, is the total elimination of Christian mission from the church's portfolio. Carey fought this impulse, and perhaps it is true that the church has fought it in every age.

THE EFFECTS

So what were the lasting effects of William Carey's approach to Christian mission? Of *An Enquiry into the Obligations to Use Means for the Conversion of the Heathens*? Of Carey's mission work in India? Of the influence that developed, for whatever reasons, around his story? Let's consider five areas.

Legacy

A common appellation for William Carey is "Father of the Protestant Mission Movement." There are some compelling reasons to question the truth of that ascription. He probably can't be considered the first Protestant missionary, even the first Protestant missionary to India. Bartholomaeus Ziegenbalg surely preceded him with a Denmark-sponsored mission in South India. And the contributions of many Protestant mission workers over the years outshine what Carey did in terms of the effective spreading of the gospel—the "children" have put the "father" in a bad light.

But Carey is a "father" because he confronted the apostolic inaction of the church of his day and changed things. Amissional churches became missional churches. He showed the way. And he modeled how to do mission.

Use Means

He put to rest the "do-nothing" approach to mission of his day. Whether inaction stemmed from theological conviction, or laziness, or provincialism, or greed—Carey showed that all arguments against mission were fallacious. In each instance he convincingly made the case that every lawful method should be put to use to tell people the story of Jesus.

Mission Societies

As we have seen, because of the foot dragging of the official church institutions and denominations of his day, Carey organized like-minded missiophiles to support foreign mission initiatives. These groups were the precursors of the modern, independent mission societies, without which the Protestant mission effort would be only a shadow of what it is.

Statistics

A case can be made that Carey's work was a shot in the arm for a burgeoning field that has been called missiometrics (Barrett 2000). The use of statistics in mission work to define successes, failures, and challenges to be met—Carey

159

SIDEBAR 10.3
ANTIMISSIONARY: TOMÁS DE TORQUEMADA, GRAND INQUISITOR

Practice: Consistency—Striving for consistency between methods and goals

It may seem unusual to place the Inquisition in the context of the church's mission work, but the logic of the Inquisition—that unbelievers can be brought to faith through physical torture—is the worst manifestation of the idea that human efforts by human beings can bring about conversion in another human being.

Tomás de Torquemada was appointed to the task of defending the faith through whatever means necessary by Pope Sixtus IV on February 11, 1482. Because of his enthusiasm for his job, Torquemada became the face of the Spanish Holy Office of the Inquisition.

Torquemada was the son of a Spanish theologian, Juan de Torquemada, who was also the archbishop of Valladolid. Tomás de Torquemada was known for two things: his personal austerity—he never ate meat, wore only linen clothing, and refused all honors—and his extraordinary cruelty as an Inquisitor. A Dominican friar, Torquemada was known by his admirers as "the hammer of the heretics, the light of Spain, the savior of his country, and the honor of his order." History has judged him differently.

The gospel story that all of us as Christians know and are meant to convey acknowledges in some form or another the fact that God is in control, that we are all sinners incapable not only of bringing about the salvation of others but of even bringing about our own salvation. Only God can do that.

Any means that we use in mission that does not acknowledge that it is God who saves is a method inconsistent with Scripture. Of course, it is easy to identify this inconsistency in the case of something as radical as the Inquisition and its use of torture. It is more difficult to identify the same inconsistency in the case of more subtle means that might appear at first glance to be simply overly enthusiastic but when examined more closely reveal themselves to usurp God's power and prerogatives as surely as the Inquisitors' methods did.

REFLECTION AND DISCUSSION

1. How should we respond to the fact that the Inquisition is part of our Christian history?
2. Where do you draw the line between pushing people to accept Christ against their will and persuading them to overcome their hesitation to embrace the gospel?
3. Write a short prayer that acknowledges God's power to save and your own longing for everyone to embrace the gift of Christ's salvation.

knew this was a fruitful way to proceed and devoted a large section of the *Enquiry* to outlining the challenge. Of course, his statistics, from an era without telecommunications and global networks, were seriously flawed, but they revealed the future. Carey based his mission actions and his mission strategies on them, and in so doing anticipated the high-tech missions of today.

Redefinition of Success

Inadvertently, Carey redefined the standards for success and failure of modern missions work. Based on the number of converts, his mission in India was a failure. If mission success means that one's work leads to the conversion to Christianity not just of a few isolated individuals and villages but of a majority of a culture, then Carey failed. At most, India today has a Christian population of 2 to 3 percent. And the future does not look much rosier. Yet still in the minds of missiologists and mission workers today, Carey succeeded. He sounded an important alarm, reminding the church that God's goal was for the church to do mission. He motivated an important segment of the Christian church to do mission work and see that work as its obligation. He declared that many lawful means, consistent with missionary goals, could be used. And he devoted his own life to the cause in India, modeling the best in self-giving in the service of the gospel.

11

Variety

Communicating the Gospel in Many Forms

Mission Exemplar: Catherine Booth
Location: Europe, England
Audience: Nominal Christians
Time: Nineteenth century

Timeline
- 1829 Born in England
- 1835–43 Is homeschooled
- 1844 Joins Methodist Church
- 1855 Marries William Booth
- 1859 Writes *Female Ministry*
- 1878 Begins the Salvation Army
- 1880–84 Open-air preaching campaigns
- 1890 Dies of cancer

Resources to Consult on Catherine Booth's Mission

Catherine Booth, *Aggressive Christianity* (Wheaton: Worldwide, 1993).

Mildred Duff, *Catherine Booth: A Sketch* (Whitefish, MT: Kessinger, 2004).

Andrew Mark Eason, *Women in God's Army: Gender and Equality in the Early Salvation Army* (Ontario: Wilfrid Laurier University Press, 2003).

Roy Hattersley, *Blood and Fire: The Story of William and Catherine Booth and the Salvation Army* (New York: Doubleday, 2000).

Norman H. Murdoch, "The 'Army Mother,'" *Cross Point* 8 (Fall 1995): 36–39.
Diane Winston, *Red Hot and Righteous: The Urban Religion of the Salvation Army* (Cambridge, MA: Harvard University Press, 1999).

When people seem impervious to the good news of the gospel, when they are in great need, and when the means of alleviating their distress seem out of their reach, innovative methods of preaching the gospel can be created. The life and ministry of Catherine and William Booth exemplify the possibilities inherent in the practice of preaching the gospel in many forms, verbal and nonverbal.

THE SETTING

The Salvation Army began in London in 1878. It was an outgrowth of the Christian Mission and established itself in the heart of the slums of London's East End. Within eight years, the Salvation Army had 2,271 officers and 1,039 corps in the cities of the United Kingdom and 1,921 officers and 747 corps overseas (Eason 2003, 47). The success of this outreach program was due in large measure to the practice of preaching the gospel in many forms.

Catherine Booth lived in a time of ferment and change in England during the nineteenth century. The Industrial Revolution had changed the face of the cities, bringing thousands of people into them to find work. The exploitation of this abundant labor source in the factories of London's East End created severe hardship and resulted in vast slums. The change was swift. In 1810 only 4 percent of England's population lived in cities. By 1840 it had risen to nearly 50 percent.

As a young woman, Catherine was swept up in the urgencies of the evangelistic movement of the day. An active member of the Wesleyan Methodist Church, she was expelled in 1850 for refusing to condemn Methodist Reformers (Murdoch 1995, 36). When Catherine met William Booth, a new preacher for the Wesleyan Methodist Reformers, she was impressed by the young man's preaching abilities and his message of abstinence from alcohol (Eason 2003, 36; Murdoch 1995, 36). They began a friendship, one that was to shape Catherine's life in dramatic ways. Catherine and William married in June 1855.

In William, Catherine found a partner who seemed favorably disposed to female ministry and gender equality (Eason 2003, 36). She herself argued that a proper reading of Scripture showed that anyone called by God could work in public ministry and that sexual equality was a God-given right (39). She and William also shared a concern for the salvation of the many poverty-stricken people in London's East End. They joined forces around those two central issues. A talented preacher, Catherine had the ability to stir the hearts of many who would never enter a church. She gave her first "word" in 1860 in a revival meeting after William had finished preaching. He immediately announced that she would preach the next evening (110).

That action alone attracted attention from both the middle-class church and the working poor. John Wesley had supported certain women preachers in the late 1700s, and Primitive Methodism was also influenced by women leaders in the early 1800s. Although a few women preachers were still effectively operating in the Primitive Methodists, the practice had waned by the 1850s (Eason 2003, 15). Catherine's "word" to the large gathering and William Booth's announcement broke through the polite structures of middle-class Victorian society, a society that isolated women in a male-dominated world, keeping women and men in separate spheres (15). Catherine invaded the public world of men, and her husband supported her.

An Innovative Ministry

Catherine and William's concern for the poor took them in new directions. They saw the destitution and dissolution of the inner-city poor. Crime and alcoholism compounded the misery of deplorable living conditions, overwork, and hunger. In Catherine's perception, these people were unable to find God on their own. They were in need of rescue and salvation, but because their hearts were hardened, they could not hear the message of the good news of the gospel (Booth 1993, 27). This view was reinforced by the behavior of many members of the working class. Their own actions—violence, substance abuse—perpetuated their poverty, and their effects on individuals and families were all too evident in London's East End.

Seeing the poor as needing God but resistant to hearing God's word was one side of the problem. The other was the church's lack of response to the plight of those adversely affected by the Industrial Revolution. When William Booth applied to the church to do traveling evangelism, church leaders refused to support his call. Catherine and William consequently left the Methodist New Connection in 1861 (Eason 2003, 39; Murdoch 1995, 37). Catherine saw the church as unresponsive to the plight of the poor, self-serving, and stagnant. Seeing the rejection of William's call by church leaders reinforced this view in her mind. Here was the dilemma: "The poor would not go to the churches, and the churches did not want the poor" (Eason 2003, 43).

As Catherine and William experienced this dilemma, the gospel story took on a whole new dimension. The good news of the gospel needed to be good news for destitute people. It needed to speak to those living in the dissolute state of advanced alcoholism. It needed to transform unemployment, poor living conditions, and the resulting depression into hopeful productive action. For the Booths "saving souls" did not lose its importance for the hereafter, but it did become a path to a better life in the here and now.

"Catherine demonstrated that disciples of Jesus Christ could meet the physical needs of people while simultaneously ministering to their lost and broken souls" (Booth 1993, 10). She argued that "for the sake of the children and for generations yet unborn" standards of Christianity must be kept high. "Show the world a real, living, self-sacrificing, hardworking, toiling, triumphing religion, and the world will be influenced by it" (21). Catherine herself set this example in her work of combating the exploitation of women and children. Revival meetings were held, but job training, relocation programs, and antialcoholism campaigns also became part of the way Catherine and William Booth communicated the gospel.

CATHERINE BOOTH'S THEOLOGY

Catherine's theology was built on concepts of holiness and sacrifice. Faithful Christians were to be "devoted to the Lord, and separated from the world, living so that their lives were a reproof to all ungodliness" (Booth 1993, 29). This lifestyle would evoke persecution from others. Self-sacrifice would be required. Catherine based her preaching on the denial of self, recognizing that God could work through human weakness.

The sacrifices expected of Christians were rooted in a connection between knowledge and responsibility. Catherine believed that Christians were responsible for the salvation of souls. If people were preoccupied or seemed uninterested, the Booths felt it was their responsibility "to go and force it upon their attention" (Booth 1993, 27). The Christian's approach should be firm and loving. "Let them realize that you feel their danger, and are in distress for them. God will give His Holy Spirit, and they *will be saved*" (28).

THE METHODS USED

The Booths, along with many Christians of their time, understood the methods of evangelism to be relative, not something that was God-ordained. During the 1840s, long before they met, each had embraced Charles Finney's theology of conversion. This "American method" of evangelism used scientific means to achieve soul-saving ends. Like Finney and others before them, Catherine and William devised novel ways of reaching the masses that were unlike any methods that had been used before.

Pragmatism and effectiveness were the gauges of success. "Compel them to come in." Catherine preached, an approach she justified by a belief that the poor could not see clearly themselves. "Confront them at every turn" was her motto.

The Booths began doing this "aggressive evangelism" in many ways. Catherine and William Booth traveled to speak at many revival meetings, at first together and then later in the 1860s, due to a great demand for their preach-

---

SIDEBAR 11.1
THE VARIETY OF THE BOOTHS' MINISTRY

Because of the urgency of spreading the gospel to everyone, Catherine and William Booth aggressively sought innovative ways to do so. These innovations included the following:

- Renting a dance hall for revival meetings
- Training new converts—poor working-class men and women—not to be too intimidated to attend church
- Training new converts to do street preaching
- Preaching to wealthy West End residents and getting them involved in supporting and volunteering at East End missions

- Utilizing the talents of women called to preaching ministry
- Using militaristic symbols and forms, which were culturally attractive to working-class people
- Taking different speaking routes (Catherine and William) to reach more people

---

REFLECTION AND DISCUSSION

These are all verbally centered forms of outreach or forms of facilitating verbal presentation of the gospel. What nonverbal forms did Catherine use?

---

ing, separately. A complementarity developed between their venues as William preached to the poor in rented dance halls in the East End and Catherine preached to the wealthy in the West End.

Many of those she reached became benefactors of the Booths' mission work in the slums. Their holistic ministry provided an outlet to many middle-class Christian women who had time and money to do philanthropy. Others participated in the Sunday-school ministry established in poor neighborhoods. Wealthy converts who were convicted by Catherine's preaching on deep commitment and self-sacrifice gave generously to their work.

Pragmatic reasons lay behind William Booth's support of women's preaching and leadership ministries. While working with the Primitive Methodists as a traveling evangelist, he had heard Miss Buck, one of a few women evangelists of that group and a seasoned traveling preacher. William was impressed by her ability and success. Catherine, although she had not preached before, had spoken to William of her own views on the subject. She was convinced that equality between the sexes was biblical and that women were endowed with all the spiritual gifts. Catherine's preaching also became the main source of income for their growing family. In effect, both his marriage and his ministry benefited from William's departure from tradition in the area of women's leadership.

But the radical Christian work in the East End slums was not welcomed by everyone. Violence was not uncommon during preaching services in the early days. Some church people attacked the methods of the Booths, claiming that they were undignified and rude. The loud marching bands, the street preaching, and the training of poor people for ministry offended their sensibilities. They worried about getting into trouble with the authorities. Catherine responded by arguing that the "dignity of the Gospel" was not human dignity but divine dignity—ultimately the dignity of love (Booth 1993, 30). Although some Episcopal Church leaders wanted to sponsor the Salvation Army, the "undignified" activities of women preachers and outspoken women leaders caused opposition that thwarted the proposal.

Going where the people are became a central method for the Christian Mission and a few other evangelical missions established in the East End during the middle decades of the nineteenth century. Since the poor would not darken the door of a church, Christians must go to the poor. They did this not only with preaching services but also with "free and easy" evenings at a music hall. This kind of pub-theater evangelism was an adaptation of a popular secular mode of entertainment. The Christian Mission acquired an old market in the East End that became its headquarters. Eventually, this became the church for the converts. The poor themselves worked and worshiped together in their own setting. Goods and services were brought in from philanthropic sources in the middle class. Sunday-school ministries were set up. The gospel took root in the East End and flourished there.

In 1878 the Christian Mission restructured and changed its name to the Salvation Army. It adopted a military motif in organization and dress. Military symbols were popular, especially among working-class men who wanted to celebrate the physical side of life. Salvation Army workers formed corps, wore striking military uniforms, and developed bands that would play on street corners to draw a crowd for a preaching service. Women preachers and the "Hallelujah Lasses" attracted crowds, both because of their novelty and because they conveyed a sympathetic attitude that led to philanthropy and training classes for women and children.

THE METHODS ANALYZED

Tracing the process of developing the ministry of the Salvation Army reveals crossroads and choices that led to the success of its mission. The method usually involved taking three steps.

Getting People's Attention

Before a mission work can grow, it must get the attention of the target group. In this case, there were two target groups: the poor and the rich. William got the attention of the poor by doing revivals in the slums, presenting the gospel in creative ways that appealed to the laboring classes of the East End, attracting crowds with women preachers and bands, and setting up the Christian Mission in the heart of the East End. Catherine got the attention of

167

the rich by preaching in their churches about the responsibility of people with knowledge and means to take the gospel to those without either.

In both instances, a kind of creative dissonance was formed. Those dissonances created a stir. Revival meetings in the East End were covered in the press. Women's preaching was hotly debated among the middle class. Catherine and William Booth got the attention of both of their target audiences.

Filling a Need

The focus on meeting the needs of the poor occupied a central place in the process of developing the Salvation Army ministries. The numbers of

---

SIDEBAR 11.2
THE AMAZING SUCCESS OF THE ARMY

Why did the ministry of Catherine and William Booth succeed and expand so quickly? Examining their work reveals several possible reasons for their success.

Compatibility: Rather than seeking to bring people from the slums into "respectable" churches, Catherine was determined to take the gospel to them. To do so, the Booths sought venues compatible with the lifestyle of the people. Renting a dance hall for revival services brought people into a familiar environment in their locality. "Free and easy" evenings were also held locally and mimicked the secular entertainment that East Enders enjoyed regularly. Compatibility was established from the beginning in the work of the Salvation Army. The Booths bought an old market, where they set up their administrative offices. They settled solidly into the cultural milieu of the people they sought to reach.

Complexity: There was no simple way to accomplish their goal. Because the Booths' financial base lay with people of means, Catherine's preaching had to appeal to the needs and sensibilities of the wealthy. A complex theology

developed that secured the support of middle-class Christians and made them feel responsible for the welfare of the poor. Further complexity developed as the Booths adopted the military symbolism popular at the time. This led to a restructuring of their organization, along with a theological rationale for this change. A rationale for the preaching and leadership of women also needed to be established. A theology that included caring for the physical well-being of people and empowering them to improve their economic status through training both for work in the Salvation Army and for other means of employment added another dimension to the work.

Relative advantage: Although it was not a simple process to develop the mission work in the East End, the means of doing so held an advantage over the mission efforts of other churches. First, the Booths were ministering to people who would not attend church otherwise. Regular churches could not reach East Enders with regular ministries. Charitable work could be done in the slums, but that did not change the hearts of the poor. The energy and sympathy that Catherine and William

---

people living in substandard conditions in London grew exponentially during the mid-1800s. Christians in the rising middle class noticed and cared about those living in poverty. The question was how to reach those people while upholding the politeness and refinement that were characteristic of the Victorian era's middle class.

Catherine's aggressive evangelism campaign sensitized wealthy Christians and provided outlets for charitable giving and Sunday-school ministry. Good moral values were upheld even during "free and easy" evenings in the East End. Preaching and nonalcoholic beverages replaced vulgar jokes and drinking. Catherine led people in protesting the oppression of women and

put into their ministry to the poor made their preaching and mission work not only more accessible to this group but also more attractive. The motives of good will and the longing for salvation for the people showed in their mission efforts.

Trialability: The strong calling to work with the poor that Catherine and William felt did not ensure success. They took risks and made progress through trial and error. Workers of the Christian Mission were physically attacked on occasion in the early days. Catherine had to try new ways to reach the rich with the message of support for the inner-city ministry. The Booths tried new approaches. They refined those approaches, continuing the successful aspects of the ministry and discarding others. They found that women's preaching and leadership were effective. Attracting people with music and entertainment also worked if it imitated the local cultural style. The "undignified" behavior of Salvationists was tried and found to be effective. Catherine cared little for the approval of others if the ministry brought people to Christ and alleviated physical suffering. Trial and error, revisioning and restructuring were a part of the process in the development of the Salvation Army. Because methods were considered relative, new actions

could be tried and kept or discarded based on their practicality.

Observability: Charting the success of the Christian Mission and the Salvation Army was not difficult. Numbers of converts and new workers grew quickly. Results could be seen: the naked were clothed; the poor heard good news; the acceptable day of the Lord was proclaimed. Because success was visible, it increased even more quickly. Catherine insisted that visible results were crucial to any Holy Spirit–driven effort. In her opinion, if the church was successful in carrying out the mandate of the gospel, the world would be much changed (Booth 1993, 28). In the days of the apostle Paul, preaching the gospel caused an uproar. Turmoil ensued. The same should be true of successful Christian work in the present, according to Catherine. If one could not see changes in the world, if one did not experience the persecution that comes with preaching the gospel, not much was accomplished.

Those reasons for the success of the Booth's ministry in no way diminish the work of God in their lives and labor. But we can see that compatibility, complexity, relative advantage, trialability, and observability were all factors that contributed to the success of their ministry.

children. She agitated for improved living conditions and worked to rehabilitate alcoholics.

The process emphasized the transformational changes that the good news of the gospel could work in people's lives. People found meaning in the gospel. That meaning gave them hope that their lives could change.

CASE STUDY:
MANITOWISH COMMUNITY CHURCH

A successful holistic ministry that uses a variety of context-appropriate methods and theologies can be seen in a ministry of a growing church in northern Wisconsin. Manitowish Community Church is a Presbyterian congregation situated in a small rural community that depends for its livelihood on summer and winter tourist trades. Fishing and water sports in the summer and snowmobiling in the winter are the main industries. Retired people and families who run businesses make up the permanent residents of this small community.

The cultural milieu is conservative, patriotic, and hardworking. Core values of community, love of nature, and independence thrive. Honesty, hard work, and loyalty to neighbors and nation are highly valued.

The needs of this community are not evident to the tourist populations that move in and out of town. Although middle-class tourist businesses thrive, Manitowish Waters is located in an economically depressed area. Some year-round people live in poverty. Family abuses such as neglect or violence easily develop in such situations and are not uncommon.

Interests and entertainment for this local community include flea markets and craft fairs, fishing, and baseball in the summer. Eating is a popular entertainment, so community picnics thrive in the summer; fish fries, feasts, and supper clubs draw people all year.

Manitowish Community Church tuned in to the cultural style in this area, making several adjustments to its particular context. As part of a small town where a few year-round residents must carry the identity and spirit for the community, it devised ways to bring the people together. Avoiding the divisive connotations of denominational labels, this Presbyterian congregation calls its church a community church. Understanding the appreciation for nature in this rural area, it made a wide and winding blacktop path from the highway to the church parking lot. Appreciating the types of entertainment the community enjoys, it developed ministry outreaches that appeal to the interests of the north woods culture. Identifying the economic and social needs of the year-round community, it developed ministry programs that support local outreach.

Rummage sales are a popular form of summer entertainment for both tourists and year-round residents in this area. Many towns have community-wide rummage sales on a particular day. The nearby town of Mercer, Wisconsin, designates a community-wide sale day organized by the chamber of commerce. Maps are provided, and residents spend a leisurely day going from house to house, meeting neighbors and exchanging money for used goods. "One person's trash is another's treasure" is the lighthearted motif of the day.

Manitowish Community Church picked up on this idea and sponsors an annual "Flea-zaar," a daylong sale of donated used items. This major outreach program of the church fits into its cultural milieu and meets many of the local needs of both church and community.

For months before the event, community is built among the congregants because they are working together: collecting goods; organizing and pricing things; setting up silent-auction sheets for the boats, bicycles, and larger items. On the day of the sale, the women all wear colorful aprons that ask, "Have you hugged a Presbyterian today?" Men and women with an interest in sports, electronics, dishes and glassware, furniture, art, antiques, and other items become salespersons for that section of the Flea-zaar.

People in the larger community benefit from the sale by coming to the church and making purchases. Good feelings are created through ordinary conversations, bargaining, and relaxing together. The youth group sells ice cream, and the women's fellowship provides hot dogs and iced tea. People eat lunch while they wait for the silent auction to conclude at 1:00 p.m. At

about 2:00 p.m. the remaining items go on sale for one dollar a suitcase or bag. People buy the suitcase in the luggage department for a buck and fill it up. This not only helps with recycling the not-so-good items, but it also, in a quiet way, aids the poor. In this proud rural community, it becomes a way of giving that can be received with pride.

The Flea-zaar is a mission event. Proceeds from the sale are donated to church mission efforts, local ministries, and international mission efforts. Local ministries such as DOVE, a shelter for abused women, benefit. Although the proportion of money given to local ministries is the largest, international hunger relief, disaster aid, and Christian mission programs also receive funds. In 2004 the Flea-zaar raised thirty-eight thousand dollars for Christian mission.

Every year this event gets bigger. People hear about it and bring donations to the church. Local people put it on their summer entertainment calendar. Tourists stop to see why so many cars are parked along the highway. The Presbyterians in Manitowish, Wisconsin, have started a ministry that just keeps expanding.

How did they do it? Interacting with the local culture, honoring core values of the community, reducing denominational divisiveness, finding an activity that draws people together in work and fun, sponsoring causes that local people care about, and having a heart for the needs of the world are a few of the steps they took.

The Booths would have approved.

Striking a Chord with Culture

Finally, the process of developing the Salvation Army ministries struck a cultural chord that seemed irresistible. The rationalism of the eighteenth century, although still alive and well in the middle class, was yielding to the more romantic influences of the nineteenth century. Romanticism flourished, giving the age a mood of emotionalism and sympathy. Salvationists capital-

---

SIDEBAR 11.3
ANTIMISSIONARY: JOHN RYLAND

Practice: Variety—Communicating the gospel in many forms

When William Carey was a young man, hard at work at becoming the "Father of Protestant Missions," his main opponents in the task of making mission the focus of the Free Churches of England were a group of Calvinists who taught that mission was not necessary. They were Particular Baptists, men such as John Ryland, John Sutcliff, and Andrew Fuller. They were the ones whom Carey had to convince of the centrality of the mission task.

The story goes that one Sunday, Carey was invited to preach regularly in a church in the village of Barton. This was the church where Carey had been baptized on October 5, 1783. That Sunday he was leading a minister's meeting in the church and raised his standard theme: the duty of all Christians everywhere to preach the gospel in the hope that others will become saved. After Carey had made his case, John Ryland is reported to have said, "Young man, sit down; when God pleases to convert the heathen, he will do it without your aid and mine."

Men like Ryland used the following theological rationale in defense of do-nothing missions: God is all-knowing. He knows all things that have happened and all things that will happen. Thus he

knows who will be saved and who will not be saved. He knows this already, before it even happens. Therefore, what point is there in our doing mission, when the case has already been settled once and for all?

Carey's message, as we have seen, is that we should use all means at our disposal to convince the lost to accept the gift of the gospel and become Christians. Of course, one can go overboard in "using all means." It is, after all, God's mission. And nothing happens unless God wills it to happen. But Carey saw that part of God's will is that we should be ambassadors of the faith, tellers of the story. It is significant that John Ryland Jr., son of the critic John Ryland Sr., became one of Carey's strongest supporters in Particular Baptist circles.

REFLECTION AND DISCUSSION

1. Compare the approaches to mission of the Grand Inquisitor Torquemada (the antimissionary example from the last chapter) and John Ryland. Critique each theologically.

2. Chart a middle way for Christian evangelism that doesn't err on the side of either coercion or passivity.

3. List the verbal and nonverbal ways of communicating the gospel implied by the middle-way evangelism outlined in your response to question 2.

---

ized on this, emphasizing the sorrows of the deprived masses, advertising in ways that tugged at the heartstrings, using drama, creating excitement, and stressing images in their presentations.

Many middle-class people were sensitive to the plight of the poor but didn't know how to address the issue. Catherine showed them that Christians could model the best of England's values while standing against oppression and helping the poor. She touched the hearts of the middle class and encouraged them to show their sympathy to the poor. "Let them see the tears in your eyes," she admonished (Booth 1993, 28).

WHAT WE CAN LEARN

Analysis of the Salvation Army ministries offers directions for contemporary mission efforts. How can we bring the good news of the gospel to cultures today? What kind of approaches to preaching the gospel, both verbal and nonverbal, fit the pluralistic contexts of the contemporary era? Studying how the Booths accomplished their mission helps us create a checklist of questions we can use to assess a potential ministry.

Process
- What societal groups are important to reach and why?
- What is at the cutting edge of the target culture and context in terms of attitudes, interests, felt needs, values, hopes, and fears?
- What are the core values of the communities involved: national, local, church, families?

Methods
- What methods will reach people in your targeted groups? The Internet? Circus arts? Music and theater? Dialogues about other religions?
- What barriers to adopting those methods do you see in your faith community?
- How can those barriers be broken down?

Theology
- What differences in the cultural milieu lead to different theological emphases for our own time?
- What appropriate theologies of interacting with people of other faiths in your context need to be developed?
- What biblical theologies can be used to support the effective methods you have devised?
- How will interaction with people of other faiths influence your theology and the theology of your faith community?

12

Respect

Not Disparaging Others in Order to Champion Your Own;
Not Disparaging Your Own in Order to Respect Others

Mission Exemplar: William Sheppard
Location: Africa
Audience: Adherents of African traditional religions
Time: Nineteenth and twentieth centuries

Timeline
- 1865 Born March 8 in Waynesboro, Virginia
- 1886 Graduates from Tuscaloosa Theological Institute in Alabama
- 1888 Is ordained by Atlanta Presbytery as pastor of Zion Presbyterian Church
- 1890 Is commissioned as missionary to Congo
- 1891–92 Establishes the American Presbyterian Congo Mission at Luebo
- 1893 Travels to United States via London, where he is honored with membership in the Royal Geographic Society
- 1894 Marries Lucy Gantt in Jacksonville, Florida
- 1900 London *Times* publishes Sheppard's eyewitness report of King Leopold's atrocities
- 1905 Visits President Roosevelt at White House; tells of Congolese plight
- 1906 Sheppards return to Congo

174

- 1910 Requests retirement
- 1912 Takes pastorate of Grace Presbyterian Church
  in Louisville
- 1912–26 Develops youth ministry in Louisville
- 1927 Dies and is buried in Louisville

Resources to Consult on William Sheppard's Mission

Joseph Conrad, *Heart of Darkness* (New York: Harcourt, Brace and World, 1967).

Adam Hochschild, *King Leopold's Ghost: A Story of Greed, Terror, and Heroism in Colonial Africa* (New York: Houghton Mifflin, 1999).

Pagan Kennedy, *Black Livingstone: A True Tale of Adventure in the Nineteenth-Century Congo* (New York: Viking Penguin, 2002).

William E. Phipps, *The Sheppards and Lapsley: Pioneer Presbyterians in the Congo* (Louisville: Presbyterian Church [USA], 1991).

William E. Phipps, *William Sheppard: Congo's African American Livingstone* (Louisville: Geneva, 2002).

William H. Sheppard, *Pioneers in Congo* (Wilmore, KY: Wood Hill, 2006).

Dinitia Smith, "A Black Adventurer in the Heart of Darkness," *New York Times*, January 8, 2002.

I n 1893, William Sheppard, the first African American Presbyterian missionary to Africa, returned to tell the church in the United States about his mission work after three years in the Congo. His mind was full of images of life along the Kasai River, of adventures he'd had with chiefs of an indigenous people who nearly killed him on their first encounter but later became good friends. His task now was to tell the Christians who had sent him to Africa about how the work of God was progressing in the Congo under his leadership. He pondered this task as he arrived at the home of an influential Waynesboro, Virginia, woman. The invitation was unusual: a white woman inviting a black man to her home for afternoon tea. But Sheppard was a missionary of the church, and the post–Civil War times allowed for new kinds of interaction between whites and blacks in the South. Still, Sheppard probably mulled over the situation in his mind. How should he approach this social engagement, one with so few precedents?

After a moment's hesitation at the gate, Sheppard went around to the back door of the house. He knocked. A black kitchen worker opened the door. Was the lady of the house at home? William Sheppard was then ushered into the front parlor to visit with her. Later she remarked to her friends. "He was such a good darky. When he returned from Africa he remembered his place and always came to the back door" (Kennedy 2002, 152).

To our twenty-first-century sensibility, this incident seems preposterous. Here was the first African American Presbyterian missionary returning from years of service in the Congo. During that time he had risked his life for the Christian faith; he had conversed with kings and gone on hunting expeditions with the best warriors of the Kuba tribe. Now, returning to his church people in the United States, he went to the back door like a slave. What could have motivated him to act in such a way?

Sheppard lived at a unique time in American history. The subjugation of African Americans as slaves to white plantation owners came to an end in 1865, the year William Sheppard was born. The next twenty years saw transformations in African American and Caucasian relations that both dislocated African Americans and gave them opportunities unprecedented in American life. Sheppard's childhood and youth were spent during the expansive era following the war, but he lived his adult life during the backlash that followed. When northern armies left the South, Jim Crow laws separating black and white services and intense discrimination, including lynchings, took hold. Churches divided into black and white denominations, and the Presbyterian Church was no exception. The liberating window began to close.

Was Sheppard's action of going to the back door borne out of fear? Did it come from his socialization as a subservient African American in a white context? Or was it a sign of something else? Seen in the larger context of Sheppard's life and work, we propose it can be seen as an act of respect—respect for a different way of viewing human relations. No doubt Sheppard knew that the system of white supremacy was wrong. He was visiting this person to talk about his work as a missionary leader, a pioneer of Christian outreach to a remote and dangerous part of the world. Yet he acted in a way that showed respect for the person he was visiting and the social structure that she embraced, even though he thoroughly disagreed with it. That practice of respect for difference is the subject of this chapter.

THE CONTEXT

The nineteenth-century Protestant mission movement coalesced around a unique set of cultural ideas and social/economic conditions. The Great Awakening of the eighteenth and nineteenth centuries spawned by evangelists such as Charles Finney and fueled by Methodist pietism resulted in an unprecedented evangelical fervor in the late nineteenth-century United States. Denominations set up mission boards; congregations saved pennies for mission work; parents dedicated their children to God's service in mission. With increasingly efficient sea travel and communication techniques, Christians became excited about reaching the ends of the earth with the gospel. Many left home and family, following a call to mission service. About one-third of those stalwart missionaries were to die before getting a chance to return home.

A strong identification of Christianity with civilization in the intellectual climate of the day fostered cooperation among business ventures, European colonial efforts, and Christian missions. Taking the Christian message to faraway "primitive" peoples included building schools and hospitals, establishing communities and churches that fostered Western values, and supporting economic ventures that brought wealth to entrepreneurs in Europe and the United States. Evolutionary theories of the superiority of the white race and the idea of Manifest Destiny, that Western cultures were destined to civilize the world, sometimes blinded Christians to the exploitation of indigenous peoples.

This context made it difficult if not impossible for Caucasians to conceive of sending an African American to the mission field as a leader. The expansiveness of the post–Civil War era did give some churches the ability to think in terms of sending an African American to Africa. After all, many whites regarded sending African Americans back to Africa as a solution to the race problem in the United States. Freed slaves were perceived by many as a threat to social life in the South. An African American missionary might encourage other African Americans to follow. Blacks, too, heard Marcus Garvey championing a movement of African Americans to return to their place of origin.

In this context, Sheppard had applied for missionary service to Africa and although turned down, continued to wait for the blessing of his denomination, refusing other offers. Still, the leaders of the church could not envision him going to the field alone. They waited until Samuel Lapsley, a young white Presbyterian, applied for service in Africa. Sheppard and Lapsley set out together in 1890 to take over the mission station in Luebo, Congo. No doubt it was assumed that Lapsley would be the person in charge.

Lapsley had been encouraged to apply for Congo service by his father's former law partner, General Henry Shelton Sanford, who lived in Belgium and had connections with Belgium's reigning monarch, King Leopold. While preparing for the trip to Africa, Lapsley had the opportunity to visit both Sanford and King Leopold in Belgium. Leopold was busy gaining power over as much of the Congo as he could. Styling himself as a philanthropist, Leopold sent workers to the interior of Africa, workers who brought back ivory, forced Africans to work on rubber plantations and to build a railroad to the interior so that those goods could be exported. It was, in fact, King Leopold who suggested to Lapsley that he and Sheppard set up a mission station in the Kasai region, the heart of Leopold's kingdom.

General Sanford knew of Leopold's vicious tactics to exploit the Congo, but they were certainly unknown to Sheppard and Lapsley as they slowly traveled upriver, encountering the horrors of Leopold's exploitation along the way (Kennedy 2002, 30). Railroad workers were literally worked to death. To account to Leopold for the bullets they used, Belgian overseers sent the dried hands and feet of murdered Africans to the king. These could be seen

177

hanging in the sun to dry at the central station. Africans who fell sick were merely allowed to die without help or pity. Joseph Conrad took the same trip to the Congo interior only a few weeks after Sheppard and Lapsley traversed the area. His novel *Heart of Darkness* (1899) describes the trip upriver in graphic detail.

Interestingly, Sheppard's autobiographical sketch of his first years as a missionary in the Congo, *Pioneers in Congo* (2006), mentions none of those harsh realities. One can only guess at the reaction he must have felt to the atrocities he witnessed on that first trip up the Kasai River. His account, instead, emphasizes the physical challenges of the trip, his impressions of the indigenes (almost always positive), and the establishment of his mission work with Lapsley. Their goal was to establish a mission station and begin a church. Sheppard's autobiography tells of his travels to nearby regions, his encounters with various chiefs, and his impressions of local customs and cultures.

THE MAN AND HIS WORK

William Sheppard was born in 1865 in Waynesboro, Virginia, and died in 1927 at age sixty-two. His mother was a free black, so, by the old rules, he could not be sold into slavery. When William was only a month old, the Civil War ended and slavery was abolished. Even so, his mother's manumission papers were treasured by the family, kept locked in a safe, so that no one could ever mistake the fact that William and his siblings were free blacks for all time (Kennedy 2002, 8).

William's dad was a stern man, the sexton at the local Presbyterian Church, who ran a well-disciplined home. Attending Sunday school each week, William began to learn about the mission efforts of the Presbyterian Church. He was fascinated by the stories of far-off lands and was a quick learner.

When William was eleven or twelve years old, he was offered a position helping as a stable boy at the home of a dentist in Staunton, a town twelve miles from his home. William left his family to live with the Henkels. In their employment, he swept the stables, learned to read and to feel at ease with whites, and in the process learned dentistry skills.

The good relations he had with the Henkel family began a pattern of relating to whites that provided Sheppard many opportunities in the years to come. Perhaps it was a core of self-confidence and strong identity received from his parents that gave William the ability to seek out influential white leaders and relate to them in ways that showed respect both to them and to himself. At age fifteen he found his way to Hampton Institute's innovative night school run by Booker T. Washington. He graduated in the first class, dubbed "The Plucky Class" by Washington. He then traveled south to study at Tuscaloosa Theological Institute, now Stillman College. Despite the hardships presented by his poverty, he gained self-confidence, and as a top student at Tuscaloosa

Seminary, he became a favorite of Charles Stillman, the white founder of the school for black ministers. Later associations with the Presbyterian Church, with Lapsley as a fellow missionary, and with powerful world leaders both in Britain and in the United States followed the same pattern. Respect for himself and those different from him was a core value for William Sheppard.

After graduation, Sheppard was ordained by the Atlanta Presbytery and served at Zion Presbyterian Church. He soon met Lucy Gantt and began a ten-year engagement to her. Gantt was a schoolteacher, intelligent and talented in the musical arts. Sheppard's first trip to the Congo was made during their engagement, but when Sheppard returned for his second stint, he went with Lucy as a married man. Lucy worked with the music and education ministries of the new church, developing a hymnal suited to the African context that was later published.

Unlike Lapsley, who died not long after he and Sheppard arrived in Africa in 1891, Lucy spent many years in Africa with William. They had four children. The first two died in their first year of life due to harsh conditions in the Congo. Consequently, Lucy took Wilhelmina, their third child, back to the United States to be raised by her sister. Max, their fourth, was a youngster when the Sheppards retired from the field.

Sheppard and Lapsley began their work by exploring the upper and lower sections of the Kasai River, searching for a place to establish a new mission station for the Presbyterian Church. They spent the first two years exploring the area and setting up the mission station at Luebo. After Lapsley's death, Sheppard worked with two other white missionaries, S. Phillips Verner, a duplicitous man who later left the mission to work in the slave trade, and William Morrison, a strong-minded idealist who refused to keep silent about the violations of human rights occurring in Leopold's Congo (Phipps 2002, 150).

After Sheppard had worked with Morrison for a couple of years, it became clear that each was a primary leader and Luebo was too small a place for them both. Sheppard moved off to set up a new mission station about twelve hundred miles from the coast, in the dangerous Kuba area, where he had nearly been killed several years earlier.

It should not be surprising that some ethnic groups were so hostile to Westerners. The Kasai River Company workers routinely plundered villages along the river if villagers were unwilling to freely provide them with food and supplies. One group, the Zappo, worked with white slave traders, capturing Africans and taking them down the river to the port. Even captains of steamboats carrying missionaries often beat their workers if they returned empty-handed from a village. On their first journey up the river, Sheppard and Lapsley met a group of workers, weakened from overwork on the railroad, whippings, and lack of food and water, who were huddled together waiting to die.

In 1898, Sheppard recorded in his journal that he had come across a hut in which eighty-one hands were hanging to dry, being prepared for shipment

179

to Belgium. His coworker William Morrison took this journal entry and sent it off to London. Within a few months the account appeared in the *Times* of London, and the battle for the human rights of indigenous peoples in the Congo assumed international dimensions.

Sheppard had felt the terrors of the slave trade, had sympathized with villagers who had lost their land and often their lives; now he had the chance to fight for their rights in the public realm. He went on dangerous fact-finding expeditions, first for Morrison and then with the Congolese consul from Britain. He spoke against Belgian atrocities both in London and in the United States and met with President Theodore Roosevelt in 1905. Sheppard and Morrison were both sued by the Kasai River Company and faced the possibility of years of imprisonment and huge fines. Eventually both were acquitted, but changes in the plight of the indigenous peoples were slow in coming. On his return to the Congo in 1906 after a furlough, Sheppard was discouraged to see how little conditions had altered for the Kuba. But due to the international pressure created by the missionaries, eventually more just conditions were imposed on the Congo. Sheppard's courage in investigating abuses and standing up for the Congolese shows the depth of his respect for humans different from himself.

The missionary career of the Sheppards ended in 1909, when Sheppard requested retirement due to failing health and family concerns. Wilhelmina had been in the United States with Lucy's sister for some years. Their youngest child Max was with them in the Congo, and his life continued to be threatened by equatorial diseases. Although passionate about his work with the Africans, respect for himself and his family led him to give up the work. In 1912 he took a post as pastor of Grace Presbyterian Church in Louisville, Kentucky, where the Sheppards spent the last years of their ministry. They established the largest Sunday school in Jefferson County, working successfully with nearly one thousand children.

THE RESULTS OF SHEPPARD'S MISSION

Sheppard reinvented the idea of respect for himself as he traversed between those different contexts. In particular, this way of showing respect led the way to a social-justice aspect of missionary work, an anthropological appreciation for other cultures. It has been reinvented in the holistic ministries of many missionaries who care not only for the soul but also for the body. Christian love is based on respect. Sheppard's way of demonstrating that respect in his mission work paved the way for other missionaries to reduce their sense of superiority and engage those to whom they were sent as full human beings, made in the image of God.

Because of the respect he showed his white contemporaries in the United States, Sheppard went to Africa and planted churches there. This began the practice of sending African Americans as foreign missionaries.

Respect for African American missionaries grew in the white Presbyterian Church as well. Despite continued racial discrimination in Louisville, Kentucky, Second Presbyterian Church of Louisville supported Sheppard's ministries both in the Congo and later in Louisville. After his death, it held a memorial service that brought together African Americans and Caucasians to commemorate Sheppard's life and death.

SIDEBAR 12.1
CIRCLES OF RESPECT

Instructions: Draw concentric circles with arrows going from the inner circle to the next and then the next and also arrows going from the outer circle to the inner, next and next. Label each circle and indicate an incident in Sheppard's life that exemplified that type of respect.

Reason: To show the influence of self on society and society on self in developing respect for self and others.

Inner Circle

Label: Respect for self

Examples: Post–Civil War climate influenced Sheppard's sense of self-worth; many African Americans were succeeding in new areas. (Arrow from outer to inner circle)

Sheppard went to back door of lady's house. This allowed her to maintain her self-respect in changing times and a unique circumstance. His sense of self-respect allowed him the grace to do this. (Arrow from self-respect to second circle—community)

Second Circle

Label: Respect in community

Examples: Sheppard went to work for a dentist, did not do just barn chores but learned dentistry. This shows the reciprocity of respect. Henkel respected him enough to teach him. Sheppard respected Henkel in return.

In Africa, when Lapsley was away on a trip, Sheppard saved a missionary from a hippo, went hunting, and gained the respect of the whole community and Lapsley on his return. His own sense of self-respect also increased as community affirmation was forthcoming.

Third Circle

Label: Public respect

Examples: Sheppard gained the position of missionary to Africa, which showed the respect of the Presbyterian denomination. A nearly all-white church sent Sheppard as its first African American missionary. (Arrow from third to second and first circle)

Experience of freedom in London, when public respect was shown to Sheppard. He was not discriminated against in public settings. This was a huge boost to his own self-respect and self-confidence. (Arrow from third to inner circle)

181

Because of his respectful treatment of the Congolese, the church grew in Africa. Sheppard's influence spread to other areas, marking the beginning of Christian congregations among the Congolese.

Sheppard also modeled a culturally sensitive approach to local religions, thus influencing mission practices of future generations. Indigenization was not just a concept to Sheppard. His respect for indigenous practices and Lucy's use of African musical themes allowed such practices to be appropriately incorporated into the congregational life of the Kuba church. This led to an indirect influence on theology as the African church grew and incorporated many African cultural forms into its worship and community life. Lucy Sheppard's African hymnal, *Musambu wa Nzambi* (*Songs of God*), became the first printed material ever made in the Tshiluba language and marks a beginning of hymnody that includes the music, thoughts, and attitudes of the church as it grew theologically in African cultural soil.

Because of his respect for the indigenous cultures, Sheppard's collections of artifacts and his book on Congolese cultural rituals became known in the United States and are now housed at Stillman College. Other artifacts from Sheppard's African ministry are held at the Speed Museum in Louisville. Sheppard was one of the first Westerners to document in an honest and honoring way the cultural practices of another group.

His respect for the Africans also led Sheppard to protest the senseless maiming and killing practiced by the Belgian colonial government and plantation managers. And because of his respect for the white leaders in the United States and Britain, he was invited to Britain and to the White House to speak of those atrocities at an international council that had the power to end them. This early critique of colonialism influenced others to begin to see the disastrous results of oppressive forms of exploitation in Western expansion.

Those actions not only helped the indigenous peoples of the time but indirectly influenced the social system of the United States. The international attention to slavery in Africa prompted people in the United States to look at racism here. Although slavery had been abolished, discriminatory practices were rampant in the South at the beginning of the twentieth century. Christian churches that appreciated the work of William and Lucy Sheppard rose above some of those discriminatory practices and set the stage for even more attention to racism in the United States.

William Sheppard, a black American, thus became a model missionary for African Americans and for the Presbyterian denomination. He became an international figure in the struggle for justice for the Congolese. He provided a model for anthropological studies of cultures and furthered knowledge of Congolese culture for the whole world. And he exemplified the changes in racial relations that were needed in the United States.

Sheppard achieved those results based on an innovative form of respect: a respect for human beings however different they were from him, however

SIDEBAR 12.2
ANTIMISSIONARY: DAVID DE SILVA

Practice: Respect—Not disparaging others in order to champion your own; not disparaging your own in order to respect others

Respect for other people's belief systems contributes to good mission; using sarcasm, incredulity, or misrepresentation of other people's beliefs results in bad mission.

David de Silva was a Sri Lankan Christian convert whom Western missionaries recruited as a debater in a series of public debates with Buddhist *bhikkhus* in the late nineteenth century. In these debates each side would attack the beliefs of the other side and attempt to make convincing presentations of their own doctrines related to each subject.

David de Silva became known as a debater who excelled not only in presenting the Christian understanding of what it means to be created in the image of God as human beings but also in attacking the Buddhist doctrine of *anatta*, or no-self, with unparalleled energy. Presenting the Christian doctrine of *imago Dei* did not qualify Silva as an antimissionary, but the way he attacked *anatta* did.

According to reports on some of the debates, Silva had refined this attack to the point where he claimed that the Buddhist teaching reduces human beings to less than human or to animal status. Needless to say, this was a highly offensive way of talking about this Buddhist teaching to people proud of their religious heritage; it was also an inaccurate characterization of no-self.

In the very short term, these tactics may have seemed effective. The Christian missionaries won the early debates. However, the Buddhist *bhikkhus* learned their lessons well and soon were attacking Christian doctrines with an energy—and inaccuracy—that more than matched Silva's forays. So adept did they become that on August 26 and 28, 1873, in the Sri Lankan town of Panadura, the *bhikkhus* won the debate by public acclamation—a first.

Many scholars see the long-term effects of this kind of strategy as destructive to the Christian mission effort and Christian-Buddhist relationships. Elizabeth Harris in her book *Theravada Buddhism and the British Encounter: Religious, Missionary and Colonial Experience in Nineteenth Century Sri Lanka* makes a convincing case that anti-Christian mission sentiment in Sri Lanka today—feelings that have resulted in frequent attacks on missionaries and the burning of churches—are a direct result of nineteenth-century Christian antimission practice.

REFLECTION AND DISCUSSION

1. Give two reasons to explain why disparaging the Buddhist view of no-self might result in Buddhist disrespect for Christian teachings.
2. Devise some ground rules for worldview or doctrinal debates with adherents of another religion that would prevent the development of mutual disrespect.
3. How could contemporary missionaries in Sri Lanka work to heal anti-Christian mission feeling among Buddhists?

wrong their views might seem. William Sheppard demonstrated this full-orbed respect in the midst of swiftly changing violent times, both in the United States and in the Congo. No matter what situation faced him, he showed respect for others and for himself. He championed his own cause without disparaging the beliefs of others. Sheppard's life shows how respect can be practiced in every situation. Each person is created in God's image and thus deserves the respect of all Christians. Sheppard's life demonstrates the far-reaching results that such a radical practice of respect can have.

13

Charity

Loving Those to Whom We Witness

Mission Exemplar: Mother Teresa
Location: India
Audience: Hindus
Time: Twentieth century

Timeline
- 1910 Born to Nikola and Drana Bojaxhiu in Skopje, Serbia
- 1922 Call to "belong completely to God"
- 1928 Is accepted into religious order of Loreto Sisters and sets sail for India as Sister Mary Teresa of the Child Jesus
- 1937 Takes final vows on May 24 as a Sister of Our Lady of Loreto
- 1946 "Call within a call" on September 10: call to leave the convent and consecrate herself to helping the poor by living among them
- 1950 The Order of Missionaries of Charity is authorized by Rome.
- 1952 The home for dying destitutes is opened in Kalighat.
- 1965 Pope Paul VI decrees the praiseworthiness of the Missionaries of Charity, and new homes are opened around the world.
- 1970–79 International awards: the Good Samaritan Award, the Templeton Award for Progress in Religion, the Pope John XXIII Peace Prize, the Nobel Peace Prize

- 1980–89 Missionaries of Charity expand, opening new homes in Lebanon, West Germany, Yugoslavia, Mexico, Brazil, Peru, Kenya, Haiti, Spain, Ethiopia, Belgium, New Guinea, Argentina, Southern Yemen, Nicaragua, Cuba, and Russia.
- 1990 After a brief retirement due to ill health, Mother Teresa resumes her post as superior general of the Missionaries of Charity.
- 1996 President Bill Clinton signs legislation making Mother Teresa an honorary US citizen.
- 1997 Mother Teresa dies.

Resources to Consult on Mother Teresa's Mission

Becky Benenate, ed., *In the Heart of the World* (New York: Barnes and Noble, 1997).

Becky Benenate and Joseph Durepos, eds., *Mother Teresa: No Greater Love* (New York: Barnes and Noble, 1997).

Teresa de Bertodano, ed., *Daily Readings with Mother Teresa* (London: HarperCollins, 1993).

José Luis González-Balado and Janet N. Playfoot, eds., *My Life for the Poor: Mother Teresa of Calcutta* (New York: Ballantine, 1985).

Brian Kolodiejchuk, ed., *Mother Teresa: Come Be My Light* (New York: Doubleday, 2007).

Joly Le and Jaya Chaliha, eds., *Mother Teresa's Reaching Out in Love* (New York: Barnes and Noble, 2002).

Malcolm Muggeridge, *Something Beautiful for God: Mother Teresa of Calcutta* (New York: Harper, 1971).

Kathryn Spink, *Mother Teresa: A Complete Authorized Biography* (San Francisco: HarperCollins, 1997).

During her first years as a Loreto sister in Darjeeling, Mother Teresa worked part-time at a medical station. "On one occasion a man arrived with a bundle from which protruded what the young novice at first took to be two dry twigs, but which proved to be the emaciated legs of a boy so weak he was on the point of death." Mother Teresa recalls, "The man is afraid we will not take the child, and says, 'If you do not want him, I will throw him into the grass. The jackals will not turn up their noses at him.' My heart freezes. The poor child! Weak, and blind—totally blind. With much pity and love I take the little one into my arms, and fold him in my apron. The child has found a second mother" (Spink 1997, 15).

Mother Teresa, known worldwide for her work with the dying in India, found herself drawn to caring for the poor even before she arrived in India. But it was during those first years as a novice in the order of the Loreto Sisters in Darjeeling that she began her lifelong practice of loving those to whom she witnessed by caring for the poorest of the poor.

Christian love did not begin with Mother Teresa. But the way that she loved the poor and showed love was a mission practice that has captured the imagination of Christians around the world. She loved the poor one by one, passionately and totally. She saw in everyone the image of God, the dignity of personhood. And she looked upon every sick and dying person as if he or she were the suffering Christ himself. She saw, not sores nor emaciated faces nor grime, but the face of the suffering Christ in each one.

WHO WAS MOTHER TERESA?

Mother Teresa began her journey toward that practice of caring for the dying poor of Calcutta when she was still a child. Born in Serbia of middle-class Albanian parents in 1910, she experienced poverty herself after her father died when she was eight years old. The financial struggles of her widowed mother, Drana, resulted in physical deprivations that must have been hard on the frail health of little Agnes. Her mother would sometimes remark to her other two children that Agnes would probably not be with them long. Either a call to a religious vocation or an illness would take her from them.

Despite their own poverty, Agnes witnessed her mother, Drana, showing special care for the poor. She visited an elderly alcoholic woman named File every Saturday, sometimes taking Agnes along with her. Drana would sometimes remark that the worst of File's problems was not her poverty but her abandonment by her son. She was unloved. Drana once brought six children of a poor widow into their family when the children's mother died, an act of mercy that demanded considerable sacrifice. Yet, she would say to her children, "When you do good, do it quietly, as if you were throwing a stone into the sea" (Spink 1997, 7).

Prayer also played a large role in shaping Agnes's habits and desires. Praying together kept the family close, her mother felt, so earnest prayer times marked their everyday life. The impact of her mother's example and teaching and the prayerful nature of family life contributed to a spiritual experience at age twelve. Agnes felt the call of God on her life to become a missionary. Serving the poor of India was one of her dreams. Agnes's mother was pleased.

Six years later, when the time came for her to follow through on this dream, her mother found it difficult to let her go. At age eighteen Agnes, with her mother's reluctant blessing, accompanied by a friend with a similar intention, began the long train journey to Paris, where they were accepted by the Loreto Sisters. Immediately afterward they went to Dublin, where they spent a mere two weeks at the convent Rathfarnham before they embarked on a ship to India. Agnes's native language was replaced by English, of which she knew little. Her mother and siblings were lost to her as she traveled to a country both distant and different from her native land. Yet family ties remained strong, and it was her mother who, years later, reminded Teresa of her original intention to serve the poor when she was at risk of forgetting that call.

An energetic learner and naturally gifted teacher, Sister Teresa was assigned to work in the convent school during her training in Darjeeling. She also spent a short time working at a medical station. This work took her out of the convent and brought to her senses the sights and sounds and odors of the poverty of an Indian urban setting. She probably recalled her own childhood days of want, and her heart went out to the poor with a special earnestness.

After completing her training and taking final vows, Sister Teresa continued her work of teaching, which she loved. But then a second call accosted her. That "call within a call" insisted that she leave the convent and go to live and work totally among the poor. This radical step proved to be the foundation for an amazing witness of love to the poor of India. There were no limits on whom she would love and no restrictions on how deeply she embraced them.

Working with the authorities of the Catholic Church meant that Sister Teresa could not immediately begin her work. Cautious leaders took time to evaluate her intentions, studying her correspondence and relationships with others. They tried to measure the impact of a young, single woman moving into the slum. They considered various ways that she might identify herself in this new work, through perhaps a leave of absence from the convent or a total separation from the Loreto Sisters, including a refutation of her religious vows. After a year of waiting, Sister Teresa's plan was approved, and she was not required to renounce her vows. A joyful Sister Teresa then spent a few short months in training at a medical center before moving to one of the poorest slums in Calcutta.

Sister Teresa found that caring for the poor energized rather than drained her, just as it had in her earlier experience of embracing the blind child. Enfolding that child had been the "crowning point of her day." That continued to be the case as she cared for the dying. Whether the person was a Hindu or a Muslim, Sister Teresa saw the face of the suffering Christ in each sick and dying person. And it was that face that she loved. It was that embrace of the suffering Christ that energized her. Here was a theology of loving those to whom she witnessed that could sustain her in the grueling work of caring for the demented, those suffering from bleeding sores, those too weak and dirty to care for themselves, and those with little hope that a loving hand would be laid upon them.

A SIMPLE MISSION FOCUS

The mission of loving that Mother Teresa practiced by caring for the dying poor had several characteristics that made it unique. First of all, it was simple. She found dying people on the streets and gave them succor. It addressed a very real need, a need that everyone could see. She did not formulate a complicated rationale; she did not address systemic causes of poverty. She did not organize a movement; she did not decry the unjust acts of others. She simply helped one person after another.

That simple act was symbolic. So many poor in the huge city of Calcutta were left to die in the streets. The famine of 1943 had made the situation even worse. Many of those poor were abandoned by their families. Some believed that they must live out their bad karma as best they could without interference. Others simply had no resources to care for them. Still others were shunned by their families for personal reasons. Sister Teresa's action of loving them through caring for their physical needs was simple and direct.

Her focus in that care was on comfort, not on cure. She impatiently appealed to leave her training at the medical station after only a few months. Although she gave medical care to many who would obviously benefit from it, especially as her ministry grew, Mother Teresa was most interested in helping unloved people to feel loved. Giving an embrace to an abandoned one, providing a clean pallet for someone sick, sending a smile across the room to a confused elderly person—those practices showed the true charity to which Mother Teresa felt called.

Her theological rationale also focused on the simple needs of people and our connection to God through the poor. Scripture, especially the Gospels, played an important part in her theology of loving the poor. "I thirst," Jesus cried out on the cross. Every cup of water given to a dying person addresses that cry. The aim of the congregation established by Mother Teresa was to "quench the infinite thirst of Jesus Christ on the Cross for love of souls" (Spink 1997, 14). Missionaries of Charity would be carriers of food and drink, for Christ identified himself with those in need: "For I was hungry and you gave me something to eat, I was thirsty and you gave me something to drink, I was a stranger and you invited me in, I needed clothes and you clothed me, I was sick and you looked after me, I was in prison and you came to visit me" (Matt. 25:35–36).

Not only did Mother Teresa desire to care for the poor; she also insisted that the Missionaries of Charity live as the poor lived. At first, she wanted her sisters to eat only rice and water since that was the daily fare of the poor, if they got anything at all to eat. But her superiors pointed out that the sisters themselves would soon be as ill as the poor, so a more substantive diet was imposed. Still, it was simple food, and the sisters were required to eat enough to nourish their bodies but not so much that their vow of poverty would be threatened. Accommodations were sparse, as were possessions. Each sister had, in addition to her simple blue and white sari, a bucket for washing clothes and a few simple toiletries. Many times generous donors wanted to improve living conditions for the sisters, but Mother Teresa refused this help, believing that the sisters should live as the poor lived insofar as it was possible.

Although Mother Teresa's call focused on Christian charity, there was, paradoxically, a religious inclusiveness to her focus. Regardless of your beliefs

---

SIDEBAR 13.1
HABITS FOR LOVING THOSE TO WHOM WE WITNESS

Love cannot be programmed or separated into distinct components. We can, however, formulate habits that, with consistent practice, nurture the relationships between missioners and those to whom they are sent.

1. *Initiate contact.* Rather than waiting to be approached, learn the cultural forms of approach for the relationship. After learning the cultural meaning of establishing a relationship with the other person or community, approach them in culturally fitting ways. This may mean going through an intermediary in some cases, performing certain rituals of honor in approaching the other, and using customary language and proper forms of address for a particular relationship.

2. *Pay attention to the response.* Listen, watch, and feel the other's response to your initiation of contact. Rather than anticipating or trying to control the person's response to you, learn the cultural meaning of your action by seeing how that person responds to you. Adjust your behavior accordingly. If a friendly approach yields a distancing response, investigate how others navigate the initiation of friendship and try a different approach.

3. *Affirm the other.* As the other person responds to you, seek ways to affirm the person. Consider her response to you a genuine expression of care by a person of worth. Verbal and nonverbal expressions of affirmation show the genuineness of your care and also augment your sense of love for the other. Negative responses or criticism have the opposite effect, diminishing the sense of value of the interaction.

4. *Appreciate the other person for himself or herself.* Recognize the complexity and mystery of the other person. Do not assume that you know him thoroughly and can predict his responses to you. Inadvertently, that stance may become a self-fulfilling prophecy because people tend to act as others expect them to act. Instead, make a habit of appreciating the person for who she is. What she does for you, or how her faults offend you, or whether her actions help or hinder her own growth may be of concern to you, but these do not form the basis of your love for the other person.

---

or the spiritual path you followed, Mother Teresa would take you in and love you. She offered comfort and the last rites of whatever religion you followed, but she did not see Kali or Muhammad or Buddha in the face of the poor. She saw the face of Christ. Religious distinctions didn't matter. Christ was present in each one; Christ sustained her in this grueling work.

SPREADING CHARITY

Sister Teresa's actions spoke to the consciences of people in Calcutta. Government officials were embarrassed by the number of dying poor on the streets.

5. *Act for the good of the other.* Making the welfare of the other a priority in our relationships entails many forms of interaction. Playfulness and serious expressions of concern, gentle and forceful engagements, cooperative and competitive behaviors—this is a short list of the many types of interactions of loving relationships. As each person in the relationship seeks to act for the good of the other, love deepens. Sometimes the best action is clearly one that pleases the other person.

6. *Pay special attention to the weak.* It is more difficult to recognize the important elements of relationship when the other person is weak. Economic imbalance, lack of education, age difference, and ethnic, cultural, and religious differences can interfere with our ability to establish relationships of mutuality and respect. By paying special attention to the weak, we compensate for tendencies to self-importance and pride that arise because of the power differential resulting from those differences.

7. *Give gifts.* This general habit flows through all of the practices of mission included in this book. Giving gifts as part of loving relationships, specifically, involves understanding the gift-giving customs of the culture that we enter. Gifts that are given sincerely, with an awareness of those customs and power dynamics, bring people into closer relation with one another, setting up mutual obligations that deepen the relationship and help the people feel the love and care of others.

8. *Receive gifts.* The mutuality that characterizes loving those to whom we witness is sustained by receiving gifts. It is the strong who give and the weak who receive. It is the homeowner who gives hospitality and the stranger who receives it. By receiving gifts, the missioner leaves the comfortable zone of helping, comforting, and advising and enters an uncertain realm of receiving and incurring obligation. This binds the missioner to the community in ways that allow the gospel to be taken up by the people while also bringing good news to the missioner.

The practical problems of sanitation and removal of the corpses were a drain on government resources. Middle- and upper-class people of the city were bothered by the frequent sight of dying people or starving children in their midst. Somehow, the Hindu doctrine of the necessity of people living out their given role in society, even a role of starvation and sickness, was not enough to salve the conscience of the city. People were bothered. And here was someone taking action, helping anyone who needed it.

People soon began calling Teresa "Mother." Her actions were so filled with love that those she served felt a mother's love coming from her. But her practice of love went far beyond her own hands and heart. Her spiritual fire soon spread, and others came to join her. The first ten women to walk with Mother Teresa in Calcutta were former pupils of hers at the Sisters of Loreto convent schools. Her passion for the poor had already been transmitted to young women, some of whom had enough courage to leave their normal life and follow her into the slums. While the number of novices in other orders dropped, the Missionaries of Charity grew.

Young women were attracted by her desire to do "something beautiful for God." Mother Teresa's focus was not on the stunning poverty all around her in the slums of Calcutta. She focused on the one person in her arms, the one dying baby she asked a young novice to hold through a whole day. No one should die without being loved, she believed. And being loved was something beautiful for God. Every act of loving care showed the world that God loved each person.

Men too were attracted to Mother Teresa's dedicated ministry. Father Van Exem caught her vision from the beginning. Archbishop Perier came on board, approving the new congregation of the Missionaries of Charity. Later, with Brother Andrew, with whom she did not always see eye to eye, she established the Missionary Brothers of Charity. Working alongside the sisters in some places, forming their own ministries in others, the brothers worked with the poorest of the poor. Brother Andrew led the congregation for twenty-eight years.

Mother Teresa's vision captured the imagination of others because it was a focused, evangelistic witness without words. She centered her life on a single goal. Rather than talk about it, she acted. Certain personal qualities, both positive and negative, contributed to her witness. Mother Teresa was dogmatic and persistent, insisting on doing mission her way. That approach often worked. The positive side of the same trait was commitment and confidence in what she was doing. She was not eloquent or smooth in her interactions with those interested in her ministry, but her directness and stark truth telling won the day. When Malcolm Muggeridge interviewed her for the BBC, the directors at first thought that the interview was barely worth airing. Mother Teresa's answers to Muggeridge's questions were terse, almost to the point of rudeness. But it had a remarkable effect on the listeners, bringing Mother Teresa's ministry to international attention. Her theology was not complicated, but it was profound.

It was an apt message for the times. And the message reached people. It reached the sick person being held, or given a bath, or tucked into a bed near the window to finally rest, away from the dirt and clamor of the streets. It reached the sisters who did the caregiving and the people in the neighborhood who saw them carrying away their dying poor. It reached the government officials, whose embarrassment intensified because this one small woman gave herself sacrificially to the destitute whom no one else would touch. And it reached the world. The message touched people of good will all over the globe, those who believed that such intense poverty was unfortunate, unjust, uncompassionate, and deplorable.

Mother Teresa exuded confidence in God. She worked persistently to get her new congregation approved by the Vatican. Father Celeste Van Exem, her ally in this work, pestered Bishop Perier time after time on her behalf. She felt strongly about the parameters of her ministry and developed the rules of the order that ensured the continuing witness of living with the poor and not

---

SIDEBAR 13.2
SAYINGS OF MOTHER TERESA

Benenate (1997); Benenate and Durepos (1997); Le and Chaliha (2002)

ON LOVE

When we all see God in each other, we will love one another as He loves us all. That is the fulfillment of the law, to love one another. This is all Jesus came to teach us: that God loves us, and that He wants us to love one another as He loves us.

We must know that we have been created for greater things, not just to be a number in the world, not just to go for diplomas and degrees, this work and that work. We have been created in order to love and be loved.

Where God is, there is love; and where there is love, there always is an openness to serve. The world is hungry for God.

ON ACTION

Our mission is to convey God's love—not a dead God but a living God, a God of love.

Then do some small things with great love. Help somebody. Maybe just smile. Is there a person who has hurt you? You go and forgive that person. Is there some bitterness? Go and say it is forgiven. And you will find Him. God cannot be found when we are unforgiving.

Whatever you do, even if you help somebody cross the road, you do it to Jesus. Even giving somebody a glass of water, you do it to Jesus. Such a simple little teaching, but it is more and more important.

When we handle the sick and the needy we touch the suffering body of Christ and this touch will make us heroic. . . . We shall need the hands of Christ to touch these bodies wounded by pain and suffering. Intense love does not measure—it just gives.

ON CONTEMPLATION

To me, contemplation is not to be shut up in a dark place but to allow Jesus to live His passion, love, and humility in us, praying with us, being with us, sanctifying through us.

In the silence of the heart God speaks. . . . It is only when you realize your nothingness, your emptiness, that God can fill you with Himself. Souls of prayer are souls of great silence.

Prayer is the very life of oneness, of being one with Christ. Therefore prayer is as necessary as the air, as the blood in our body, as anything, to keep us alive to the grace of God. . . . If we don't pray, our presence will have no power, our words will have no power.

above them. The structure she developed served the Missionaries of Charity well in Calcutta. The ensuing years saw an expansion of her ministry to other countries. The structure of the order of the Missionaries of Charity translated well into those new contexts.

Mother Teresa believed that God's providence would supply her needs. She said, "We have no income, no government grant, no church maintenance: only divine providence" (González-Balado and Playfoot 1985, 61). She had no trouble making the needs of her ministry known. But she never asked for money. Although she accepted help for her ministry from the government, from churches, and from individuals, she was quick to refuse gifts that she thought would compromise the witness of the Missionaries of Charity in any way. Mother Teresa realized that many missionaries began by serving the poor but went on to become rich themselves. She even had Kathryn Spink, her biographer, cutting hair in the women's ward of Nirmal Hriday, the home for the dying in Calcutta (Spink 1997, 146–47). Mother Teresa wanted helpers, and she believed God would send them, along with the financial resources that were needed.

In India, however, Mother Teresa learned to beg. And she taught her order, the Sisters of Charity, to beg for the poor. Why should she be ashamed to claim for them the food and shelter that their human dignity required? Why should she be hesitant to plead for whatever she needed to make the poor feel loved?

Those two seemingly contradictory approaches to making the needs of the Missionaries of Charity known were each effective in the spheres in which she used them. Begging from rich Westerners would have been humiliating. The missionaries needed an approach that gave them the opportunity to help, to see that God wanted them to participate in this ministry. And in India, where there were beggars everywhere and people who could fulfill the needs of those beggars, asking for resources for the poorest of the poor was just the approach that was needed.

Mother Teresa found that many people wanted to help. And she somehow found a way for each one to contribute to the ministry. To see the face of the suffering Christ in the poorest of the poor in India, one did not necessarily need to join the Missionary Sisters in India. One could help by volunteering in other ways.

Her British friend Ann Blaikie, who had worked with her in India, spread the word of her ministry throughout England. She gathered many people all across the British Isles to hear what Mother Teresa was doing and to contribute to the work in some way.

Jacqueline de Decker, who had gone to India with a vision very similar to Mother Teresa's, could not stay because of health issues. Mother Teresa embraced her from afar, naming Jacqueline her "other self." Here was a sick and suffering woman who could never return to India to help. To her, Mother

Teresa gave the ministry of identification—it was her own suffering that contributed to the welfare of the poor.

Those individuals and many others across the world formed a network of coworkers who, by praying, giving, and volunteering, pushed the ministry forward as it expanded in many directions at once. Mother Teresa tells the story of an Australian man who made a substantial contribution but then said, "This is something external. Now I want to give something of myself." By regularly volunteering at the house of the dying, this man gave of himself (Benenate 1997, 69).

Mother Teresa said that she often asked for gifts that had nothing to do with money since there were so many other things one could give. She wanted people's love and the sacrifice of their hands. So she always helped people who wanted to give of themselves to find a place in her ministry. There was room for everyone in the ministry of loving the poor. This was a giftive mission of the highest order.

Mother Teresa also made good use of the government resources that she uncovered in Calcutta. Her first home for the dying was housed in two rooms of a Hindu temple dedicated to the worship of Kali. Those accommodations were offered to her by the government, and she accepted them gratefully. Later interactions with local officials brought resources to her ministry as well as good feelings and protection as she worked for the betterment of their city.

Mother Teresa found a way to make her message compatible with the culture around her. Rather than keep the traditional black robes of Catholic sisters, she had her Sisters of Charity dress in white saris much like the Hindu women wore and modest enough not to offend Muslim sensibilities. She worked with the people at the temple of Kali where she housed her first center for the dying. She allowed people to die without heroic medical interventions, a practice understood by her Hindu neighbors. Rather than contest local customs or set her ministry apart from local religious centers, she worked with them, finding acceptance through her sensitivity to social norms and religious practices.

It is not surprising, then, that her coworkers included Hindus. Once a Hindu leader remarked that when he saw the sisters serving the lepers, he felt that Christ had come once more to the earth and that he was going about doing good. Another Hindu man who visited the house for the dying in Calcutta said, "Your religion must be true. Christ must be true if he helps you to do what you're doing" (González-Balado and Playfoot 1985, 92). That part of the work was very beautiful to Mother Teresa. "It had created a concern and awakening that the poor are our brothers and sisters and they have been created by the same loving hand. That oneness is more and more coming into reality" (92).

Of course, some people opposed her ministry. Mother Teresa and those she accepted into the order were often criticized by the local people. At first, the priests at the temple of Kali persistently opposed housing the shelter

SIDEBAR 13.3
ANTIMISSIONARY: KING RICHARD THE LION-HEARTED

Practice: Charity—Loving those to whom we witness

Mission success, at least long-term success, is directly related to the degree of love one has for the people to whom one does mission. Less love means less faithful Christian witness.

King Richard I of England (1157–99, reigned 1189–99) was called the Lion-Hearted because of his military expertise. He was undoubtedly a great warrior. His military exploits have made him a man of legend in the history books of England.

He was less than effective as a Christian missionary. And make no mistake, he self-consciously dedicated his military talents to the promotion of the Christian gospel. He chose to raise an army and travel to the Middle East to recapture the Holy Land from the infidel Muslims. This military foray came to be called one of the Crusades of that period of church history, a time when Christian mission workers saw no conflict between a gospel that preaches self-sacrificing love for all human beings and all creation and the use of the most violent military force possible with the weapons of the day.

This discrepancy marred not only his warrior image but also the code of honor held among military men of the period. Richard professed to respect the skill and honor of his main Muslim antagonist, Saladin, a general of comparable military skills. Saladin also respected Richard, so much so that when at one point he had Richard and his army pinned down in a fortress town by the Mediterranean Sea,

he offered Richard safe passage before his final attack. For his part, Richard, when he had a similar chance later in the war, went back on his word for safe passage for some Muslim civilians.

Steven Runciman, in his magisterial work *A History of the Crusades*, best captured Richard when he wrote, "He was a bad man, a bad son, a bad husband, a bad king, but a gallant and splendid soldier" (1987, 127). Perhaps we could add, he was a bad representative of Christianity, a bad missionary.

It is too much to lay at Richard's doorstep all the missteps of Christian mission workers throughout history who have been tempted to use violent and coercive means to tell people the story of Jesus Christ. But the very success of his military exploits increases his level of responsibility for influencing all missionaries who carry out their calls with less than full love for their non-Christian neighbors.

REFLECTION AND DISCUSSION

1. Find three Bible passages that show the incompatibility of love of neighbor and coercion.

2. What do you think Jesus meant when he said, "I did not come to bring peace, but a sword" (Matt. 10:34)? Explain this verse in the context of the whole chapter.

3. How would you synthesize Jesus's teaching from Matthew 10 with the three passages you documented in the first question?

for the dying at their temple. Not until one of their own leaders became ill, was refused hospitalization, and subsequently came under the care of the sisters did the Hindu priests become more accepting of Mother Teresa's work in their temple. Demonstrations against her ministry were not infrequent in those early days. Some criticized her for a naive belief that she could affect in any significant way the huge problem of poverty in India. To them she replied that she did not do business the way they did. She didn't add up the number of India's poor and try to influence it. Rather, she only subtracted, taking from the total number of the poor one person after another.

Probably the fact that Sister Teresa was only one person, and a person of delicate health at that, also gave her innovative practice an advantage. For that one person began a loving practice that grew and grew—that changed not only people's attitudes about poverty and Christianity but also the way people understood poverty.

14

Missional Ecumenicity

Practicing Mission as the Joint Project of the Church

Mission Exemplar: Billy Graham
Location: Global, United States
Audience: Secularists
Time: Twentieth century

Timeline
- 1918 Born near Charlotte, North Carolina
- 1939 Is ordained as Southern Baptist minister
- 1943 Graduates from Wheaton College
       Marries Ruth Bell
- 1948 Becomes president of Northwestern Bible College,
       St. Paul, MN
- 1949 Cofounder, Youth for Christ
- 1950 Founds Billy Graham Evangelistic Association
- 1956 Founds *Christianity Today* magazine
- 2007 Opens the Billy Graham Library

Resources to Consult on Billy Graham's Mission

Lewis Drummond, *The Evangelist* (Dallas: Word, 2001).
Billy Graham, *A Biblical Standard for Evangelists* (Minneapolis: World
   Wide, 1984).
Billy Graham, *Just As I Am* (San Francisco: HarperCollins/Zondervan,
   1997).
Billy Graham, *Peace with God* (Dallas: Word, 1984).

Billy Graham, *The Secret of Happiness* (Dallas: Word, 1985).

William Martin, *A Prophet with Honor* (New York: William Morrow, 1991).

William G. McLoughlin, *Billy Graham: Revivalist in a Secular Age* (New York: Ronald, 1960).

Curtis Mitchell, *Billy Graham: The Making of a Crusader* (New York: Chilton, 1966).

John C. Pollock, *Billy Graham: The Authorized Biography* (New York: McGraw-Hill, 1966).

By its nature, mission is an activity that attempts to include. Mission draws wider and wider circles including more and more people. The apostle Paul taught us that the gospel of Jesus is for everyone. Patrick included everyone in fellowship, regardless of their backgrounds or spiritual maturity. Cyril and Methodius thought everyone should be able to understand the Scriptures and the liturgy and the writings of theologians and pastors, and that the work of mission was to make those literary manifestations of God and God's work available to everyone. By and large, mission down through the ages has been an inclusive affair with the goal being the growth of the kingdom of God.

Yet in modern times, as social observers such as Robert Bellah and H. Richard Niebuhr have shown, cultures have become so complex and personal loyalties so diverse that any endeavor calling for inclusiveness runs into a cultural buzz saw that threatens to tear it apart. Even issues of personal religious identity are fragmented by related cultural demands. Sometimes churches get caught up in this complexity and forget the oneness of the message of God's love for all people. And sometimes what seem to be competing Christian missions get caught up in the fragmentation as well.

Mission exclusions have extended not just to nonmembers but to other Christian groups as well. Where once mission was the one thing that united different sectors of the church in the task of proclaiming the gospel story, uniting different denominations and agencies and national churches in the same task, in the nineteenth and twentieth centuries mission has become something that further divides, a competitive affair in which the languages of growth and membership have come to refer not to those who want to be included in the gospel story but to those who want to join our denomination, our way of doing church, our cultural expression of Christianity. Growth and membership have sometimes come to refer to institutional successes, not to gospel successes.

William Franklin Graham, better known as Billy Graham, has been a voice calling for the oneness of the gospel message. In our list of mission innovators, he joins Mother Teresa as one of the twentieth-century mission figures who

199

has gone against the ecclesiologies of exclusion and recaptured the universality of the gospel story. They used very different vehicles to accomplish this task. As we have seen, Mother Teresa used the medical-mission approach, helping the poor and sick. Billy Graham used the public-preaching approach. Perhaps the sign of their being on the right track is that people recognized them as rarities, as people going against the trend of exclusion. Both were named on the Gallup Poll list of most admired people of the twentieth century (Mother Teresa was number 1; Graham was number 7). They became spiritual icons because in their work they pointed people not to an ideology or to an institution but to Jesus.

WHO IS BILLY GRAHAM?

Billy Graham was born near Charlotte, North Carolina, on a dairy farm. His parents, William Franklin Graham and Morrow Coffey Graham, were members of a Presbyterian church. Although Graham was active in that church and although he later in life became a Southern Baptist (in 1939 he was ordained as a Southern Baptist minister), denominational religion was not his focus. From an early age, he seemed to instinctively know that the church served the gospel, not the other way around. This insight, as much as anything else, was the root of his mission innovation.

In addition to raising him in the church, his parents apparently took Graham to other religious meetings, because he became a Christian by commitment (not by inheritance) during 1934 at a revival meeting. Revival meetings, usually held in large tents set up in open fields, were a staple of southern religion in those days. This particular meeting was led by evangelist Mordecai Ham. It became the occasion not just for Graham's spiritual dedication but for his choice of career as well. He determined, at the age of sixteen, that he would also become an evangelist.

Graham's college education began at Bob Jones College (now Bob Jones University), but finding the strict lifestyle rules of that institution too restrictive, he transferred. He became a college hopper, moving from Bob Jones to Florida Bible Institute (now Trinity College of Florida) and finally to Wheaton College in Illinois, where he graduated in 1943. Billy Graham is well educated and reads widely but has never considered himself a scholar. His self-identity is as a preacher. He pastored a small church in Western Springs, Illinois, his last year in college.

While at Wheaton College he met Ruth Bell. The two later married and remained together for the next sixty-five years. "I saw her walking down the road towards me and I couldn't help but stare at her as she walked. She looked at me and our eyes met and I felt that she was definitely the woman I wanted to marry." Ruth Bell Graham died in May 2007 at the age of eighty-seven. Together the Grahams had five children, nineteen grandchildren, and twenty-eight great-grandchildren. Their two sons, Ned Graham and Franklin Graham, are both active in aspects of their father's ministerial pursuits, as is one of their daughters, Anne Graham Lotz.

Graham developed a type of public evangelistic ministry he called a crusade, which was really his version of a tent revival. His special stamp on the form of the revival grew as the years progressed: once he and his team identified a city for the revival, he angled for an invitation to come from the local pastor's association. He combined a large local choir (as many as five thousand people) and professional gospel music singers with an explicit evangelistic message. His big break came early in a series of meetings he held in the Los Angeles area. Newspaper mogul Randolph Hearst, looking for a conservative, anticommunist public preacher, tapped Graham to promote in his newspapers. This backing drew thousands more to the meetings, and Graham's enormous public-speaking skills did the rest.

Throughout his life but especially in the early years, Graham had a restless energy that led him to lead or start several important ministries. At age thirty he became the youngest sitting president of a four-year college when he took the reins of Northwestern Bible College in the Twin Cities of Minnesota. He also helped found and promote an extremely important ministry to teenagers called Youth for Christ in 1949. Seven years later he saw a need for evangelical theologians and pastors to display academic and scholarly acumen and founded a magazine for that purpose, *Christianity Today*.

In 1950 he founded what became his flagship organization in Minneapolis, the Billy Graham Evangelistic Association (BGEA). Originally a place to organize his crusade meetings, the BGEA became a multifaceted institution with diverse ministries such as Worldwide Pictures, a feature film company; *Decision Magazine*, a popular magazine with human-interest vignettes; *Hour of Decision*, a weekly radio program that ran for over fifty years; "My Answer," a newspaper column of spiritual self-help advice; and later, Passageway.org, a Web site for teens.

The BGEA was headquartered in Minneapolis, but Graham lived in the mountains of North Carolina. Later he moved the BGEA to a large plot of land near Charlotte, North Carolina, home ground for him. Throughout the years of his ministry, he expanded his crusades to include foreign cities, and he became a world-famous religious personage. In the last couple of decades, he rethought calling his meetings crusades, as overly aggressive mission methodologies have come under serious question. Instead of associating Christian mission work with warfare (and wanting to avoid the increasingly politically incorrect association with the Crusades of the tenth and eleventh centuries), he began calling his revival meetings "festivals." His last meeting was held in New York City in 2005, although he made a later appearance at a revival meeting led by his son Franklin in New Orleans for the victims of the Hurricane Katrina disaster.

> ## SIDEBAR 14.1
> ## BILLY GRAHAM NOTES
>
> - Number 7 on Gallup list of most-admired people of the twentieth century
> - Member of the Southern Baptist Convention
> - Registered Democrat
> - Preached to live audiences totaling 215 million in 185 countries
> - Held over forty-one evangelistic crusades from 1948 to 2005
> - Received Congressional Gold Medal
> - Received Templeton Foundation Prize for Progress in Religion
> - Received Ronald Reagan Presidential Foundation Freedom Award
> - Inducted into Gospel Music Hall of Fame
> - Honorary Knight Commander of the Order of the British Empire
> - Spiritual advisor/friend to US presidents

One of the public's most enduring images of Graham is as a friend of United States presidents. As the evangelical Christian voting block Graham represented grew in numbers and influence, political figures lined up to be seen as supporters of Graham's ministry. Presidents beginning with Harry Truman met with Graham and sought his support. Although Graham for much of his life was a registered Democrat, he met with all the presidents and offered them spiritual counsel.

One of his closest friendships was with Richard Nixon, a relationship that proved embarrassing for Graham when the Watergate tape recordings showed Nixon to be a less than saintly person. The association with Nixon also created a political firestorm when a young Graham was revealed on some of the Watergate tapes to be exchanging with Nixon less than flattering comments about high-profile Jewish leaders in the United States. It was an especially incongruous revelation since Graham had been one of Israel's strongest supporters, was especially friendly with American Jewish leaders, and refused to join the call for the conversion of Jews to Christianity. The flap was one of several Graham endured; from the time he chose the role of public preacher, he has been asked regularly to comment on highly volatile social issues of the day. He has been willing to address such issues and has handled them with an unusually sensitive combination of commitment to conservative Christian values and compassionate social awareness. But occasionally he has misspoken.

As he approaches ninety years of age, Graham is beset by several major physical maladies, and his public appearances are declining in number. He is not fully retired, however. Always a prolific writer of popular spiritual self-help books, he continues to minister through the written word to an adoring American public.

MISSIONAL ECUMENICAL COMMITMENTS

One way to discuss Graham as a mission innovator would be to say that he managed to make the public preaching of the gospel to world audiences that were increasingly suspicious of any sort of religious self-promotion an acceptable, even admirable, endeavor. In a century of secularism, religious unbelief, atheism, and suspicious confusion of religious missions and jihads as being politically motivated, Graham manages to preach, comment on the issues of the day, and not needlessly offend or appear to be a pawn of United States government agencies. That would be a major accomplishment, but perhaps not an innovation of the caliber of the others we have noted in previous chapters.

But Graham has stood for an innovation that may well become determinative of the success or failure of the church in the twenty-first century. We call it missional ecumenism and by that mean finding a way to tell the gospel story in a world beset by two competing forces, globalization and tribalization. Graham has increasingly functioned in a world pulled by market and scientific forces toward a homogenization of interests and at the same time pulled in the other direction, toward an insistence of distinct cultures to have their say and their way. This situation has created a politics torn between global interests and national interests, between statecraft and worldcraft. The clashes between these political forces are changing the world at a rapid pace.

The same thing is happening in the world of religion. The religious realm is manifesting struggles that in many ways mirror the geopolitical struggles: conflicts within Christianity itself, what we might call intrareligious struggles; conflicts that Christianity has with its own history, with Judaism especially; conflicts that intertwine race and religion in volatile mixtures; and conflicts among the religions of the world. With such a plethora of competing religious forces across the religious spectrum, it is easy to despair of the possibility of preaching a single religious text as the only correct one. Billy Graham has done more than any other twentieth-century religious figure to show us how to combine the preaching of the single gospel story in a way that unites rather than divides. We choose to call this innovation *missional ecumenism.*

Missional ecumenism is the capacity to focus on a single religious story as the true one while at the same time recognizing that that story takes many cultural forms, both whole and partial. Billy Graham has shown great skill in doing this. Whether he would acknowledge this as a skill or a goal, he has in practice done it. Consider just the four areas we mentioned in the last paragraph: intra-Christian interactions, Judeo-Christian interactions, interreligious interactions, and racial-religious identity. Graham has consistently shown us the way forward in all these areas.

203

Intra-Christian Interactions

Graham has instinctively resisted the religion of exclusion. He began his college career at Bob Jones College in Greensboro, North Carolina. Bob Jones is known for insisting that students conform not just to religious and educational standards but to social ones as well, and not just social standards such as no dancing, no card playing, no use of alcohol or tobacco, but also standards such as no dating and no fraternizing with the opposite sex. Graham realized this was not the way forward for modern Christianity and transferred to colleges that were equally conservative theologically but less conservative socially.

Perhaps more significant was his growing understanding of world perceptions of Christianity and its mission effort. Increasingly in Graham's lifetime, the history of Christian missions came under critique for its associations with the West's colonial and imperial political history. Critics noted that perhaps the most common metaphor for twentieth-century Christian missions was the warfare metaphor. Although most Christian missioners restrict, in their minds at least, the warfare imagery to what they call spiritual warfare, the distinction between that kind of warfare and militarism is lost on most outside observers, particularly those of other religions. It does not help that the history of Christian mission is full of military associations with Christian missions. And of course, the Crusades of the tenth and eleventh centuries were explicit attempts to use military might for Christian mission purposes.

Billy Graham called almost all of his forty-plus major revival meetings "crusades," meaning by that battles against evil in the world by providing the answer of Jesus Christ. At the end of his revival career, he began to see the problems with this designation, and his son Franklin now calls his meetings "festivals," a word with much happier connotations.

Further, Graham had specific requirements of the local Christian community before he would consider having a revival meeting in a city. We have mentioned already that he insisted on an invitation from the local pastors. He further insisted that those pastors and their churches work together to make the revival happen. The five-thousand-member choir was also an occasion for unity: it was made up of all the choirs of the sponsoring churches. The Protestant Graham also insisted that Roman Catholics be included in preparations and platform ministry during the meeting weeks.

Judeo-Christian Interactions

Graham has consistently been a supporter of the Jewish community and an advocate of better Jewish-Christian relations. Early in his career he went out of his way to form friendships with American Jewish leaders. He was a strong supporter of the State of Israel and its right to political existence. For these efforts he has been cited by Jewish groups such as the Anti-Defamation

League of B'nai B'rith and the National Council of Christians and Jews for his contributions to positive Jewish-Christian relations.

Further, Graham has always resisted targeting Jews as objects of conversion. In fact, Graham has always spoken of people who need Christ in generic terms, refusing the judgment of specific religions and ideologies that seem to inevitably accompany such targeting and simply insisting that the gospel is a positive story of redemption aimed at everyone regardless of religious background. When Graham speaks at all of the people he thinks of during his revival sessions, it is of hurting people who need the help that God through Christ offers. He seems to identify his audience as all people who need Christ, secularists especially.

Interreligious Interactions

Although he doesn't do so as specifically, Graham seems to extend the way he sees Jews to people of other religions. He refuses to target other religions, even when he has had crusade meetings in countries where he knows his audience is composed primarily of members of other religions. This posture is a bit trickier to hold than the one he maintains toward Jews. Whereas Christians and Jews share a common and close history, Hinduism, Buddhism, Islam, and other religions are more distant from Christianity.

The difficulty of this posture is illustrated by a statement Graham made regarding people of other religions: "I fully adhere to the fundamental tenets of the Christian faith myself . . . but as an American, I respect other paths to God." Critics of Graham suggested that this might mean that he accepted other religions as valid paths to salvation. Although Graham did not say this in his statement, this is the kind of scrutiny and speculation a person of Graham's high profile receives—and the statement quoted here is filled with provocative possibilities. What he fully meant, of course, only he can say. But at a minimum, Graham's statement shows a respect for people of other religious traditions that many who are committed to the twenty-first-century mission task do not yet hold. It is a further indicator of his realization that mission in the new millennium will of necessity have to take a new, more religion-friendly posture if it can hope to be a witness to God's universal love for all people.

Racial-Religious Identity

Graham has been at the forefront of battles surrounding racial identity, perhaps *the* issue of the twenty-first century, along with religious pluralism. He has always been a champion of racial equality. In the United States this has taken the form of being a strong supporter of the civil rights movement. A favorite story of Graham watchers recounts how he once bailed Martin Luther King Jr. out of jail after one of King's arrests during a civil rights demonstration. For many decades, Graham refused to hold any of his public-preaching meetings in South Africa because apartheid laws would not allow full representation of black Africans in the crusades.

In his United States crusades, Graham always insisted on the black religious community's support before he would accept an invitation to hold a crusade in a city. Evidence of the way black religious leaders view his support comes from groups such as the George Carver Memorial Institute, which recognized him as a contributor to better race relations.

Graham's commitment to evangelism and to worldwide mission has been a hallmark of his ministry. He has always understood his call to be to evangelism in the revivalist tradition. He married the daughter of medical missionaries to China, and his international commitments to worldwide crusade-style evangelism has confirmed his understanding of the church's global focus. He has spent his life preaching for conversion to Christ, the Savior of the world. His commitment to public media—television, radio, magazines, newspapers—shows his view of the gospel's province as all of life, not just church life.

MISSION AND THE WHOLE CHURCH

Because missional ecumenism is an innovation, it is not uncontroversial. As we have seen from our other mission innovators, the *missio interna* is almost always as difficult as the *missio externa*. That is to say, missional ecumenism has its critics. Indeed, it is a position that receives strong criticism from both ends of the Christian theological spectrum.

People on the left end of the spectrum are suspicious of Graham's unquestioned commitment to classic Christian doctrines and of his unwavering conviction that people need to hear the gospel story and have their lives changed as a result of it. They are also suspicious of Graham's so-called ecumenism, because given his conservative theological stances, they naturally assume he is opposed to what is sometimes called the unity of the church. How can one be ecumenical when one believes there is a single gospel truth that has universal application?

People on the right end of the Christian theological spectrum also criticize Graham for being "soft" on too many issues that they deem central to the faith. They are frustrated because Graham rarely joins in public denunciations of blocks of people, even when he disagrees with them on a specific issue. His statement on other paths to God, for example, which we cited in the last section, gives support to people in their religious quests, separating that support from a specific evaluation of the beliefs involved. This is a separation people on the right end of the spectrum have difficulty making. (Actually, people on the far left have the same difficulty.)

Since missional ecumenism is an innovation for our day, perhaps it would be helpful to use the four categories of the previous section to comment on what this innovation is and what it is not in reference to each of these four categories.

Intra-Christian Interactions

Almost all sectors of the church pay lip service to the idea of Christian unity. The scriptural injunction that the church be one is clear enough so that different denominations, associations of churches, and even independent churches would probably agree that at some point church unity will change from a desired state to a realized outcome. At issue in the unity-of-the-church matter, then, is not the goal but the question of what unifies Christians of different cultures, races, religious backgrounds, beliefs, worship practices, and so on.

It should be obvious that the self-identification of the label Christian is not enough. Christians around the world are embarrassingly eager to dismiss other self-identified Christians as not really Christian or not Christian enough.

For many Christian groups, the question of what unifies disparate Christian groups is historical: is this group in the proper line of apostolic succession? For many other Christian groups, what unifies disparate Christian groups is a set of doctrines: those who believe our list of beliefs are Christians; those that don't are not. For still others, what unifies disparate Christians is simply the idea of unity itself: unity is such a good thing and such a clear scriptural goal that the idea of having a unified church alone should be enough to bring us all together.

Each of these positions has strengths, and each has weaknesses. This discussion is not the place to debate them. It is enough here to say that there is a fourth factor that missional ecumenists consider the unifying factor. The factor is mission itself. Those who join us in promoting the work of God among those who have not heard are displaying the distinctive mark of God's church. Missional ecumenists believe that God will bless such efforts, no matter what form they take, and that will be the basis of an enduring unity.

Judeo-Christian Interactions

There are two givens regarding the interaction among Christian groups and Jewish groups in the last couple of centuries. One given is that the Jewish people occupy a privileged position among ethnic groups in the world today. They were God's original chosen people. God made agreements and promises with the Jewish people. God honors such agreements and promises. Non-Jewish people must respect those covenants if they are trying to honor God.

A second given is that God has extended certain privileges originally afforded to Jews alone to all people, non-Jews or Gentiles. The promises God gave to Gentiles are just as binding and just as important as those God gave to Jews. Non-Gentiles, Jews, must respect those covenants if they are trying

207

to honor God. One of the reasons for the persistent Jewish-Christian conflict down through the ages (and there are many reasons for this conflict) is that most Jews and Christians believe only one of the two givens.

Missional ecumenists believe that the story of Jesus is a salutary and salvific story for all people, all ethnic groups, all races, all cultures, all religions. Thus, all people need to be told the story in the hope that they will see its salvific power. Yet people are outside the story not because of their ethnicity, race, culture, or religion but because they deny God and God's designs for all humanity. God desires relationships with all people, and that is what unifies Christians and Jews.

Interreligious Interactions

It is also what unifies Christians and Muslims and Buddhists and Hindus and Confucians and Taoists and adherents of indigenous religions and new religious movements. All people are made in the image of God, and God desires that all people and all peoples become part of a reconciled relationship with God. God made promises to all these peoples. Reconciliation with all peoples of the world is God's deepest desire. God made this reconciliation possible through Jesus.

Missional ecumenists believe that Christians are united not in their denunciation of other ethnic groups, other religions, or other cultures, but in their hopeful message that God desires all of us to be in a reconciled relationship with God and with one another through Jesus Christ. Missional ecumenism focuses on the possibilities each of us has because of who made us and how we were made. God made us in the image of the divine. We have rejected the implications of that image to be sure. That has made reconciliation difficult. But through Jesus it again becomes possible.

Racial-Religious Identity

Conflict among the religions of the world is currently exacerbated by racial tensions. Racial identity is as powerful a factor as religious identity in the world today. Add to that other functioning "identities"—national, occupational, ideological—and one can see why the question of identity is crucial in the twenty-first century.

Missional ecumenists are beginning to see the difficulty of targeting various identities to overcome with a single Christian identity and to recognize that the future of mission lies in making the Christian story a way of defining, interpreting, and embracing a complex of identities that most people today carry. Put another way, the challenge is not to do away with all of a person's identities in favor of a Christian identity but to use the gospel story as a way of refining complex identities. The story of Jesus is a way of making sense of the complex of identities in which we all participate.

CONCLUSION

It is quite clear that some kind of mission innovation is needed in the twentieth century. Billy Graham and Mother Teresa seem to have shown us the way forward in their enormously productive lives of mission service. Both took advantage of technologies, medical and communicative, that were not available to earlier Christian mission workers.

Conflict abounds in the world today, both political and interreligious. Often politics and religion seem indistinguishable. That conflict abounds is not unique in history. Humanity seems destined to conflict as surely as the sparks of a fire fly upward. What was different about late twentieth-century conflict and continues to be different about conflict in the twenty-first century is its increasing power to destroy. Nuclear weapons will soon fall into the hands of nonstate agents (if they have not already), and the world will be forced to deal with religious terrorists whose worldview admits no negotiations of the traditional political sort.

Like it or not, mission has become part of this complex of religiously based problems. Mission has become associated with starting conflicts, with perpetuating conflicts, and with raising them to unacceptably risky levels.

In such a situation, we have a limited number of options. We can continue to operate on what has become a conflict model of missions. We can roll the mission dice and assume that Christianity will be the more powerful religious force in the world, backed as it is by large numbers of adherents and political associations with the world's one remaining superpower, the United States. If we choose this option, it is most likely we will find ourselves in a war that is at least in part religiously motivated. This option does not seem consistent with the message of the gospel.

A second option is to give in to the clamor to abandon religious missions altogether. Both legal and theological options toward this end are being developed and implemented as we write. Anticonversion laws are being proposed and sometimes passed in many parts of the world. The usual aim of these laws is to do away with Christian mission efforts. And some Christian theologians have bought into this option and are writing and advocating theologies that essentially eliminate the need for Christian mission. This option also does not seem consistent with the message of the gospel.

Missional ecumenism seems to be an innovation that offers a third option. It does not abandon the scriptural mandate to tell the world the story of Jesus. But it attempts to do it in a way that dramatically reduces confrontation with the many identities people of the world hold dear.

15

Jesus, Mission Innovator

Jesus's Model of Giftive Mission

If we could get all of our mission exemplars into a room together, they would find they have much in common. Paul's insistence on the universality of mission would resonate well with Billy Graham's missional ecumenicity. Patrick's focus on the importance of fellowship would sound familiar to Mother Teresa, with her insistence on charity for everyone, and vice versa. Matteo Ricci's creative contextualizations in China would light up Catherine Booth's recognition of the needs of both rich and poor in nineteenth-century England. And so on.

But the point on which they would have the most agreement would not be a mission strategy or a theoretical insight; it would be a person, Jesus Christ. All of them—Paul, Patrick, Cyril and Methodius, Aquinas, Las Casas, Ricci, Carey, Booth, Sheppard, Mother Teresa, Graham—would quickly acknowledge to one another that without the anchor of Jesus, they would all be adrift in a sea of confusion. It was because of Jesus, they would all surely say, that they did what they did.

Probably they would say more than that. Jesus was the reason for it all, to be sure. But Jesus was also the model of how it should be done. Jesus was a mission innovator of the highest order. He showed how to bring a new message to an old religion. The message was for the members of the old religion, and this *missio interna* was painful. It aroused anger, bitterness, hostility, persecution—all this from those who should have understood his message best. Jesus eventually paid the highest human price for his willingness to carry out this mission.

Jesus's message, however, was intended for more than the members of the old religion. It was for all human beings. This *missio externa* was also difficult. It also aroused anger, bitterness, hostility, persecution, fear, and bewilderment. But this resistance did not stop Jesus. He persevered, and eventually his offer of the free gift of salvation to everyone who would accept gained a toehold in the first-century Middle East. Eventually it grew to be the largest religion in the world. One in three people in the world today claims to have accepted the story of Jesus as true and unique. They have accepted the gift.

But two out of every three people in the world today do not make such a claim. And so Jesus is still looking for mission workers to carry the story further. Would you like to volunteer? Have the stories of Paul, Patrick, Cyril and Methodius, Aquinas, Las Casas, Ricci, Carey, Booth, Sheppard, Mother Teresa, and Graham inspired you to become a gift giver to the people of the world? If so, you can begin by noticing how each of them first relied on Jesus.

Pay attention to how they relied on Jesus's teaching about God, how they unfailingly went back to mine the story of his ministry to learn how to do it. Do not be afraid to measure what you do against what Jesus did. You do not have to measure up, but you have to measure. Your mission may be a pale imitation of Jesus's mission, but it needs to be an imitation all the same. Begin by noticing that Jesus was an innovator, make no mistake. He wanted to change things both within and outside the religious communities of his day. He went right to the heart of the matter, the amazing story of God's love. Love is the place to start, the root of all mission. And it is where we end—with love. Love is the fruit of all mission, if our mission is blessed by God.

JESUS THE INNOVATOR

How can one be an innovator when it comes to love, you might ask? Well, consider that no human society can possibly express perfect love. So any culture with which the Christian gospel comes in contact will have an expression of love, but it will be a flawed expression of love, sometimes a seriously flawed expression of biblical love.

Jesus came in contact with a culture that had a good expression of love—not a perfect expression, but a good one. The people of this culture had guidelines. First for *neighbors*, presumably for those who were of the same people, but not of the same household: For neighbors the guideline was to love them by not seeking revenge or bearing grudges against one of your people. Instead, love your neighbors as you love yourself (Lev. 19:18). This is a high standard in collective societies, where revenge for wrongs endured was often considered a point of honor and served as an important method of societal control for people who did not have a professional police force. Love was more important than honor or social control, however.

Second, they had a love guideline for people who were not neighbors but were strangers in their midst, presumably for a short period of time: *Aliens* is what they are called in the biblical texts. These were people who worshiped other gods, people of other religions. The guideline for these aliens stipulated that they were to be loved also—loved as you love yourself (Lev. 19:34). This is a very high standard of love, indeed. How could Jesus possibly offer an innovation to that, a new message that would show a way to go beyond culture and attempt to inhabit the heavenly places with regard to love?

Jesus's love innovation was to add a third category to neighbors and aliens. It seemed there was a loophole regarding people one was to love in the culture into which Jesus was born. The loophole was *enemies*. Presumably, all people who were not part of our group, our people, could be considered aliens and fall under the guideline for loving aliens as oneself. But a new category had come into being: enemies. If people were enemies, one did not have to love them as oneself. And how quick were Jesus's neighbors to turn aliens into enemies—perhaps even turn some neighbors into enemies (Mic. 7:6)? Enemies did not need to be loved but could be fought and persecuted and belittled and dismissed. They could be forced to submit, coerced into compliance. The pure pleasure of hate at last had an outlet.

Jesus innovated. He said enemies were to be loved. Here are his exact words:

> You have heard that it was said, "Love your neighbor and hate your enemy." But I tell you: Love your enemies and pray for those who persecute you, that you may be sons of your Father in heaven. He causes his sun to rise on the evil and the good, and sends rain on the righteous and the unrighteous. If you love those who love you, what reward will you get? Are not even the tax collectors doing that? And if you greet only your brothers, what are you doing more than others? Do not even pagans do that? Be perfect, therefore, as your heavenly Father is perfect. (Matt. 5:43–48)

Can you imagine the uproar? What if we were to say that Hindus and Buddhists and Muslims were to be loved, even as we love ourselves? Can you imagine the uproar? This is a radical teaching, a hard teaching. It is impractical to begin with, and . . . the arguments against loving one's enemies go on and on. Jesus's teaching on love for enemies has been argued and discussed and dissected for two thousand years. But it is still there, still the goal toward which we all—including all mission workers—strive.

The loophole Jesus taught against in the culture into which he was born is still with us. It is very nice to have enemies to not love. It is convenient. It is a nice pigeonhole into which we can stuff all kinds of our less-than-perfect behaviors. Instead of Baal worshipers and Babylonians and Samaritans and Romans—the enemies of Jesus's day—we have Jews and blacks and homosexuals and communists and Muslims. The loophole of Jesus's day is alive and well today. And so for us to pay attention to what Jesus did in regard to our enemies is very relevant mission practice indeed.

But today our sin in this area leaks out in other ways. In our culture, the culture into which we were born, we not only have a loophole we can use when it is convenient to avoid the commandment to love our neighbors as ourselves, but we have done something to love itself: we have trivialized love. In our culture love has become a synonym for sex; love has become the word of choice for any moderately positive feeling we might have throughout the day—for an ice cream cone, for sitting for a moment in the sunshine, for a new blouse or shirt.

It is a shame, really, this trivialization of love. It is not as if we do not have the resources in our cultural history that extol the virtues of love. Treatises and poems about love have filled tomes throughout human history. The Bible itself defines love in many ways, from the descriptions of human love in the Song of Songs to the new commandment to love as Christ loves in the Gospel of John. The everlasting love of God is described in the Psalms and contrasted to the fickleness of human love in the book of Hosea. In the Greek tragedies love is a cause of war; the Upanishads tell stories of the ruler Ramachandra seeking his beloved; romantic poets lament the fleeting emotions of this most mysterious experience. Friendship and affection become a focus of Aristotle's reflection on the good life and provide material for reams of greeting cards in the modern era.

Is it any mistake that hardly a wedding goes by these days that doesn't include a reading of the whole paean to love in 1 Corinthians 13? We have a sense and a longing for the real thing. But we read it as if it were an icon, a ritual that one must go through in order to tie the knot of marriage. Then we are bombarded the minute we step out of the wedding chapel with Madison Avenue trivializations of the word or newspaper headlines that list the people groups we can safely put in the categories of enemy, that is, the people we don't have to love as neighbors and aliens.

Jesus's mission innovation was showing us that love is the greatest thing. Love of neighbor means love of all people, even Samaritans, and if you want to enter the mission business, then get ready to love. Because you cannot do mission without loving the people to whom you tell the story.

JESUS THE MISSION THEOLOGIAN

One of the criteria for a person becoming a mission hero is that he or she must recognize that love is the key commandment. The eleven examples of mission heroes we chose to highlight in this book all recognized this. And thousands

213

of faithful mission workers we were unable to mention recognized it also. Mission begins and ends with love.

The paradigmatic teaching of this, of course, is in Matthew 22:34–40. Ironically it occurs in an unloving context. A group of experts in religious law, the law of Moses, who had become uneasy with Jesus's radical teaching got together and strategized on how to trip him up in public. Jesus answered by quoting the law of Moses right back at them, specifically Deuteronomy 6:5 about loving God and Leviticus 19:18 about loving neighbors:

> Hearing that Jesus had silenced the Sadducees, the Pharisees got together. One of them, an expert in the law, tested him with this question: "Teacher, which is the greatest commandment in the Law?" Jesus replied, "'Love the Lord your God with all your heart and with all your soul and with all your mind.' This is the first and greatest commandment. And the second is like it: 'Love your neighbor as yourself.' All the Law and the Prophets hang on these two commandments."

Notice that Jesus uses the term *love* here in reference to two relationships: the people to whom we witness, and God, about whom we witness. Loving the people to whom we witness can include many interrelational dynamics. Affection, service, sharing, mutual help, friendship, and communication geared to understanding can each be a part of loving those to whom we witness. God is the third party in this relationship. As our lives intersect with others, God is the focal point of our loyalty, the one to whom we witness. We want those to whom we are sent to discover and develop a loyalty to God. God becomes our common loyalty in giftive mission.

This is the key insight that mission workers must have. Look at the key relationships of the mission heroes of the past eleven chapters. Patrick loved the people of Ireland so much that he went back to tell them the gospel story, even though they had enslaved him for six years. From their earliest boyhood days in the marketplace of Thessalonica, Cyril and Methodius knew they wanted to give the gift to the Slavic peoples, whom they loved so much they devoted their lives to their service. Las Casas loved the Native Americans who were being decimated by his countrymen. Catherine Booth loved the poor—and the rich. Mother Teresa loved the sick and the dying. William Sheppard loved the Africans. Billy Graham loved the people of the twentieth century who lived under modernist conditions that seemed to make it easy to forget God. All of them loved the people to whom they were called, but they all put their love in the context of their primary love for God.

JESUS THE STANDARD

There is one more way of looking at Jesus's love innovation: to look at love as a Christian phenomenon. It is not, after all, as if Jesus had a monopoly on love. Human beings have been behaving with love toward their friends,

---

SIDEBAR 15.1
COMPARING MISSION WORKERS

Compare the views of the missionaries we have studied in part 2. For each mission hero, answer the following questions:
1. What is the mission hero's theology of God?
2. How does he or she view human beings?
3. What is this missionary's view of the world?
4. How important is the Bible to the mission hero's work? How did he or she use Scripture?
5. What is his or her eschatology? What is going to happen in the future?
6. How would this missionary describe the interaction between God and human beings?
7. What is her or his goal of Christian mission?

---

neighbors, strangers, and even, on occasion, enemies for all time. We don't have to resort to Christian literature to find moving portraits of human love of neighbor.

Yet part of Jesus's mission innovation was to make love of neighbor the standard against which all mission workers were to measure their successes and failures. And part of Jesus's mission innovation was to define what Christian love was over against human love. Christian love begins with a love of God; love of our neighbor is then a reflection of that primary love relationship. Christian love is Christian because it is rooted in love of God.

"'Love the Lord your God with all your heart and with all your soul and with all your mind.' This is the first and greatest commandment. And the second is like it: 'Love your neighbor as yourself.' All the Law and the Prophets hang on these two commandments" (Matt. 22:37–39). All our mission work hangs on these two commandments. Go and do likewise.

PART 3

Method

How Do We Do It?

The stories of missionaries throughout Christian history inspire us. Each mission hero highlighted in the previous section developed a way of sharing the gospel that reflected Jesus's way yet fit into his or her unique historical and cultural context.

How did they do that? What wisdom did they gain that helped each discover an innovative practice that furthered the cause of Christ in an alien situation? How did they arrive at their unique way of spreading the message of Jesus?

The stories make it clear that the insight each gained did not come to them instantly as they reached their mission destination. Quite a bit of learning preceded those insights. Patrick arrived in Ireland as a slave and had to escape before he could even think about forming a community. Bartolomé de Las Casas lived in the New World for years before he recognized the harsh consequences of the *encomienda* system. Mother Teresa taught school in India for some time before receiving her call to live among the poor.

The process of coming to the insight that helped each to develop a fitting practice of giftive mission may not have been the same for each missionary.

But we can identify some overall characteristics of the journey that inspired their innovative practices.

They each arrived on the scene with experiences they had gathered from their childhood, their social conditioning, and their culture. Reflecting on those experiences in a new setting is the first step in developing the sensitivity required for presenting the good news in a way that reflects the attitudes of Jesus.

The second step in the process of finding Christian mission practices that suit a particular context is to lay aside, temporarily, one's own cultural interpretation of life. Developing an appreciation of others—and the strange customs and religions of another place—requires a nonjudgmental attitude. Matteo Ricci didn't discount the philosophies and religions of the Chinese. He centered on Confucianism, studying it, finding the parts of Confucian teachings that were compatible with Christianity, and finally developing a rationale for utilizing Confucianism to spread the gospel. He could not have completed that process without bracketing his own convictions of what is valuable and important, his own ways of interpreting the world, his own cultural responses to concrete situations.

Now one is ready for the third step in the process of learning to do giftive mission: encountering the new culture and religion with an open attitude. The apostle Paul did not rush into Athens and begin criticizing the goddess worshipers. He did not castigate the philosophical seekers for their constant quest of some new and titillating idea. Instead he quoted their own philosophers and visited their temples. He showed respect for the unknown god that they worshiped.

Paul not only encountered the religion of the Athenians with openness, but he also evaluated their religion on the basis of his own understanding of God. This is the next step in the process of developing practices of giftive mission. Paul evaluated the religions of the Athenians according to what he knew about God. At this stage the convictions previously bracketed in order to encounter the other religion with openness are brought back into the dialogue. On the basis of that evaluation, Paul told the Athenians the gospel story, revealing to them the name of that unknown God, Jesus Christ.

The learning process culminates in an integrating phase in which the knowledge of the other culture merges in many ways with one's own interpretations of the world. New meanings are created, and the missioner finds a way to do giftive mission that fits both the gospel and the setting. Aquinas not only studied Aristotle's thought with openness, laying aside his own convictions for a time, but he also then evaluated Aristotle's thought on the basis of his Christian understandings. The integrated wisdom that he presents in his writings sets out a new way of looking at the world that is no less Christian but is broadened by his study of Aristotle. The limits of his thought have been expanded. He knows much better now how to present the gospel in ways that can be appreciated in his Greek-influenced world.

The process of learning described in this section deepens one's knowledge of oneself and knowledge of the other culture. It starts with reflecting on one's experience. It sets aside convictions and meets the new culture with an open attitude. Then it evaluates that new culture and religion on the basis of Christian understandings. Finally, it integrates new ideas and insights with original understandings. Giftive mission practices develop from participating in this spiral of knowledge, outlined in this section.

16

The Spiral
of Knowledge Acquisition

Learning about New Cultures and New Religions

The practices of mission described in part 2 move beyond competitive and cooperative endeavors, resulting in a form of mission that brings gifts both to the community encountered and to the messengers and their community. The missionary does not reach a point of exhaustion through perpetual giving while receiving little. Both communities give and receive gifts. By calling this process giftive mission, we stress the rewards received by both the messengers and the receivers.

Paul describes this process in 2 Corinthians 9. He encourages the Corinthians to give generously to support other churches and their work, indicating that such acts of giving will be rewarded. First, Paul says, when communities share with one another, all will have enough (9:13–15). Second, when people give to supply the needs of others, expressions of thanks to God overflow (9:12). In addition to those results of equitable sharing and praise to God, prayers for the givers of those gifts by the receivers will follow, and relationships between the communities will develop. "Their hearts will go out to you, because of the surpassing grace God has given you" (9:14). The results

---

SIDEBAR 16.1

PROCESS OF GIFTIVE MISSION—2 CORINTHIANS 9

In this letter to a newly planted church, Paul encourages the Corinthians to give generously to support other churches and their work, assuring them that they will also receive in this process. The results of this giftive approach will be many:
- When communities share, all will have enough.
- Thanks to God will overflow.
- Prayers for the givers by the receivers will follow.
- Healthy relationships between the communities will develop.
- God's grace will be received by the givers.

---

of giftive mission are themselves a gift of God, mirroring God's gift of Jesus to the world (9:14, 2:14).

The process can be thought of as a reciprocal relationship in which giving and receiving flow into each other, creating a synthesis of giftive mission. On the giving side, one becomes aware of the gifts one receives through giving. The missionary also develops the art of giving as a spiritual practice that includes sensitivity to the cultural forms of gift giving in a particular setting. A theology of giving as receiving then develops within that setting. For example, we find that we see Christ in the face of the poor, we begin to understand the theological value of suffering, or we discover serving is actually a path to fulfillment.

On the receiving side of the relationship, the missionary learns to express need. Rather than taking a stance of constant confidence or control, the giver learns to ask for and receive gifts. The dependence of the missionary on the community to which he or she is sent increases the interpenetration of giving and receiving. Although this sounds simple, it calls for a good deal of humility. Can a teacher really ask for help? It is difficult for foreigners to admit that they long for a taste of their home-country food, be it rice or potatoes. Showing need in appropriate ways prepares one to graciously receive gifts from the other—even as one is giving the greatest gift of all, the gift of the gospel. Expressions of need give power to the local community, allowing them to become givers in the situation. Developing daily practices of receiving gifts fosters interdependence with neighbors. It lifts up those in need by granting them the status of givers. Receiving a banana or a cup of water from a villager can spark an interaction that builds communication and begins to establish friendship between guest and host.

THREE BASIC CONVICTIONS

Three basic convictions, if acknowledged, provide the fertile soil in which giftive mission can grow and develop. First, *mission grows out of experience.*

SIDEBAR 16.2
THE RECIPROCITY OF GIFTIVE MISSION

Reciprocity: Receiving through both giving and getting gifts

GIVING	RECEIVING
Oneself as gift to others	Expressing need in context—dependence
Awareness of receiving through giving	Graciously receiving—others hold power
Giving as spiritual practice	Daily practices of giving and receiving result in
Theology of giving as receiving:	
See Christ in the poor	interdependence with neighbors;
Value of suffering	interdependence with the needy.
Serving poor as path to fulfillment	

Often lost in the modern missiological clamor to learn about other cultures and religions as a basis for doing cross-cultural mission is the recognition that faithful mission begins with a penetrating knowledge of ourselves. No one has objective knowledge of the world. Rather, our understandings are framed by our background and experiences. The personal experiences and "situated" knowledge that have shaped our social and religious reality also shape our approach to mission. Awareness of our own ways of looking at things sets the stage for interchange with others. Personal awareness makes room for mutual understanding and begins the giving/receiving process.

Second, *mission is two-directional.* The heyday of taking the gospel along with Western civilization to people in majority world societies (imperial mission) has given way to an era in which receiving missionaries and theological insights from non-Western sources is becoming increasingly common (reciprocal mission). Western missionaries receive insights from Christians in the communities to which they are sent. Western churches receive missionaries from Africa, Asia, and Latin America. Not only Christians in other places but people of other religions have gifts to share with Christians. Recognizing mission as a two-directional process fosters an attitude of openness to both people and ideas of other cultures, theologies, and religions.

Third, *mission is Spirit-directed.* God's Spirit moves people and works in the social structures of every culture and every religion. How God works in another society may not be readily perceived by the guest, the missionary from another culture. Believing that God's Spirit is working in that society enables the missionary to seek understanding of God's work in that place. Recognizing the work of God's Spirit in how people receive the story of Jesus,

223

SIDEBAR 16.3
CONVICTIONS UNDERLYING GIFTIVE MISSION

- Mission grows out of experience.
  My experience → New experience → Giftive mission practice
- Mission is two-directional.
  Christian missionary shares gifts. ←→ Receivers share gifts with Christians.
- Mission is Spirit-directed:
  God working in missionaries
  God working in culture/religion
  Christian seeing work of God in interaction

---

how communities organize worship and religious institutions, and how we ourselves are changed through the interaction with another culture and religion is crucial to giftive mission.

THE SPIRAL OF KNOWLEDGE ACQUISITION

Becoming a giftive mission worker may mean developing a new way of learning. It may be one of the most difficult things you have ever experienced. Many of us have been trained to learn in a one-way process, in the imperial mode. We have all the answers—isn't that what our education was all about? We understand the world perfectly—isn't Western civilization, the Western worldview, the peak of all human endeavors? We understand the gospel story perfectly and never need correction—how can we possibly be Christian mission workers if we are not perfect Christians?

The process of becoming a giftive mission worker grows out of mutual understanding with people of the new culture. The missionary moves toward that mutual understanding by progressing through five stages. Those stages recur, overlap, cross over, and merge with each other. Rather than being a static or linear set of prescribed actions, the process of acquiring knowledge of a different culture or religion moves dynamically, builds on intuitive insights, and continues to deepen and broaden through time and interaction between the two cultures. Rather like a spiral, learning and interacting with a new culture builds on past insights and reaches toward the unknown. That process moves us toward mutual understanding with the people to whom we are called, preparing us for engaging in giftive mission.

Although the process itself is fluid and dynamic, delineating five distinct stages can help us to identify and pay attention to crucial aspects of the interaction. Let us preview each of the five stages in turn. We will then discuss each in more detail in the next five chapters.

224

Stage 1: Recognizing and Understanding Our Past Experience

The missionary engaging people of another religion begins that interaction by recognizing his or her own experience. Those experiences include the influences that have shaped us, the features of our ways of understanding the world that are formed by our society, and the particular communities in which we have lived. By clearly articulating to ourselves our own beliefs and commitments, by understanding our preferences and convictions, and by understanding that those convictions are formed in our specific context, we prepare ourselves to recognize and appreciate the different features of another culture.

For example, some Muslim girls and women in Indonesia wear headscarves as a symbol of their devotion to God. Reflecting on a Christian use of symbols, such as wearing a cross or placing a Bible on the living-room table, might help us appreciate the religious importance of veiling to Islamic women. Without that reflection, it is easy to oversimplify the significance of Islamic veiling from a Western perspective as oppressive to women or as a form of government control.

Exploring our own culture and recognizing that our experience is not universal but is bounded by family views, social mores, Christian theologies, economic expectations, and other cultural influences is a first step toward valuing the differences we will find in another society.

Stage 2: Bracketing Our Convictions

The second part of the process is laying aside the convictions that result from the influence of our past experience. We do this so that we can meet the person of another culture with an open attitude. By "bracketing" we do not mean forgetting one's culture or devaluing our deeply held convictions or becoming theologically "soft" on our commitment to Christian truth. Bracketing one's convictions means, rather, a temporary setting aside of those formative features of experience that result in our particular point of view on a range of topics, in order to appreciate the different values and customs of another people. When missionaries encounter a strange custom, instead of immediately evaluating it from their own perception of Christian standards (or more often Western standards), they should attempt to accept the custom as a valued expression of the other's culture.

While living in Indonesia, Frances had to "bracket" her conviction that the best way to engage a colleague in conversation was to speak frankly and openly, maintaining a warm presence and making eye contact. The Javanese pattern of polite interaction differed drastically from this learned and valued custom of hers. In Indonesia it is polite to remain composed, make one's point indirectly, and avoid eye contact. If she hadn't set aside her valued style of conversation, she would have encountered not only resistance to her ideas but misinterpretation from her male colleagues, since making eye contact with someone of the opposite sex sends a dubious moral message.

Recognizing the cultural framework of one's experience and bracketing that framework in order to open oneself to the other culture are the first steps toward developing giftive mission practices.

Stage 3: Encountering the Other with Openness

Recognizing features of our own cultural formation allows us to see the different ways of others in a similar light. Their customs and habits are formed in communities and societies just as ours have been. Their symbols and rituals are formed in religious communities just as ours have been. Understanding the boundedness of our own culture and perceptions helps us open ourselves to the differentness of others. And of course, it also explains their attachment to their way of looking at things.

An open attitude forms the basis of learning about another culture and prepares the way for acceptance of people different from ourselves. Many times we judge practices to be wrong when they are merely different from our own practices. If we refrain from evaluating behaviors and rituals from our own point of view, we give ourselves a chance to truly understand the meaning of those actions as the people who participate in them understand them.

On a visit to the state mosque in Kalimantan, Malaysia, we noticed that, as in many mosques throughout the world, women are not permitted to enter the main worship level. As Western Christians, we might have immediately judged this custom as oppressive to women. Maintaining a more open attitude led to further investigation. We learned that the entire upper level of that mosque is reserved for women. Set apart from the intense midday heat of the tropics and the possible harassment of men on the streets, devout widows and poor women can rest and worship here. Because this custom of separation of women and men for worship differs from American Christian customs, we might have judged that Malaysian Islamic custom as inadequate or oppressive. Instead we found that this setting for worship and rest can be both normal and beneficial to Malay women. An open attitude gives the missionary a chance to understand the customs of another religion or society.

Stage 4: Evaluating through Reengaging One's Convictions

While openness to other religious ideas and customs produces knowledge and empathy, one cannot embrace every idea and practice of another culture or religion. Balancing periods of openness with evaluations of the meaning and results of the practices of others fosters mutual understanding while maintaining one's Christian identity.

At this stage one might ask where God's presence and work is evident in this culture. One has learned some of the perspectives and values of the other culture or religion. Using theological insights as well as the tools of social science, the Christian now evaluates the religious and cultural situation from his or her own perspective. Reengaging one's convictions, one now views the culture from one's own Christian perspective. In this process, the missionary can assess the values of the other culture and design ways to introduce the story of Jesus into the belief structures and societal mores of the people.

The indigenous belief in a high God, beyond the understanding of humans, helped one missionary to Africa reframe the gospel in terms that dovetailed with the religious beliefs of the people. Like Paul at the Acropolis telling people that Jesus revealed the unknown God (Acts 17), this missionary told villagers that the high God had sent Jesus to the earth so that people could understand the love and goodness of the God beyond human understanding (Donovan 2000).

At the same time, insights from the other religious practices and the customs of people of other religions influence the Christian. For example, the African practice of long religious meetings full of praise can become a positive influence on the missionary's views of worship. The sincere and specific prayers of Indonesian Christians may teach the Western missionary to rely more heavily on God in everyday affairs. The Buddhist practice of meditative silence can help the Christian learn a new attitude of prayer. The evaluative process reaffirms Christian identity and suggests patterns of growth while marking areas of religious need and outlining possibilities of creative connection.

Stage 5: Integrating Our Horizon of Meaning

As Christians begin to understand the situatedness of their own customs, encounter those of another religion or culture with openness, and evaluate that culture on Christian terms, change occurs both in the people of the other culture who interact with the missionaries and in the Christians relating to the culture.

The people are influenced by the story of Jesus as it is related to them in culturally appropriate ways. Their perceptions of wealth and poverty may change; their ideas about individual autonomy and social groups may be altered. Their views of the supernatural and how powers beyond human control relate to the world may change. They may openly accept Jesus as Savior. A church may be formed bringing new social forms and religious ideas to the culture.

The Christians are also changed by the character and forms of the culture they encounter. For example, missionaries returning to the United States after living in Java, Indonesia, may find that the value they place on polite, refined, and indirect communication has increased. They may depend less on frank communication and more on nonverbal cues. They may resist openly addressing conflict. In short, they have changed under the influence of refined Javanese culture.

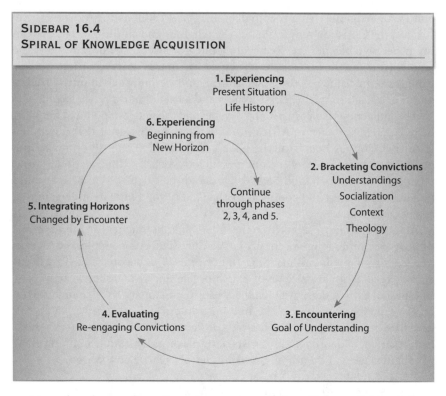

SIDEBAR 16.4
SPIRAL OF KNOWLEDGE ACQUISITION

1. Experiencing
Present Situation
Life History

6. Experiencing
Beginning from
New Horizon

2. Bracketing Convictions
Understandings
Socialization
Context
Theology

Continue
through phases
2, 3, 4, and 5.

5. Integrating Horizons
Changed by Encounter

4. Evaluating
Re-engaging Convictions

3. Encountering
Goal of Understanding

Mutual understanding about the customs of the religions of the missionary and the new culture can augment understanding of both religions. For example, Christians coming to Indonesia who immediately evaluate the Muslim call to prayer as a pagan rite will be disturbed by the loudspeakers that call Muslims to prayer five times a day, beginning before dawn. A missionary with an open attitude may respond with questions about the meaning of the call, explorations of how people in the community respond to the call, and discussions with Muslims about the place of prayer in their lives. Rather than a disturbance, the call to prayer may become a reminder to the missionary to seek God frequently as Muslims are calling themselves to prayer. And as Christians describe their ways of prayer, both private and communal, Muslims may discover that Christians are not as *kafir* (religiously coarse and inept) as they may have thought.

The meeting of two cultures can change people even when both parties are Christian. Those changes may be conscious or unconscious and are likely to be a combination of the two. Two Presbyterian congregations in the United States were asked by a Brazilian seminary to embark on a project to help rebuild the seminary curriculum. June and Jack Rogers, Presbyterian mission coworkers, went to the Institute for Theological Education of Bahia (ITEBA) to start the process. The seminary learned new methods of teaching and learning. Brazilian lecturers from ITEBA visited the two congregations and held lectures and seminars. The congregations learned about the African Brazilian culture in northeastern Brazil with its history of slavery and oppression. The process of mutual understanding necessitated that both parties examine their own past experience, bracket their points of view, encounter the other with openness, and evaluate their own convictions as the process developed. The result was a changed seminary, contextually oriented to Brazilian culture while biblically sound, and changed congregations in the United States, with an understanding of liberation theology from a Brazilian point of view. As mutual understanding grew, relationships developed. Brazilian and American Christians experienced joy in this new understanding of one another, and faith deepened on both sides.

The spiral of change continues. As the horizons of meaning of two cultures meet and influence each other, new experience shifts one's focus and changes ideas and habits. Social groups reform; societal mores are revised; social structures change. As mission groups and cultures continue to interact, changes in both societies and both religions occur. Based on our new understandings, we develop new practices, giving gifts to one another.

The next five chapters outline this spiral of knowledge acquisition, focusing on the steps involved in each stage and how they overlap and influence one another. Studying this process can help us see how the story of Jesus becomes woven into the lives of peoples and cultures. As mutual understanding grows, relationships develop with people from another society. Religions and cultures also expand through this process of knowledge acquisition. The process will enable us to formulate new practices of giftive mission appropriate to our new setting. That positive result will revitalize our Christian faith as we learn to witness to our own beliefs and grow from contact with people of other religions.

17

Experiencing

The Influence of Our Personal Histories

It may seem a bit odd, selfish even, to begin exploring how to go about doing giftive mission by talking about personal experience. But it is not at all odd in the Judeo-Christian traditions and the ways we have appropriated them. For example, Christians read Psalm 139 with delight. We experience a sense of comfort as we ponder the many ways that God knows us. "O LORD, you have searched me and you know me" (v. 1). The psalmist goes on to enumerate the details of that knowledge: "You know when I sit and when I rise; you perceive my thoughts from afar" (v. 2). "Before a word is on my tongue, you know it completely" (v. 4). "You hem me in—behind and before" (v. 5). "If I go up to the heavens, you are there; if I make my bed in the depths, you are there" (v. 8). The psalmist believes that God's love for us finds expression in thorough knowledge, and in that we take comfort.

We find knowing ourselves in the same deep ways rather difficult. Often we act in ways we don't understand. Sometimes we mistake our own cultural style or social conditioning for a deeper expression of personality or values. Sometimes we do the opposite: mistake our personal uniqueness for cultural influence. We often consider the ways we do things to be the best or even the only acceptable ways. Becoming aware of our cultural conditioning and

---

How can I know myself better?
1. Begin by reflecting on the ways that God knows you:
    Knowing you before you were born
    Knowing your daily habits
    Knowing your thoughts
    Knowing the things you say
    God's presence in your life includes knowing you thoroughly. How can you begin to know yourself better?
2. Next, reflect on the following influences that helped shape who you are:
    Inherited characteristics from your parents
    Family influences and patterns of interaction
    Social influences from where you grew up and where you live (location)
    Economic status of your parents and yourself (class)
    Influence of society (culture)
    Education
    Church life
    Personality traits
    Each of these influences had an impact, both positive and negative, on your life.
3. Now, make a list of the values you have adopted due to the above influences.

---

personal idiosyncrasies is important as we seek to understand those of other cultures and religions.

WHY KNOWING OURSELVES IS DIFFICULT

If we embark on an encounter with another culture without a thorough knowledge of ourselves and the history, culture, values, and genes that have shaped us, we encounter two major difficulties. First, we may mistake our own cultural views as the true and only way to understand the world or present the story of Jesus. Beliefs and customs of others may automatically be dismissed as ignorance. Ways of expressing and practicing Christian faith that are unfamiliar may be labeled heretical. Communication with those we are trying to understand breaks down if differences are judged instead of explored.

Second, we may lose our distinctive way of understanding ourselves and our faith by overidentifying with either our own or another cultural group. Forgetting the importance of our own cultural framework to our practices of faith, we may lose our particular cultural and Christian focus. Attempting to embrace all facets of another culture may result in a loss of meaning and values in our own lives.

To avoid those pitfalls, we need to begin the mission task with personal reflection. Reflecting on our experience, the ways that we understand, and

---

SIDEBAR 17.2
LOSS OF MEANING

Paul Rabinow argues that the cultural anthropological approach of attempting to affirm all values of another culture is not possible without a loss of meaning. As one attempts to embrace contradictory values, one cannot hold any value as universally good. This leads to a nihilism that denies all values.

Read his "Humanism as Nihilism" (1983).

---

the sources of that understanding becomes the first step in developing giftive mission.

QUESTIONS TO ASK OURSELVES

We can begin this process by asking a series of questions in five categories (see sidebar 17.3).

A relationship with a person of another religion, a neighborhood in proximity to another faith community or place of worship, an interreligious family background, a curiosity about different cultures, a *kairos* moment, or a sense of calling are all examples of experiences that might engender interest in other religions. For example, when the woman at the well, whose story is told in John 4, encounters Jesus, she has a moment of insight. She sees her life clearly; she recognizes Jesus's knowledge of her and care for her. As this *kairos* moment affects her, she becomes excited about sharing her faith with a community in which she doesn't fit easily. She runs back into town declaring, "Come, see a man who told me everything I ever did. Could this be the Christ?" (John 4:29).

Separations that are part of a call to a particular mission may include not geographical distance but separations from friends or distance from one's

---

SIDEBAR 17.3
SIXTEEN QUESTIONS

Questions about who I am

1. *Who am I* as a messenger of good news?
2. How do I understand the salient *features of my personality?*
3. What *community* do I spring from, and how has that community shaped me?
4. What *talents* do I bring to the mission enterprise?

Questions about my convictions and values

5. What are the *convictions* and distinctive points of view that I bring to the mission enterprise?
6. What *values* do my convictions represent?
7. What are the *sources* of those convictions?

Questions about goals

8. What *goals* do I bring to the task of Christian mission?
9. Why am I *committed* to those goals and not other mission goals?
10. How are my goals connected to my *convictions*, values, and sense of identity?
11. How do I intend to *fulfill* those goals?

Questions about my experiences

12. What salient *experiences* have moved my life toward an interest and commitment to Christian engagement with people of other religions?

Questions about separation

13. What must I *leave behind* to follow the call to this particular mission?
14. How do I feel about the *separations* I may face, perhaps from family, community, and/or nation?
15. What *resources* for nurturing myself and my faith will I look for in my new setting?
16. How will leaving behind facets of my life encourage me to *change?*

---

comfort zone of ideas, everyday routines, economic lifestyles, or cultural behaviors. What resources for nurturing myself and my faith will I look for in my new setting? How will leaving behind facets of my life encourage me to change?

WHO AM I? IDENTITY, COMMUNITY, AND CULTURE

Theologians through the ages have mused on the nature of the self and its relationship with God. Perhaps our individual personalities have been known to God since before we were born (Ps. 139:13). Perhaps God holds an image of each one of us (Ps. 139:15–16). Or maybe the self changes as we interact with God (Ps. 139:3, 19–24).

Identity for contemporary people presents additional complexities. Charles Taylor argues that the self is not only personal and identifiable; the modern self is social and corporate. Taylor's work *Sources of the Self: The Making of Modern Identity* (1989) analyzes historical events, intellectual and social trends, values, and religious sensibilities in terms of their impact on the individual's sense of self. He argues for a moral component to that socialized self. People make strong evaluations about what they value, he claims. Those moral evaluations, made within societies through social interaction, also shape individual identity. For North Americans, values of the goodness of liberty, equality, fraternity, and justice shape not only our society but our individual sense of self.

That view holds implications for one's understanding of one's self, God, and other cultures. But Taylor presents only one of many contemporary theories that shape the sense of identity that we hold. Arguments about the essentialist versus the social self (A. Smith 1982; Mead 1934), analyses of cognitive versus relational development patterns (Kohlberg 1981; Gilligan 1993), and the relation of those and other theories to Christian faith (Fowler 1995; Taylor 1989) bring the many facets of self-understanding to our attention.

The situation is further complicated by theories of the self presented by modern societies that are not Western. Christian theologian Roland Chia (2002) argues that Singapore's experience of modernity has been uniquely shaped by its recent origins and survival-oriented, pragmatic policies. Furthermore, although identity issues have been pondered philosophically in many societies,

---

SIDEBAR 17.4
EIGHT QUESTIONS FOR REFLECTING ON IDENTITY

1. Where were you born, into what ethnic community and stratum of society? How have your ancestry and social location influenced you?
2. How have your family and social community, including extended family, friends, and social groups, influenced your sense of self and direction in life?
3. How have the schools you attended and the peer groups you joined shaped your personality? Describe the result by listing the major features of your sense of self.
4. Describe the influence of religion in your life, including personal experiences, studying religions through books, and/or friendships and church communities in which you have participated.
5. List all the ways that you think being a North American (or a Singaporean or a Canadian or an Australian or whatever) has shaped you as a person.
6. Describe the unique things about yourself that you believe are part of your personality and will remain unchanged through interaction with another culture.
7. Outline areas of your sense of identity that you believe will change through cross-cultural interaction. Include things that you think can benefit from interaction with another culture.
8. How has the story of Jesus become part of your own life story? Recount your journey of faith to this point in your life.

not all the cultures involved in Christian mission are modern societies that have developed theories of identity.

Consequently, although some understanding of theories of identity can be helpful in the process of self-reflection, a thorough knowledge of all the theories isn't necessary for doing Christian mission. What is necessary is recognition of key features of identity theories commonly used in one's culture, since it is through the lens of those theories that one's self-understanding develops, and self-reflection on the question of identity fosters deeper self-understanding.

CONTINUUMS OF IDENTITY THEORIES

Some common parameters of personal identity have emerged in the literature of self-understanding. The parameters of self-definition in a particular society influence how one is expected to interact with others. And on that question, societies differ markedly. Outlining the continuums of identity theories helps us process the different expectations of individual behavior that we may encounter in another culture. Where do you and your society fall on the following continuums?

Individualism—Communalism

The basic unit of social interaction may be the individual or the community, depending on the society. The agrarian nature of ancient Chinese society, for example, along with Confucian teachings, has resulted in an emphasis on family and clan membership as a key element in a person's identity (Hu Wenzhong and Grove 1999, 1). Since the advent of psychology as a field of study in late nineteenth-century Europe, Western theories have focused on the individual and how relationships and social groups influence the individual and his or her sense of identity. That individualistic emphasis has reached China as globalization and the market-economy model influence Chinese society. A recent return to teaching Confucianism in elementary schools shows the contemporary search for balancing those identity theories in China today.

Another example of the movement between individualism and communalism in understanding identity can be seen in Indonesia. In that traditionally communal society, individualism is sometimes seen as an insidious part of westernization that should be avoided. One of Frances's Indonesian doctoral students, concerned about the dominance of men in Indonesian society, decided to study psychology to better understand *bapakism*, the power of the father figure. She wanted to develop a counterbalance to Freud's male emphasis with a study of the role of the mother in family life. Locating her studies in the family, rather than focusing on the individual, illustrates the communal orientation of Indonesian society. Yet, a study of the role of mothers, of necessity, deals with individual mothers and their relations with individual fathers. The heavier weight of social identity and one's position in the community, in this research, had to be balanced with the importance of individual agency of women in family life (Adeney 2003a).

Is your personal outlook influenced more by individualism or communalism?

Belonging—Independence

The social location of the self in Western theories is explored in many ways, but the stress has been on an autonomous and independent entity. This contrasts with theories of the self that focus identity mainly on the social group or even the nation. "I belong to Pakistan," a student began her paper for an evangelism class. That statement indicates a distinct difference from many self-oriented North American views. The student did not seek to explore the *question* of belonging. Rather, she *assumed* belonging as her starting point.

Recent studies by Carol Gilligan have challenged the individualistic stress in decision making, particularly for women. Rather than make their ethical decisions on the basis of a continuum that puts individual autonomous decision making at the top of a hierarchy of maturity as Kohlberg and others have argued, her research shows that women make decisions in the context of important relationships in their lives (Gilligan 1993; Kohlberg 1981).

Belonging in Pakistan, as Frances's student illustrated, is centered on the national community for Christians and Muslims alike. This student believed that she was destined to do evangelism in Pakistan because she belonged to her country. Even though one can be executed for converting to Christianity in Pakistan, this student will return to her country and seek ways to bring the story of Jesus to her people while avoiding that disastrous consequence. She is committed to that path because her sense of identity is bound up with her nationality.

After God, to whom do you belong?

Achievement—Ascription

Many Western theories of the self emphasize achievement. A faith in progress combines with evolutionary views, producing stage theories of development (Fowler 1995), hierarchies of human needs (Maslow 1994), and a myriad of self-help theories. Firm believers in change, many Americans add to this a bootstrap theology that believes in the individual's ability to change himself or herself.

Those theories contrast with social theories of the self that posit self-identity as a response to the actions of others. George Herbert Mead (1934) and Archie Smith (1982) both focus on that interactive component of self-development. Systems theory in psychology and pastoral studies also emphasizes the social dimension of self-identity.

SIDEBAR 17.5
CONTINUUM OF IDENTITY THEORIES

Identity theories may place primary importance on the individual or on the group. Some theories emphasize accepting a given role in society depending on the social status of the group and the place one holds in the family. Others emphasize individual autonomy and the importance of socialization in developing one's ability to choose a life path. Societies therefore vary in their emphasis on which behaviors are appropriate for an individual depending on where their emphasis falls on the following continuums:

Individualism ←→ Communalism
Belonging ←→ Independence
Achievement ←→ Ascription

Bringing these more communal theories into play is important as one moves into another culture. Using personal achievement to effect positive change is a philosophy that is not appropriate for certain kinds of relationships in some cultures. That perception of individual change and achievement in social life stands in contrast to the Chinese view, for instance, that the chief determinant of relative power is seniority. The older sibling has more status; the older person's comments in a meeting carry more weight. Younger people defer to older ones, and severe social sanctions may be applied to those who disrespect those guidelines (Hu Wenzhong and Grove 1999, 7). Indonesian society, in many instances, bases honor on one's ascribed status, as a grandmother, for instance, or as a member of a highly respected clan, or as an inheritor of a particular vocation. Some religious communities in the United States, the Amish and the Plymouth Brethren, for example, also rely on age and gender qualifications for undertaking community leadership. Understanding both ascription and achievement orientations as cultural influences fosters understandings of social relations and self-improvement attitudes among people of different cultural backgrounds and religions.

Is your personal development influenced more by your own efforts or by the group(s) with which you associate?

Recognizing that individualism, belonging, and achievement (or communalism, independence, and ascription) form a nexus of assumptions on which personality theories develop is crucial for Christians planning to work in another cultural setting. If one can see that those assumptions are developed in societies and are peculiar to particular ways of understanding identity, we can perhaps begin to fathom the differences regarding identity presented by other cultures.

By reflecting on our own views of identity, belonging, and location in social structures, we begin to understand ourselves in relation to our own culture. In this reflection process, we might focus on the influences that have shaped our emphasis on individuality or communal identity. We might explore a personal sense of belonging or a strong pull toward independence and investigate its sources. We might examine our ascribed status in a particular setting, contrasting it with areas of achievement and explore how those influences form a sense of possibility for personal growth and change.

These questions not only help us to understand our own sense of self and place it in our social location, but the same questions also can aid reflexive understanding as we ask them of another person or culture. In chapter 19 on encountering the other, we will frame questions that aid understanding of the cultural forms through which others understand their identity. We will ask the same questions of adherents of other religions we encounter: how do *they* evaluate the importance of individualism and community, belonging and independence, and achievement and ascribed status?

Of course, we value our own ways of doing things, and that is as it should be. As we think about how we understand ourselves, how we fit into our communities, and how we interact with roles that are ascribed to us and areas of life in which we strive to achieve, we can evaluate our own strengths and talents. Perhaps you are a good observer and will quickly attune yourself to the characteristics and preferences of others. Maybe you are skilled in social graces, able to make others feel comfortable and accepted. Or your talent may be an ability to process and compare differences between one culture and another. Thinking about what you may be able to bring to an interaction with those of another religion helps prepare you to take on the role of listener and guest in another milieu or that of gracious host in your own.

HOW ARE MY VALUES CONNECTED TO MY CONVICTIONS?

We usually take for granted the values that generate our convictions. We may not articulate our values clearly, and most of the time we don't try to identify their sources. We think little about the broader concepts that underlie our values and link them together. When we make ethical decisions, we don't always identify the intellectual, social, practical, and affective influences on our choices.

Yet the values we hold form an important part of identity and greatly influence our experience in life. Although we may think that our actions are logical or natural, our choices are influenced by a number of factors: authorities we trust, principles we hold, the ends or goals that we believe are good for ourselves and our communities, the context in which we operate, our everyday behaviors, and our own character, even our genes.

When values clash, some people assert religious reasons for their convictions; others appeal to communal sensibilities; still others rely on individual choice. Most values occur in multiple societies, yet the overall pattern, the hierarchy

238

of values and the emphasis on the value of certain goods over others, differs greatly from one society to another.

Hu Wenzhong and Cornelius Grove identify three fundamental values of the Han Chinese, an ethnic group that makes up more than 90 percent of the Chinese population. Collectivism, which began in the interdependent life of agrarian society, was strengthened by the policies of the People's Republic of China. Large power distance, a concept that refers to the extent to which people in a society accept the fact that power is distributed unequally, also characterizes the Chinese. The ascribed status of older people is only one among many factors that lead to a tolerant deference across lines of unequal social status and authority. A third fundamental value of the Chinese is intra-group harmony. Like people in many Asian societies, the Chinese avoid overt conflict in interpersonal relations. Maintaining harmonious relationships with family members, close friends, and colleagues is of supreme importance to the Chinese, who comprise almost one-quarter of the world's people (Hu Wenzhong and Grove 1999).

A very different set of core values characterizes North American peoples, according to Charles Taylor. Individual evaluations of the good are important to the Canadian and United States societies that Taylor addresses. Human rights, another individual value, also rank high among this group. Justice and equality among communities, exhibited in values of antiracism and equal opportunity, are also basic values in the modern West according to Taylor (1989).

Comparing lists of values from the Han Chinese and the Canadian/United States Caucasians reveals the variance in basic convictions about the good. This example highlights the importance of understanding our own values and their cultural/historical sources when we begin to interact with people whose history and culture differ markedly from our own. We encounter this situation when we engage people of another religion.

As a Western Caucasian woman from the United States, Frances values individual decision making, gender equality, and direct communication in social

---

SIDEBAR 17.6
SOCIAL VALUES: COMPARING CHINA AND THE UNITED STATES/CANADA

HAN CHINESE VALUES	UNITED STATES/CANADIAN VALUES
Filial piety; tolerance of others; humility; observation of rites and social rituals; kindness (forgiveness, compassion); wealth; industry (working hard); harmony with others; loyalty to superiors; reciprocation of greetings, favors, and gifts (Hu Wenzhong and Grove 1999, 7)	Individual moral evaluations, human rights, liberty, equality, fraternity, justice, democracy, antiracism, equal opportunity (Taylor 1989)

interactions. If she interacts with a Chinese Buddhist, she will encounter a different set of primary values that stress the good of the group, harmonious relationships, and humility in social affairs. Those different primary values lead to different points of view on what constitutes a good conversation. Convictions about how to behave in concrete situations also differ. Understanding her own value structure helps her to *recognize* and respect difference rather than react as though the Buddhist is just wrong. She can lay aside her convictions temporarily in order to learn from and appreciate the values of a Chinese Buddhist. This "bracketing" of convictions will be taken up in the next chapter.

SOURCES OF VALUES

Identifying the sources of our values can aid us as we encounter different values held by those of another religious or cultural group. By understanding the source of a conviction we hold, we can compare it to the convictions and sources of another's value. The assumed "naturalness" or logic of our own appraisal reveals its cultural bias in this process. And that helps us see our own values in a more relative light, opening the way for us to learn appreciation of another's point of view. Let us examine five important sources of our values: authorities we trust, principles we hold, the ends or goals that we believe are good for ourselves and our communities, the context in which we operate, and our own character.

Authorities

As children we learn to look to authorities to guide us in our choices. Parents and teachers tell us what is good, how to behave, and what to value. As adults we participate in this socialization process, helping our children learn values and proper behavior. We also expand the authoritative sources to which we appeal. Religious texts and rituals, historical figures, philosophers, political leaders, community mores, and the voice of our own wisdom and conscience become authorities in our lives. Instead of spending energy on every decision, we turn to these authoritative sources to help us live in a consistent and upright manner. People of different religions and cultures appeal to authorities that may offer different counsel than the ones to which we appeal.

Compare these two proverbs: "Be sure you're right—then go ahead," and "When two men are one in heart, they will get the strength to cut metal with ease." The first, a maxim of Davy Crockett, American pioneer and folk hero, appeals to an inner authority and shows the virtue of self-reliance. The second, a Chinese maxim, appeals to unity between two people and shows the virtue of consultation and discourse. Neither is "right" or "wrong," but each appeals to a different authority.

Religious texts and leaders provide authority for strong evaluations in most societies. Muslims derive dictums of family law from the Qur'an. Christians appeal to the Bible to frame their notions of marriage. The different lifestyles that arise from these religious authorities may be difficult or impossible to reconcile. Understanding their source in religious authority, however, helps people to be more understanding of the customs of others.

Besides internal authority, authority in relationships, and religious authority, other authoritative sources may be operative in the development and maintenance of values. Social institutions, political forms, and even economic authorities come into play as a community makes strong evaluations about its life. Protection of the rain forest may not be as important to an Indonesian villager as it is to an affluent American college student. The authority of economic need influences both of their views. Freedom to speak out on issues of gender equality may not be as important to a fundamentalist Christian in the United States as it is to a post-Taliban Muslim woman in Afghanistan. The institutional authorities that have influenced their lives and the changes in those authorities inform the strong evaluations made by those women.

Principles

Many people hold strong principles on which they base their actions. Ideas of fairness, retribution, compassion, and equality are a few examples. Principles may be developed in different settings, as part of a religion or as part of a national identity, for example. Some Christian communities, such as Mother Teresa's sisterhood in India and World Vision, have been known to emphasize the principle of compassion. Some Buddhist communities, such as the Tibetan Dalai Lama's group, are known for acceptance of diverse ideas. Others are centered on right living, such as the Soka Gakkai Buddhist community. Building national character based on secular freedoms, as in France, or on religious purity, as in Iran, also shows how principles can become a source of religious or national values.

Holding principles as a source of values implies a universal value. If something is right or good in principle, it is not culturally or geographically limited but is considered right or good for all people at all times. The principle of just retribution held by the policeman in the novel *Les Misérables* became such a central part of his identity that he could not go on living after Jean Valjean, the "criminal," was shown irrefutably to be a good man. Being a person of principle implies a consistency of behavior that rests on unchangeable ideas of what is good and right.

Because of this universal understanding of principles, they offer a stability and consistency in the value judgments of individuals and communities. They are clear, identifiable, and implementable ideas that undergird morals. Broad principles such as justice or respect for elders can be drawn upon to help communities develop specific good actions acceptable to everyone. Most cultures

241

and religious groups value multiple principles but are often characterized by an emphasis on one or two.

Sometimes those principles are misunderstood through a facile interpretation by a person from a different religion or culture. Equality, for example, can be understood as a principle that ensures an equal voice for everyone in a community. Sometimes that principle is projected onto communal societies or religious groups. Because everyone has a voice in a Society of Friends meeting, for instance, this does not mean that the voice of a youth is equal to the voice of an elder. In fact, an elder's voice may be the definitive one in coming to the "sense of the meeting." If we don't understand the hierarchy of power in a communal setting, we may project equality of voice onto the community when another principle is more primary. In the case of the Friends, the voice of the Holy Spirit is considered the primary voice, and it is heard most forcefully in the opinion of the elder members of the community.

Goals

Aristotle associated the goal, or "end," of action with moral reasoning. In his *Ethics*, he argues that reasonable thought about a subject includes reflecting on the end or goal of the idea or project under consideration. As individuals and communities gear their actions to good results, human well-being results.

Consider how thinking about the end results of an action helps you to make good decisions. If you have three exams coming up in the next week, you may decide to study late on Saturday evening rather than visit with family or friends. Your decision rests not on principle—exams are more important than family and friends—but on goals: you want to do well on all three exams.

Rarely is the result of an action the single consideration in making a moral decision or deciding how to act. For example, if you see a young child fall into deep water at a swimming pool, you may automatically jump in to rescue the child. This decision is based on the result: saving the child from drowning. But it may also be connected to principles: the value of human life, for instance, or the special claim that the weak or innocent have to the aid of able members of society. The person who jumps into the pool to rescue a child doesn't take time to reflect on the sources of the good act. Those sources make their impact quickly and mainly unconsciously, showing how deeply connected we are with the sources of our strong moral evaluations.

If the goals or ends of action become the sole consideration, decisions may become morally confused. For example, if one chooses only profit in business as the end to which all behaviors are oriented, unfair business dealings, lack of community and family life, and poor working conditions for employees may result. Considering religious and social authorities as well as ethical principles in addition to the goal of building a profitable business makes for a healthier enterprise. "The ends do not justify the means" is a maxim that illustrates this point.

Context

The context, the particular setting of the business in the above example, also influences the moral sources relevant to making business decisions. The surrounding community with its history and culture contributes as a source of valuing. If the profit motive is the goal of a collective, rather than a single business owner, that would make a difference. If the context was one of abject poverty in which profits would be equally shared, good working conditions and community/family life might become secondary considerations to making enough money to feed people. Would that poverty also mean abdicating the principle of integrity in business practices? How far does context go in changing one's perspective on principles?

When thinking about context as a contributing source of values, it is sometimes difficult to separate oneself from one's milieu. When my (Frances's) oldest daughter was fifteen years old, she went on a choir trip to New York City. When she returned home to Berkeley, California, she declared, "I always thought Berkeley was the center of the world, but now I know about New York!" Understanding the shared viewpoints and attitudes of one's community may require "leaving" that community in order to recognize the unique points of view held by one's own group. This can be done through studying other texts, viewing films, meeting people from other cultures, visiting nearby religious sites, and learning about other contexts without geographically removing oneself from one's context.

H. Richard Niebuhr has said, "We are in history as a fish is in water" (1967, 48). In a similar way, we are in our cultural and religious context. Understanding how that context influences our values requires effort to disengage from that context and then look at it from a new perspective. What has your study of other cultures and religions shown you about how your own society and religion influence your values?

Frances had an Indonesian student from Sumatra who came to Java to study. After a few weeks, she said that she had begun to realize that Sumatran Christians were more *terus terang*, frank and open about their opinions and needs. Javanese, she continued, were more indirect, relying on nonverbal cues to communicate dissatisfactions to others. This student valued open discussion of disagreements because of her culture of origin and the context of the Batak Christian community of Sumatra. The Javanese Christian with whom this student was sharing an apartment instead valued a refined and indirect form of communication that avoided direct confrontation. Was one better or more moral than the other? Each student's context had shaped her moral sensibilities about handling conflict in different ways.

243

Character

Added to this growing list of sources for individual and community values is the character of the individual. Whether our character is shaped mainly by environment and socialization or whether we primarily inherit character traits is a source of debate among social scientists. Whether nature or nurture is the primary source of our character, how one's character influences everyday behavior and ethical decisions and shapes our values is the issue we want to address here.

Honesty, harmony, fidelity, integrity, and courage are a few examples of character traits that become sources for values. Aristotle advanced the idea that character is developed through practicing certain actions over and over again. By acting in the same way consistently, we develop habits that shape our character. To become courageous, one must act despite fear. To become honest, one must tell the truth in small and large matters. To become prudent, one must act repeatedly in careful ways. Developing everyday practices that reinforce one's values builds our character.

Chinese wisdom advocates similar patterns to develop character. "Fighting is a test of courageous spirit." "The virtuous are unbeatable." "Frivolity leads to a lack of strategy." These maxims display the same values of courage, honesty, and prudence, showing how they may be fostered by repeatedly choosing the virtuous action.

GOALS OF MY MISSION TASK

Another important area of reflection on our own experience is how we understand our task as people who desire to interact with those of another faith. Various goals of Christian mission and the reasons for those goals have been explored in chapter 3. Reflecting on your own and your community's choice of mission goals and examining how those goals are connected to your values and identity can lead to a deeper self-understanding.

Where do your mission goals fall on the "wipe them out" versus the "do nothing" spectrum of approaches presented at the beginning of this book? Are your goals for Christian mission attuned to a Trinitarian view, or are they more Jesus-centered? Do you take a service orientation to mission, or are your goals more focused on a witness through words? How do your mission goals fit with your church tradition, your values, and the kind of person you are now and are striving to become? Articulate for yourself your particular mission task in interacting with people of another religion.

Many factors have probably influenced your viewpoint of the mission task: a sense of calling by God, your church tradition, your congregation's understanding of mission, a curiosity about other religions, and many more. If your goals include an emphasis on giving and receiving from others, you are making a commitment to giftive mission.

In organizing this book around practices, we have focused on day-to-day lifestyle choices that influence both character and community. A commitment to giftive mission involves an acceptance of the formative power of those everyday practices. As we develop those practices in our lives during our interaction with people of another religion, we both bring and receive gifts. Both the giver and the receiver are changed through the process. That change becomes both the source of and one of the reasons for the commitment to giftive mission.

Mother Teresa's Sisters of Charity remind themselves daily that the giving they do allows them to become recipients of God's grace. They make promises of obedience, chastity, and poverty, and yet they feel free, fulfilled, and wealthy. These sisters take a fourth vow, to meet with the poor as a path to spiritual fulfillment. They claim to see the face of Jesus in the face of the dying on the streets of Calcutta. They believe that suffering has redemptive value. They receive spiritual gifts through giving. Not the least of these gifts is a sense of deep gratitude for life and for the poor.

The other side of giftive mission is receiving. Becoming a receiver, indebted to others, is difficult for people of means or those who wish to feel independent. Learning to receive from those the missionary serves allows true interdependence to grow between the missionary and those of another culture or religion. It is important to ask for what one needs as long as it is something that can be provided in that setting. Asking poor people for money would be inappropriate. But asking for a place to sit down, a drink of water, or an occasion to dialogue are appropriate requests. Learning to receive graciously what the community can provide balances the power between the giver and the receiving community.

When Mother Teresa left the Loreto convent to live on the streets of Calcutta, she went through the city streets asking for a room to live in. Four Muslim brothers named Gomez gave her a second-story room above their flat. Here she could lie down in safety and begin her ministry with the poor. When she was hungry, Mother Teresa would leave the Gomez family a note asking for food. She was never disappointed. These expressions of dependence on the people of Calcutta opened many doors for Mother Teresa's work with the poor. Later, when other sisters had joined her and a larger place was needed, another Muslim man sold a large house to the Sisters of Charity for less than the price of the land. He said, "This house was given to me by God, and now I am giving it back to God." Mother Teresa's expressions of need and willingness to receive began the process of giftive mission that allowed this person from another faith to serve God in his own way.

Learning to graciously receive and becoming aware of the gifts one receives through giving sets up a dynamic process that allows trust and mutuality to grow between the missionary and the people of another religion. The missionary is enabled to serve a community that welcomes and interacts with him or her. Both parties are enriched as they receive gifts both through giving and accepting gifts.

CONNECTING MISSION GOALS TO VALUES AND IDENTITY

If the process of giftive mission described above resonates with you, you might reflect on how that dialectic relates to your sense of identity and your values. Are you oriented to relationships? Do you value mutual sharing? Are you looking for a deeper spirituality in your life? Does keeping connections with your church as well as making new friends seem important to you? Answering these questions for yourself can help you shape the kind of giftive mission that will feel comfortable to you. It will also prepare you for some of the jolts you will experience as you leave behind familiar ways and engage a new culture.

For example, one of the qualities of giftive mission practiced by Mother Teresa was a practice of staying connected to others around the world. She did this by including them in the mission. She learned about a person's particular interest in her work with the poor. Then she outlined ways that the person could serve the mission. It might be through participating directly, praying for the mission, providing needed items, or even suffering with a personal illness. Explaining how each of these tasks served the mission of the Sisters of Charity, Mother Teresa formed a global network of coworkers that expanded her work exponentially.

This part of her work necessitated a love for people, an understanding of the breadth of God's work with the poor, an ability to communicate clearly and frequently with people far away from the mission, and good recording and accounting skills. Your talents may lie in this area or in another. How can your skills be used in giftive mission?

Looking at your own gifts and talents is one side of the coin. Identifying the gifts you are receiving from those you serve is the other. If you highly value your own spiritual growth, you will want to look for the spiritual gifts you receive from those you serve. Mother Teresa has written of many examples of her experience with receiving spiritual gifts from those she served. If you are oriented to achievement, you may receive great satisfaction from working on a project with people in the community. If you enjoy leadership, the appreciation of a congregation in another cultural setting may become a gift to you.

As you go through this reflective process, your attention may be drawn to formative experiences that have shaped your identity, values, and orientation to giftive mission. Perhaps you were raised in a cross-cultural setting. Maybe your parents practiced different religions. A *kairos* experience that gave you a sense of being called by God to mission may be important in your life. Clearly framing those salient experiences in your mind and thinking about their centrality in your life will be important later when your sense of connection to the mission work becomes strained by culture shock and cross-cultural misunderstandings.

The Israelites were reminded by God through the prophet Jeremiah to remember their salient experiences with God. Remember how God brought you out of bondage in Egypt. Remember how God delivered you from your enemies. Tell these stories of deliverance to your children. Make a habit of retelling them as you walk with your children or sit around in the evening. These reminders can help those who practice giftive mission today. Living in a foreign country or entering a strange community can be a disorienting experience. Telling ourselves the stories of our Judeo-Christian heritage can encourage us. Reminding ourselves of how God has put us there, and how God has delivered us in the past, can help us through the rough times.

WHAT WE LEAVE BEHIND

Embarking on a mission project or sustained interaction with people of another religion means that we are leaving many things behind. We choose to exit our comfort zone and enter the world of another. This may mean moving across the ocean, putting our children in different schools, learning a new language, and appreciating new customs and foods. Or it may mean entering a community nearer home through interaction with neighbors, participation in community activities at a nearby temple or mosque, and making friends who are considered strange by people in our primary community. In either case, it will involve trying to understand the sacred texts of another religion and learning to see the world from a different perspective.

It is not easy to anticipate the things we will miss as we place ourselves in close contact with a strange and new culture. Sometimes things don't seem very different in the new place. England, for instance, seems similar to the United States to many North Americans who travel there. But a few months at

---

SIDEBAR 17.7
WHO IS MY NEIGHBOR?

The well-known parable of Jesus found in Luke 10:33–37 describes the reactions of religious people to a person who has been attacked, robbed, and hurt on a lonely road. Jesus tells this parable in response to the experts in the law who wanted to test him and show their own righteousness. The story illustrates how cultural/religious views can be so limited that the values of the religion itself become obscured. Both the priest and the Levite walk by the beaten and needy one. But then we see a view from *another culture* that illuminates the value of loving one's neighbor. The Samaritan, whose people the Jews believed were less holy than they, embodies the value of love of neighbor forgotten in the Jewish cultural milieu. The story shows how giftive mission works reflexively—in cross-cultural interaction we are giving *and receiving* the gospel.

SIDEBAR 17.8
WHAT IS MOST IMPORTANT TO ME?

Identify the ten most important values in your life. Articulate your point of view about that value. Identify the source of the value. The first example is done for you.

VALUE	POINT OF VIEW	SOURCE
1. Daily prayer	Prayer keeps me in touch with God.	Bible: Paul's letters; church teaching; family life
2.		
3.		
4.		
5.		
6.		
7.		
8.		
9.		
10.		

Cambridge University showed Frances how very different the social expectations for professors were. Frances's children learned how different the language and customs of British schoolmates were. They even had to learn to drive on the "wrong" side of the road.

While we can't anticipate every disruptive change, we can prepare ourselves for dealing with certain "deficiencies" in our new situation. If our mission destination is far from home, we will miss family and friends. Even if we aren't geographically separated, as we immerse ourselves in a new community we will find the lack of friendships trying at times.

Christian ideas differ from context to context, but the differences among them are not as great as the differences that we will encounter as we engage people of other religions in their own settings. Reflecting on your experience in all these ways prepares you to understand what you must hold at bay if you are to encounter another religion and culture with openness.

18

Bracketing

Putting Convictions on Hold

Recounting our experiences and recognizing the influences that have shaped us show us both the limits of our knowledge and the richness of our personal resources. The learning process begins not with universal knowledge but with the experiences we have accrued in our life. We test that accumulated experience by adding new experiences that either confirm or correct the conclusions we have drawn from our experience up to that point. What our experience has taught us is valid, until a new experience causes us to reassess our knowledge. That reassessment becomes the basis for evaluating future experiences. In this way, we build our store of knowledge, confirming and correcting, always changing it as we go along.

Realizing that we constantly revise our knowledge through processing new experiences prepares us for learning something new. We become better able to entertain the idea of changing our views on a certain topic. We begin to question and test our knowledge against new experience. Often what we learn does not meet our expectations. We may not encounter what we expected in a new experience. But whatever we gain from that experience changes our orientation. The new knowledge we gain through it changes us.

This process teaches us a lot about ourselves, about the perceptions that we held and how they change by encountering a different view of things. If a new

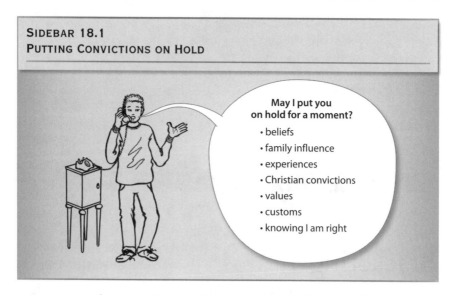

May I put you
on hold for a moment?

- beliefs
- family influence
- experiences
- Christian convictions
- values
- customs
- knowing I am right

experience confirms our view, we deepen our trust in the way we have perceived that subject. On the other hand, when new experiences disconfirm our former view, we see more clearly how our former understanding was shaped by our past. We revise it. And we understand ourselves better in the process.

The next step is to free our grip on the way we understand things right now. Holding too tightly to our own convictions can hinder our ability to understand another point of view. It can prevent us from listening to others whose viewpoint differs from our own. It can result in a defensive attitude toward people of another religion or culture. Rather than viewing it as an opportunity to learn, we can perceive the difference in the customs and rituals of others as a threat to our own understanding or even to our identity. Those attitudes stop the flow of communication and the self-corrective process of learning through experience.

To avoid that impasse, the next step toward engaging those with different beliefs and habits is to temporarily lay aside those convictions. This chapter will demonstrate the necessity of putting one's convictions on hold, outline ways to do that, and explain how laying aside one's convictions results in positive give-and-take with those different from ourselves.

REASONS FOR LAYING ASIDE ONE'S CONVICTIONS

It may sound strange to suggest that people who have given their lives to Christian mission should lay aside their convictions as they meet those to whom they were sent. Even though this bracketing of convictions is a temporary stage, an intentional withholding of judgment for purposes of seeking understanding, it is still awkward. Being willing to go through this process of withholding judgment about the customs and beliefs of others, however, brings positive results that far outweigh the temporary discomfort we experience.

Consider four reasons for putting convictions on hold.

1. To communicate the story of Jesus effectively, an *understanding* of the worldview, attitudes, and convictions of the people one engages is essential. If one's own convictions are not laid aside, evaluation of the other's customs is made so quickly that an understanding of the other's convictions is blocked. The depth of beliefs cannot be explored, complex reasons for behaviors elude the missionary, and appropriate language and metaphors for introducing the gospel story escape notice.

2. A willingness to listen and understand the other's convictions and customs leads to *communication* about those beliefs by the people in the culture. If, on the other hand, they feel morally judged by a foreigner's religious convictions, they are likely to cease explorations of their own. The salient problems that the story of Jesus could address in that culture or religion remain hidden.

3. *Relationships* are built through conversation about deeply held values. As people sense a true interest on the part of visitors from another culture or religion, those conversations can develop into friendships. The practices of fellowship and love, discussed in part 2, can be enacted only if Christians do not barricade themselves behind walls of judgment about the values of those whom they have come to serve.

4. *Contextualization* of the gospel can occur only within the culture itself. Understanding the cultural forms and religious expressions of the people allows the contextualization process to occur without judgment or intervention by Christians from another society. If the missionaries do not lay aside their convictions, they cannot see the value in the cultural forms of the religion or society they encounter. Appropriating the story of Jesus into those cultural forms, as the people accept that story and make it their own, is complicated by the shallow understanding of the missionaries. Outsider Christians can resist contextualization in conscious and unconscious ways if a true understanding of the values and beliefs of the society is not developed.

LOCATING UNDERSTANDING IN CULTURAL FORMS

Although our own ways of doing things seem natural and right to us, we are sometimes unaware just how connected to our experience and socialization those habits are. Sociologist Peter Berger (1990) suggests that most of our knowledge is formed in our social location through interacting with our community and our environment. He describes how societies construct social worlds of meaning. This process creates a world of meaning that later seems natural and unchanging and becomes incorporated into the structures of thinking and reflection of individuals. The realm of religion is particularly subject to this process as religious ideas are formed, communicated, acted upon in communities through rituals and religious practices, and internalized in thoughts, prayers, and conceptions of the divine.

Jesus repeatedly attempted to show those he met that the cultural forms as well as many of the values of the people were not exclusive ways of worshiping God but had developed in societies. He explained to the woman at the well that both Samaritan and Jewish forms of worship were not absolute but relative to their situation. "A time is coming," he said, "when you will worship the Father neither on this mountain nor in Jerusalem . . . but in spirit and truth" (John 4:21, 23).

Although Jesus told the woman that the Jews had knowledge of the object of worship, his point was that God seeks worship by those who seek spirit and truth. Once freed from humanly devised rules of worship, worship becomes a well of living water, springing up in each heart. Religious symbols and rituals are essential to religious worship, but they do not totally encompass God, the object of worship.

Just as the Jews and the Samaritans began to worship in places that held special meaning for their social groups, so various Christian forms of worship developed in response to historical situations. The church where Calvin preached in Geneva was deliberately plain to correct what Calvin saw as excessive attention to images in the Christian worship of his day. The simplicity of many Protestant churches today reflects that radical change. Both the artistic images and the reaction of simplicity are cultural forms, developed in specific situations to express worship to God in ways that were thought to be right and good.

Our own experience of Christianity has been shaped by those or other cultural forms. That wealth of experience, lodged in Christian traditions, predisposes us to perceive things in a certain way. What we hear and see in interaction with others is closely related to how we have experienced our religion in our own community. Experience prepares us to see and learn. But experience also *directs* our learning. We see the world *through* the eyes of our experiences and the cultural forms that shaped those experiences.

When learning about something new or strange, past experiences can get in the way. Because of our past, we view the new topic from a particular point of view and with a certain set of predispositions. Consequently, we see a certain portion of the subject: we weigh its components in a fashion consistent with our own perceptions.

As we project our own experiences on theology in this way, we quickly evaluate the worth and veracity of the topic according to our own standards. We may not even "see" with any clarity the ideas or practices presented to us. We are "blinded" by our own pre-texts—the sum of our experience and the predispositions that experience has effected in us.

> ## SIDEBAR 18.2
> ## THE PROCESS OF MEANING MAKING
>
> *Berger (1990, 3—28)*
>
> Meaning is constructed through world-creating activity, a dialectical process between human collectives and the material world.
> 1. Humans are born into a world of meaning.
>   - Humans are unfinished at birth.
>   - They inhabit an open world and are not totally governed by instincts like other mammals.
>   - Therefore, humans are born into a world of possibilities.
>   - Humans in a world are produced by that world.
> 2. Yet, at the same time, humans produce a world of meaning through a give-and-take process of world construction.
>   - Externalization: Humans create meaning and structures of society.
>   - Objectivation: Created meanings become external to humans and have power over them.
>   - Internalization: Human productions seem "natural" and inform structures of consciousness.
> 3. The result of this process of world construction is culture, the totality of human products.

Jesus understood this when he spoke to the Jews about a new and radical way of being religious in his own day. He told the would-be followers of this new way that they could never understand it, could never enter the kingdom of God unless they became "as little children." Little children do not have much experience. They have not had time for narrow views or disappointed expectations to filter and direct their perceptions. Little children have fewer obstacles standing in the way of learning new ideas or trying a new path or life direction. Their lack of experience allows them to open themselves to new ways of looking at things.

As adults we, in contrast, have learned much through experience. We have practiced our faith and honed our understandings of the world in ways that have produced knowledge and wisdom. But at the same time, we have developed filters that pattern and structure new experiences that we encounter. Some of us have been taught that all religions other than Christianity are spurious or even idolatrous. Some of us have negative impressions of a particular religion or even a particular Christian denomination. Such prejudices will hamper our ability to understand another religion.

Prejudices of a more positive kind may also deter us in our search for understanding. Firsthand knowledge of the goodness of God, who cares for each

253

person and has shown care to us, may block our understanding of a religion that sees, not God, but emptiness at the center of the universe. Unless we find a way to open ourselves to other ways of seeing things, we will be unable to perceive that other religion accurately or appreciate it fully. And if we cannot understand the other religion, we cannot understand those who practice it. Both learning and communication cease. We see instead our own reflection, a predetermined pattern of understanding created by our experience that may have little to do with the way of life we are trying to understand.

We cannot go back and undo our experiences. Without the faith that Jesus spoke of, we cannot become as little children, as Jesus suggested. The best we can do is consciously attempt to lay aside what we have learned through our experience and encounter with fresh eyes the "other" that confronts us. We bracket our prejudices. We intentionally lay aside the filters our experience has generated. This includes the ways we understand our own religion, the things we appreciate about our own culture, the values that our own society has taught us, and the expectation that whatever is valid will conform to our own views.

It is important to note, however, that this laying aside of our convictions is an ideal, something we attempt but do not expect to reach. We learn only by projecting a set of convictions on the world and seeing whether our experience confirms or rejects them. By attempting to bracket our prejudices, we hope to allow what is being communicated by others to reach us. But we never totally succeed in laying aside our own views. Nonetheless, repeated attempts to do so, along with a growing awareness of our own pre-texts, can aid us in perceiving more clearly the parameters and meaning of the beliefs and practices of another religion.

OBSTACLES TO LAYING ASIDE OUR CONVICTIONS

Understanding the cultural-conditioned nature of many of our religious rituals and customs frees us to explore the religions and customs of others without fear. We understand that we are not bracketing God's power or reality. We are not bracketing truth. We are not removing ourselves from God's care. We are not rejecting God's goodness or the wisdom that we have been given. In temporarily laying aside our convictions, we are putting on hold the socially constructed forms through which we understand God and the world.

This general recognition, however, does not break through the many barriers to bracketing our prejudices that stand in our way. Let us look at three major obstacles confronting us as we try to lay aside our convictions.

Prejudices as Lenses

It is difficult to examine our pre-texts when it is *through* those viewpoints that we understand our world. We bring meanings—be it a text, a religion, or a personal encounter—to our new situation. Those "foremeanings" form the

---

SIDEBAR 18.3
PREJUDICES

Gadamer (2005, 267–71, 351–56)

Hans-Georg Gadamer defines the term *prejudice* as the sum total of our experiences and the predispositions or attitudes that this whole body of experience has influenced us to adopt. He points out that the term *prejudice* did not have a negative connotation before the Enlightenment. With the rise of the scientific method, which attempts to ascertain "objective" truth through experimentation, the term *prejudice* took on a negative connotation. "Subjective" knowledge, gained through experience, did not attain the universality to which the scientific method aspired. Therefore "prejudice"—knowledge gained through experience—was relegated to an inferior status. Gadamer argues, however, that understanding through experience is the primary way of attaining knowledge of the world.

---

backdrop against which we assess the content of what we encounter. Without them, we would not be able to focus on important aspects of our new situation or judge their influence on the total picture. Yet, by looking through them, as a pair of glasses, we see the new text in a particular way.

The foremeanings that are crucial to understanding Christianity may differ from the lenses we need to understand Taoism, for instance. The Chinese maxim "Try to protect society from dangers when alive. Die a heroic death to illustrate the Way" is probably incomprehensible to a teenage Christian girl living on a farm in Iowa. The foremeanings that she brings to the text—perhaps of the importance of diligence in providing food to the farmhands or patience with the hardships of a long winter—hinder rather than help her in understanding the meaning of the text. If her projections are too far off the mark for understanding the context and content of the maxim, she may become frustrated or interpret the text in a way that bears little resemblance to the intended meaning.

The nearer our projections come to the foremeanings in the text, the fuller our understanding will be. Becoming aware of the lenses of meaning that we look through, though difficult, can greatly advance our understanding of a strange text or situation. Our task in understanding the text must be geared to the framework of meanings of the text itself rather than to our own foremeanings. This second step of analyzing the context and content of the text or new situation itself can best be accomplished if we are aware of our own set of foremeanings and attempt to bracket them as we encounter the text.

Prejudices as Part of Our Identity

The convictions we hold are not merely ideas but form part of our identity. Attempting to lay them aside may engender fear or a sense of confusion. Who am I without my treasured convictions about Christianity? Will bracketing my convictions lead to a loss of faith? Will my understandings of Christianity become syncretistic?

These fears are normal and need to be addressed. We can rest assured that God will not abandon us if we decide to look at another religion with as much openness as possible. The bracketing process is an attempt to see another religion more clearly rather than to reject our Christian faith. The process of understanding not only moves through the spiral of knowledge acquisition, but all its phases operate simultaneously. Thus even when we are trying not to evaluate on the basis of our foremeanings, that evaluative process is working in the background as part of our learning experience. The bracketing task merely mutes the evaluative exercise, giving us a chance to understand the foremeanings of the new context.

We can expect to be changed by our contact with another religion and culture. But our identity will develop in concord with our Christian faith as the encounter with the other produces self-understanding. We will see ourselves in a new light after our interaction with people of another religion. We will understand our own Christian faith better. Some aspects of our theology may change. But no text or community can take our identity from us. Rather, we grow and change in and with God, as Christians, no matter where we are or what texts or communities we encounter.

Prejudices as Community Values

Our socialization patterns us to see the world through the eyes of our culture and religion. Our communities are heavily invested in our success in passing on that tradition of values. By bracketing our convictions and becoming open to the values of others, we may feel that we are betraying our community and even our faith. Not attempting to influence the values of another religion— even listening to them without correcting them—may leave us with a sense of wrongdoing. We may feel that we are compromising our integrity by listening to the values of others.

How does an African Christian appreciate the Islamic sharia law that states that a man may take up to four wives? How does an Indian Christian listen well to the Hindu doctrine of seeking sensual pleasure as a religious task? How does an Indonesian Christian respond to the village shaman's custom of blessing the water used to make Coca-Cola? In considering these and similar questions, we need to understand that bracketing does not mean giving up our treasured values. Bracketing is not *practicing* values that are at odds with our Christian convictions but only putting aside our convictions long enough to really *hear* another point of view.

New experience often gives one the sense that "something is not what we supposed it to be" (Gadamer 2005, 354). That very experience of dissonance helps us to see more clearly both our own point of view and that of the other. By bracketing our pre-texts, we give the voice of the other a chance to be heard.

Bracketing our convictions as a mission community may not be possible in every situation. In reflecting on his mission work in Africa, Vincent Donovan stated that "the church is destroying the possibility of mission by its own structures and restrictions on missionizing" (Donovan 2000, 7). Donovan felt that he was prevented from putting aside his cultural prejudices, that he was hindered from evangelizing by church strictures, that he could not "hear" the questions and perspectives of the Africans he encountered because of the form in which the Christian message had been structured over the past two centuries.

We too may encounter resistance to bracketing prejudices in our communities. The church or mission society that sends us to another culture may place restrictions on the kinds of activities in which Christians may participate with people of different religions. Or there may be pressure to preach or plant churches before the missionary has a chance to "hear well" from the people. There may also be pressure from Christians in the new community to remain separate from people of "the other religion." Sensitivity to both of these communities is necessary in the process of bracketing pre-texts.

How to Bracket Prejudices

How can we "break the spell" of our foremeanings that so strongly predispose us to see things from a certain perspective? Often the new situation itself brings us up short, shocking us into seeing the difference between our own predispositions and those of the other. Certain customs may seem "meaningless" to us. Or the meaning that we perceive may be contrary to our expectations. In either case, the shock of recognition that we did not find the meaning that we expected can help us identify and then bracket our own prejudices.

When this occurs, we do not need to forget the content of our own ideas but rather must recognize them and see how they predetermine our interpretation of the text or situation. Becoming aware that a certain childhood experience, or a particular pattern of socialization, or a point of view that we learned in our own culture makes the text or situation we meet seem incomprehensible or reprehensible provides a clue to what we need to bracket. For example, an Indonesian Christian woman seeing an American woman on the beach in a scanty swimsuit may be startled. She may immediately assume that this woman could not be a Christian because of her immodest attire. Alternatively, an American Christian woman, seeing a veiled Indonesian Muslim woman, may assume that she is oppressed by her religion. These opinions are based not on the situations but on the foremeanings constructed in the communities from which the two Christian women came. If, after the shock of misunderstanding, each became aware that the cultural meanings of her own context might not be applicable in the new situation, they could bracket their pre-texts and begin to learn the meaning of swimsuits or veils for the women they are observing.

To begin to learn the meaning of the other's behavior, the learner needs to *remain open* to the many possibilities of meaning that present themselves in the situation. Different meanings are possible. Wearing a swimsuit might indicate a permissible freedom of movement for a sports activity, or it might show a cultural activity of sunbathing, which may be new to the Indonesian. Wearing a veil could indicate religious devotion, or it might signal recognition that the person belongs to a particular religious community. Keeping our prejudices at bay allows us to situate our reinterpretation of the text or behavior in relation to the whole of our own meanings. Although the Indonesian woman has a dress code that the American woman does not uphold, she may be able to reinterpret the meaning of the American woman wearing a swimsuit into her realm of meanings for sports or cultivating personal beauty. Although the Christian woman may be shocked by a veiled Muslim, she may be able to reinterpret her understanding on the basis of her own devotion to God or acceptance in a church community. Remaining open to other meanings and reinterpreting the text within one's whole range of meanings can aid us in understanding the other.

Another way to break the spell of our foremeanings is to *ask questions* when misunderstandings arise. Clarifying the meaning of the action on the other person's terms helps us reinterpret the action in a way that suits the intention of the other rather than conforms to our former prejudices. We must take care not to ignore the actual meaning of a text or topic until it breaks through our imagined meanings. Rather, by bracketing our prejudices when misunderstandings arise, we can prepare ourselves for the text/other to tell us something.

Finally, we can recheck our foremeanings to conform with the things themselves. *Constantly reassessing* perceived meanings is part of the learning process. The meaning of an action may differ from one situation to another; the meaning of a text may differ from one religion to another. Putting ourselves in a new situation and learning from new experiences involves this constant process of reassessment.

As that reassessment recurs in our examples, the Indonesian Christian woman will become more tolerant of the swimming attire of the American woman. The American Christian will see a devotion and sense of belonging in the veiling of the Muslim woman. When people use the occasion of being startled by the strangeness of the other to become aware of their own prejudices, remaining open and reassessing their knowledge on the basis of other possibilities, the result is greater understanding between the cultures. At the same time, interpretations that are truer to the situations from the viewpoint of those doing the action result from this process of bracketing and remaining open (Gadamer 2005, 267–70).

Gadamer (2005)

When we have a new experience, we come to it with perceptions that we have acquired through past experience. Like looking through a set of glasses, these "foremeanings" and pre-texts tell us what is important. Gadamer claims that interpretation begins with those foremeanings. But those meanings are replaced by more suitable ones as the process of understanding and interpretation progresses. As one's expectations are not met by a new experience, one revises the foremeanings or projections that were formerly used, replacing them with different meanings that conform to the new experience (267).

As new experience corrects our foremeanings, we become more open to other new experiences. G. W. F. Hegel asserts that conscious experience should lead to a self-knowledge that no longer has anything other than or alien to itself. Without going that far, Gadamer claims that the person of experience becomes radically undogmatic and better equipped to have new experiences and to learn from them. Openness to new experience, then, is made possible by experience itself (355).

WHAT SHOULD WE BRACKET?

How can we identify those convictions that are culturally formed by our experience and lay them aside? Here are several important areas to consider.

Obvious Differences

Some of the more obvious differences include modes of dress, behavior, attitudes, values, forms of community, patterns of authority, political organization, laws, and customs.

Dissonance Signaled by the Culture

These are cultural cues that our behaviors and attitudes are inappropriate, for example, students indicating to Frances that walking fast and perspiring in Indonesia was not appropriate for a woman professor. Ways of behaving that seem incomprehensible to us might be relationships to older and younger family members or to persons of different status, economic class, or religion that differ drastically from the way we normally interact.

Internal Warnings

Sometimes we sense that our views are interfering with our ability to understand the ways of the culture we have entered. This is the shock of recognition that we described above. For example, questions about ways of thinking: Why either/or, not both/and? Why monogamy, not polygamy or polygyny? Or, alternatively, feelings of discomfort with expressing our views may alert us to the need to bracket them, for example, requesting communion with wine in a situation where alcoholism is a social danger or asking for grape juice in a place where it is not available or the cost is prohibitive.

Religious Differences

Bracketing our beliefs when other beliefs are dominant in order to gain an understanding of the perspective of others can be difficult but is worth the effort in the long run. Indonesian Christians believe in spirits that can both help and harm individuals and communities in their everyday life. As a missionary in Indonesia, Frances was initially unaware of this belief among highly educated Christians. When she indicated openness to considering belief in the reality of the spirits herself, graduate students and professors began telling her their stories of spirit encounters. It wasn't until she bracketed her own prejudice, based on the scientism of the West, that she could begin to explore the real views of spiritual forces held by Indonesian Christians.

POSITIVE RESULTS OF BRACKETING

Realizing that our own point of view is influenced by our experience and personal history, we attempt to set it aside in order to better understand the people to whom we are called to minister. The positive effects of this bracketing process are significant, impacting our understanding, our communication with others, the relationships built, and even the process of contextualizing the gospel in our new setting. Let us explore each of those in turn.

Understanding

If we are constantly using our own standards to evaluate the way others understand their religion, the point of view they take on cultural issues, or their way of behaving in everyday situations, we miss a lot. By putting aside our own convictions, we open the door for a deeper understanding of the ways of others.

We may first have to reach a point where we realize that we don't understand the other's point of view. Hearing a Buddhist explain reincarnation may leave us, as Christians, puzzled. To hear a Muslim speak of jihad may leave us unnerved. To grasp the reasons why a Hindu may pour milk on a statue, explaining that this is an offering to a particular god, may lead to a sense of discomfort on the part of the Christian. Our own Christian convictions block our understanding. We dead-end in our attempts to understand.

Frankly admitting that we don't understand—that our response to the beliefs of others may be discomfort—can be the beginning of a truer understanding of the other's point of view. Zali Gurevitch, in working with Palestinians and

Jews, found that realizing that they didn't understand each other's position could become the beginning of meaningful interaction (1988, 1179–99). In such situations we begin to ask ourselves, "What do they *really* think? How do they *actually understand* land ownership, the process of reincarnation, jihad, or offerings to their gods? I don't get it. But, I really do want to understand."

Openness to another's point of view takes deliberate effort, a sincere desire to temporarily set aside one's own beliefs in order to gain understanding. When Frances lived in a Muslim neighborhood in Jakarta, Indonesia, she was surprised when her Muslim neighbor took offense at seeing her Bible on the floor next to her low bed. After her neighbor explained the holiness of the actual written text of the Bible, part of which is included in the Qur'an, Frances could read the Qur'an with a new attitude. Now she could understand not with her mind only but also with her emotions—she "got it" that the Qur'an was the holy word for her neighbor Masooma. More than a book, the Qur'an, for Masooma, was a physical embodiment of the words of God. With this new attitude, Frances could read more openly, ferreting out the holy meaning. Setting aside her own understanding of how God speaks in dialogue with humans in the Bible, she now tried to literally "hear God speaking" in the words of the Qur'an. She understood better why Muslims did not consider English versions of the Qur'an the literal words of God, how Arabic, the holy language, must be understood to really hear the words of God. And she made sure to keep her Bible off the floor.

Communication

That experience led to better communication with Masooma. She invited Frances to sit in on her after-school class, where she taught children from the International Pakistani School of Jakarta to read Arabic. The class took on new meaning for Masooma as she saw Frances's appreciation of her work to instruct children in the language of her faith. And Frances's openness to Masooma's explanation about why the Judeo-Christian Bible should not touch the floor somehow opened both her understanding of Masooma's view of Holy Scripture and her willingness to communicate with Frances more of her beliefs and religious practices. It was not that Frances hadn't known that Arabic was the holy language of Islam. Of course, teaching the children Arabic was important to Masooma. But as Masooma shared its importance with Frances not only verbally but by including Frances in the daily teaching practice, the importance of Arabic to her as a Muslim became more clear.

Relationships

Relationships can deepen from bracketing one's point of view and opening oneself to understanding the other from her or his point of view. As understanding deepens, communication opens up, and relationships are thereby developed. Masooma and Frances began to have conversations about their beliefs. Masooma began to share with Frances the foundation for her generous hospitality. When she took in her servant's sister who was out of work, Frances warned her that this could become a long-term situation that might strain her family's financial resources. Masooma replied with a smile, "Food and shelter do not belong to me." They are given by Allah and belong to him. "I am not sharing what is mine, but what belongs to God," she said. Frances could not imagine Masooma speaking to her in so personal a manner about her religious convictions had Frances not showed openness to how Masooma perceived the world, even being willing to be chastised by Masooma about leaving her Bible on the floor and accepting her invitation to attend the afternoon Arabic classes. Those incidents began a process of learning about Islam and Pakistani culture for Frances. They also led to a deeper relationship with Masooma, who soon declared that she would be Frances's "mother" in Indonesia since her own mother was far away in the United States.

Contextualization

Deepening relationships with those of another religion and culture opens the door to discovering the metaphors that might be most apt for communicating the gospel. God goes before us into another culture. God's wisdom can be found in many aspects of another religion. Those points of contact can become the links that lead a person or a community to find the pearl of great price, to embrace the gospel, and to find life in Christ.

Discussions with Masooma over the course of a year ranged over topics of work, home, family, and religion. Frances learned to make Pakistani tea and to participate in the customs of tea drinking with her husband and children. She shared her kitten with Masooma's daughters and learned why cats were not allowed in Masooma's house. They talked of Jesus and the differences in how their religions understood his life and work. After Christmas, Masooma asked Frances if she could have her Christmas cards. She said she liked them, especially the pictures of Jesus.

Was the gospel being contextualized for Masooma? Did her view of Jesus change over the course of this friendship? In this case we don't know. What we do know is that the gospel was preached, not in one-way communication but in giftive mission, not in words but in actions. The most important of those actions may have been Frances's openness to really listen to Masooma's point of view, to lay aside her own way of looking at culture and religion and open herself to Masooma's way, to receive her hospitality, to respect her role in her religious community, and to appreciate her religious convictions as she herself understood them.

19

Encountering

Learning from a New Culture and Religion

Reflecting on our experiences and our gifts and setting aside our convictions prepares us for encountering those of another religion. We are preparing to do giftive mission. We are ready to listen and discover the questions of meaning that arise from this new context. Rather than jumping to conclusions or judgments, we will focus on trying to understand.

If we realize that all our knowledge is seen through the lens of our experience, it may be easier to understand the views of people with different backgrounds and experiences. What we know is interpreted through our foremeanings. What others know is interpreted through the lens of their perspectives, through their foremeanings. Understanding is always interpreted understanding, knowledge that points to universal truths but sees them partially.

As we seek to understand people who are different from ourselves, we do well to remember our overall objective. Whatever our specific mission objectives—teaching, social service, evangelism, church planting, or serving a congregation—the overarching modus operandi of Christian mission is love. The second commandment, to love our neighbor as ourselves, weaves its way through the biblical text. Learning the way of love, both human and divine, becomes a central part of the mission task.

We cannot love without understanding—without *knowing* the people we serve. Communication that focuses on mutual understanding becomes part of the way we learn to love the stranger. In this kind of communication, we use human reason not to control, build, or exploit the relationship, but to foster understanding. The resulting action is action between *subjects*, people who have value in and of themselves.

In the sixteenth century, Sepúlveda thought he could prepare the Indians in South America for the gospel by conquering them. Subduing them would make them more receptive to the love of Christ, he reasoned. But Sepúlveda did not know the Indians. He didn't learn their language; he didn't explore their culture; he didn't respect them as human persons. Because he lacked understanding, Sepúlveda could not love the Indians or show them the love of Christ. Sepúlveda used a pragmatic kind of reasoning to argue that the indigenous peoples must be conquered to prepare them to accept Christianity. He didn't use reason to foster his own understanding of the Indians and their culture.

The kind of reason geared toward understanding will set the stage for loving practices. That "communicative reason" can be used in a cross-cultural situation or with a strange text as well as in one's own context. Communicative reason seeks to understand for the sake of interacting with the other. Jürgen Habermas contrasts that communicative reason with technical reason, which is communication that seeks to achieve or control (see sidebar 19.1).

For example, as an ethicist, Frances studies Aristotle's *Ethics*, not to alter, use, or manipulate it, but primarily to understand Aristotle's point of view. She approaches the text with the confidence that what Aristotle describes will be *valid* for his audience. She thus becomes part of Aristotle's audience. She trusts that his judgments will be *right* and suitable for his context. She believes that Aristotle is *sincere* in presenting his discourse. Those assumptions of truth, rightness, and sincerity underlie communication geared to understanding (Habermas 1985).

As we encounter another religion or a strange community, we strive for communication that yields mutual understanding. We can assess our ability to reach this goal by examining our assumptions. Do we accept that the truth expressed in this text is valid for the people to whom it is addressed? Do we trust that the values communicated are suitable for that group? Can we count on the sincerity of the author or community to which we are called?

For example, as a scholar of religion, Terry studies the life and teachings of Siddhārtha Gautama Buddha, not to alter, use, or manipulate them, but primarily to understand his point of view and the point of view of those who follow the Buddha as a religious outlook. He approaches these texts assuming that those who have followed the teachings of the Buddha for 2,500 years have a valid outlook on life, one that has produced some good in their lives. He trusts that Gautama's judgments were in important ways right for the context of fifth-century BCE India. He believes that the Buddha was a sincere teacher of religious philosophy. By making those assumptions, Terry understands modern Buddhists better and puts himself in a better position to communicate with them—to tell them the story of Jesus in a way that appeals rather than repels.

Christian missionaries need to struggle with these presuppositions that are so important to developing mutual understanding. In the last chapter we

---

SIDEBAR 19.1
HABERMAS ON REASON

The hermeneutic philosophy of Jürgen Habermas developed out of the critical school of philosophy in Europe. He followed Max Horkeimer and Theodor Adorno in arguing that the European tradition of reason led to unreason. What was the European tradition of reason?

Aristotle's dimensions of reason—theoretical, technical, and practical—were separated by Immanuel Kant, who developed different criteria for each. Separating technical reason from practical reason allowed individuals to choose their own ends, deciding which goals they would work toward, without the necessity of appealing to any moral authority. This allowed Enlightenment thinkers to separate themselves from oppressive church authorities. However, it also led to the separation of practical or ethical reasoning from the reason used to create, build, or craft something in the world. In this way, technique became separated from ethics.

Habermas argues that separating practical/ethical reason from technical/ how-to-make-something reason allowed modern societies to develop huge economic and political structures without regard to human well-being. Money and power, tools of technical reason, were set free from moral constraints. This led to a modern world that allows economic and political forces to operate unchecked by the demands of the good of humanity.

According to Habermas, there are two realms or types of reason operating in the contemporary world. The first is *technical reason*, which is geared to the demands and rewards of money and power. The other is what Habermas calls *communicative reason*. This type of reason is geared to human understanding. Habermas believes that every individual, ideally, would like an equal voice in decisions regarding his or her welfare. Communicative reason occurs when people talk with one another with the goal of mutual understanding. In that way, every voice can be heard, and human beings can flourish.

Habermas believes that technical reason is overshadowing communicative reasoning in the contemporary world. He advocates the development of nongovernmental institutions—educational systems, social institutions, community projects—that foster communicative reason. Only by reasserting the centrality of communicative reason in the world will we escape the destructive forces of materialism and political oppression, the fruits of unchecked technical reason.

265

SIDEBAR 19.2
STEPS IN ENCOUNTERING

Choose a practice (something regularly done in a specific way) that you don't understand from another religion or a culture that you have encountered. Answer the following questions on the four steps of encountering. Your answers will help you develop an encountering strategy for the practice in question.

1. *Listen:* What would you need to listen to? To start, religious understandings, social interactions, body language, and so on.
2. *Discover their questions:* Imagine what concerns might lead them to act in the way they do.
3. *Get the message:* Rather than evaluate how good their practice is, try repeating their explanation for it to yourself with the attitude of trying to understand.
4. *Walk with the other:* Imagine yourself doing this practice. Walk through each step in your own mind. How does it feel?

---

emphasized the importance of putting one's convictions on hold. The goal of mutual understanding demands that bracketing. How can I understand another's way of life if I cannot accept that it carries truth that is beneficial for them? How can I understand them if I cannot accept that morality as well as sincerity are present in their way of life and in their communication with me? The goal of mutual understanding can only be reached if I suspend, temporarily, my judgment of another's religion and way of life.

That goal will be easier to reach if we divide it into smaller units that can be analyzed. In this chapter we suggest steps to take that will enable missionaries to foster mutual understanding with the community to which they have been called.

STEPS IN ENCOUNTERING

Listening is the first and most basic step. Rather than focusing on whether we *agree* with the text or idea expressed or considering how to respond to it, we focus on *hearing the meaning* the other intends.

An American missionary who was leaving Indonesia after working at a university for years said to Frances, "You never know what the Javanese are thinking. They may say very nice things to you while they are covering up their true feelings. You never know who might be your enemy and who is your friend." That disappointed missionary had not learned the skill of listening in the Indonesian context, where much of the communication about feelings toward others occurs nonverbally. Instead, he listened only to words and missed the facial cues and sidelong glances that in Javanese society communicate dissatisfaction clearly and effectively. Learning to listen includes learning how others communicate. Their forms of relaying information may be quite different from our own.

Second, we attempt to *discover their questions*. As we mature, we learn to ask certain questions of meaning of ourselves and our communities. Questions of meaning arise in every religion and culture, but the questions differ. Listening with an ear to hearing the basic questions about truth, values, productivity, beauty, origins, the transcendent, or other fundamental topics will help reorient our knowledge to the structure of knowledge used in that society.

While teaching sociology of religion to graduate students in Indonesia, Frances read many very long research papers. Students told her that they needed to write longer papers because more words were required to express an idea in Bahasa Indonesian than in English. As she read the papers, however, she noticed that many of them began, not with the topic itself, but with a long prologue about how the situation came about. By the time the topic itself was introduced, Frances had already read ten to twelve pages of text. As she questioned each student about this introductory material, she learned that Indonesians are very interested in the question of origins. How a situation began and how it developed must be understood before the topic itself could be addressed.

Third, our attention will turn to *getting the message*. Here we will explore ways of checking whether the understanding we are building of the other reflects things as that person understands them or whether our understanding is clouded by our own worldview and projections.

In the case of the question of origins for Indonesian graduate students, Frances realized that intellectuals everywhere ask those questions. But including that material in the research paper indicated that the question of origins was more integral to Indonesian understanding than perhaps to her own. She preferred a paper that limited its parameters to the topic itself. The origins of the question, while interesting, were not part of the assignment in her mind. As she focused on the students' questions of meaning, Frances got the message. She began to understand that they framed their research topics to include the question of origins because that was crucial to their own understanding.

Finally, we learn the process of *walking with the other*. Understanding prompts us to respond. As we acquire knowledge, the practices we outlined in previous chapters become the basis of our actions with people in this new community. Giving those general practices a particular cultural form enables us to walk together with those who are different from us. When Frances got the message about the importance of the question of origins for her Indonesian students, she began to reframe assignments in a way that took their question of origins into consideration. She was learning to practice giftive mission.

267

ZECHARIAH: AN EXAMPLE FROM THE BIBLE

What happens when two cultures, two communities of different religions, interact in an open way? The book of Zechariah gives us an example of just that sort of interaction. Here we see a vision of God gathering many nations together and living among them (Zech. 2).

That joining together of the nations would not, however, eliminate Judah's chosen status (Zech. 2:12). But it would have two important effects on their interaction. First, these very different people would gather together as neighbors. Everyone would invite their neighbor to sit with them under their vine and fig tree (3:10). Strangers would welcome one another, sit and talk together, receive hospitality from one another. Given the hostilities between the Jews and the surrounding nations at this time of exile, such a vision seems miraculous.

A second effect of this gathering of the nations together in Jerusalem would be that those very neighbors of different nationalities would begin to see that God is with the Jews. Many people would come to Jerusalem. They would seek out the Jews, grabbing their cloaks and asking them about God (Zech. 8:20–23). The strangers themselves would take the initiative to explore the story of how God met the Jews, how God came to dwell among them, sharing with them wisdom, and covenanting to be their protector.

Because the Jews, in this vision, would practice truth and peace with their neighbors, it is those who are strangers to the covenant who would ask the Israelites their questions of meaning (Zech. 8:16–22). How well the Jews would have to listen for the needed trust to develop so that those questions of meaning could be asked! How accurately the Jews would have to reflect the understandings and worldview of the strangers for them to be able to discuss their questions of meaning; how well they would have to walk together, sharing conversations, meals, and their lives with one another to facilitate that deeper communication. The mutual understanding that Zechariah envisioned could develop through this interaction. It could result in the strangers longing to hear the narrative of Israel and meet the God who had rescued and protected them throughout the generations of their history.

Those events could come about only if the Jews opened themselves to the presence of other nations in their holy city of Jerusalem. It could come about only if the Jews showed hospitality to the strangers who became their neighbors, sitting together, chatting, learning of the things that mattered most to one another. Zechariah's vision was a grand vision of peace among nations. It is a vision built on trust in God, moral actions, and mutual understanding. Let us explore the four steps to encountering the other with openness, keeping in mind this biblical example as a model.

LISTEN

Studies of listening have, at times, been relegated to linguistic theory or pastoral-care studies. Listening has been viewed as a methodological tool in communication. What if we were to envision listening differently: as a central part of developing our identity, individually and communally, and as an essential dimension of our understanding of God and the world?

The Old Testament story of Nineveh can serve as an example. Nineveh was doomed. God had decided to destroy the city because of the great evils practiced by the people. To announce that destruction, God sent Jonah as a missionary to the people. Jonah resisted the call, but God's insistence eventually led him to the gates of the city. There he fulfilled his task. Here the story takes a different turn. The people listened to the pronouncements of God's judgment. They realized their wickedness and repented. They turned to God, begging for forgiveness. And God changed directions, forgave them, and did not destroy the city.

Jonah was unhappy. But for everyone else, the story has a happy ending. The people listened to the word of God and were changed. God listened to the repentance of the people and changed directions. Judgment was averted; the people were saved. God's mercy won. In this example, we see listening as part of God's character and way of interacting with humans. Listening is not a sideline. God does not listen just to be a good communicator or an effective counselor.

Jonah is a different story. Jonah wanted to see the destruction of the strangers to the covenant of Israel. He did not trust in the validity, rightness, or sincerity of their communication. He did not listen to them with the goal of mutual understanding. He did not value any part of their way of life. All he could see was the wickedness. Perhaps Jonah was right. The text tells us that the wickedness of the city was great. But God passed over Jonah's stiff-necked attitude. God sent his message through Jonah. God listened with understanding to the people's repentant response. The goal of mutual understanding was reached. Listening changed the world: the people repented, God changed plans, and the city was saved.

HOW TO LISTEN

Perhaps we don't listen well because listening is difficult. It seems to be a skill that is overshadowed by learning how to talk. Parents can't wait until their infants develop enough to begin talking. You rarely hear a relative ask a mother of a toddler, "Has she learned to listen yet?" "What were the first words he listened to?"

Listening is a skill that can be improved by paying attention to some simple guidelines.

SIDEBAR 19.3
THE LISTENING SELF

Levin (1989, 24–26)

Does God interact with us as we listen to others?

David Michael Levin, following Martin Heidegger, criticizes the correspondence theory of Being (or God), which assumes a disinterested, dispassionate, and disembodied position as paradigmatic of the "essential truth" of Being.

Levin suggests, instead, a notion of Being (or God) as it appears to show itself in relationships, a nongrasping, nonrepresentational construct. Being in this sense is attempting not to control or relate theoretically but rather to "be with," a way that lets go and allows for movement and change.

To what extent is this the way God "listens" to us?

Utilize Dissonance

Sometimes when we think we are listening to someone, we actually hear only our own projections. We hear what fits with our way of ordering our world. We hear what strikes a note of resonance with our own feelings. We hear what the person would say *if he or she were us*. Then, when a moment of dissonance occurs, we are shocked. We thought we had understood the person. We thought he or she was like us. Here our discomfort can provide a shock of recognition for us. We suddenly recognize that our hearing has been geared to our own point of view. This is the moment to look at our own viewpoint, to back up a bit and bracket our prejudices.

A few years ago, Frances and Terry visited a temple in Sri Lanka. At the site were Hindu, Buddhist, and indigenous shrines. Just outside the temple grounds was a mosque. Our guide told us that people came here to pray for a child or to seek healing, returning annually to express gratefulness for receiving positive responses to their request. The peacefulness of the scene impressed us. Here were people of different religions living together in harmony, requesting, receiving, and expressing gratefulness for blessings received.

Our idyllic view was shattered when we came to the "cursing stone." A small enclosure about waist high contained a large boulder. Men and women gathered around this shrine were hurling coconuts against it and shouting. They seemed enraged. Some left in tears after smashing their coconut against the rock. Flies buzzed in the heat as the coconut milk ran down the stone. Seeing the cursing stone in a worship setting that had seemed so peaceful shocked us both.

Study the Context

Next, we try to determine what about this new setting, in comparison to our own, may be influencing the different perceptions that we became aware of in a moment of dissonance. Does the view of the world and the place of humans in it differ from our own? Are there different values informing actions in this community? Is our own understanding of the divine interfering with our ability to comprehend what has been said? Does the economic or political situation demand a special kind of listening? Separating our interpretations of what we hear from our usual context and looking carefully at the way the present context informs the communication are crucial at this point.

At the moment of dissonance we experienced at the interreligious temple in Sri Lanka, we faced the obvious fact that not all the people who worshiped at that temple came for blessings. Some came to curse. We learned from our guide that curses invoked here were believed to have special power to harm with a lasting effectiveness. Now we could see how our own perception of a loving God, our own "prejudices" about worship, and our understandings of prayer clouded our perceptions of worship at the temple. We had seen the worship through the lens of our own Christian understandings. To begin to understand seeking divine intervention for cursing others, we had to relinquish our own convictions about God, worship, and interreligious harmony. We had to study the context more closely without the interference of our own viewpoints.

Repeat What We Heard

Restating what we heard to the person or group communicating with us can encourage further clarification. If our perceptions are inaccurate, the interlocutors can correct us. If incomplete, they can expand their idea. If points are more or less important, they can clarify the central and peripheral parts of their discourse. Simply reflecting what we heard fosters communication geared to mutual understanding.

Conversing with our Sri Lankan guide about the cursing stone and the other worship occurrences at the temple we visited helped us to clarify our understandings. Harmony was present as people from different religions shared the temple space. Gratefulness was part of the day's pilgrimage to the temple for many whose requests for children or healing in previous years had been granted. But there was also an opportunity to release anger, to curse one's enemies, to display rage against what life had brought to some. We gained a fuller understanding of the temple activities and the meaning of the rites performed there by reflecting to our guide what we had seen and heard and then receiving clarification from him about how those acts were understood by the pilgrims themselves.

Reorder Our Understandings

Whenever we hear a new idea or are presented with a different way of looking at things, it influences our whole understanding. Without our even thinking about it, the experience of dissonance and clarification in listening functions as a corrective to our total view. The conscious reordering of perceptions is an *evaluative step* that we have isolated as the next step in the spiral of knowledge acquisition. But if we realize that it will, to a certain extent, occur automatically, we can make use of it and also limit its influence. We can intentionally stay a bit longer with the perceptions of the other and not jump back too quickly into our own framework of interpretation.

Our view of the worship at the interreligious temple changed as we allowed the experience of dissonance to reorder our perceptions. We realized that not only were positive human emotions encouraged at the temple but that there was also a place to express negative emotions such as frustration, anger, and even hatred. A notion of retributive justice emerged as part of the worship process for the Sri Lankans as we now understood it.

DISCOVER THEIR QUESTIONS

To more fully understand the point of view of the person of another religion or culture, we need to discover the issues they are dealing with, the life questions that are important to them. The next step in encountering the other with openness, then, becomes a search for *their questions*. This can be done in several ways.

Find a Deeper Question

One can use a Socratic method of presenting and hearing different points of view in order to uncover a deeper question. In Plato's *Protagoras*, his dialogue about education, he listens to the Sophists, who see education as a technique that advances one's own position. He listens to the one who claims that education teaches one to classify and order the world. He listens to the perspective of the one who claims education is about acquiring skills of certain crafts. After hearing them each out, Plato notes that, without coming to a conclusion about education, the dialogue reveals a deeper question: What is knowledge? It is this question that has prompted all the other questions about the purpose of education. This was Plato's way of discovering questions that might be common to the different cultures.

In the case of the cursing stone, one might ask if the discharge of emotions has a cathartic effect on a grieving person. Or one might ask a question about justice: should not the offender also suffer? Seeking answers to these questions might lead to a deeper question of the meaning of suffering in the Sri Lankan religious context.

Seek a Response to an Idea

Another way to discover the questions that are important to the people we are trying to understand is to present an idea and then ask them what they think of it. Their response will reveal what they hear in your discourse that is important to *their way of looking at the world*. After listening to their response, instead of refuting it, ask what *other issues* they think are related to this idea. In this way, a broader discussion that revolves around *their* questions of meaning can be initiated.

Vincent Donovan describes this process in *Rediscovering Christianity* (2000). Sent as a missionary to East Africa, he discovered that after fifteen years of Catholic mission work, the Masai people still did not understand the Christian gospel. The missionaries working there had separated themselves from the people in living compounds. They had developed educational and health-care institutions that served the people. But they had not explored the religious beliefs of the people. They had not talked with the people about Christianity in their religious context. There had been little communication about ideas or understandings of ultimate reality. The missionaries had not listened to the people. Hence, there was no mutual understanding between them about religion.

Donovan requested that the church allow him to proceed in a different fashion. Understanding his call to be one of an evangelist, he sought permission to travel out to the villages rather than live in the Catholic compound. The church approved his plan. Thereafter, he went to a village and presented the Christian gospel. Then he asked for the people's response.

On the basis of their response, Donovan changed the way he told the gospel story. When he heard that they believed in a high God, beyond the realm of spirits and the gods they could name, Donovan declared that the high God was the God whom Jesus brought news of into the world. By aligning his gospel message with revelation the people already had about God's mystery and power, Donovan connected the Christian gospel with their own way of understanding the supernatural.

GET THE MESSAGE

Sometimes, in some villages Donovan visited, the people didn't get the message. Or maybe Donovan didn't get the message from the people. Maybe he didn't understand their questions of meaning well enough to see how the vastness of God's goodness in sending Jesus could address their questions. Getting the message is a two-way street. Without mutual understanding, communication from both sides is blocked.

When we first encounter another religion, we look for commonalities. What do its adherents believe that we can relate to in our way of ordering the world? The Christian may find a resonance with the Buddhist notion of emptiness.

Through silence or meditative prayer or repeating the Jesus prayer, a connection with a Buddhist way of life can be made. This connection can start the Christian down a helpful path to mutual understanding. Conversations can begin. Appreciation for Buddhist concepts can develop.

It won't be long, however, before this way of finding commonalities begins to encounter difficulties. The silent worship of God for a Christian is Presence-filled, not empty. The Buddhist emptiness is, however, much fuller than a Christian idea of emptiness. "The way of the common" falters. Misunderstanding occurs. The Christian discovers that he or she cannot understand how a Buddhist can long for emptiness. The Buddhist discovers that a personal God does not seem big enough to embrace. Both sides come to a point of not understanding the other's viewpoint.

That nonunderstanding may be difficult to accept. The purpose of seeking mutual understanding is to achieve it, not to accept a dead end of nonunderstanding. The point of disconnection, however, may be necessary as a starting point for a deeper mutual understanding.

Zali Gurevitch, a sociologist at Hebrew University in Jerusalem, did research with groups of Palestinians and Jews who were attempting to communicate (1988). The groups were made up half of Jews and half of Palestinians who met for four days. Their task was to discuss their differences on the land issues in Israel, not the easiest task, given the land disputes in that area.

Gurevitch found a recurring pattern in these four-day sessions. During the first two days, the conversations took the "way of the common." People introduced themselves, discussed their lives, found that they shared certain attitudes and opinions, and discussed those. About halfway through the dialogue, however, something usually occurred that brought hidden tensions into the foreground. Whether this tension was initiated by a single person, focused on a point of disagreement, or was sparked by general discomfort didn't seem to matter. In every case, the result was a shock of recognition that the parties, indeed, did not understand each other. The Palestinians could not understand the Jews' claim to their land. The Jews could not understand Palestinian rejection of that claim. The impasse was real.

Gurevitch found that those groups that could accept that they could not even understand each other's position, much less agree, somehow found a way through the impasse. They began to develop real communication that led to mutual understanding of their differences. The acceptance of nonunderstanding set them on a new course, the "way of the strange." These groups began to discuss the hows and whys of their nonunderstanding. This process took them to a level of understanding of their differences that could not be achieved by groups that refused to recognize their total nonunderstanding of the other so they could begin again from the acceptance of that fact (Gurevitch 1988).

Donovan must have encountered a similar experience with villages that chose not to accept Christianity. He felt disappointed as he left those villages.

SIDEBAR 19.4
THE SOCIAL SELF

SIDEBAR 19.4
THE SOCIAL SELF

During the 1930s, George Herbert Mead developed his idea of the social self (1934). This theory argues that the self is not individual or autonomous but is developed through social interaction.

Josiah Royce, an earlier American philosopher, had developed the notion of a triadic system of communication in which every person is connected to the person with whom he or she is communicating, and both are connected to a third "common loyalty." The communication between the two persons or communities depends on their understanding of and commitment to that third entity—the common loyalty. Mead builds on this idea and draws from John Dewey and C. S. Peirce, American pragmatists, to develop his idea of the social self.

When a person says something to someone else, Mead argues that the meaning of that communication is not fully known to the speaker until the other party responds. For example, if interlocutor A tells a joke, and recipient B begins to cry, this tells A that their communication was not a joke but had another meaning. One's sense of identity is developed through social interactions that define to the person his or her sense of self. The self, thus, is not an essential entity but develops through social discourse.

Language and communication become central in Mead's view of the social self. One cannot be the person one is born to be or the person one decides to be. Rather the self is developed through time and interaction with others.

H. Richard Niebuhr, a German American Christian theologian, developed the theological implications of this notion in *The Responsible Self* (1999). In this work, Niebuhr argues that teleological ethics, geared to the good end, and deontological ethics, geared to right principles, need to be augmented by a third type of ethics, responsibility ethics, in which a person responds to input from others in finding/living the good life.

But he was able to accept nonunderstanding. He and the people of the village took "the way of the strange," discussing their differences to a point at which they could accept not understanding each other. Although those villages did not become Christian communities, a level of mutual understanding was achieved through the acceptance of nonunderstanding. And it left them more open to possible future presentations of the gospel story, rather than closing them forever to God's grace.

WALK TOGETHER

How far can we walk together when our discussions have led to the conclusion that we do not, indeed cannot, understand one another? Donovan decided to move out from a village when he became convinced that the people did not

275

want to embrace the good news of the gospel. Gurevitch's four-day consultations between Jews and Palestinians ended, while the controversy over land in Israel continues unabated.

Would new breakthroughs of mutual understanding have occurred if Donovan had continued the discussions after the acceptance, on both sides, of nonunderstanding? The same question might be asked about a more ongoing study of Palestinian-Israeli dialogues.

A guide to developing giftive mission cannot dictate how far mutual understanding can go and when a parting of the ways becomes necessary. What it can do is outline ways to walk together. The situation itself determines whether walking together is the appropriate response to a situation. The wisdom of Ecclesiastes tells us that there is a time to sow and a time to reap, a time to embrace and a time to refrain from embracing. There is a time to walk together and a time to part ways. During the time for giftive mission to operate, how can we walk together with those of a different religion?

The middle section of this book outlined eleven practices of giftive mission. We will turn to those practices to find the tools to utilize in encountering another religion. Those practices can be clothed with particular cultural forms as we encounter others and learn to understand their point of view.

But to develop specific forms of those practices, we need to return to our own way of understanding the world. Reconnecting with our own convictions to evaluate the ways of the community we encounter is the topic of the next chapter.

20

Evaluating

*Appraising the New Culture and Religion
from a Christian Viewpoint*

I n the first stages of the knowledge-acquisition spiral—recognizing experience, bracketing convictions, and encountering with openness—we have described how to engage people in *their* context and understand them through *their* ways of viewing the world. We have bracketed our own viewpoints and refrained from making value judgments. Learning about the other's point of view necessitates comparisons against the backdrop of what we already know, so bracketing our convictions has been an imperfect and incomplete process. Nonetheless, our openness to the perspectives and opinions of the people with whom we are interacting has been expanded by this attempt to withhold judgment. Encountering the other—through the processes of listening, discovering their questions, learning to accept points of nonunderstanding, getting the message, and walking with them—provides us with information and new perspectives on a range of subjects.

The process of evaluation, which we will explore in this chapter, brings those new understandings and old convictions together. At this stage we bring back into our thinking in a conscious way *our own point of view*: the understandings, values, relationships, and perspectives from our past experience that we reflected on and then put aside in order to encounter those of another religion with openness. We reengage our own convictions, comparing

277

SIDEBAR 20.1
TRANSFERRING BRACKETED CONVICTIONS

List the sources of the values in the culture you are learning about on the left and the sources of your own culture's values on the right.

NEW CULTURE'S SOURCES OF VALUES	MY CULTURE'S SOURCES OF VALUES
Authorities (e.g., ancestors, parents, older brother, God, community, self):	
Principles (e.g., appearance is paramount, intention is paramount):	
Life goals (e.g., fulfill one's given role, chart a new path):	
Context (e.g., fit into context and community, be different from surroundings):	
Character (e.g., nonoffensive, internal strength, forthright, outgoing leadership):	

---

what we have learned through the open encounter with the other with our own cherished beliefs and values.

FINDING A SET OF MEASURING TOOLS

To evaluate means to measure. And to measure we need a norm or statement of the good, a way of measuring, and a measuring instrument. To evaluate a person's height, for example, we need to know what height is normal and good, we need to devise a standard way to measure height (inches or centimeters or whatever), and we need a ruler, a measuring instrument. All three elements—norm, standard, and measuring instrument—are required for any evaluation.

What set of tools—norm, standard, and measuring instrument—can we use to evaluate our experiences of the other religion's traditions that we have so intentionally gathered in the first three phases of the spiral of knowledge acquisition? In one sense the Bible, for the Christian, provides all three tools for evaluation. The Bible gives us norms, telling us what is good. Our interpretation of the Bible's pronouncements, our theology, gives us the standard by which to measure how closely a belief or custom conforms to the good. Also, we use our personalities and attendant experiences, as seen through our own gospel lenses, as our measuring tools. The perspectives we acquired through our experience and study of the Bible influence us as we evaluate the very different cultures and religions that we encounter. We use those tools in a specific setting, and that context and the people in it also influence our evaluation.

SIDEBAR 20.2
MEASURING TOOLS

Norms (biblical themes—statements of the good)	Love Holy Spirit Personal God Other
Way to measure—contextual standard of measurement	Utilize context—measuring standard found in new situation. Focus on their questions and issues. Find points of contact with the norm—the good as I understand it.
Measuring instrument	Have conversation between contexts. Engage in dialogue about the norm. Use the norm to address their needs.

Reappraise one's own views in dialogue with the other culture's views (integration).

As we have seen, the Bible has a great deal to say about the Christian's responsibility to people who belong to and believe in other religions. Different theologies emphasize different aspects of biblical teaching. It becomes extremely difficult to comprehend the whole gospel all at once. And it does seem true that at different times and in different places, different facets of the gospel gem need to be polished. What is needed in one situation may be quite different from what is needed in another context or era.

In the face of this complexity, we often choose a theme that serves as an entrée to the rest of the gospel truth. As we saw in chapter 2, many solid scriptural themes are useful for this purpose. None is exhaustive. None of the ones we mentioned can be left out. It is possible, however, to use one or another in a faithful rendering of the word of God today.

THREE BIBLICAL EXAMPLES

Consider just three themes: love, the Holy Spirit, and a personal God as an overarching standard of evaluation.

Love

The apostle John speaks of the process of evaluating religious beliefs and practices in his first pastoral letter. He warns the churches about false teachers, advising them to "test the spirits to see whether they are from God, because many false prophets have gone out into the world" (1 John 4:1). John makes

279

EVALUATING

ight "enlightens every person coming into the all teachings are sound. Christians need to ıth from error, sin from righteousness. John's

valuation tools we have described. The *norm* ve. The *critical standard* for determining the s considered to be love in that context reflects e is from God; everyone who loves is born of NRSV). The *measuring instrument* to test ....ve in a teaching or practice is a person's response to Jesus. This measuring instrument is used because the primary manifestation of God's love is that God sent Jesus into the world so that we might live through him (4:9). John tells us that we can recognize when love is *not present* by looking at how people respond to Jesus, the bearer of and witness to God's love. John tells us that false prophets can be exposed if they directly deny that Jesus has come from God (4:2–3).

As we reengage our convictions and begin evaluating what we learn from another religion and culture, this advice from the Bible proves helpful. Where love, the overarching good, can be seen, practices of the other community can be embraced. The community's attitude toward Jesus can also be determined. Often people of other religions recognize the importance of Jesus to Christians and respect our reverent attitude toward him.

Denial that Jesus is sent from God is a specific point, relevant in John's epistle for evaluating those who *claim* to be Christian leaders but are not. That context-oriented measuring instrument may not be as relevant in our new context since we are not looking for false prophets coming to teach in the church. Instead we are evaluating the love of a community to discern how active God already is in that community.

John outlines specific criteria by which we can ascertain the presence of love. Love is life giving (1 John 4:11–16), active in doing good (4:17–18), and confident, displacing fear (4:17–18). We learn the source and meaning of love when we embrace Jesus, sent to be the Savior of the world (4:14–16). But the fruits of love can be seen in other cultures and religions even if they have not embraced the gospel, as the light of God has enlightened every person (John 1). It is those fruits that will aid our evaluation. Although we cannot ignore life-denying activities and false teachings, we can look for the manifestations of God's love at work in the "foreign text," the communal and religious practices of the new culture.

The Holy Spirit

Jesus promised that God would send the Holy Spirit into the world in a special way after his death. "I will ask the Father and he will give you another Counselor to be with you forever—the Spirit of Truth" (John 14:16–17).

Besides believing in the "light that enlightens every person," Christians believe that since the death and resurrection of Jesus, God's Spirit has pervaded the world in a special way. As we embrace that idea, we begin to see God's activity in many places, social structures, teachings, and practices of communities around the world. The activity of the Holy Spirit can become a critical standard for evaluating the presence and work of God in another culture or religion.

Lee Snook, a North American Lutheran theologian who worked as a missionary in Africa, revised his view of the Holy Spirit during his time in Africa. His understanding changed for two reasons. First, he saw the activity of God's Spirit in the beliefs of the Africans *before* they ever heard the name of Jesus. He saw love demonstrated in the community. He saw faith in God. He saw trust in the power of God to change reality. Second, Snook saw the work of the Holy Spirit *after* the people accepted Christianity. This second work of God was more direct and more powerful than the first. Building his theology of the Holy Spirit on the "light of God that enlightens every person," Snook began to see the specific work of the Holy Spirit: building up the body of Christ, encouraging healthy living, enabling people to change direction and move from darkness into light (Snook 2000).

A Personal God

Vincent Donovan presents us with another example of a Christian missionary who found that God was active in the culture when he evaluated it on the basis of a reengagement of his Christian convictions. Donovan worked with the Masai in Africa, where he discovered that the religion of the people focused not only on spirit activity and animistic worship but on a God who was personal. That concept of a personal God led to a deep sense of brotherhood among the people. Donovan found that deep loyalties and a sense of the value of all people were inherent in their religion.

Donovan discovered those qualities by bracketing his prejudices and encountering Masai culture and religion with openness. Through discovering the people's questions and discussing the gospel with them in terms of their own beliefs, Donovan came to the conclusion that the good news of the Christian gospel was relevant to them. In fact, the personal God of the Bible had somehow enlightened their hearts to a certain extent. The universal nature of the good news was evidenced by the hints of the gospel embedded in both their questions and the practices of their religion.

Donovan found God's presence in Masai society. He used that standard of a personal God as an entry point for telling the gospel story to the Masai. He found that knowledge of a personal God was a good that could be used to evaluate Masai beliefs. The instrument for evaluation became how practices conformed to or departed from that standard. The Masai needed the good

281

news of the gospel. Not all their community practices conformed to the standards of the personal God of the Bible as Donovan knew God. The process of evaluating Masai culture and practices depended on the measuring tools of the good, as defined by the personal God of the Bible, as measured by the practices developed by the Masai.

USING TOOLS OF EVALUATION TO SPREAD THE GOSPEL: A CONTEXTUAL METHOD

Finding an overarching biblical theme to use as a critical standard is the first step in evaluating another culture or religion. A second step is seeing how that theme is demonstrated in the culture as a manifestation of God at work in the world. What beliefs or cultural forms can be understood as a witness to God's love? What political ideas or social structures can be shown to have been influenced by God's Spirit? What metaphors and parallels can be used to show that some of the religious practices bear witness to a personal God? How can those ideas already present in the religion of the people be used to communicate the gospel through the story of Jesus?

Those questions cannot be answered in general but can be addressed specifically only for a certain religion and context. Not every critical standard developed through Christian theologies will be found in every context or religion. Not all practices in other cultures witness to God's love, the work of the Holy Spirit, or the reality of a personal God as Christians understand those concepts. The apostle John outlined ways to evaluate the presence of God's love in a community. Snook found the idea of the Spirit's presence in all things as a force for life and goodness to be compatible with presenting the specific work of God's Spirit in redemption. Donovan found the motif of brotherhood helpful as he reengaged his convictions and evaluated Masai culture. He used this theme in presenting the good news of Jesus Christ to many small communities. As missionaries reengage their own convictions, evidence of God's work in the world will direct their evaluation, showing what cultural constructs support the message of the good news of Christianity.

WHERE AM I? CONSIDERING THE CONTEXT

Using an overarching biblical theme to evaluate the wholesomeness of practices, beliefs, and social structures gives us a standard. But the process of evaluation happens not in a vacuum but in a particular location. We also need a method, a way of going about the process of evaluation that will focus our attention on the crucial dimensions of the interaction between our convictions and prejudices and the beliefs and values of the people in that particular context.

We have been investigating the culture and religion of a particular community. That research has been performed *in a field*, *by* someone, and *for*

SIDEBAR 20.3
QUESTIONS FOR EVALUATION

How can I reengage the areas of my experience that I bracketed in order to encounter a new culture with openness?

1. List specific ideas, feelings, and convictions set aside during the encounter phase:

   Understanding: What I thought about the other culture, how I understood ethics, manners, and religion.

   Socialization: Ways to learn and act; habits learned in my family, school, and church.

   Context: Things that were important in my hometown, region, and nation.

   Theology: What I believed about God, the world, and humans.

2. Now juxtapose those convictions with knowledge gained about the new culture and religion. Here I use my own understandings to evaluate the new culture using the measurement tools described in this chapter:

   Understanding: What do I think about the other culture in comparison to my own? What strengths and weaknesses do I see in its convictions about ethics, manners, and religion?

   Socialization: What differences do I see between the ways I was taught to behave and believe and the patterns of personality formation and learning in this culture? Are there aspects of my own upbringing that are better than the ones I'm encountering? Worse? Different but not better or worse?

   Context: What aspects of life are important here that were not central in my own home place? Are the different values that arise in this context compatible with what I believe? How can I learn from this new context? What things learned back home could be helpful here?

   Theology: What parallels can I find between my Christian convictions and the beliefs of the people in my new setting? What beliefs about God and the world and the way humans interact that I hold to be true are not reflected in the religion I'm engaging? Where can I see God already working in this religion? How can I approach people here about Christian truths?

3. How can I fit what I have learned about this culture with my own views? How have my convictions changed by learning about this religion and culture? How would the people change if they embraced Christ?

4. What practices can I develop to engage this religion in ways that show Christ's love and appreciate how God has gone before me into this place?

someone. Looking at each of those dimensions provides a structure in which to evaluate the presence of God's love in the community.

The Field

The "encounter with openness" toward another text, religion, or culture has taken us to a context that differs from our own. Paying attention to that "field" becomes crucial as we evaluate what we have encountered. If we have

283

listened with openness, our perceptions of the other religion, although not complete, will be true to the religion itself. We have uncovered questions that are important to that community. Now we put the specific knowledge from that context into dialogue with our own views.

The Researcher

As the researcher (or learner, as we might think of ourselves in our encounter with the people of the other community), we now bring our views back into play. What we believe about God, the world, humans, becomes important as we evaluate how God may be working in this particular culture. We have seen places where God is at work in this religion. We have found areas that display God's action—where life is enhanced, where good actions predominate, where fear is displaced. Reengaging our values and convictions now gives us a basis on which to understand how God's work can be furthered in this setting by introducing the gospel in relevant ways.

The Audience

Our learning is not only for ourselves; it is also for others. We want the church that sent us to this place to understand the people and how God is working among them. We want to develop mission goals that are appropriate to this context, theologies that are compatible with what God's Spirit is already doing there. We also want the people to whom we are sent to understand the good news of the Christian gospel. We want the church to be established and to grow. Communicating with people where we see God working in their society, grappling with their questions, drawing parallels, and using metaphors that make the gospel story clear in their setting are important facets of the evaluating process.

KŌSUKE KOYAMA AND WATER BUFFALO THEOLOGY

Because this process of evaluation is tied not only to the convictions and prejudices of the missionary but to the context and questions of the community to which he or she is sent, we will explore this process in the life experience of a person who encounters another culture and then evaluates that culture in terms of Christian beliefs and cultural influences. By looking at a specific case, we can see the process of evaluation in action, tied to a particular context.

Kōsuke Koyama, a Japanese theologian who studied theology at Tokyo Union Theological Seminary and Princeton Theological Seminary in the United States, realized the importance of integrating his views with his context as a missionary to villagers in northern Thailand. To bring Christianity into a new setting, we must "let theology speak in and through that context," he says (1999, 21).

As we bring our theology into conversation with the questions and context that we encounter in another religious setting, we allow the context itself to assume a primary place in our reflections and actions. The result of that process, a life engagement in the new context, is critical accommodation, a more difficult task than mere cultural accommodation, according to Koyama. He asserts that it is only through critical or prophetic accommodation that authentic contextualization can occur.

By contextualization, Koyama means developing a Christian theology that is appropriate to a particular context. It is during the stage of evaluation that such a meeting of ideas and cultures can happen. According to Koyama, theology resembles poetry more than science, and a concrete narrative of his experience in Thailand displays an open-ended *lived methodology*. The twenty-fifth anniversary edition of the book detailing the local theology he developed in Thailand, *Water Buffalo Theology*, describes Koyama's struggle to integrate his already bicultural experience and education with the life he experienced in northern Thailand.

In tracing that story, we see the experiential learning of the knowledge-acquisition spiral occurring. The evaluative phase of that process recurs throughout, but we will attempt to extract it, describing the steps Koyama took when he brought his own convictions into dialogue with the views of the Thai farmers.

During his time of study at Princeton, Koyama did not attempt to integrate his theological training with his Japanese identity. When he arrived in Thailand as a missionary, he was presented with yet a third definitive culture and another religion: Buddhism. In addition to reengaging his convictions in order to evaluate what he experienced in Thailand, he had to simultaneously determine what those convictions and prejudices were. Koyama calls his *Water Buffalo Theology* the outcome of a "three-cornered conversation" among his contexts of Tokyo, New Jersey, and Chiang Mai.

In the contemporary global context, people often have bicultural or tricultural backgrounds to begin with, even before they intentionally encounter another religion. If one has not reflected on one's experience before encountering the other culture or religion, it will need to be done as evaluation proceeds. The conversation with the worldview and practices of the other can be two-way only if one understands and embraces a worldview and practices of one's own.

When Koyama arrived in Thailand, he began a journey through the knowledge-acquisition spiral. He first began to study the language; he found it most difficult, which led him into a state of repentance. His "humiliation" at not understanding or being able to communicate showed him his own weakness, leading him to a commitment "to see the face of God in the faces of people." By realizing that he did not understand the people, he began to look for God in that context and community.

Seeing God in the face of the other includes bracketing one's own ideas and convictions about how God is seen in the world. The humiliation of being unable to understand and his frustration at being unable to communicate helped Koyama bracket his sophisticated theologies and cultural backgrounds and become open to the encounter with the other: the Thai farmers living in a Buddhist/animist culture.

Respect for that culture and its religion became a central practice in that open encounter. Using the Buddhist vocabularies and interacting with Thai Buddhists and Christians without a sense of superiority or inferiority led Koyama into interreligious dialogue "naturally." Mutual enrichment, rather than replacement, became a goal of interreligious dialogue in this setting.

Koyama's goals included more than interreligious dialogue, however. He wanted to develop a relevant theology for that local community. He outlines this process in three steps. First, we must identify the issue at hand, articulating *the people's* questions. We discussed this as part of the encounter phase of knowledge acquisition. Second, we must see how our views relate to *their questions and needs* that have been identified as crucial to them in their context. That is, we must put our theology at their service. This is the stage of evaluation. And third, we must use the new knowledge we gain by *reappraising our own views* in light of their questions and issues to serve them in their setting. This process of integration is the next step, to be explored in our next chapter. Then we continue traversing the spiral, beginning again with a reformed horizon of meanings to inform our experience.

It is the evaluation part of this process that we highlight as we reflect on Koyama's water buffalo theology. How does he reengage his pre-texts and Christian convictions, placing them into dialogue with the questions and issues presented by his new contexts? In applying his theological knowledge and understandings from Tokyo and New Jersey, Koyama evaluates the Thai context and develops a local theology. Having done theological training with Western texts, Koyama asks, for instance, how Thomas Aquinas's and Karl Barth's theologies could benefit the farmers of northern Thailand, where he was serving a congregation. He brings his understandings into conversation with the context of the Thai farmers.

He goes further, insisting that he did not *understand* those theologies that were part of his old horizon of meanings until he understood their relevance to the new context in which he served. That is, Aquinas's and Barth's ideas needed to be *reshaped* and reembodied in light of the concerns and lifestyle of the rice-farming communities of the Buddhist northern Thailand context that Koyama sought to understand. He could not make this evaluation outside the controlling influence of that context. Aquinas's and Barth's old meanings, at least as he understood them in Tokyo and Princeton, were deemed irrelevant here. New understandings, realized by bringing those theologians into dialogue with Thai culture and concerns, would become the true meaning of those texts in this situation.

But in order to find any relevance for his learned theologies in Thailand, Koyama needed to integrate those theologies into his own life experience. What parts of the theological traditions that he had studied were relevant to his own life? How could he integrate his theology with the culture in Thailand unless he understood what was important and what could be discarded from his bicultural education and experience? Koyama's seven years of "theological floating," during which he ignored his own culture and language, came to an end in Thailand, where he could no longer ignore the need for integration. To do that integration, Koyama needed to evaluate his own theology as well as the Thai culture and religion.

In looking back on his life experience and learning, Koyama realized that his existence had been marked by the continual violence of wars. Raised in a Christian family, he was baptized by a minister who told him that the God of the Bible is concerned about the well-being of nations, including Japan and the United States, which was bombing Japan at the time. This first ecumenical lesson linked Koyama's theology with the leitmotif of the importance of removing violence from the world. He identifies violence as his biblical theme, the critical standard that he then uses in his evaluation. Whether a religion, including Christianity, contributed to the lessening of violence became the critical standard for evaluating its truth and relevance. "What if the *karman* doctrine were to bring forth a less violent world than the Semitic doctrine does?" Koyama asks. "The final test for the truthfulness of the *theologia cruces* is whether this Christian teaching truly contributes toward the removal of violence in the world" (1999, 179).

This concern is not only an ethical standard but has become part of Koyama's identity as a Christian theologian. Charles Taylor suggests that modern people search for something outside themselves that resonates with deep personal longings and experiences (1989). When one makes a connection between the external and the inner life in this way, strong moral evaluations develop as part of one's identity. Koyama's life narrative shows marks of this process. As a youngster, his life was shadowed by war. As a college student in Tokyo, he suffered hunger as a result of the devastation of war. The violence against Jews and blacks in New York City was another kind of "bombing" that threatened Koyama's sense of self-identity. The issue of violence needed to be understood and integrated into his theology and his sense of self, becoming his point of entry into the whole gospel.

As a young man, Koyama turned to the Bible and the study of the life of St. Francis of Assisi as he worked through this problem. In this way, he related that central identity experience of the problem of violence to the Christian faith. When he brought his theological and experiential views into dialogue with Buddhism in Thailand, this central motif was an important facet of his

287

experiential understanding, which he used in evaluating his experience of the other. His reconstruction of knowledge, the integration of horizons, which we will explore in the next chapter, was heavily influenced by the critical standard of the importance of removing violence from the world.

The evaluation process, then, is based on processing one's own experience and encountering the other with openness. Others, going through the same external stimuli as Koyama, might interpret the process differently, through different life experiences. As James McClendon shows well in *Biography as Theology* (2002), someone like Martin Luther King Jr., for example, processed Christian theology through the lens of justice instead of violence. A different theology emerges. The process of evaluation itself includes reconstructing one's knowledge in light of the issues and context of the other. Relating those two aspects of knowledge to one's central sense of identity and the moral evaluations that arise from that sense of identity is a third step in the process. As one's sense of identity links an inner longing or sense of self with an external event or reality, the evaluation process proceeds.

Koyama studied the stigmata of Christ, developed a theology of Christ's suffering, and related those concepts to the struggles of Thai peasants as part of his growing understanding of what a contextualized Thai peasant theology might become. His experience of the violence of war and its connection with his Christian experience helped form a self-identity and a theology that were integrated in his own life. That nexus of experience, theology, and identity could then come into conversation with the people of Thailand—Buddhists and Christians.

PRIVILEGING THE CONTEXT

Koyama's lived methodology also shows the importance of the context itself in the evaluative process. Only by allowing the context to govern one's understandings and reshape one's views will the next phase, integration of horizons, become possible. Koyama's insistence that Aquinas and Barth only made sense to him now if they could be understood in the Thai context and used in the service of the church there illustrates this central concept. By privileging the context, Koyama allowed a reordering of his theological concepts and priorities to inform his views. If the context is not given this privileged position, a reentrenchment of one's former understandings or, alternatively, an uncritical acceptance of the new cultural context, along with a rejection of one's former views, will result. Allowing the new context to re-form knowledge from another setting allows the integration of horizons to proceed unhindered. Moving through the evaluation phase and into integration of horizons leads to what Koyama calls "authentic contextualization."

The third step for Koyama is using that new understanding of Aquinas and Barth in this example to serve the farmers in Thailand. That is, having

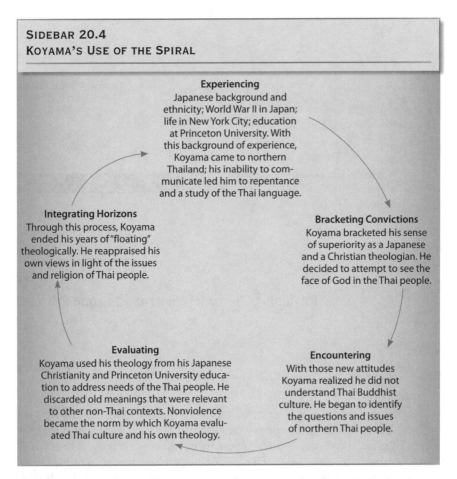

SIDEBAR 20.4
KOYAMA'S USE OF THE SPIRAL

Experiencing
Japanese background and ethnicity; World War II in Japan; life in New York City; education at Princeton University. With this background of experience, Koyama came to northern Thailand; his inability to communicate led him to repentance and a study of the Thai language.

Integrating Horizons
Through this process, Koyama ended his years of "floating" theologically. He reappraised his own views in light of the issues and religion of Thai people.

Bracketing Convictions
Koyama bracketed his sense of superiority as a Japanese and a Christian theologian. He decided to attempt to see the face of God in the Thai people.

Evaluating
Koyama used his theology from his Japanese Christianity and Princeton University education to address needs of the Thai people. He discarded old meanings that were relevant to other non-Thai contexts. Nonviolence became the norm by which Koyama evaluated Thai culture and his own theology.

Encountering
With those new attitudes Koyama realized he did not understand Thai Buddhist culture. He began to identify the questions and issues of northern Thai people.

allowed their concerns to reshape his ideas through the evaluative process, the new horizon formed by this interaction becomes a contextualized theology that is then put into service in his congregation in Thailand. Here Koyama moves beyond the integration of horizons and begins to traverse the spiral of knowledge acquisition again. He allows the new understandings that form his new horizon of meanings to inform his actions.

He describes this application by bringing his readers into his daily life. As he walks toward the church one morning, he realizes that he must preach not from the Bible as he knew it, not from Aquinas's or Barth's theologies as he learned them, but from the metaphors of the rice farmers whom he watched working in the fields. Bananas, sticky rice, and water buffalos would be his metaphors. With Luther he would find his theology not in reading books or speculating but in living and dying. The suffering of God and the suffering of the farmers, and his own suffering, would become the stuff of theology.

21

Integrating

Reshaping Our Own Views and Mission Practices

As we have seen in the preceding chapter, reengaging our convictions and evaluating the culture/religion that we encounter shows that the ideas and values of one context are not so insular that a conversation across cultures is impossible. The case-study evaluations show that God's loving presence influences religions other than Christianity; God's Spirit is active throughout the world. Our interaction with another culture changes as we reconnect with our own faith and values. We ourselves are changed in the process. Our approach to mission can now be reshaped.

This chapter focuses on *how we are changed* in the process of knowledge acquisition. Our experience with another religion changes our perceptions of our own religion and culture. We gain insights into God's work in the world. We identify social structures and values that carry the gospel in another culture. Our understanding of the church in our own context and in its relationship to the community of the other also changes. Our knowledge of ourselves expands. Now we are ready to integrate our knowledge with the knowledge gained and reshape our mission practices in clearer, more compassionate ways. We are ready to begin practicing giftive mission.

Making those changes, like evaluating, requires reflection. Missionaries are people in fields or settings. They have their own deeply held convictions

SIDEBAR 21.1
QUESTIONS ON HOW WE CHANGE

Answer the questions below to help you understand how you are changed in the process of knowledge acquisition.

1. How has your experience with another religion changed your perceptions of
   - your religion?
   - your culture?
   - the way you were brought up?
   - the differences between your social life and the life of the people with whom you interact?
2. What insights into God's work in the world have you gained from your open encounter?
   - Where did you see love operating in the society you encountered?
   - How do you think the Holy Spirit has been active in the religion before Christianity was presented?
   - What did the people's attitude toward or response to Jesus tell you about their culture?
3. What social structures, values, or ways of behaving in the new culture are compatible with the Christian gospel? How has that knowledge affected your understanding of the gospel?
4. How has your knowledge of yourself been expanded?
5. How has your approach to mission changed? How has it remained the same?
6. How has your understanding of the church in your own context and in its relationship to the community of the other been changed?

coming into a new situation for the purpose of communicating with people different from themselves—people of another culture and religion. To assess the changes made by that process of interaction in a general way misses the specificity of the interaction. Generalizations fall short of the goal of showing how integration brings the knowledge of two parties together. So the integrating process is best described with case studies, concrete examples of missionaries who got involved with people of another religion or culture, bracketed their convictions in order to begin to understand that culture, encountered new ideas and practices with openness, and evaluated them on the basis of their Christian faith. How were these people changed? What new forms did their mission practices take?

WAYS OF RESPONDING TO KNOWLEDGE IN A NEW CULTURE

The integrating process brings together a person's broadest perspectives with some of the knowledge gained from traversing the spiral of knowledge. A fusion

291

of those horizons shifts the perspectives of the missionary. We reorganize our former views, taking into account new knowledge gained in the interaction with another way of looking at the world. Naturally, the fusion of horizons can take different forms.

Integration

The experiences of living with Muslims in Indonesia, for example, changed Frances's understanding of Islam. Frances discovered that not all Muslims were like those from the Middle East. She learned that the Indonesian patterns of Islamic life flowed from a cultural base that was deeply influenced by Hinduism. The style of dress for women reflected cool pastel colors. Short headdresses revealed, rather than covered, the faces of smiling and calm Indonesian women. Her contact also reshaped her view of prayer. The dedication of Muslims arising at dawn to pray, praying in the fields in the heat of the day, and closing their day with praise to God impressed her. She began to reshape her Christian prayer life, responding to the call to prayer with a prayerful attitude. Allowing herself to be influenced by the Islamic society around her changed her horizon of meaning, re-forming the ways in which she understood not only their religion but her own.

Terry had a similar experience while studying Buddhist *bhikkhus* in Sri Lanka and their approach to moral living. Monks in the Theravada tradition live by a set of 227 rules that shape a life in communal living in some detail. They call living by the rules morality and consider that kind of moral living a prerequisite to advancing to higher spiritual planes. This insight helped Terry expand his understanding of rule-based Christian living. Rules of morality are often seen in Christian practice as requirements rather than as foundations for further and higher spiritual insights. While moral living does produce the fruits of the Spirit, it can also be helpfully seen as a foundation, a root, for further growth. Studying and interviewing Buddhist monastics gave him insights into Christian moral living that he might otherwise not have had.

Rejection

A harmonious integration or fusion of horizons does not automatically result from encountering another religion and evaluating it in terms of our own convictions. Alternatively, we can reaffirm ourselves in the views that were bracketed. Rather than finding something God-honoring in another religion, we discover beliefs that are not biblically supported and must be rejected. In that case, change occurs but the change reinforces the former views, perhaps strengthening them. Usually, as a result of the encounter, we hold to these views in a deeper, richer, often more compassionate way. The value of the spiral of knowledge acquisition is just as important, even though the end result differs.

For Terry, the Buddha's insistence that there is no ultimate God on whom one can rely for spiritual succor did not agree with biblical faith in a personal God who can be trusted and relied on for the graceful gift of salvation. Although it was obvious that the Buddhists he met, who insisted on their spiritual autonomy and the necessity of disciplined meditative effort, were enriched by that belief and developed worthwhile spiritual practice as a result, Terry's experience of the grace of God was too central to his faith to be changed by the sincere testimonies of his Buddhist friends to the contrary. Because, however, he came back to a reaffirmation of this belief after going through the steps of the spiral, his "rejection" of the teaching did not diminish his respect for the Buddhist friends with whom he disagreed. In fact, it deepened that respect.

Frances had a similar experience. She found many laudable expressions of modesty in Muslim forms of dress and behavior for women. But her conviction that women as well as men are created in God's image kept her from affirming the secondary place to which women are relegated in most forms of Islamic sharia law.

Other Outcomes

There are, of course, other possible outcomes. One could change religions. One might call this the *replacement outcome*. If the biblical parable of the talents teaches us anything, it is that God calls us not to bury our spiritual talents in the sand but to invest them in a risky world market in our efforts to tell the story of Jesus in hopes that God's kingdom will grow as a result. Playing it safe with God's gifts to us is not part of God's plan.

Or one could decide that all religions are pretty much the same, that one is as good as another, and that it really isn't necessary to choose among them. Call it the *relativistic outcome*. A relativistic view of all religions can result from interaction with another way of life. "True for you" becomes the motto of this response. In this case, one retains one's original convictions, but somehow they lose their power. Now they are placed alongside the views of the other as "equally valid." Paul Rabinow explains how a tolerance of other's views, without a correspondingly deep commitment to one's own way of thinking, can lead to a leveling of all claims to truth (1983).

Our experience with the spiral, however, is that among committed Christian missionaries, integration and rejection are far and away the most common outcomes of the fusion of horizons that takes place. And this fusion occurs in an almost bewildering variety of forms. Because of the infinite variety of contexts and personalities involved, one must really hear everyone's story to begin to get a sense for what might take place. Put another way, it is what does take place. Our only option is to become more cognizant of the dynamics involved so that we can take better advantage of the mission opportunities they create.

With that in mind, it might be helpful to end with three case studies of missionaries who have in one form or another raised the spiral of knowledge acquisition to a conscious level where they can self-consciously integrate it into their mission theology. The three studies we have chosen come from across the Christian denominational spectrum.

CASE STUDY 1: KOYAMA AND WATER BUFFALO THEOLOGY

We saw in the last chapter that when Koyama began evaluating Thai culture and the emphasis on nonviolence in Theravada Buddhism, he pushed himself to take another look at his own convictions. Reflecting on his experience of violence during his youth, as his nation fought in World War II, led him to question some of his own religious convictions. His adoption of the Western theologies of Aquinas and Barth also came under review.

Not only did Koyama evaluate Thai culture and religion, but he also allowed Thai culture and religion a role in evaluating his own convictions. Here the process of integration is already begun as one evaluates the cultures side by side. Koyama sees value in the Buddhist notion of nonharm. He recognizes the integrity of the peaceful practices of the Thai villagers he encounters. As he contrasts those values with views of war from his Japanese culture and his Christian convictions, he finds his perspective changing. Nonviolence becomes a central theme of evaluation for Koyama, not from his own culture or religion per se but from the life dialogue he holds with Thai culture.

During this evaluative process, Koyama's horizon of meaning changes. Because he critiques his own views in light of the values he encounters in Thailand, he is simultaneously integrating while evaluating. The water buffalo theology Koyama develops is not a theology from Japan alone. It is not a theology from his education at Princeton alone. It is not a theology from Thai culture and Buddhism alone. Rather, as Koyama himself states, his theology arises from a three-way conversation among parts of his life. The influence of his Japanese heritage converses with his theological education, which talks with his Thai context. He no longer sees meaning as he once did. In fact, he cannot revert to his former horizon of meaning. He is permanently changed—changed by the evaluation of Thai culture and religion from his Christian point of view and changed by his critique of his own convictions from the Thai perspective as he experienced it.

For Koyama, the integration of horizons occurs along with his evaluation of Thai culture and religion. As he articulates his water buffalo theology, he does not separate evaluating Thai culture from integrating some of those influences with his former point of view. The process becomes a seamless web. In this case, the integration phase is not singled out as a separate step but flows out of the other phases.

294

CASE STUDY 2: TIMOTHY RICHARD'S CONTEXTUAL THEOLOGY IN CHINA

Alternatively, the integration phase can be formed from distinct decisions to put aside some of one's former views because of the influence of one's new setting. Timothy Richard, a Baptist missionary to China, exemplifies this more conscious fusion of horizons. Our summary of Richard's story is taken largely from Andrew Walls's account (2002, 236–69).

Living at the height of the nineteenth-century missionary movement, Timothy Richard felt a strong calling to serve as a missionary in China. He was attracted to the China Inland Mission but eventually went to China with his own denomination as a Baptist missionary. Like most missionaries of his time, Richard understood theology as unchangeable. The purpose of mission work was to bring as many souls to Christ as possible in the shortest amount of time. The Bible was the guide for bringing those conversions about as well as the source of wisdom for people who accepted Christ.

As Richard lived in the countryside of China, however, he found it difficult to evangelize during the periodic famines that struck the area. People ran out of food; farm animals starved to death; people were hungry; children died of malnutrition. His preaching became ineffective as basic human needs overwhelmed the people's interest in religious ideas. Richard responded by returning to the United States and studying agriculture. On his return to China, he began writing articles for

newspapers on advanced farming techniques. His mission practices now focused on helping people find ways to reduce the devastating effects of famine. Through his work many were saved in this life. As he integrated his knowledge of the Chinese context with his understanding of the gospel, he diverged from his original plan of only helping people to find salvation in the next life.

Richard's horizon of meaning changed as he integrated his experience with the Chinese experience, one of suffering and starvation. From that understanding, he reframed his mission. His focus became advancing knowledge of agriculture in a society that needed that knowledge to survive. Richard did not "lose" his faith in Jesus as Savior of the world. But his experience in China reframed how he practiced that faith, not through preaching but through journalism. Educating the Chinese on how to avoid famine by producing more rice became Richard's focus. He integrated his experience of life in his new context with his Christian convictions and emerged from the process with a new goal and a new set of mission practices. Richard's form of giftive mission became one of staving off hunger in a famine-prone area of China. His practices reflected his understanding of his new context.

Some of Richard's colleagues questioned his new form of mission to the Chinese. Without experiencing the suffering of famine themselves, they evaluated

Continued

Timothy Richard's—Continued

Richard's new giftive mission practice and found it wanting. Some even questioned his Christian faith. But understanding the knowledge-acquisition spiral allows us to see how Richard shifted the way he framed the gospel to a pattern meaningful to the people to whom he was ministering. That reformulated practice in no way calls his Christian faith into question. The ubiquity of the gospel stands out clearly in Richard's life. His practices preached well. His words of advice on agricultural techniques saved lives. Healthy people could then listen to the words of an evangelist in a later period. Missionaries in the next generation could establish churches among people who were not starving because Richard's giftive mission practices helped communities survive.

Richard not only changed his mission practices but reformulated his theology in dialogue with the religions of China. He used his life text, Matthew 10:11 ("Whatever town or village you enter, search for some worthy person there and stay at his house until you leave"), to expand his vision of an Asian Christianity that could be spread throughout China by the Chinese, an Asian Christianity that could someday helpfully enrich Christianity in the West.

Let us look more closely at the theological integration Richard did as he lived and practiced mission work in China. Beginning with a traditional evangelical theology of evangelization as the preaching of God's word to the lost millions of China, Richard was influenced by China itself to expand his vision in several ways.

What is evangelism? Richard's growing sensitivity to Chinese culture soon taught him how barbaric those traditional customs of evangelization seemed to the Chinese. Yet, Richard, in his many years of missionary work, never lost his vision of Christocentric evangelism, though his vision expanded.

He focused on Matthew 10:11, noticing how Jesus admonished his disciples to find those who are worthy of hearing the gospel in a new place. Richard surmised that the Buddhist religious scholars were the worthy in China. They were the ones who were searching for truth, looking for religious answers, and sensitive to religious ramifications in society. Rather than continue the old missionary methods, Richard began to focus on cultivating the literati of China. Those worthy ones would be his listeners. They in turn would spread Christianity throughout China.

He learned about Chinese Buddhism. While never abandoning his commitment to biblical truth, Richard came to the conclusion that God was active in pre-Christian Asia. The Chinese Pure Land Buddhist notion of grace, its idea of a Savior, was not something learned from the West. While Richard was not a systematic thinker, his writings on Chinese Buddhism show a willingness to learn from that religion even while he attempted to convince Buddhists of the truth of Christianity.

How does the context influence the tasks of Christian mission? Richard worked in the days when much of the missionary movement was synonymous with verbal evangelism. It was difficult to integrate the idea that social service or political action could become part of the mission task along with proclamation. The context in China changed all this for Richard.

Although at first he was able to use the famine itself to draw converts to

Christianity, Richard soon realized that the famine was of such proportions that it demanded a response from him as a Christian. His response was to examine the structure of food distribution in the area and attempt to change it. This meant getting involved with local officials; it meant appealing to Christians at home for funds; it meant focusing on feeding the hungry in addition to preaching.

Richard turned to scientific knowledge to provide the tools that could overcome famine. If scientific knowledge was not part of the Christian gospel per se, it certainly was part of a Christian view of nature. If China could appropriate scientific knowledge, it could not only feed its people but could also prevent famine in the future.

How could Asia influence Christianity in the West? The context taught Richard not only how to present the Christian gospel but also how God was active in the world for good. His expanded vision included not only social service but peace and justice issues. On the basis of his mission experience, he critiqued the West in its quest for material goods and more and better armaments. Asia not only benefited from the Christian gospel but could, in its turn, critique Western views.

The fusion of horizons experienced by Richard meant that he held on to his Christian convictions but, at the same time, expanded his vision to include issues and dimensions of thought that he learned in his encounter with China and Chinese religions. His calling as a missionary sent to preach the gospel in China never wavered. But his understanding of the tasks of mission expanded. His reliance on the Bible for interpreting how the gospel should be preached remained central, but his interpretations, especially of Matthew 10:11, expanded. Finding the worthy led to a strong emphasis on Chinese intellectuals and the reflexive evangelism that he participated in with them. His understanding of Christ and the crucifixion as central to the Christian message did not change, but his emphasis on God as Creator and the Holy Spirit as harbinger of God's acts of goodness expanded his theological focus. The wisdom of the East met the wisdom of the West in the life and work of Timothy Richard, and God's world is richer for that fusion of horizons.

CASE STUDY 3:
VINCENT DONOVAN IN AFRICA

As we learned in the previous chapter, Donovan's mission experience was almost the direct opposite of Richard's. His experience of the church's work in Africa convinced him that the missionaries were doing primarily social work and little preaching for conversion. It seemed to him that the latter was called for in the Masai African context. Once he opened himself to African traditional religions and saw the rich store of biblically compatible

Continued

297

Vincent Donovan—Continued

knowledge and instincts in their belief systems, he realized that a fusion of horizons between his Christianity and the Africans' acknowledgment of a high God, a moral universe, and a life to come could result in a very successful Christian mission. As you can see from sidebar 21.2, Donovan's experience as he describes it in *Christianity Rediscovered* (2000, 31–33) matches step for step the spiral of knowledge acquisition.

SIDEBAR 21.2
DONOVAN'S USE OF THE SPIRAL

The circle below shows how Donovan used the spiral of knowledge acquisition to change his methods of mission. His mission goal was to establish the church in the rural villages of East Africa, where animism was the major religion.

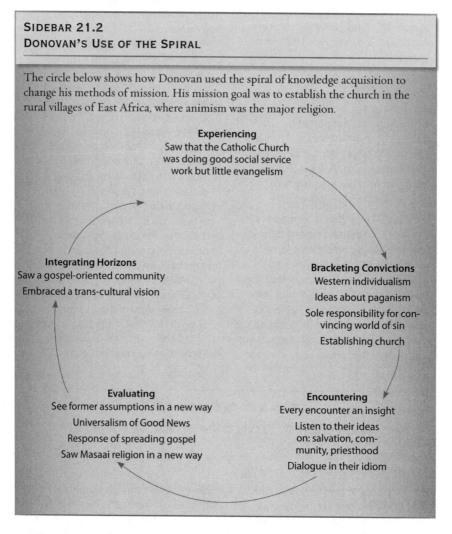

Experiencing
Saw that the Catholic Church was doing good social service work but little evangelism

Integrating Horizons
Saw a gospel-oriented community
Embraced a trans-cultural vision

Bracketing Convictions
Western individualism
Ideas about paganism
Sole responsibility for convincing world of sin
Establishing church

Evaluating
See former assumptions in a new way
Universalism of Good News
Response of spreading gospel
Saw Masaai religion in a new way

Encountering
Every encounter an insight
Listen to their ideas on: salvation, community, priesthood
Dialogue in their idiom

The process of integrating new knowledge can go wrong; new views may be uncritically adopted or the temptation to consider all perspectives as equally valid may dominate, reducing the vitality of both. Or integrating new knowledge with one's own convictions can be done successfully as we bracket our convictions, encounter the new religion with openness, evaluate our experiences, and reflect on how new knowledge can be incorporated into our ways of understanding life and Christianity. In that way we develop new theologies that are true to God's word and new mission practices that focus on giving and receiving gifts.

PART 4

Giftive Mission

Because world religions, economic conditions, and political conditions are changing, Christian missioners need to explore new metaphors for what it means to do mission in the twenty-first century. We suggest that one of the primary biblical images that can help in the process is the idea of giving gifts. The metaphor of giving gifts can be a helpful way to describe what we are doing when we tell the story of Jesus. We think that gift giving, along with other traditional biblical metaphors, should be in the toolbox of mission workers around the world. We call this giftive mission.

Giftive mission has several strengths: (1) It is biblical. The Scriptures are filled with references to God's gifts to us and our resultant giving of similar gifts to other people. (2) Christian theology, the theology of grace, seems to mesh particularly well with the idea of gift giving. (3) All the world's cultures share the experiences of gift giving. Although different cultures view gift giving in sometimes very different ways, the fact that it is a ubiquitous practice means that it can be used as a fruitful common ground for discussion and relationship building. It is also fertile ground for teaching others the meaning of the gospel story.

22

Metaphors for Mission

As a boy, Terry was a featured soloist in his dad's evangelistic campaigns. His biggest number was "Bringing in the Sheaves," and it is easy to see in retrospect that the message of that song, more than anything else, shaped his understanding of Christian missions. Christian missions meant harvesting lost souls.

Several things over the years, however, have been instrumental in changing the harvesting image as his most important metaphor for missions. For one thing, a voice change meant he could no longer hit high C, and he quit singing "Bringing in the Sheaves." More importantly, theological study convinced him that the mission impulse is wider and deeper than the idea of reaping lost souls, although he has not abandoned the idea of fields "white already to harvest" (John 4:35 KJV). And study has taught both of us that a metaphor is only effective when it relates to its cultural context, and our culture—a global, interdependent, technological, multicultural, urbanized society—demands a new key metaphor (or metaphors) to communicate the world mission of the church. (Throughout this chapter, we use the general term *metaphor* to refer to metaphors proper, similes, and other literary devices of that sort.)

It seems such a simple thing, changing a metaphor we use to describe something. We usually see ourselves using language to communicate clearly, and if one way of talking about something doesn't communicate accurately and well to our listeners, we search for a different way of talking about it. If

SIDEBAR 22.1
RIPE FIELDS

Jesus said, "Do you not say, 'Four months more and then the harvest'? I tell you, open your eyes and look at the fields! They are ripe for harvest. Even now the reaper draws his wages, even now he harvests the crop for eternal life, so that the sower and the reaper may be glad together. Thus the saying, 'One sows and another reaps' is true. I sent you to reap what you have not worked for. Others have done the hard work, and you have reaped the benefits of their labor" (John 4:35–37; see also Matt. 9:37; Luke 10:2; 1 Cor. 9:7–12; 2 Cor. 9:9–10; Gal. 6:7–10; Heb. 12:11–13; James 3:17–18; Rev. 14:13–16).

The harvest imagery in these passages refers to a harvest of righteousness, a harvest of material benefit given in exchange for spiritual direction, and a harvest of eternal life. The focus is on the readiness of the fields—it is time to harvest—and on the cooperative nature of the efforts in sowing and reaping. We cooperate with God in God's work of harvesting the ripe earth.

The agricultural image has probably been the most frequently used mission metaphor in the history of the church. Matteo Ricci, in his journal of his mission efforts to China in the sixteenth century, commended one of his coworkers, Father Cattaneo, by saying he "managed well and increased the harvest" by winning "many converts" from among the Chinese (Ricci 1953).

I, for example, say that a lawsuit is a gravamen, and my listeners have no idea what a gravamen is, then I change the metaphor I use to talk about a lawsuit: a lawsuit is a matter of sour grapes, I say. My listeners know what sour grapes mean, so I have successfully communicated. A simple thing.

Is it really so simple though? In changing a metaphor for something, am I really just making a harmless change in the way I talk about it so that my listeners can understand what I mean? I might be doing that, but I might also be doing much more. Some say that a metaphor—the words related to one thing that we commandeer to talk about another thing—is a much more powerful tool than we tend to realize.

Change the way we talk about something, they suggest, and we go a long way toward changing the thing itself. All of a sudden we are in deeper water (to use a metaphor). Metaphors are very powerful tools. Words like *indispensable* and *determinative* and *ideological* begin to creep into our minds when we think about metaphor this way.

We want to think about metaphors for mission in this deeper way. Our hypothesis is that we are using metaphors for mission that do not communicate as well as they once did. Many of the metaphors we use actually communicate the wrong things about mission to a suspicious public. People of other religions get a false impression of what Christianity is because of some of the metaphors we use.

We think we should change our metaphors. We need to communicate better what it means to tell the gospel story in our twenty-first-century world to people of other religions. But this is not just a literary exercise. It is serious business. To do it well, we need to first understand more clearly what metaphors are. We must then take a look at the way the Bible uses metaphors for mission and, third, suggest some alternative metaphors—biblically based metaphors—for this time and this place.

WHAT IS A METAPHOR?

As you might expect given the above discussion, the concept of metaphor can be a confusing thing. Our Scrabble dictionary defines metaphor as "a figure of speech." My *Oxford English Dictionary*, on the other hand, goes on and on about the different levels of meaning of this "simple" word. Clearly it can be understood on many different levels. To simplify, let's say for heuristic purposes that there are three primary ways to understand the concept of metaphor.

The first level is *metaphor as literary device*. Metaphor on this level is what you learned about in English composition class in the fifth grade. My English composition text said something like this about metaphor: A metaphor is the use of language referring to one thing to describe the nature of another, totally different thing. "My dad is strong as an ox" is a metaphor. It uses a prime characteristic of an animal, an ox, to describe the physical strength of a human being, my father. "Naty Alvarado is quick as a cat" is another metaphor. Again, it uses the characteristic attribute of an animal to describe and illustrate a characteristic of a human being, in this case a handball player. Animals do not supply us with our only metaphors. "He is dumb as a post" uses an inanimate object. A television news anchor intoning that "The White House said today that . . ." is using an architectural reference to refer to the president and his staff.

Metaphor as literary device is the most basic level of metaphor. Metaphors at this level are used by everyone. They fill our speech. We don't even think about their use. Every culture has a large store of metaphorical conventions that are commonplace parts of our language. Of course, there are metaphor "experts" who are not satisfied with commonplace metaphors, sometimes calling them clichés. These metaphor experts, otherwise known as writers and poets, pride themselves on coming up with new, unique metaphors that no one has ever thought of before. T. S. Eliot describing the London fog moving about the town as prowling on cat's paws is a good example of a metaphor expert in action.

Even at this most basic level of metaphor, however, certain assumptions are being made about reality, assumptions that are important to acknowledge if we are to fully understand the other ways the concept of metaphor is used. One assumption is that the phrase "My dad is strong as an ox" describes reality in a, well, real way. Both my dad and an ox are real things. In fact, they are the most real things. The job of language, and in this case the metaphor, is to as accurately as possible tell us about those two real things. The language we use is a servant of the real things in the world, and the test of good language is the extent to which it can be said to accurately describe that real world. You may be saying, "Duh!" at this point. This is all common sense. And for you it might be.

But consider a second level of metaphor. We might call this *metaphor as reality itself* or *metaphor as everything*. In this view, metaphor is not simply a way of talking about real things; metaphors (that is, human language itself) *are* the real things. We cannot, as human beings, say that anything really exists until we talk about it. In a sense, when I relate my dad to an ox, I am creating both by the act of describing them. And because I relate them to each other, I am creating a reality of relationship that would not exist except for the fact that I have spoken of them in this way. Reality, in this view, is not something concrete "out there" but is something I create in my mind, by thinking and talking about it.

Thus a metaphor is not just a literary device to make my descriptions of reality out there more accurate and interesting. It means something much more important: that everything is a metaphor. The English language itself is one big metaphor, or more to the point, an unending series of smaller metaphors. It is not just the language about an ox's strength that is a metaphor; the word *dad* is also a metaphor. It is not just a cat's quickness that is a metaphor; the name Naty Alvarado, used to describe my handball-playing friend, is a metaphor.

In this view, a metaphor's value (or success, we might say) does not lie in the extent to which it is interesting in a literary or poetical way. Nor does it succeed because it helps me understand my father in a more accurate way, that is, a way that corresponds to reality out there. In the view of metaphor as reality itself, a metaphor succeeds to the extent that other people around me agree that this is a good way to talk about reality and begin to use the same metaphor(s) themselves. As listeners and readers, other people hearing or reading my "metaphors" decide for themselves what they mean, using their experience as the judge. If it turns out that their experience is well described by my metaphors, then we have shared meaning. Shared meaning leads to communities and cultures of like-minded (perhaps better, like-experienced) people. In this way, the reality we all share is constructed in our minds, using metaphors (language) as the building materials.

This view of metaphor may sound a bit strange. Whereas the first view, metaphor as literary device, probably made sense to you, this one might seem odd. Who could formulate such a view? And why would one do so? What value does this way of looking at metaphor have? This "metaphor as everything" view has become popular because it emphasizes what is known as the subjective view of reality, that is, the view of reality that focuses on the human being as knower. In the minds of linguists and philosophers who emphasize this view, the objective way of looking at reality is overemphasized in science, neglecting how important a human being and his or her emotions and prejudices and cultural background and religious views are in determining what is real and true.

But we suggest that this subjective view of reality perhaps has gone too far. We certainly think that when applied to the concept of metaphor it is unhelpful. If everything is metaphor, if all language is metaphor, then the concept becomes unwieldy for our purposes. So we suggest an understanding of metaphor that goes beyond the metaphor-as-literary-device understanding, but we stop short of becoming idealist philosophers, saying that all reality is constructed in our minds and is determined by our language. We use a view located somewhere between the *metaphor-as-literary-device* view and the *metaphor-as-everything* view.

We need a name for this position. Let's call it the *complex view of metaphor.* In this view, metaphors do have literary properties in that they are interesting and insightful ways of talking about something. They enable us to learn more about an object than if we insisted on sticking to what we might think is purely descriptive, scientific language. But metaphors do more than illumine. They also have creative properties. When we use a set of related metaphors to describe a human activity, what were at first simply ways of talking about that activity over time gain strength and become themselves determinative of the activity itself. For example, if we talk enough about politics as a "dirty game," we are in no little way contributing to a perception that becomes reality (or that heightens and reifies a reality already there), whereas if we talk about politics as an essential component of an overall lifestyle of public service, then it is more likely to become that. The way we talk about things contributes to their reality and nature. Metaphors have great creative power.

We like this way of talking about metaphor because it seems to address some serious problems today in the way we talk about, and thus think about, and thus act about, Christian mission. How does the way we talk about mission, the metaphors we use, affect mission activity itself?

METAPHORS WE LIVE BY

In 1980 George Lakoff and Mark Johnson published *Metaphors We Live By*, in which they convincingly make the case that metaphors are not optional ways of describing things poetically but are essential to the way human beings form concepts and clusters of concepts: "Our ordinary conceptual system, in terms of which we both think and act, is fundamentally metaphorical in nature" (3).

This may sound like a new idea. Lakoff and Johnson acknowledge that it does seem new. But they attribute this to the fact that normally the way we

---

SIDEBAR 22.2
WAYS TO UNDERSTAND METAPHOR

1. *Metaphor as Literary Device:* One thing describes another.
   She is pretty as a picture.
   He is strong as an ox.
2. *Metaphor as Everything:* Image determines perceptions of reality.
   She is pretty as a picture. (woman as a beautiful object)
   She is smart as a whip. (woman as quick and accurate)
   He is strong as an ox. (man as strong and plodding)
   He is strong as a bull. (man as strong and powerful)
3. *Metaphor as Complex Image:* Reworking metaphors to influence society.

   Politics is a dirty game ———————→ Politics is like a chess game
   (Simple, dishonest, dishonorable)   (Complicated, demanding, honorable)

   She is pretty as a picture ———————→She is like a fine wine
   (Static, young, simple)   (Changing, maturing, complex)

---

structure our concepts and ideas is largely an unconscious process and reality: "Our conceptual system is not something we are normally aware of. In most of the little things we do every day we simply act more or less automatically along certain lines" (3). For Lakoff and Johnson, metaphor is not just a matter of lively, interesting language, but our human thought processes are largely formed along metaphorical lines.

This way of thinking is a matter not of an accumulation of random discrete metaphors but of "metaphorical concepts," that is, large groups of related metaphors clustered around single ideas. As an example, consider the metaphor that "argument is war." This in itself is a metaphor, one you have probably used. But it is a metaphor expressed in much more complex ways than just the simple statement that "argument is war." As a concept it is supported by a whole range of related metaphors. Lakoff and Johnson list a few of these related metaphors (see sidebar 22.3).

Since we use this extended metaphor—argument is war—to describe the actions we take when we disagree with someone's position, we act, in the process of disagreeing, as if we were engaged in warfare. That is because we—in our culture at least—consider argument to be analogous to war; we find it very difficult to have a disagreeing discussion in any way other than a warfare mode. We may talk about agreeable disagreements, and we may occasionally approach them that way in our behavior, but our default way of acting when we are in the verbal process of disagreeing with someone is verbally confrontative. Because we use the language of war to describe arguments, we engage in what can only be called verbal battles.

308

Metaphorical concepts are so common we hardly notice them. Consider, for example, our concept of argument. Two definitions may be seen in comparison:

Cognitive Definition of Argument: Argument occurs when two or more people disagree about a subject. In an argument, one person states his or her view of a subject; then the other person states his or her view of the same subject, and conversation proceeds in like fashion.

Affective Definition of Argument: An argument is a conversation during which opponents resort to heated emotional and often inaccurate statements of their positions.

We can also see two ways to metaphorically conceive of argument:

ARGUMENT AS WAR	ARGUMENT AS SPORT
Your claims are indefensible.	She took an end run around my point.
He attacked every weak point in my argument.	I got hit below the belt on that one.
His criticisms were right on target.	We volleyed for over an hour on that topic.
I demolished his argument.	We were coming up to match point.
I've never won an argument with him.	He hit a hole in one there.
You disagree? Okay, shoot.	She threw a curve ball at me.
If you use that strategy, he'll wipe you out.	Showing I was right was a slam dunk.
He shot down all my arguments.	When he said that, he hit the ball out of the park.

If this is the way we talk, and if the way we talk is to some extent determinative of the way we act, then consider for a moment what it would mean to decide that we do not like the metaphorical cluster that talks about argument as war. What could we do about it, theoretically at least? Two theoretical courses of action come to mind. The first would be to say that the root of the problem is not being as clear as possible about what argument is, that by resorting to the metaphorical language of warfare we have gotten too far away from the real thing, which we might call an exchange of disagreeing ideas. We simply need to revert to more objective, scientific language to describe arguments and thus solve the problem of importing alien ideas into the concept of argument. Let me suggest you try this. I did. I came up with a paragraph something like this:

309

> Argument occurs when two or more people disagree about a subject. In an argument, one person states his or her view of a subject; then the other person states his or her view of the same subject, and conversation proceeds in like fashion.

Notice the sparseness of this "objective" description. Notice what it does not answer. Most lacking is any description of how this exchange of disagreeing ideas is carried out, whether it is done with love or hate or indifference, and it does not describe the desired goals of an argument, whether it is to win or lose, or collaborate, or mutually soliloquize. Since these questions are all of a subjective nature—that is, people would answer them quite differently according to personal preference and cultural context—it is difficult to make up hard and fast objective descriptions of them. And you would find if you attempted to answer them how natural it is to resort to metaphorical language, language that would reveal what you really thought about the nature of argument and how it should be carried out. You would find the pull to subjective description very powerful, indeed necessary, to making the statements you would want to make about the nature of argument.

So what does this have to do with mission? It is time to return specifically to the subject of mission and metaphors and to begin by going to the fount of all mission metaphors, the Bible and the way the Bible uses metaphors to describe mission.

BIBLICAL METAPHORS FOR MISSION

The Bible uses many metaphors and metaphor clusters to describe mission activity, a fact that has not gone unnoticed by biblical scholars over the centuries. Terry remembers a text he read in seminary, written in the late 1800s, describing in some detail the metaphors the New Testament uses to describe mission activity. The author described five principal ones—agricultural, military, architectural, athletic, and market—citing them with approval, implying that they are just as good today as they were when first used by Jesus, Paul, and John in the first century CE.

Many books have been written over the years to describe biblical metaphors for mission. In 2006 Stanley Skreslet published an excellent book on mission in the New Testament, *Picturing Christian Witness: New Testament Images of Disciples in Mission,* in which he discusses the primary "images" (Lakoff would call them metaphor clusters) used to describe mission activity. The five images he discusses in depth are announcing good news, sharing Christ with friends, interpreting the gospel, shepherding, and building and planting. Skreslet chooses these five because they seem most appropriate to him in our time. Although he does not spend a great deal of time discussing other images that he implies are not that helpful today, such as military imagery and marketing imagery, the strength of his work is his acknowledgment that the images we use must be rooted in the biblical text.

Skreslet's book in many ways is an improvement on Terry's nineteenth-century mission text because Skreslet acknowledges the context-specific nature of metaphor clusters. Some metaphor clusters communicate more readily in certain cultural contexts than others do. Although Skreslet's work is complete in relation to what he set out to do, he left for others the task of being more specific about how some biblical metaphors seem more appropriate for twenty-first-century missions and how others seem to have lost their metaphorical value in the two thousand years since the biblical writers first used them.

Since our view of complex metaphors specifies that metaphors work on a case-by-case basis from cultural context to cultural context, it is difficult to say that some metaphors are appropriate for today and others are not in a universal sense. An agricultural image may still be appropriate in a certain rural-dominated cultural setting, while in an urban one it might not. Perhaps the best way to proceed is to consider a certain number of specific biblical metaphors and discuss their appropriateness or inappropriateness for today's mission climate.

Agricultural

If a few metaphors could be considered universally applicable at the time of the biblical writing, the agricultural metaphor would be in that small group. In Jesus's and Paul's day, over 90 percent of the people made their living by farming or subsistence hunting and gathering. In such cultures talking about mission in terms of that kind of activity makes a world of sense. Consider samples from the biblical metaphor cluster used to describe this in relation to mission:

The harvest is plentiful but the workers are few (Matt. 9:37).

The kingdom of heaven is like a mustard seed (Matt. 13:31).

And I will make you fishers of men (Mark 1:17).

I planted the seed, Apollos watered it, but God made it grow (1 Cor. 3:6).

Whoever sows generously will also reap generously (2 Cor. 9:6).

At the proper time we will reap a harvest (Gal. 6:9).

The harvest of the earth is ripe (Rev. 14:15).

The agricultural metaphor is still powerful today, but since almost half of the world's population now live in cities, not in the country, many people no longer relate as readily to agricultural and pastoral imagery as they did in Jesus's day. Thus this imagery needs to be used more selectively. Since I am an urban dweller in a highly technological society, I have, as I mentioned above, quit singing "Bringing in the Sheaves." I need to find a new song, and many of us working in such cultures have switched our "songs," that is, our primary metaphorical clusters vis-à-vis mission.

Military

A close second in frequency to the agricultural imagery used to communicate mission in the Bible is military activity. Unfortunately, military activity is as ubiquitous today as it was in biblical times; military activity has always been a standard feature of human life on this planet. And, unfortunately, it is not difficult to get an emotional rise out of people by asking them to sing a religious, military song. Do you remember singing "Onward Christian Soldiers" in church and the tingle it created? Consider this biblical language:

Because he fights the LORD's battles (1 Sam. 25:28).

I did not come to bring peace, but a sword (Matt. 10:34).

Waging war against the law (Rom. 7:23).

The helmet of salvation and the sword of the Spirit (Eph. 6:17).

Fight the good fight of the faith (1 Tim. 6:12).

With us like a good soldier of Christ Jesus (2 Tim. 2:3).

With justice he judges and makes war (Rev. 19:11).

Human capacity for violent disagreement has remained static; what has changed most dramatically has been the increase in weapons of war and their destructive capacity. Violence used to be limited to the damage one person could do to another person with handheld weapons such as knives, swords, and spears. Now we find ourselves able to kill thousands of people with a single bomb blast and theoretically able to destroy life on our planet with nuclear weapons. It is clear that in such a world, military metaphors for mission bring more baggage than the concept can bear. They do communicate, but they communicate the wrong things.

It is fair to say that even biblical writers had reservations about using warfare imagery. Paul noted in his second letter to the Corinthians that "we do not wage war as the world does" (10:3). Paul wasn't ready to give up on the metaphor, but he relativized it somewhat. We need to give it up. Billy Graham

312

has ceased calling his evangelistic meetings "crusades" and "campaigns" in an attempt to distance himself from this metaphorical concept cluster.

Architectural

A third image of mission is not the most prominent, perhaps, but important all the same. It is used especially in Paul's first letter to the Corinthian church. It is the concept of building, both physical buildings and institutions. Some of the elements of this metaphorical concept include:

Unless the LORD builds the house (Ps. 127:1).

The stone the builders rejected (Matt. 21:42).

We should not think that the divine being is like gold or silver or stone—an image made by man's design and skill (Acts 17:29).

You are . . . God's building (1 Cor. 3:9).

I laid a foundation as an expert builder, and someone else is building on it (1 Cor. 3:10).

James, Peter and John, those reputed to be pillars (Gal. 2:9).

In him the whole building is joined together (Eph. 2:21).

Whose architect and builder is God (Heb. 11:10).

Are being built into a spiritual house (1 Pet. 2:5).

This is still a powerful image, useful in today's complex cultures, where building large buildings has become a technological wonder and an artistic achievement. Complex cultures are also, by definition, institutionally diverse, and the concept of "building" can apply to both old and new institutions. Thus, we have an appropriate image here, one that resonates well with a prominent metaphor used to describe the New Testament church, the kingdom of God. The challenge with this metaphor involves showing the resonances while pointing out the dissonances: "The kingdom of God is like a human institution, but it is different in important ways."

Athletic

This is a metaphor cluster used heavily in Paul's letters to Timothy, but its ideas also appear throughout the New Testament. It is important, however, because it is one that might have increased, rather than decreased, in cultural appropriateness today. Athletics are so important now that perhaps this metaphor could be used more profitably today than in the past. Here's how the biblical writers use it:

Everyone who competes in the games goes into strict training (1 Cor. 9:25).

You were running a good race (Gal. 5:7).

Similarly, if anyone competes as an athlete (2 Tim. 2:5).

Correcting and training in righteousness (2 Tim. 3:16).

I have fought the good fight, I have finished the race (2 Tim. 4:7).

No discipline seems pleasant at the time (Heb. 12:11).

They may be won over without words (1 Pet. 3:1).

Like the architectural metaphor, the athletic image carries some baggage. Not all people like sports. Not all people like the sports offered on television. Not all people like the athletes who represent sports such as football, baseball, basketball, and hockey. Abuses in sports—greed, steroids, cheating, and so on—make this a metaphor that needs nuancing to effectively communicate gospel values. But it definitely has more potential today as a metaphor than it did even in biblical times.

Market

As we mentioned in chapter 1, nothing could be more relevant to today's world than the marketplace metaphor. With democratic capitalism becoming the world's default political/economic system, images that relate gospel mission to that kind of thinking are definitely useful. Buying and selling are the stuff of everyday life. We measure everything by what we consider to be their cost and benefit to us. Consider how the Bible uses this image:

Every tree that does not produce good fruit will be cut down and thrown into the fire (Matt. 3:10).

Like a merchant looking for fine pearls (Matt. 13:45).

The man who had received one talent went off [and] dug a hole in the ground (Matt. 25:18).

You should have put my money on deposit with the bankers (Matt. 25:27).

SIDEBAR 22.4
NEW TESTAMENT IMAGES OF DISCIPLESHIP IN MISSION

Here are some New Testament passages that depict Stanley Skreslet's (2006) metaphor clusters:

Announcing good news	Jesus in the temple (Luke 4:16–21)
	The Great Commission (Matt. 28:16–20)
Sharing Christ with friends	Parable of the banquet (Luke 14:16–24)
	Jesus eating with the disciples on the Damascus Road (Luke 24:28–32)
	The disciples sharing in community (Acts 4:32–35)
Interpreting the gospel	Paul's letters to the churches (e.g., Rom. 1:1–7; Gal. 1:1–3; Eph. 1:1–14)
	Paul arguing that the "Unknown God" is Jesus (Acts 17:22–31)
Shepherding	Jesus pleading with Simon Peter, "Feed my sheep" (John 21:15–18 TNIV)
	Priscilla and Aquila instructing Apollos (Acts 18:24–26)
Building and planting	Growing into a holy temple for God (1 Pet. 2:5)
	God's servants work together: Paul plants, Apollos waters, God gives the increase (1 Cor. 3:5–6)

They are like children sitting in the marketplace (Luke 7:32).

You were bought at a price (1 Cor. 6:20).

Unfortunately, many think that perhaps the modern church has already overused this image and has used it as far more than a metaphorical image, succumbing to some of the more unsavory aspects of the marketplace that have penetrated the operation of the institutional church itself. The Bible is very cautious about this image. Jesus was appalled at the extent to which the money changers had affected temple life. "How dare you turn my father's house into a market!" (John 2:16); Paul carefully distinguished between a regular business and gospel "business." Our religious institutions need to heed their warnings. The marketplace metaphor has gained too much creative power over the reality of the church in our culture. In too many cases the image is becoming reality.

This is just a sampling. Note that other important metaphor concepts are used in the texts to describe mission: the rescue metaphor cluster, the healing metaphor cluster, the storytelling metaphor cluster, just to name three. And one we discuss more fully below, the gift metaphor cluster, is often used. But before we take up that discussion, we should spend just a bit of time with an important question: Can we really change significantly the way people think metaphorically about an activity like mission? And if we can, how might we go about doing so?

CHANGING MISSION METAPHORS: *SIC ET NON*

In some important ways, metaphor clusters cannot be changed just because someone thinks they are inappropriate. Metaphors become part of the air we breathe. Our everyday life is immersed in the metaphors of our age and cultural context. To just one day up and decide that the bald eagle is an inappropriate symbol of the United States does not change much; there may be ways to change or modify an enduring image, but we cannot do it alone.

That is the first thing to realize about metaphor clusters. By their nature they are *communal, not individual, images*. As such, individuals like you and me cannot really change them. They are out of our hands. At the beginning of our book, we noted that the current dominant image used to describe the community of religions in the world and how Christians relate to them is the marketplace of religions metaphor cluster. Those are the images our Western cultures have determined to be most understandable and appropriate to our time. We cannot change the way culture at large envisions these mission themes.

That is not to say that we cannot critically evaluate them. We may determine that these images are theologically inappropriate in one way or another. We may decide that the marketplace image reduces the interaction of Christianity with the other religions to economic dynamics, for example, in a way that does not do justice to the good news. Or like Paul we may decide that there are some good things about such an image as long as it is properly nuanced. Making theological judgments about the ways people come to talk about the work of God is part of our task as public theologians. But it would be a mistake to think that we can summarily change the way we and others think about them.

A second problem with thinking that we can easily change mission metaphors is that they are *holistic, complex sets of ideas*, not single, focused, one-time metaphors. Take the journeying metaphor, for example. A whole complex of ideas surrounds this idea, not just the single verbal metaphor about religion being a life journey. This metaphor cluster includes ideas about how one takes such a trip, about helping others along the way, about what difficulties we can expect, and many other facets. Consider that John Bunyan was able to write a whole book, *Pilgrim's Progress*, that is basically an expansion of the journeying metaphor cluster and you begin to realize how complex an idea it has become.

Again, this is not to say that we cannot challenge such an idea just because it is complex, but we should not underestimate the size of the job. We should be prepared for a major dissecting task first of all, to fully understand the depth and width of the image, and then after we have laid bare its elements, we can begin to appreciate how each must be addressed. As Bunyan showed us, the journeying metaphor can be used to great advantage. But as modern New Agers have demonstrated, it can be used in inappropriate ways that must be challenged.

Just because we need help with this kind of metaphorical problem does not mean that we should not attempt it. To the question, can we really choose our metaphors about mission? the answer should be a qualified but clear yes. Given enough time, theological argument, and help from our church counterculture, we can make a difference in the way people talk (and subsequently think and act) about mission. Just because these very complex ideas have become embedded in our culture like intricate tree root systems spreading out over hundreds of square feet underground does not mean that we cannot take steps to uproot and modify them. Two reasons give hope.

First, *metaphors are human constructs*. And it is the nature of human constructs and cultures to change. Nothing human is static. Nothing about what we do can even approach the eternality of God and God's word.

Second, *metaphors by their nature change and develop*. It should be obvious to anyone who reads the current literature on mission that some images are used more often than others. As we have suggested, the marketplace image is perhaps the most common one. As Christians we are in a marketplace competition with the other world religions. Christianity is growing (gaining market share), especially in the majority world, but the other religions (Hinduism, Buddhism, and Islam) are also growing quickly. We are competing with these other religions to reach the unreached and the nominally committed with our religious product first. We must be aware of what the competition is doing, the methods they are using, and the successes they are having so that we can counter those gains and replace them with gains of our own.

This marketplace model is becoming more common than, say, the agricultural model (the most common biblical model) for reasons mentioned above. It fits modern, economic culture better than the agricultural model in many parts of the world as more people move to the city. The agricultural model is still important in many contexts, but the marketplace metaphor works well in more globalized areas.

Mission metaphors do change "on their own," so to speak. That is, they change in response to changing cultural contexts. Mission metaphors can be "encouraged" to change by our efforts also. This is desirable; as the Bible models by having a large number of different metaphors designed for the different cultural contexts encountered in Scripture, so a savvy mission agent needs to have several metaphors at his or her disposal for use in different cul-

317

SIDEBAR 22.5
CHARACTERISTICS OF METAPHORS

Metaphors have five characteristics:

1. *Metaphors are communal.* Metaphors are located in society, not in the individual. Public theology can speak to metaphors of our times. *Example*: The term *clean bombs* refers to weapons that kill people but leave buildings intact. Christians can clarify the meaning of "clean bombs," illuminating their destructiveness and disassociating them with the positive connotations of "clean."

2. *Metaphors are complex.* Metaphors represent a set of ideas, not a single idea. Components can be analyzed and evaluated. *Example*: The term *illegal aliens* refers to people residing in the United States without the proper legal documentation. *Aliens* in popular culture refers to strange creatures from outer space. *Illegal aliens*, then, becomes a complex term with connotations of criminality, strangeness, and even perhaps inhumanness. Looking closely at the language used can lead us to an evaluation that gives better understanding and reduces prejudicial connotations.

3. *Metaphors are human constructs.* Language puts together metaphors and strengthens them. Societies then understand those metaphors to be part of reality. *Example*: "His mind is like a steel trap." This metaphor implies that knowledge is cold, objective, and static. It can be captured and kept by men (males). Repeated use of this conceptual metaphor can result in a devaluation of the subjective, communal, and fluid aspects of knowledge. It can reinforce a common but erroneous belief that men are more intelligent and unemotional than women.

4. *Metaphors are changing.* Metaphors are constantly changing. Humans can become aware of the relativity of metaphors. Human groups can construct metaphors in new ways. *Example*: The horsepower of cars used to indicate in a visual way how strong the engine of a car was. Today that metaphor is much less in vogue since communities are at a great historical distance from using horses for transportation. We have dropped the metaphor and merely speak of car cylinders, forgoing the use of a metaphor. A new metaphor for the power of an automobile could be modeled on airplanes or rockets or the speed of light.

5. *Metaphors are provisional.* Metaphors can outlive their usefulness. Metaphors can be evaluated and nuanced by Christians. *Example*: The warfare metaphor for mission—speaking of battles, crusades, armor, and marches—probably does more harm than good in contemporary society. It can be spiritualized, referring to a Christian's inner struggle, it can be downplayed, or it can be put aside altogether.

---

tural contexts. In one context the agricultural metaphor might work best; in another the athletic metaphor; in another the marketplace metaphor; in still another, the journeying metaphor.

The Bible guides us in this in another way. In addition to modeling the need for several mission metaphors, the Bible shows how to handle the fact that all metaphors are provisional and imperfect. That we have choices of more or less appropriate metaphors in different settings, and that the ones we have evolve, means that none of them is perfect for all times and all places. This reminds us that the eternal, unchanging gospel story is unavoidably made real to us in temporal, changing forms.

This is not a weakness, but it can be made into a strength. It helps us to communicate to others that even though the gospel story can be told in many ways (using many metaphors), the story itself is in a class apart from human language and experience. The Bible is our teacher in how to do this. In using metaphor clusters for mission, the biblical writers almost always use what we might call the "Yes, but . . ." metaphor approach. "*Yes*, mission is like growing crops, *but* it is more than that." Consider the following three examples of the "Yes, but . . ." approach to mission metaphors.

As we saw in chapter 2, in 2 Corinthians 2:12–17, Paul uses a version of the marketplace metaphor. Standing in the city of Corinth's agora, the marketplace, where he is surrounded by merchants who have set up their booths to sell their wares, he says, "Christianity is like selling religious goods in a booth, just as you are doing." This is the "yes" part of the "Yes, but . . ." approach. Then he adds that "Christian teachings, however, are more like the incense that surrounds a successful booth than it is a product itself." This is the "but" part of the "Yes, but . . ." approach. Paul uses the marketplace image to make a valid point about how it resembles Christian mission but then shows how mission goes beyond any human conception or activity.

A second example is found in Paul's second letter to the Corinthians, when he references the military metaphor, which elsewhere he has used with approval (Rom. 7:23; Eph. 6:17). Here, however, he says, "Yes, but . . .": "For though we live in the world, we do not wage war as the world does" (2 Cor. 10:3). We do "wage war," Paul says, but it is different because it is the gospel we are talking about here, not land acquisition or world dominance or an expression of human violence.

A third example is Paul's well-known speech to the Athenians in front of the temple dedication to the unknown god (Acts 17). Paul's "yes" here is an acknowledgment that there is a god to worship and not everyone is sure just what or who that god is. Paul's "but" here is that that god is not unknown to him and doesn't need to be unknown to them, and that God is unique, not one of many.

Metaphors for mission are many. They can be used interchangeably, depending on the circumstances. All are provisional. Our task is to first choose the one that will communicate best. Our second task is to at some point relativize even the best metaphor, showing that although it directs us toward understanding, the story it points to is unique and transcendent, going beyond any human metaphor cluster.

GIFT AS MISSION METAPHOR

Using gift giving as a principal metaphor for doing mission today has some unusual strengths. We would like to make the case that today it might be one of the best for communicating the gospel cross-culturally to people of other world religions. In the next chapter we will show in some detail the universality of gift giving in human cultures, even though the concept has distinct features in different cultures. But first, let's begin by noting that gift giving is a metaphor used throughout the biblical texts. Gift giving as a metaphor for mission has strong biblical warrant.

Old Testament

Giving. The primary question of the Old Testament is the question of creation. Why would an all-powerful, self-contained God create a world, an act of giving to human beings that really has no justification or rationale, at least as seen from our limited human point of view? This is a nice theoretical question to ask on the salad days of life when things are going well. It becomes a crucial question when things are not going so well, when the giving of life seems more problematic. Job asked the question in the midst of his suffering: "Why is life given to a man?" he laments (3:23). The only conclusion one can reach is that giving is part of the nature of God; and since we are created in God's image, it must be a part of our nature also, if we are to realize the divine intent inherent in our being. To be fully human, we must give.

Gift(s). The question then becomes, what to give? And to whom? In all religions, the paradigms for living are set by the gods or God. For Christians, therefore, the place to answer the question of what to give starts with examining what God has given to us in this life on earth. The paradigmatic gift in the Old Testament is God's gift to Abraham: the promise of a line of descendants as numerous as the stars in the sky and the grains of sand on the beach (Gen. 15:4). God didn't just give us life; God gave us the resources to flourish in all the ways God meant for us. The summation of these sustaining gifts is the earth itself: "But the earth he has given to human beings" (Ps. 115:16 NRSV). Yet how can we imitate a gift (life) that only God can give? Two ways of accomplishing this are by attempting to give something back to God and by giving ourselves to other human beings.

The Old Testament is clear about what we are to return to God: a symbol called the tithe. It is a symbol because God doesn't need our gifts, but to be related to God, we must give something back. The paradigmatic return gift to God is the tithe. Remember Jacob's vow of this return gift: "Of all that you give me I will give you a tenth" (Gen. 28:22). And what of humans? We cannot give them life. We cannot give them the whole earth. But we can give them parts of it. We can contribute wherever possible and wherever the occasion presents itself to support the well-being of humans. The proverb sums it up well: "If he is thirsty, give him water to drink" (Prov. 25:21). As God's agents of mercy, however, we can give more than material sustenance. We can also give spiritual gifts. Many Sundays we end our worship services with a shorthand summary of these spiritual gifts with which we bless one another: "The LORD bless you and keep you; the LORD make his face shine upon you and be gracious to you; the LORD turn his face toward you and give you peace" (Num. 6:24–26).

Getting (receiving). Much is said in the Old Testament texts about our human response to God's great gifts and how people receive human gifts. Overall, however, the emphasis is on the giver. Giving a gift initiates a relationship. We can see three important effects of a gift on the receiver. First, both giver and receiver prosper, the receiver by the gift of course, but the giver will also prosper: "Good will come to him who is generous" (Ps. 112:5); "A generous man will prosper" (Prov. 11:25); "A generous man will himself be blessed" (Prov. 22:9). Second, a gift provides the access needed for establishing a relationship: "A gift opens the way for the giver" (Prov. 18:16). And third, a gift can provide what we might call relational lubrication for already established relationships that have fallen on hard times: "A gift given in secret soothes anger" (Prov. 21:14).

Generosity. Why are people generous? First, because God models generosity. Psalm 112 tells us that God "has given freely to the poor" (v. 9 NASB). Therefore we are to give freely to the poor. Proverbs notes that this is a characteristic of a person wholly given over to God: "The righteous give without sparing" (21:26). One of the best Old Testament illustrations of this is the building of the tabernacle, a story related in the thirty-fifth chapter of Exodus. When Moses came down from Mount Sinai after meeting with God and getting instructions for the people, he called the Israelite community together and told them that they were to build a tabernacle in which to worship God. That tabernacle was to be built from the material gifts brought by individuals in the community, gifts such as gold, silver, bronze, yarn, linen, goat hair, dyed ram skins, wood, olive oil, spices, and gems. Also, they were to give the gift of their time and skills. That is, they were to build the temple themselves, with everyone pitching in as they were able. The connection here between generosity and the ability to wholeheartedly worship God is unmistakable.

Gratitude. Finally, the attitude of response to receiving gifts is captured in the often-used phrase, "I will give thanks to the Lord." We find this phrase in a variety of forms throughout the Old Testament texts, but most often in the Psalms (for example, see Pss. 7, 28, 30, 35, 75, 100, 107, 118, 136). Another phrase of gratitude that reveals much about what our response should be to God's gifts in general describes appropriate gratitude as being captured by giving one's heart to God. Proverbs 23:26 says, "My son, give me your heart." Numbers 8:16 says we are to be given in our entirety, "to be given wholly to [God]." In one case this giving was made literal by Samuel's mother, who

---

SIDEBAR 22.6
GIFT AS MISSION METAPHOR FROM THE OLD TESTAMENT

GIVING	GETTING
Giving as part of God's nature	Receiving a gift opens the way for a relationship:
Life as a gift of God in good and bad times	giver and receiver both prosper;
	a gift gives access to both for a relationship;
Resources of the earth as God's gift to humanity	a gift fosters an already established relationship.
Giving as part of human nature made in God's image	Examples of people receiving gifts in the Old Testament and the relationship established:
Giving as part of human development	Ruth receives her livelihood from Boaz→Ruth and Naomi taken into Boaz'
Giving back to God through tithing and worship	family
Giving back to God by giving to others	Elijah receives bread from the widow at Zaraphath→Life for widow and son
	Rebecca receives gifts from Isaac→Marriage
	Jacob receives birthright and blessing from Isaac→Relationship of Jacob's descendants with God

GENEROSITY	GRATITUDE
God models generosity for humans.	Giving thanks to God
The righteous give without sparing.	Giving one's heart to God
The community brings gifts to build the tabernacle.	Giving ourselves to God
The Israelites give their time and talents to the construction of the tabernacle.	Fulfilling promises to God
Generosity leads to ability to wholeheartedly worship God.	

promised to give her son to the temple for God's service if her prayers for a child were answered: "Then I will give him to the LORD" (1 Sam. 1:11).

New Testament

Giving. Acts 20:35 tells us that it is more blessed to give than to receive, and this sums up the biblical and Christian stance on gift giving. As with all things Christian, (1) giving begins with the model of God's gifts to us. It proceeds then (2) with us giving back to God what we can: "Fear God and give him glory" (Rev. 14:7). And then (3) we attempt to imitate the model set for us by God by giving generously to other human beings: "Let him give generously" (Rom. 12:8). The Bible recognizes, however, that pure altruism is impossible for fallen humans, so it talks at length about some of the inherent benefits of giving. For instance, it says we personally receive much in return for giving. Giving gives great joy, Paul tells us in 2 Corinthians 8:2. Giving increases our understanding of the world and its needs—and its blessings—as the early deacons who helped with the distribution of food to widows learned in Acts 6:1–7. Giving teaches us important work values—before learning to give, Zacchaeus took and suffered for it (Luke 19:5). Philippians 4:12 assures us that giving and getting lead to personal contentment for both giver and receiver. And blessings of all kinds come to the giver of gifts:

Whoever sows generously will also reap generously (2 Cor. 9:6).

He [God] . . . will enlarge the harvest of your righteousness (2 Cor. 9:10).

You will be made rich in every way so that you can be generous (2 Cor. 9:11).

Gift(s). The Bible is also clear about what kind of gifts we receive from God, either implying or stating explicitly that we should then consider passing those same kinds of gifts (to whatever extent we are able) to others. Of course, some of the gifts we receive from God we can only tell others about in the hope that they will seek them on their own, such as the gifts of the Trinity: as Christians we receive the gift of God (Matt. 10:40), Jesus Christ (Col. 2:6), and the Holy Spirit (John 20:22). We also receive several specifically spiritual gifts: forgiveness of sins (Acts 10:43), the kingdom of God (Mark 10:15), and eternal life (1 Tim. 1:16). We receive behavioral gifts: righteousness (Matt. 10:41), wisdom (Rev. 5:12), and comfort (2 Cor. 1:4), for example. And of course we receive material gifts, the kind easiest for us to pass along to others, gifts such as wealth (Rev. 5:12) and power (Rev. 4:4). In fact, we receive anything we ask for (1 John 3:22), and most of us ask for material things. A special category of gifts we receive from God are called spiritual gifts, referring to the spiritual and psychological talents God has given to each of us so that we can serve God better (1 Cor. 14).

Getting (Receiving). According to the biblical texts, knowing how to receive gifts is an essential part of the gift-giving process. Although in the overall scheme of things, the New Testament teaches that it is "more blessed to give than to receive" (Acts 20:35), the texts say so much about receiving that we ignore it only at our peril. We can summarize what the New Testament says about receiving in the form of the four receiving principles:

323

1. We should ask God and God's agents for things (Matt. 7:8; 1 John 3:22). Part of the dynamic of not asking is stubborn human pride. Asking and receiving are part of the acknowledgment of our dependence on God. A common mission mistake is to think that we are in mission work only to give and forget that we also are there to receive mission gifts from others.
2. We should use what God and God's agents give to us: "Each one should use whatever gift he has received to serve others" (1 Pet. 4:10).
3. We should consider reception of gifts a stimulus to give to others: "Freely you have received, freely give" (Matt. 10:8).
4. We should believe that we have received many gifts from God and God's agents (Mark 11:24). Part of the dynamic of receiving is to believe that God and God's agents supply our needs. Without this belief we become in the asking either beggars or greedy people.

Generosity. There is no better summary of the attitude that makes gift giving Christian and biblical than the eighth and ninth chapters of Paul's second letter to the Corinthians. In these two chapters Paul explains how the Macedonian churches discovered the joys of giving and modeled this for the rest of the church. He describes that attitude of generosity, reminding us to give *freely*: "Then it will be . . . a generous gift, not . . . one grudgingly given" (9:5). Christian gifts are given *voluntarily*: "Entirely on their own, they urgently pleaded with us for the privilege of sharing" (8:3). Christians give *faithfully*, Paul tells us: "Each may give what he has decided in his heart to give" (9:7). Christians give *gladly*: "God loves a cheerful giver" (9:7). Christians give *sacrificially*, that is, even poor people give: "Their overflowing joy and their extreme poverty welled up in rich generosity" (8:2). In short, for Paul, generosity is a sign of Christian living, a fruit of the Spirit of God: "Just as you excel in everything—in faith, in speech, in knowledge . . . see that you also excel in this grace of giving" (8:7).

Gratitude. The locus classicus for gratitude, the response of the receiver of gifts, might be 1 Thessalonians 5:18: "Be joyful always; pray continually; give thanks in all circumstances, for this is God's will for you in Christ Jesus." Is this injunction to be thankful *in* (not necessarily *for*) all circumstances realistic? Modern studies seem to point in that direction. Studies of people who score high on measures of gratitude show that they are able to distill lessons even from bad experiences for which they are appreciative. Some of the benefits of gratitude include (1) opportunities: an attitude of gratitude helps people see beyond tragedies to new opportunities; (2) skills: difficult circumstances force people to develop skills for which gratitude is appropriate; (3) blessings: the ability to perceive and identify blessings is a wonderful strength only humans can possess; (4) contrast effects: a harsh winter makes an individual more grateful for a mild spring; (5) ways of coping: gratitude is an effective way of dealing with stressful life situations; (6) redemption sequences: gratitude can

SIDEBAR 22.7
GIFT AS MISSION METAPHOR IN THE NEW TESTAMENT

GIVING

God models giving for us.

We give back to God what we can.

Giving to God is part of our worship.

Giving to others imitates God's giving to us.

It is more blessed to give than to receive.

Benefits of giving:

Giving gives joy.

Giving increases our understanding of the world, its needs and blessings.

Giving teaches us important work values.

Giving leads to contentment for both giver and receiver.

Blessings come to the giver of gifts (2 Cor. 9:6 and 11).

God makes the giver righteous (2 Cor. 9:10).

GETTING

Gifts we receive from God:

Gifts of the Trinity:

Gift of God (Matt. 10:40); Jesus Christ (Col. 2:6); Holy Spirit (John 20:22)

Spiritual gifts:

Forgiveness of sins (Acts 10:43); kingdom of God (Mark 10:15); eternal life (1 Tim. 1:16); talents to serve God better (1 Cor. 14)

Behavioral gifts:

Righteousness (Matt. 10:41); wisdom (Rev. 5:12); comfort (2 Cor. 1:4)

Material gifts:

Wealth (Rev. 5:12); power (Rev. 4:4)

GENEROSITY

Attitude that characterizes Christian giving (2 Cor. 8–9):

Give sacrificially (8:2)

Give voluntarily (8:3)

Give generously (8:7)

Give freely (9:5)

Give faithfully (9:7)

Give gladly (9:7)

GRATITUDE

"Be joyful always; pray continually; give thanks in all circumstances" (1 Thess. 5:18).

Benefits of gratitude:

See new opportunities

Identify blessings

Perceive contrasts with other situations

Cope with stressful circumstances better

See redemption sequence as one moves from trouble to triumph

Become less defensive and more open to life

make the telling of life stories move naturally from trying times to triumphant times; (7) mental flexibility: grateful people are less defensive and more open to life (Snyder 2001, 467).

GRACE: A BIBLICAL WARRANT FOR GIFTIVE MISSION

Using gift giving as a metaphor cluster for mission has more than strong biblical warrant. The Christian theological tradition has recognized significant resonance in gift giving and the way the church has conceptualized God's word over the years. This is most apparent in the way the doctrine of grace has been used as a shorthand description of how God relates to the world through Jesus Christ and the Holy Spirit.

Grace in this view belongs to God. In fact, it is the very nature of God to be gracious, to give this free gift to everyone regardless of merit. A definition of this aspect of God's gift giving might be, "Divine love and protection bestowed freely on all people." The first chapter of the Gospel of John uses this language of grace to communicate who God is and how God relates to us. In this chapter we see that God is grace (v. 14); that all good things have as their fount God's grace and truth (v. 17); and that this grace of God takes the form of a gift to all human beings that results in blessings of all kinds (v. 16). We might say that one way to talk about God is to talk about grace. Many have called grace the signature doctrine of Christianity, that is, the doctrine that most characterizes the Christian religion and distinguishes it from the other religions of the world.

The mission implications of this understanding of God's grace are far reaching. Missiologists can with great profit focus on the last three words of this definition of grace, namely, "on all people." God is not just the God of

---

SIDEBAR 22.8
WHAT DOES GRACE MEAN FOR MISSION?

As God's gift, grace has missiological implications:

All people are born of God (John 1:3–4).

Grace is available to all people (John 1:16).

Through grace people are saved (Rom. 3:24).

Through grace people believe (Rom. 4:16).

Grace is God's provision for all people (Rom. 5:1–2).

Everyone has access to God's grace (Rom. 5:15).

The world is ruled by grace (Rom. 5:17; Col. 1:17).

All people are equal before God (Rom. 5:18–19).

Everyone is protected by God's grace (Col. 1:20).

SIDEBAR 22.9
METAPHORS FOR MISSION: REFLECTION AND DISCUSSION

Consider metaphors for mission by addressing these questions:
1. Describe two metaphor clusters that influence you and the subculture you identify with (for example, millennials, generation X, seniors, African Americans, working class, Latinos, and so on).
2. Analyze the two metaphors you chose:
   - What are the components of each?
   - Where do they come from, historically, culturally, and so on?
   - How do they influence you, your group?
   - What shorthand references to them are commonly used?
3. Trade metaphors with someone else and analyze *his or her* choices.
4. Evaluate the two metaphors you chose in question 1.
   - Which aspects of them are Christian?
   - Where do you see grace operating in the metaphors?
   - How could they be changed to better reflect God's grace?
   - In what ways are they incompatible with the gospel message?

Christians but the God of all people. We are all "born of God." Grace is not just a gift given to Christians; it is a gift given to all people. All people have access to this free gift, whether they be Hindu, Buddhist, or Muslim. God's grace is not a matter of "I have it and you don't," but a matter of "we all have it" through God's provision. This puts everyone on an equal standing before God: equally gifted, equally judged. Mission in this voice, using this acknowledgment of God's work and intent, pulls us together rather than divides us.

In this view, grace also describes human beings and the state in which they find themselves in relation to God. If grace is "divine love and protection bestowed freely on all people," then human beings are graced, that is, in "the state of being protected by God." As Paul points out in the fifth chapter of Romans, we are living in a world ruled by grace (v. 21) and as such are protected by that grace. When we find ourselves surrounded, overwhelmed by sin, the quantity of protecting grace increases accordingly. We don't always know it or feel it, but we are constantly protected by God's grace.

Missiologically this condition is also very powerful. Arguably there is no greater need in the world today than for people to feel safe. We all want protection from evil people, from nuclear missiles, from terrorists, from HIV/AIDS, from the bird flu. According to the biblical view of grace, we are in a constant state of protection, simply by virtue of being humans created in God's image. Is that not good news? Can Christian witness couched in those terms be viewed as anything but good? This is not a message of judgment but a message of mercy. We come bringing the news of good gifts, the grace of God. And the news is that you are already protected by God; you are in a state of grace.

There is yet another way that the Bible talks about the gift of grace. The biblical writers often talk about grace as a power in the world to which we all have access. This kind of language resonates so strongly with the way many, if not all, religious people in the world construct their cosmologies and mythologies that it becomes an indispensable missiological tool. Grace is the power that makes the world run, the *mana*, the *chi*, the *tao*, the "spirits" that invest everything. Historically people who have not heard about God's grace have observed that the world seems to run according to unseen powers and spirits that add more meaning to people and events than people and events constitute in themselves. By this grace, people believe (Acts 15:11). By this grace, people are saved (Rom. 3:23). By this grace, people do marvelous things (Acts 4:33). By this grace, we become spiritual heroes, men and women "full of God's grace and power" (Acts 6:8). All people (who are by biblical definition given grace) live in a state of grace, where the power of grace is freely available.

We can begin to see the power of this image in a missiological sense. A metaphor cluster centered around gift giving has many advantages in a world filled with suspicion and mistrust of people bearing religious messages. Yet crafting and applying this metaphor cluster to specific mission fields is not easy. Like all mission metaphors, the image of gift giving is not perfect in itself, and because of the way different cultures view gift giving, it must be applied with care. Our next chapter isolates just a few of the issues that must be addressed.

23

The Four Gifts

arcel Mauss, in his classic work *The Gift: The Form and Reason for Exchange in Archaic Societies* (1990), notes the central irony of gift giving across cultures: in theory, gifts are voluntary with no strings attached by either giver or receiver; in practice, in all cultures at all times in all places, gifts are part of highly ritualized expectations of both giver and receiver and, often, of only nominally disinterested onlookers. The rules of gift giving change from culture to culture; the fact that there are "rules" does not. Mauss's conclusion was that there are no free gifts.

Mauss was a sociologist, not a theologian. His intent was not to teach the right way to give gifts, the Christian way (or the Hindu or Buddhist or Muslim way), but to describe the way it worked. In *The Gift*, he describes the total social phenomenon called gift giving, analyzing the legal, economic, moral, religious, and aesthetic dimensions of this ubiquitous practice. But never did he say, this is the way it should be done.

The closest he came to what we would call the theological dimension is his acknowledgment that many if not most religions have a concept of the free gift; indeed, they hold up the idea of the free gift as the ideal. As Mauss observes, "In theory these [gifts] are voluntary, in reality they are given and reciprocated obligatorily" (1990, 3). But Mauss's work is not to comment on this aspect. He accepts the gap between theory and practice as a fact of social life, not as something to be decried. He focuses on the practice of gift giving and the role the practice plays in making a society viable (or not viable, as the case may be). And in *The Gift*, he focuses on what that role might be, especially in indigenous societies.

Yet it is precisely this ambiguous nature of gift in cultures—the gap between religious theory and cultural practice—that makes the concept of gift so interesting for us as we study the role of Christian mission to people of other religions in various cultures. Self-advocating Christianity in a particular culture also runs immediately into the problem of what the gospel ideally teaches and what people of a particular culture are prepared to hear about it. Not everyone practices what is preached. In fact, no one does. So in that sense, gospel giving can be seen to occupy roughly the same cultural space as gift giving, the never-never land between theory and practice, between ideal and shadow.

Faced with this reality, Mauss as sociologist chooses to largely ignore the theoretical and focus on the practice. He tells us specifically that this is his interest: "What rule of legality and self-interest, in societies of a backward or archaic type, compels the gift that has been received to be obligatorily reciprocated? What power resides in the object given that causes its recipient to pay it back?" (1990, 3). Again, he does not deny the gap, "the so to speak voluntary character of these total services, apparently free and disinterested but nevertheless constrained and self interested" (1990, 3). He chooses to study the practice, apparently because it is most available to him.

What Mauss eschews, however, we embrace. We are interested in the gap between gift theory and gift practice, because it resonates so powerfully with a similar gap between gospel and gospel as proclaimed/heard. Our interest is to explore the nature of that similarity and then to explore the possibility that the idea of gift giving might be a useful metaphor for the task of Christian mission to people of other religions, precisely because it is so similar in social role and structure.

Before we can do those two things, however, we need to learn a bit more about gift giving. Mauss tells us a great deal about gift giving in archaic cultures (what we will call indigenous cultures). Even though these cultures are by no means uniform in the way they give gifts, there are enough structural

---

SIDEBAR 23.1
CONDITIONS OF A "FREE GIFT"

Gifts, by definition, are given with no strings attached, yet:
1. Every culture has rules that apply to gift giving and receiving.
2. The "rules" of gift exchange vary from culture to culture.
3. One is required to reciprocate if a gift is received.
4. Power resides in the object, requiring that it be reciprocated.

similarities to make the development of an ideal type, called indigenous gift giving, heuristically sound. But we also need to learn about some other ideal types of gift giving. We have, again for teaching purposes, identified three others: Western gift giving, Eastern gift giving (specifically in India), and religious gift giving.

In describing these four different ways of giving and receiving gifts, we find great differences, of course, but we also find enough overall similarities to draw conclusions about human gift giving in general. Those generalizations will become useful in comparing the human endeavor of gift giving to the human religious practice of Christian mission or religious self-advocacy. In this chapter, then, we are acting as Marcel Mauss acted, simply describing the practice end of the gift-giving dichotomy. We have already, in the previous chapter, put on our linguistic hats, studying the semantic gap between theory and practice (the "Yes, but . . ." dynamic). In the following chapter we will become theologians speculating on the theological possibilities of verbally relating gift giving and Christian mission.

INDIGENOUS GIFT GIVING

Indigenous groups almost always operate according to what might be called an exchange economy. That is, they give gifts within a context of reciprocal relationships, relationships that determine the roles of gift giver, gift receiver, and gift reciprocator. Fulfilling the obligations associated with gift giving in such a culture builds trust. In an exchange economy, the act of giving gifts is more important than—or at least as important as—the gifts themselves. One does not choose whether to give gifts, and one does not choose what gift to give in an exchange economy. The exchange of gifts is expected, obligatory, and sharply regulated by unspoken protocols, and occasionally by spoken protocols (but usually not written protocols).

To call an exchange economy an economy is to use the word in its broadest sense. We are talking about not the simple exchange of money or what passes for money in a particular culture, but rather the total system of human interchange with other people, with the gods, indeed even with the natural elements of the environment. In this sense economy is almost synonymous with ecology, or the intimate integration and interaction of all elements within a system. In this sense, economy encompasses the material exchanges of a culture but also includes political, legal, moral, and ethical exchanges.

In an exchange economy, the dominant method of interaction might be called cooperation. In such a context, however, cooperation takes on a special meaning. Here cooperation does not mean the absence of competition, nor does it mean that relationships are always well meaning and harmonious. Such is not always the case. There is a particular form of indigenous gift giving common to the Native Americans of the Northwest United States, called potlatch, that is filled with rivalry and hostility, for example. Potlatch in these tribes involves well-to-do members of a particular Native American culture "giving" away expensive, valuable goods by destroying them in public displays of extravagance.

Cooperation in such a context simply means that all parties—givers, receivers, and onlookers—understand the "rules" of gift giving that exist in their culture and participate in those interactions freely, indeed with relish. By their participation they see themselves as part of a group that in large measure is bound together by such gift giving and the attendant obligations and rituals. In such groups, as Mauss observes, "marriages, inheritance of goods, legal ties and those of self-interest, the ranks of the military and priests—in short everything, is complementary and presumes cooperation between the two halves of the tribe" (1990, 6).

Although the primary goal of gift-giving rituals in tribal groups is tribal solidarity, solidarity is not the only goal of gift giving in such cultures. Other primary purposes inherent in indigenous gift giving include communication, redistribution, and honor/respect. Although market exchange (purchase and sale with reference to a price system) is only fully developed in the market cultures of the East and the West, and will be examined in detail later, some minor evidences of it can be found even in exchange cultures. For now, however, let's examine solidarity, communication, redistribution, and honor/respect as goals of exchange societies.

Communal solidarity is the number one value of gift giving in exchange societies. David Mann notes: "Gift exchanges [in African tribal groups] cement relationships. It is to a person's advantage to share with others, thus building networks of relationships resulting in mutual obligation. This continual sharing throughout the society creates a sort of social safety net for times of difficulty" (1990, 51).

The elaborate rules of gift giving in exchange societies serve to create the reality of a group of people operating according to the same guidebook. This security is the number one value and goal of exchange gift giving.

A second, related goal is communication. Bronislaw Malinowski wrote in some detail about the *kula* gift-giving practices among the Trobriand Islanders. *Kula* is a complete system of inner- and intratribal relationships among these South Sea peoples. The *kula* system (*kula* means "circle") is a "vast system of services rendered and reciprocated which indeed seems to embrace the whole of Trobriand economic and civil life. The *kula* seems to be the culminating point of that life, particularly the *kula* between nations and tribes. It is certainly the purpose of existence and the reason for undertaking long voyages [among islands]" (1953, 27). *Kula* keeps islanders informed about news and events and the needs of other islanders.

A third goal is redistribution. Although material benefit is not the primary reason for gift giving in exchange societies, it can serve the purpose of moving wealth along to those who need help. A colleague of mine once observed a gift exchange among a group of Native Americans living in Oklahoma. The item being exchanged was a handwoven blanket. The ritual involved a seemingly random passing of the gift, the blanket, from hand to hand, from person to person. Each recipient seemed to know just how long to keep the "gift" before in turn giving it to someone else. In the end, my colleague told me, the blanket ended up in the hands of the most needy person.

And the fourth goal is honor/respect. For example, "Wealth plays a determinative role in the highest levels of status in the Dowayo [Africa] culture, that of *waaryaw*. With that status comes the obligation to sponsor large festivals whenever members of his family are participating. As the *waaryaw* contributes significantly to these festivals, he gains increased status which follows him and his family throughout life" (Mann 1990, 52–53).

As we shall see, this goal can sometimes get out of hand, as in potlatch ceremonies, where the powerful and rich try to outdo one another in giving expensive gifts, often simply for destruction. Sometimes physical hostilities ensue. But this is most often not the case and only honor is sought.

Although these goals seem to be sought by individuals, a close understanding of the gift-giving function in indigenous groups reveals that the participants are really the entire collective. Everyone is involved in the obligations created by anyone's gift. And when those obligations are not met, everyone in the group suffers from the resulting vacuum. Still it is helpful for purposes of description to divide gift giving in exchange economies into three constituent parts: gift givers, gift receivers, and gift reciprocators (who become gift givers in an endless cycle of gift exchange).

In Samoa, one can begin to understand gift giving only if one first accepts the fact that the giver of gifts gives them because he or she is obligated to do so. Gift giving is not the result of a good feeling someone has about someone else, a good feeling that makes the feeler decide, "I should give so-and-so a gift." Giving gifts is an obligation. If you want to be a contributing member of a society, you give gifts. Not giving a gift is like declaring war on the neglected parties; as Mauss puts it, it is tantamount to "rejecting the bonds of alliance and community" (1990, 13).

Gift giving begins with an obligation. It continues with an invitation to someone to receive your gift. The recipient is outside the collective. Gift giving is not an inner-family affair but an engagement with the larger circles of obligation that make up the world of the group. The offer is made, and the person receiving the gift is obligated to accept (more on that below). If either the obligatory offer or the obligatory reception are for some reason not carried out according to custom, penalties in the form of censure ensue.

We should say a word about the gifts themselves. On the one hand, one could say that in such a gift-giving system the gift itself is secondary. The more important thing is to give the gift according to the tradition. But to say that

333

the gift itself is unimportant would be misleading, because the value of the gift does much to increase the prestige of the gift giver. The more valuable the gift, the greater the honor. To give a cheap gift would be a sign of lack of generosity and would defeat one of the purposes of gift giving in the first place.

All gifts in these cultures are talismans; they are spiritually alive. That aliveness creates the interactive nature of gift giving. The gifts may be blankets, abalone shells, furs, houses, boats, carvings, or other artistic works—all are alive with the spirit of their owner, and they take on the additional spirits of their new owners. Gifts are like living beings that accumulate the energies of relationship and experience. And they are spiritually related to other like objects. This spiritual power gives indigenous gift giving its tremendous grip on these cultures.

The recipient of a gift is under equal obligations. Just as the giver has an obligation to give, the recipient has an obligation to receive. You cannot say that you do not want a gift. You cannot reject a gift because for some reason you don't like abalone shells, or you already have plenty of abalone shells, thank you. Further, you cannot think that you do not want to be under the obligation to reciprocate to this particular giver of a gift, that you do not want to be beholden to that particularly unsavory person. None of this is within the rights and freedoms of a recipient. If someone gives you a gift, you accept it.

The third obligation is reciprocation. A person is obliged to give, obliged to receive, and obliged to reciprocate. Penalties are most severe for failure to reciprocate appropriately. Usually a form of "interest" is required on a gift to be reciprocated: if a single blanket is given, then two are given in return. The protocols for reciprocation are elaborate: one does not return a gift right away; there is an appropriate waiting period, or one waits for the next festival or potlatch before the gift can be reciprocated. Penalties for not reciprocating can range from social ostracism to being reduced to a state of slavery for payment of debt.

Such is an outline of the gift-giving practices of indigenous societies, using exchange economic principles. They operate according to the three obligations of giving, receiving, and reciprocating. Although sometimes the language of free gift is used to describe the generosity of the givers, in practice it is a system of social requirements designed to foster stronger social bonds. It remains for us to ask ourselves questions about what role the language of free gift, of disinterested giving, might have in societies that so obviously eschew the free gift in practice. Why maintain the language of free gift at all? And what would happen in such a culture if the concept of free gift were offered from the outside (i.e., the free gift of the gospel)? How would the members of such a culture interpret it? We can only offer some initial impressions for now, but it is worth some speculation before we discuss the other types of gift systems.

First, then, why is it necessary to have a concept of free gift even if it is never (or rarely) realized in practice? This question can be answered on several levels. The first is a functional one, the one to which Mauss and other sociologists/anthropologists might relate. It might be that having an ideal like the free gift in play gives the social dynamics some latitude to explain incongruous facts and unresolved ambiguities. No social system, particularly one related to the moral dimension, works perfectly, and having a dynamic, even transcendent, principle to which such anomalies can be assigned can be useful. The second possibility might involve the "spirit of the things given." Might it not be the case that by invoking a kind of spiritual dimension to the gifts given, a type of transcendent, ideal gift dynamic became necessary to explain the difference between inanimate objects—that is, physical objects not invested with the spirit of *hau* imparted by ownership and giftship—and those that are invested with this spirit. And a third possibility might be called theological. What if the ideal of the free gift is a residue from Christian creation perfection or a prefiguring of the free gift itself (Jesus Christ) to come?

SIDEBAR 23.2
INDIGENOUS GIFT GIVING

In an exchange economy, gifts are given and received in the context of relationships:
- Gift giver
- Gift receiver
- Gift reciprocator

Results of gift giving and receiving in an exchange economy:
- It builds trust.
- All parties cooperate by following the rules of gift giving.
- All parties participate in gift exchange.

Goals of gift giving in exchange economy cultures:
- Solidarity
- Communication
- Redistribution
- Honor/respect

The power of the gift itself:
- The receiver of the gift already "owns" it.
- The gift determines the rights of the receiver.
- The value of a gift increases or lowers the prestige of the giver.
- The "spirit" of the gift empowers its owner.
- A gift takes on the "spirit" of the new owner.

The process of gift giving:
- One has an obligation to give a gift.
- An invitation is extended to someone to receive the gift.
- The offer is made.
- The person receiving the gift is obligated to accept it.
- The person accepts the gift.

The obligations of gift giving:
- The giver is obliged to give.
- The receiver is obliged to receive.
- The receiver is obliged to reciprocate.
- The community imposes "interest" and penalties for failure to fulfill those obligations.

And then the second question: what would happen in such a culture if a true, free gift, such as the gospel, ever came and were offered? Fortunately, in the case of Mauss's populations, the South Sea Islanders, we have empirical evidence of what did happen. The gospel of grace came and was accepted en masse. Very high percentages of these populations are Christian as a result of Christian mission efforts that brought the "free gift," the gospel story. It seemed to fit. In the next chapter, we discuss in much more detail why this was so. But to tantalize here, it seems that Christianity itself fits the exchange market quite well. The ideal of the free, unrequired, unrequited gift of grace offered by God in Jesus Christ combines with a more practical understanding of what happens when one receives such a gift: we are required to reciprocate by becoming givers of the gift to others. Much of the almost miraculous spread of the gospel story among these cultures came as a result of the work of indigenous mission workers, who received the gift and then felt obligated to pass it on.

WESTERN GIFT GIVING

Typically, Western gift giving operates according to a market economy. Features of the "Western" aspect important to our discussion include an emphasis on human rights over against human responsibility; individual freedom; and equal opportunity for all, opportunity that usually (not always) trumps hierarchical roles. Or to condense it into a sentence, "Western" denotes a system of human rights emphasizing individual freedom brought about by equal opportunity. As related specifically to gifts, Western market economies place great value on the nature of the gift, that is, the value of the gift. And they, of course, place a great deal of emphasis on the importance of individuality and freedom in givers and receivers deciding whether to give gifts and whether to reciprocate.

What is a market economy? The essential features of market exchange are purchase and sale at a money price determined by the impersonal forces of supply and demand. Doesn't sound much like gift giving of any sort does it? That is because in market economies, gift giving and market dynamics have been compartmentalized, and gift giving is seen, in theory, to be something different from market dynamics. Whereas we buy and sell according to price, need, and supply, we give gifts according to personal decision, affective value, and altruism.

The theory seems to hold as far as the compartmentalization aspect is concerned. In people's minds in Western cultures, buying and selling are kept clearly distinct from giving and receiving. One does not buy Christmas gifts from their givers; one does not sell presents to a person on his or her twenty-first birthday. Similarly, when one goes to the grocery store, one does not talk about receiving the gift of laundry detergent. One compares the price and value in terms of the cleaning power of one detergent with that of another and makes a purchase decision. Little if any thought is given to exactly who has sold this product to me; in my purchase of it, I give no thought to my relationship with the corporate CEO of the store where I bought it. Buying and selling are different human activities than giving and receiving.

The theory, however, seems to fail at the point where it suggests that gifts are given in market economies according to a different set of rules than those by which market dynamics per se operate. The underlying thinking and dynamics seem to be remarkably similar even if the overt behavior and the language used are distinctly different. They are similar in both method and goal. Both seem to resemble a marketplace. We could create a spectrum of motivations in Western gift giving that range from market motivations on one end to relational motivations on the other.

Consider the office gift. At Christmas most workers in a Western employment situation are faced with the decision of whether to give presents to fellow workers. The decisions are many: to give or not to give; to whom to give; what to give. The corporate culture is an important factor—do other people give gifts to their colleagues or not? Different companies will have quite a variety of workplace practices. One can safely discount gifts that the company gives to employees. Christmas gifts coming from employers, whether gifts or monetary bonuses, are gifts in name only. They are clearly so much a part of the business transaction side of the market economy that to call them gifts is to stretch the meaning of the word beyond its conceptual limit.

The gift to a worker/colleague, however, is more instructive. The single most important feature of that gift is choice. Each individual makes a choice regarding the three main decisions: to give or not to give, to whom, and what. How those three decisions are made—that is, with what motive—determines the nature of the gift. If the giver leans toward giving a gift to curry favor, the action leans toward a business transaction with the danger of being either a payment for services or a bribe. However, if the giver leans toward making those decisions because he or she likes a person or has a friendship with the person, then it leans toward the gift end of the spectrum.

Because the marketplace model is so ubiquitous in Western cultures, however, even gifts that lean toward the relational end of the gift-giving spectrum tend to resemble business transactions. Even relationships in market economies are most often determined on a quid pro quo basis: if you give me value, I will give you equal value in exchange. Consider the giving and receiving of Christmas cards. Many people send Christmas cards to a regular list of people. Most people regularly reevaluate the extent of their list, either eliminating names or adding names, depending on whether that person sends them a card. What is intended to be a gift of Christmas sentiment is transformed into a marketplace dynamic.

The choices related to gift giving made in a Western market economy are individual choices made according to common cultural precedents but mostly related to what one would like to do. This is very different from the gift-giving practices in indigenous societies, where a common set of gift-giving practices are determinative for everyone, and individual choice is relegated to whether to participate (not how to participate), with dire consequences for nonparticipation.

Western market economies have effectively separated what in indigenous societies is part of a seamless whole: the circle of giving that includes economics, relationships, and friendships. In Western cultures this circle is broken into three or more spheres with room for overlap, but they also allow for the freedom to totally compartmentalize any or all of them. In such a setting, there is little place for common rituals, gift-giving celebrations that draw people together. And even if there are common gift-giving occasions (such as Christmas), there is little harmony of practice, and the act of gift giving too easily loses every common meaning except the market one. This is what people mean, in part, when they refer to the commercialization of these holidays.

One of the features of Western culture that gives gift giving its distinctive, individualistic features is the literate nature of its tradition. As Western culture has become increasingly literate, it has become increasingly complex. The balkanization of its various functions, especially the relegation of the relational to the private sphere, has been made possible by the analytical precision that literate cultures are able to achieve in contrast to oral cultures. Put more simply, gift giving has been discussed thoroughly in the history of Western literature, and the overall effect of this discussion has been the creation of a body of ideas on various aspects of gift giving that has added to its complexity.

As in most cultures, Western gift giving has a religious, mythological base. Although we will discuss this base in more detail in the section on religious gift giving, we should mention here that the prototypical *ideal* gift in Western religious mythology is the gift of creation itself—in the beginning God created the heavens and the earth, the perfect gift to give to human beings. Human beings are part of the gift of creation and are given dominion over it. The prototypical *human* gift is the gift of the apple that Eve gave to Adam. Western gift-giving practices are a result of the dialectic between this ideal gift (God's gift of creation and life) and this human attempt at the practice of gift giving (Eve's gift of the apple).

The major feature of gift giving in a market-based, individualistic culture is the emotional state of the individual gift giver. This can be either a strength or a weakness, but too often it is a weakness. Pride and selfishness inevitably creep into a system where a large part of gift giving is the pleasure it gives to the individual giver. In many cases the subjective pleasure of giving a gift to someone in need overshadows everything else about the act. In "Reveries of a Solitary Walker," Jean-Jacques Rousseau remembers how he felt when he gave a few apples to someone in need:

338

When I reflected back on the sort of pleasure I had experienced I found that it consisted less in a feeling of beneficence than in the enjoyment of seeing contented faces. That aspect has a charm for me which even though it penetrates my heart seems to be solely a matter of sensation. If I did not see the satisfaction I caused . . . my pleasure would be cut in half. (1959, 1092–93)

One gives because it makes one feel good.

A second feature of gift giving in a market-based, individualistic culture is the undue focus placed on the material value of the gift given. In such a system gifts are liable to become either the privilege of the rich, who can afford them, or the province of dame fortune—the rain falls on the just and the unjust alike, or should we say on some of the just and some of the unjust. Envy and jealousy over who gets the good gifts and who can afford to give them threatens to dominate the more important gesture of gift giving itself. Hospitality becomes the province of the rich, largesse the private reserve of the fortunate. On the other hand, in such a system a great deal of creativity and personal energy can be devoted to deciding on and/or crafting the most appropriate gift for the situation. In *The Consolation of Philosophy*, Boethius captures the danger of this facet of gift giving in the West: "Though God, all bounteous, give gold at man's desire and honors, rank, and fame—content not a whit is closer, but an all-devouring greed yawns with ever-widening need" (2000, 2.2). In such a setting a gift can indeed become a poison, recalling the semantic homonymy of the word *gift* in its ancient Germanic roots.

A third feature emerges when we consider a system where reciprocating a gift is not mandated. In fact, the Western gift-giving ideal is one in which a gift is given with no expectation of a return at all. After all, that is what God offered us in creation: a freely given gift, the gift of grace, with no expectation of a return. Such a system can lead one to focus solely on one's own good feelings about giving, as the Romantic Rousseau admitted. But it can also lead to the objectifying of the poor into the needy poor, the abstract class of people who need our gifts. We give to the poor because it is our religious obligation, not because we are giving gifts in the context of a human relationship. The act of giving becomes an act of charity. The occasion of the extravagant gift becomes a moment of guilt over giving the gift to someone not in need instead of selling the costly perfume and giving the money to the poor.

Finally, a fourth feature of market-economy gift giving is that it becomes easy not just to objectify the poor but to commodify the act of gift giving itself into a product of human personality, generosity. Gift giving can be measured, not just by participation, but by the quality of participation. We can measure it by how well it comports with the ideal of a virtue, generosity. We can write ballads about generous heroes, poems about selfless paragons of giving. Goethe captured this in his Faust character, the boy charioteer who reveals his identity in the following poem:

My names are Lavishness and Poetry.
I am the poet who achieves his ends
When he his inner substance most expends.
I too have riches infinite, and here
I look upon myself as Plutus's peer.
I deck his dances, I am his banquet's pride,
And what he lacks for, I provide.

(1901, 3:113–15)

Of course, it is all too common to simply point out the weaknesses of the Western approach to gift giving. We would do well to note that each of the four elements above can be seen, in their proper place, as having the potential to create great gift-giving scenarios. And we should be mindful that the very fact that we can be critical of individualized gift giving is one of its strengths. The freedom to criticize, modify, edit, or change is not a freedom available in most indigenous cultures, where the "rules" are simply a given to be faced.

It remains to briefly deal with the status of the free gift in market economies. Why is it necessary to have a concept of free gift in a culture where it is never realized? When one has the freedom to change gift-giving practices, or at least to participate at will, it is essential to have a model to strive for. Put another way, in a gift-giving system, one needs a stake in the ground to which all other aspects of the system are anchored. In indigenous societies the stake in the ground is the cultural, relational rules themselves. In a market economy, where the rules are fluid, one needs another stake in the ground: the gods' model of gift giving.

The model of the "gods" in indigenous societies is for the gods alone. In market economies, it is necessary to attempt to emulate the model of the gods. God's free act of creative grace, a gift for which no return is expected, is the model of gift giving that Westerners attempt to emulate. They don't achieve it, and the story of Eve giving the apple to Adam, immediately following the retelling of God's perfect gift, is a reminder of how far we have to go to match God's gift-giving capabilities. The free gift is needed in a context of freedom of gift giving.

Second, what happens in such societies when the gospel, the paradigm of the free gift, is introduced? When the concept of the free gift is clearly the model and goal, what happens to gift-giving practice? The answer to this question is a mixed bag. Gift-giving practices proliferate. Some are good (i.e., move us toward the free-gift model), and some are bad (i.e., move us away from the free-gift model). The danger in Western cultures is that they have mostly come to identify their cultural pattern with the gospel, since they see their cultures shaped in the Judeo-Christian framework. The question is whether the gospel is really best expressed in a market-economy model. Serious questions can be raised as to whether such a model is really any more compatible with an exchange model or, as we shall see in the next section, a redistributive model.

SIDEBAR 23.3
WESTERN GIFT GIVING

Western gift giving operates according to a market economy in the context of the following core values:
- Emphasis on human rights over responsibilities
- Focus on individual freedom
- Stress on equal opportunity for all

Gift giving operating in this context *results* in compartmentalization: economics, relationships, and friendships are differentiated:
- One may buy and sell according to price, need, and supply.
- One may give and receive gifts according to personal decision, affective value, and altruism.

The *goals* of gift giving focus on the free choice of the giver
- to decide whether to give a gift;
- to decide whom to give gifts to;
- to decide what the gift shall be;
- to receive personal satisfaction through gift giving.

The *power* of the gift itself revolves around
- the material value of the gift;
- giving equal material value in gift exchange;
- the tensions between the ideal gift of God (creation) and the practical giving of gifts (Eve's gift of the apple).

The *process* of gift giving and receiving includes the following steps:
- The individual gift giver wants to give a gift.
- The material value of the gift is decided upon.
- The gift is given, resulting in a sense of satisfaction for the giver.
- The gift is received and may or may not be reciprocated.

The *obligations* of gift giving in a market economy model:
- Give without expectation of receiving
- Give to the poor
- Give generously

The *weaknesses* of the market economy gift-giving model:
- Depends on the emotional state of the giver
- Produces envy of those who receive the most valuable gifts
- Does not redistribute wealth in the community
- Becomes relegated to personal relationships
- Is commodified

EASTERN GIFT GIVING

Indigenous gift givers have clear understandings of gift giving in implicit and oral form. Western gift givers follow market rules for gift giving, informally written and practiced according to individual choice. Eastern gift givers tend to live in societies that are highly stratified (caste based) compared with indigenous homogeneity, so they give gifts according to written rules enforced by class (caste) duty. We are going to focus on the Indian context in this description of Eastern gift giving, knowing full well that other Asian cultures (China, for example) would be quite different. India, with its well-known caste social structure, however, ideally illustrates the points we would like to make about gift giving in a tightly compartmentalized social structure.

The economic pattern followed in India has not been an exchange economy or a market economy, but an economic system usually termed redistributive. Redistributive economic systems are those in which some authority—political, religious, or moral—determines how gift giving should proceed. In such a system, clear, written gift-giving rules are necessary, since different classes or castes of people follow their own sets of rules. No one size fits all (indigenous gift giving), yet no market freedom pertains in terms of gift giving (Western gift giving).

In indigenous societies gift giving and the economic system are part of a seamless whole—one people, one system. In Western societies, the economic system and the gift-giving system have been intentionally separated; gift giving is separated from the economic system through the use of two separate vocabularies, even though gift giving is strongly influenced by the economic system, the market economy. In Eastern societies, gift giving is one-way—it is all about gifts given unilaterally and unreciprocated according to written class and caste rules. It is both congruent with the economic system and separated from it. It is congruent in the sense that gift giving is part of a total, written package of "life practices" to which one is born. One's gift-giving duties are clear, just as one's marriage duties, occupational goals, and so on are traditional and defined. Yet in the manuals describing one's duties, gift giving is a separate chapter, and in that sense some division between it and other duties is clear. It is not a seamless system in that sense.

Some examples follow, but we should note again that all our examples come from the Indian and South Asian context. The gift-giving protocols in China and East Asia would be quite different.

In Hindu cultures, gift-giving practices are codified in writings called *dharmasastras*. *Dharma* is a Sanskrit word meaning "the right way of doing things," and *sastra* means a "verbal codification of rules, whether of divine or human provenance, for the positive and negative regulation of some human practices" (Pollock 1985, 500–501, cited in Heim 2004, 8). These *dharmasastras* regulate almost every aspect of human living, producing what one writer has called "an encyclopedic synthesis of an entire way of life" (Pollock 1993, 105). In India, Sanskrit writings became particularly prominent at a time during the Middle Ages when Brahmanical life was threatened both externally and internally, externally by the Muslim invasions and internally by the rise in popularity of the bhakti devotional cults. These cultural grammars were in a sense well-articulated compendiums of lifestyle practices that had probably been more tacit in the past and were needed in a time of social upheaval.

Some of these grammars were totally dedicated to gift giving. In *Theories of the Gift in South Asia* (2004), Maria Heim lists three of the most prominent ones: Bhatta Laksmidhara, *Book on Giving* (*Dana-Kanda*); King Ballalasena, *Sea of Giving* (*Danasagara*—although this may have been written by Ballalasena's prime minister, Aniruddha); and Hemadri, *The Wish-Fulfilling Gem of the Four Aims: Gift-Giving* (*Caturvarga-Cintamani: Danakhanda*). These and other *dharmasastras* include hundreds of pages on gift giving, signifying something of the importance of the subject in Hindu social and moral life. Indeed, gift giving (*dana*) is one of the foundational virtues required for making moral and meditative progress in the religious life. In some lists of the virtues required, *dana* is the first one. In other words, if one wanted to make spiritual progress of any kind in life, the rituals of gift giving provided the indispensable foundation, in addition to the caste requirements of gift giving for social life.

In Buddhist cultures, the importance of gift giving was also emphasized, though more for the moral value than the social value. Since one of the Buddha's reforms of traditional Hindu life was the relativizing of caste requirements, at least as they applied to spiritual progress, he was naturally more interested in finding relatively universal ways of looking at things like gift giving, rather than caste-specific ones. He still saw *dana*, however, as foundational and essential to the spiritual life. His followers tended to write about gift giving from this perspective. Buddhists called these texts *sangahas*, a word meaning "compendium"; *sangahas* tended to be collections and summaries of large bodies of teachings from the extensive Pali Scriptures. Some of the most important works on *dana* were written in Pali in Sri Lanka during the Polannaruva era, especially under King Parākramabāhu I (1153–86 CE). The most important text written during this period was the *Ornament of Lay People* (*Upasakajanalankara*) by a forest-dwelling monk named Ananda. Another text by Abhayagiri Kavicakravarti Ananda, *Gift Offering of the True Dhamma* (*Saddhammopayana*), is a religious poem summarizing lay practice, including gift giving.

Many Jain texts on gift giving also exist from this period. Jains called these texts *sravakacaras*, a word meaning "lay conduct." Mahāvīra, the founder of the Jain sect, was, like the Buddha, more inclined to produce works for the entire spectrum of lay people, as opposed to caste-specific works. Jains emphasized two aspects of *dana*, one a religious aspect focusing especially on vows made by Jains to give in a religious-observance context. More general works for laity focused on generosity as a human virtue rather than a soteriological category. Jains defined dharma in a twofold manner: dharma that leads the soul to salvation and dharma that supports people in everyday life. Is this an echo of Mauss's distinction between the theory and the practice of gift giving? Some prominent Jain works on gift giving include Hemacandra, *Treatise on Discipline* (*Yogasastra*); Siddhasena Ganin, *Discourse on the Meaning of Truth* (*Tattvartha Sutra*); Devendra Suri, *Daily Ritual Duties of the Laity (Sraddhadinakrtya)*; and Suracarya, *An Exposition Beginning with Gift-giving (Danadiprakarana)*.

Together these Hindu, Buddhist, and Jain texts paint a picture of a unique approach to gift giving that is at once similar to indigenous and Western gift giving and different in important ways. One of the most important distinctions is its almost total lack of expectation about gifts being reciprocated. Whereas this is an essential element of the relational web surrounding indigenous gift giving and an unspoken expectation of Western gift giving, it is hardly mentioned in the Eastern texts noted above. Thus the four categories that Maria Heim uses to discuss Eastern gift giving do not include this category. As we follow her outline and discuss Eastern gift giving in terms of the giver, the recipient, the ritual, and the gift itself, it will become clear why the Hindu, Buddhist, and Jain pundits did not talk much about reciprocity.

Consider, then, the giver of gifts. In Indian thought the giver does not give out of obligation. In fact, many of the manuals mentioned above are clear that although *dana* is foundational for spiritual progress, one does not have to do it. It becomes clear that one does it for merit in the afterlife and the spirituality enhancing properties of gift giving. This is an important element that distinguishes the Eastern gift from the indigenous gift.

Also, in Eastern thought, the giver does not give out of a sense of freedom. One does not give because it makes one feel good to help the needy and poor; in Eastern cultures the needy and poor are taken care of by the spiritual dynamics associated with class and caste. In fact, giving because it makes one feel good is a sign of a poorly given gift. This lack of freedom and personal feelings associated with the gift in Eastern cultures distinguishes it from the Western approach to gift giving.

So what does distinguish the giver's motivations in Eastern gift giving? Because of the ubiquitousness of religious language and motivation in gift giving, one is tempted to say that that is its distinguishing feature. *Dana* is religious, not social. It has basically religious implications and no social ones. That would be, however, a dramatic oversimplification, because in the manuals gift giving is clearly given a moral (i.e., social) value. Yet what is that value when it is based on neither obligation (indigenous) nor generosity/gratitude (Western)?

Eastern gifts are based on purity of intentions. What makes a gift valuable in Eastern cultures is disinterest. The giver gives not in the hope of creating obligation or a sense of gratitude in the receiver, nor because one feels good about the giving of a gift, but because it is right. One of the *dharmasastras* defines the most righteous gift as "that which is given constantly to worthy recipients without any regard to any ends, only with the thought of giving up" (Heim 2004, 35).

When understood properly, this principle is not at odds with the religious motivations for giving, the twin ideas of merit making and eventual liberation. The quest for spiritual progress in Eastern religions is vitiated by self-centeredness or excessive grasping after the honor or value of spiritual achievement. One of the sure signs, for example, that someone is not making spiritual progress is that the person claims he or she is. Similarly, a gift given out of self-interest is a gift wasted.

Somadeva distinguished among good gifts (*sattvik*), passionate gifts (*rajasik*), and base gifts (*tamasik*). Good gifts are those given by a disinterested giver to a worthy recipient; passionate gifts are those given for ostentation and in deference to the opinions of others; base gifts are given by servants to people who may not be worthy (Heim 2004, 45).

Notice the important role that the recipient plays in Eastern gift giving. The best recipient of a gift is one who is righteous and disinterested. One does not want to give to scoundrels or to self-interested people because they will not have the spiritual maturity to accept the gift with disinterest. They may make too much of the gift, bringing embarrassment to the giver; or they may be so moved by the gift so that they feel they must return it in kind, which would also vitiate the value of the gift for the disinterested giver. As Heim perceptively states, "The ideal human relationship forged by *dana* is that of one-way regard and respect" on the part of the gift giver (2004, 54).

There are two reasons why the character of the recipient of *dana* is so important. One is religious: merit accrues from giving to those on the spiritual path. But the second is practical: it is easier for the giver of a gift to have the proper attitudes of respect if the recipient is worthy of respect. If the recipient is a bad person, then giving is most often done out of either obligation or pity, both bad gift-giving motivations.

Ritual, that is, the manners of gift giving and receiving, is very important in Eastern cultures, because proper, well-articulated procedures for giving a gift contribute to both a giver who is disinterested and a recipient who is worthy. Consider the example of Buddhist monks on their daily begging rounds for food from people in the villages. Monks are taught very specific ways of receiving this gift of food. As they offer their begging bowls as receptacles for the food, they are taught neither to look at the food (and thus display interest in its quantity, kind, and quality) nor to catch the eye of the donor (and thus display gratitude for the gift). In turn, the householders are taught to give without pride but with esteem for the worthiness of the monks, and yet not to catch the eye of the monk—the gift would lose value if it was given as a personal favor for particular monks.

And what of the gift itself? If the emphasis in Eastern gift giving is on the internal disposition of the gift giver and the worthiness of the recipient as a field of merit, then it might seem that the gift itself is secondary. In some senses this is true, particularly as the value or lack of value of the gift might be seen as a threat to the purity of the state of mind of the giver and the receiver. Disinterestedness can easily run aground on the shoals of greed or beauty or deservedness.

But the texts, somewhat surprisingly, devote quite a bit of attention to the nature of the gift, to the appropriateness of it. First, three categories of gifts emerge: material gifts of support to the religious; gifts of learning; and the gift of fearlessness (that is, the gift of rescuing others from violence inflicted either by oneself or others). The actual content of these gifts is heavily dependent on context, tradition, and class or caste requirements.

It almost seems redundant to add a section here on the questions we have been asking about the religious implications of gift giving. In Eastern cultures, as we have seen, it is hard to disentangle what we might call the religious and the secular, since religious language and motivation are so commonly referenced in the literature. And can it really be said that the same division and ambiguity obtain between the theory of the free gift and the cultural practices of gift giving in Eastern cultural systems? What cultural role, if any, does the free gift play in Eastern cultures?

In one sense, because there is so little regard for the reaction of the receiver of a gift in Eastern cultures, the idea of a free gift becomes moot. No obligation to reciprocate is implied. In that sense, every gift is totally free. No sense of gratitude is either expected or wanted. In that sense, also, every gift is totally free. Perhaps in Eastern cultures it might be more productive to ask the complementary question: if every gift is free (of obligation and moral response), can gifts be said to play any social role whatsoever, either in communal solidarity or in terms of supporting a market economy? The answer, of course, is yes, but the role is limited to clearly maintaining the classes and caste boundaries of these complex societies.

And what happens when the gospel is presented in such cultures as the ultimate example of a free gift? Perhaps the answer is that it is received as a ho-hum event; free gifts already abound, and the proper cultural response is no response. And second, it is received as something that reinforces class and caste distinctions, when the gospel really should have some role in relativizing those distinctions. Perhaps we need to rethink what free gift, what grace, means in Eastern cultures.

RELIGIOUS GIFT GIVING

Religions, as religions, concern beginnings and endings. The middle, the lived life here and now, also has religious import, of course, but it is import dependent on where everything comes from (beginnings) and where we want to ultimately go (endings). The middle can be studied religiously, but it is also accessible to anthropologists, sociologists, and philosophers. The beginnings and the endings are only accessible to the religious viewpoint. From a religious viewpoint, it is important for us to see where the pattern set by religious be-

SIDEBAR 23.4
EASTERN GIFT GIVING

In a complex stratified society, gifts are given in the context of class duty:
- There is a unified system.
- Individuals are born into a role that includes a set of life practices.

The *results* of gift giving and receiving in a class-stratified society:
- Gift-giving duties are clearly established by the system.
- Gift giving is one-way—unilateral.
- Gifts are not reciprocated.
- Written rules govern gift giving.
- Spiritual merit for the afterlife may be obtained through gift giving.
- Spiritual progress in one's present life results from gift giving.

The *goals* of gift giving and receiving:
- Making moral and meditative progress in religious life
- Following caste requirements for a smooth social life
- Having pure intentions in giving a gift

The *power* of the gift:
- Good gifts are those given by a disinterested giver to a worthy recipient.
- They have power to enrich spirituality and give spiritual merit.

- Passionate gifts may show ostentation and deference to the opinions of others.
- Base gifts are given by servants to people who may not be worthy. They lack power to enrich spirituality or grant spiritual merit.

The *process* of gift giving and receiving:
- A gift is given according to well-articulated procedures to show one-way regard and respect.
- A gift received by a worthy recipient allows merit to be accrued to the giver.

The *obligations* of gift giving and receiving:
- There is no obligation to give.
- One is obliged to give without feeling good about it.
- One is obliged to follow class rules in giving and receiving.
- One is obliged to avoid pity and obligation as motivations for giving.

Types of gifts in Eastern gift giving:
- Material gifts of support to the religious
- Gifts of learning
- The gift of fearlessness

ginnings and the expectations of religious endings lead us when it comes to gift giving in the middle, the here and now.

All three types of gift giving that we have idealized are dependent on religious beginnings and endings. As has been obvious in our descriptions of indigenous, Western, and Eastern cultures, and exchange, market, and redistributive economic systems, they are permeated with religious language and meaning. It is possible, as Mauss and other social scientists have done, to study these cultures from a sociologist's point of view, to deal with the observable practices instead of commenting on the transcendent ideas to which each culture ascribes its motivation for its actions. At some point, however,

---

SIDEBAR 23.5
BEGINNINGS AND ENDINGS IN RELIGIOUS FRAMEWORKS

Indigenous: A Divine Pattern	• The gods created the world to be modeled after themselves. • The people would try to act as the gods act. • Success or failure is measured by how well the group lives according to the divine pattern. • Endings are measured by how harmoniously the tribes are living. • Each person lives according to the role assigned by a clan or group within the divine pattern. • Stories of how the gods act and give gifts are important in tribal life.
Western: An Ideal State	• God creates free humans for relationship with God—the ideal state. • The ideal state is not realized because of human choices. • Restoration of the ideal state is the desired end. • Humans work with God to restore creation to its ideal state. • History tells the story of attempts to restore the ideal state. • The ideal state will be realized in another world at the end of human history.
Eastern: A Single Essence	• The beginning was a world undivided, of a single essence. • The world became fragmented and divided. • The goal is to restore the unified oneness of all things. • Reaching a condition of nothingness or spiritual attainment can help restore the undivided essence of the universe.

the religious ideas must be dealt with, not just as social facts, but as religious ideas per se. This section is an attempt to deal with these systems as religious systems, including the five functions of religious gift giving: alms, devotional, sacrifice, self-giving, and ritual remembrance. We will then talk about missiological implications in the next chapter.

Indigenous religious beginnings are extraordinarily diverse in detail but have some common features. For most indigenous groups, the gods originally created the world in the expectation that the way they, the gods, live would be the model for the way the people in their creation lived. People could not do it as well as the gods do it, of course, but they could try. Success or failure is measured by the extent to which the group lives according to the divine pattern. Endings in such groups are usually described in terms of the extent to which harmony prevails in the way the people are living. Harmony means everyone not only knows and understands the divine patterns but also lives according to the role assigned by clan or group within that pattern.

Note an important feature of this kind of religious system. "Endings" are most often seen in terms of here-and-now practice, not some other-worldly condition we can expect at the end of time. Although many of these groups believe in some kind of ethereal realm to which dead spirits might go, even those spirits continue to participate in life here and now. Time is mostly a function of the past and how that past relates to the here and now. The future plays a more minor role. Eschatological time is not a significant feature of these systems.

Thus the central religious feature of indigenous gift giving is the extent to which it contributes to imitating divine gift giving and the extent to which it contributes to harmony within and without the group here and now. In such a system, remembering together the original stories of how the gods acted is of extreme importance. The role of storyteller takes on a special place in group life. Where "giving" to the gods is a part of the lore, that giving is done out of gratitude for what the gods have done (devotional), in re-creating the gods' gift-giving patterns (ritual), and to some extent in supplication for the gods' help in living the life ordained by the gods' action (sacrifice). Giving for personal gain, spiritual and otherwise (alms), mostly concerns material blessing and protection from evil spirits. Self-giving is not well developed; the cultures are communal, and self-giving is emphasized as a matter of everyday participation for tribal harmony.

Western religious beginnings involve an ideal state created by a single god. This creative act was carried out by a god interested in relationship with free human beings. Free human beings don't always make the best choices, so the ideal state is never realized. The ending of such a religious system is a restoration of the ideal state (Eden, heaven) envisioned by a god in the first place. The here and now is the story of attempts made by a god and human beings to work their way back to that ideal state.

Note two features of this kind of system. First, history becomes very important as an unfolding of the continuing saga of the god's and humans' attempts to recreate the ideal state. Human beings become part of an ongoing sacred story. It is not just a matter of remembering and honoring the god's actions; it is a matter of living into the story. Second, the ideal state is part of another world that comes about only at the end of human history. There is an other-worldly denouement to the story in which we find ourselves enmeshed.

The central feature of gift giving when seen in relation to the Western religious mythos is a heavy emphasis on devotional gift giving to the god in an attempt to communicate accurately and sympathetically. Since the god is sovereign in these systems, he or she is beyond sacrifice. Alms are given in an attempt to love, honor, and obey the god's good nature. Ritual remembrance is done primarily to motivate us to action in the here and now because of what the god has already done for us in creation and restoration. Self-giving is important because we are actors in this drama who must commit time and energy to the task of restoration.

SIDEBAR 23.6
RELIGIOUS GIFT GIVING

Functions of religious gift giving and how they are fulfilled in each system:

Alms	• Indigenous: Hope for material blessing and protection from evil spirits • Western: Attempt to love, honor, and obey God's good nature • Eastern: Gain spiritual merit and make spiritual progress
Devotion	• Indigenous: Gratitude for what the gods have done • Western: Communicate accurately and sympathetically with God • Eastern: Give to the gods in order to solicit their help
Sacrifice	• Indigenous: Supplication for the gods' help • Western: God is sovereign and thus beyond sacrifice • Eastern: Not very important
Self-Giving	• Indigenous: Participation in tribal harmony • Western: Give self in action to aid restoration of all things • Eastern: Give up self to help one to rise above self
Ritual Remembrance	• Indigenous: Re-creating the gods' gift-giving patterns • Western: Motivation for action in the present world • Eastern: Not emphasized because the future is more important than the past

Eastern religious beginnings tell the story of a world undivided and of a single essence. The world we think we live in is divided and fragmented. The goal is to do whatever it takes to restore that undivided oneness even as we live in a world unavoidably divided by caste, individualism, and different levels of spiritual attainment. Hindus describe this goal as a positive oneness, Buddhists tend to describe it as a condition of nothingness, but the effect is the same. Less "me," more "our" or "all."

A central feature of such systems is the unavoidable dualism of the ideal state as compared with the here and now. Some Buddhists describe this in terms of two tiers of truth: *nirvanic* truth, concerning the ideal state, and *samsaric* truth, involving the inadequate worldview system in which we find ourselves trapped.

Gifts in such systems are heavily weighted toward almsgiving and devotion. Almsgiving is what one does to gain spiritual merit and make spiritual progress.

Devotion is what one gives to the gods in order to solicit their help. Sacrifice pales in importance because the gods are designed to be not so much givers of boons as inspirations toward enlightenment. Ritual remembrances are not emphasized because the future is more important than the past. Self-giving is central in an ambiguous way: giving up the self is a way for the self to rise above itself in an attempt to become part of the greatest Self, the oneness of all being.

DOING THE PRACTICES

Following are a few words about how we might go about relating the gift of the gospel to the specific mission context in which we find ourselves.

First, learn as much as you can about the gift-giving practices of the context in which you find yourselves. Remember that each context is unique. Never assume you know how the Trobriand Islanders practice gift giving because you have read Bronislaw Malinowski's description of it. Or that you know how Brahmanical Hindus in an Indian village give gifts because you have read the *dharmasastra* related to that particular caste and place. Religions, even if documented in texts, never exist purely in a culture. They are always modified by local cultural practice and almost always combined with a folk-religious tradition of some sort. Religions, even if reported on in some detail by competent anthropologists, change on an almost daily basis in terms of the way they are practiced. They change because people change and conditions change and religious needs change along with these contextual changes. A Christian mission worker must consider every context a new field to be exegeted.

Second, read as much as you can from the experts. The previous point is not meant to discourage study of the civilizational religion dominant in your area nor to discourage study of the ethnographic work done in your area by anthropologists and historians of religion. Preparation for mission must include this kind of description. It provides a baseline of expectation that can then be modified by your own observation of how gifts are really given and received in this place at this time.

Third, remember that what we have to offer to everyone, everywhere, is God's gift of grace. We are gospel gift givers, imitating God's original gift to us and all that implies.

Fourth, study the way other Christian mission workers have given the gift over the centuries. Begin with the eleven practices that we think have been shown time and time again to be both faithful to the gospel and effective in results. Even though these eleven appear to be universal truths, they take very specific forms in local contexts and situations. The real art of mission work is to take these eleven mission practices and make them our own, dependent on the local context and our particular gift. We are in the business of making universal truths relevant to local situations.

SIDEBAR 23.7
GIFT GIVING: REFLECTION AND DISCUSSION

1. How do the creation stories of indigenous, Eastern, and Western religions influence the goals of gift giving in each one?
2. List four things about gift giving in your own culture that you learned from this chapter.
3. After reviewing the eleven practices and their relation to giftive mission, which of the practices fit your context best?
4. Which of the practices best fit the context of the new culture/religion that you are doing mission with? Give reasons for your answer.
5. Retell the story of the Christian gospel with gift as its central metaphor.
6. Describe how three different passages of Scripture support your retelling of the gospel story using gift as a metaphor.

Fifth, and finally, try different forms of the practices with the mind-set of giving gifts. Quit doing what does not glorify God and advance the gospel. Keep doing what does. Search endlessly for new forms of the practices that will bring the truths that change the world.

24

Giftive Mission

S o how might we describe giftive mission? How might we describe mission that uses the metaphor cluster around mission as gift that is so easily discernible in the biblical texts yet so little used in mission practice to people of other religions?

We could start by challenging our own assumptions regarding giftive mission and its use by mission theorists and workers. It is surely true that even though mission theorists have not done a great deal of conscious reflection on giftive mission as we define it, mission workers in practice for centuries have seen themselves as bearers of the gift of the gospel to those who have not heard. And if we look closely at the mission innovators we have chosen to highlight in our practices section—Paul, Patrick, Cyril and Methodius, Aquinas, Ricci, Las Casas, Carey, Booth, Sheppard, Mother Teresa, and Graham—we find that all of them saw themselves as bearers of the gospel gift. So one challenge might be, what is new about giftive mission?

Yet we would see this not so much as a challenge to what we are suggesting as confirmation of it. If our imitation of God's freely given gift of grace has always been at the core of what mission workers have done, why shouldn't it be more explicitly reflected upon? Why shouldn't our language about mission focus more specifically on this reality? In such reflection and language, we might find nuances that would mitigate some of the mission excesses we see around us today. And, more importantly, it might highlight the positive practices embedded in the mission effort that can also be seen daily around the world. These positive effects must be championed to counter the influence of the antimission forces both within and outside the Christian community.

It might be that the time has come for seeing ourselves as the bearers and the receivers of gifts with regard to relationships with people of other religions. If one reason Hindus, Buddhists, Muslims, and other people of well-articulated and successful civilizational religions have resisted the gospel message is that they feel disrespected, then establishing a religious gift exchange might go some distance in remedying that problem. We come offering the greatest gift we can imagine. We come offering what is most valuable to us. And we offer this in the context, initially at least, of the gift-giving practices indigenous to the culture in which we find ourselves. We will observe rules of obligation, if that be the case. We will observe the implications of merit and disinterestedness, if that be the case. And together we will work toward the elusive ideal of the free gift that must be teased out of every cultural setting.

So how might we organize this articulation of giftive mission? In chapter 22 we noted that the biblical use of metaphor followed a predictable pattern: the "yes" phase: using a metaphor that had a good chance of relating meaning to a particular cultural group; the "but" phase: relativizing the metaphor by recognizing the limitations of any metaphor, but also the limitations of human speech in describing one of God's central acts, the mission of God; and the "still" phase: making sure that whatever language we use, it points us forward to the excess of meaning resident in any kind of God language, in the very enterprise of theology itself.

Those three phases make a good outline for talking about giftive mission, starting with the biblical core related to the metaphor we want to use and

---

SIDEBAR 24.1
WHY USE GIFTIVE MISSION AS OUR MISSION METAPHOR?

- Scripture frequently uses the metaphor of gift.
- Missionaries have traditionally seen themselves as bearers of the gift of the gospel.
- We can more consciously become imitators of God's free gift of grace.
- We can move beyond the excesses of confrontation and competition in mission.
- The gift metaphor highlights positive practices embedded in mission efforts.
- Championing those giftive mission practices can counter antimission forces.
- Seeing ourselves as bearers and receivers of gifts can improve our relationships with people of other religions.
- Giving/receiving gifts according to cultural rules in various settings honors others.
- Using the giftive mission metaphor, we discover hints of the free gift in other cultures.

moving toward ways in which that core might be applied to the various segments of our world culture today: the indigenous, Western, and Eastern segments. Needless to say, using this kind of ideal-type paradigm (indigenous, Western, Eastern) is meant to teach a method of application, not the specific applications themselves. Those applications can be done only on the field, in the context of firsthand relationships.

YES . . .

As we noted in chapter 23, the Bible has a great deal to say about gift. Much of this metaphorical language concerns more than mission. As we noted, the concept of grace, of the freely given gift, can arguably be called the signature teaching act of Christianity itself. But let's be a bit more restrictive for a moment and examine the language of grace when it refers specifically to Christian witness.

The dominant language we want to focus on involves the actual "giving of the gift of the gospel" to others. The universality of the "giving" and the universality of the scope of the "others" is revealing. As people shaped by grace, we are in the giving mode all the time, and everyone we meet is a potential receiver of our largesse (actually, God's largesse channeled through us). In other words, we give all the time to everyone.

We give to our own people, our own "tribe." Nehemiah tells us that we must be always instructing our people in the meaning of our texts, the gift of meaning (8:8). But we give our own more than meaning; we also give gifts to commemorate the mighty acts of God—giving our little gifts reminds us of God's great gift to us all (Esther 9:19).

We give to those in need: a cup of cold water to those who are thirsty, cold, poor (Matt. 10:42). We give to those in need of "power." We make people aware of the power of the Holy Spirit, at least those who have come to that important point of recognizing their human lack, their dependence on a power greater than themselves. The Holy Spirit is available for all but can be actualized only by those who have come to that place of acknowledgment. In doing what we can to make people aware of this ubiquitous power, we are the givers of the Holy Spirit (Acts 15:8).

Finally, the act of giving is a humble act. Both James and Peter use an intriguing phrase: "God opposes the proud but gives grace to the humble" (James 4:6 and 1 Pet. 5:5). This raises two important questions: What happens to those who receive the gifts we offer, the gift of grace God has given us? And what happens to us when those to whom we offer the gift of the gospel want to return a gift to us? In some cultures, as we have seen, return gifts are important. When we offer the gift of grace we will be, in turn, offered valuable gifts. The New Testament especially has much to say about receiving gifts, both from God and from others. Primary in the lessons we learn is that as we receive the gift of the gospel, we immediately begin to give the same gift to others. A distinct metaphor cluster forms around the receiving of gifts in the Bible:

A man finds joy in giving an apt reply (Prov. 15:23).

A righteous man will receive a righteous man's reward (Matt. 10:41).

Whatever you have asked for in prayer, believe you have received it, and it will be yours (Mark 11:24).

Receive the Holy Spirit (John 20:22).

But eagerly desire the greater gifts (1 Cor. 12:31).

The man [who doubts] should not think he will receive anything from the Lord (James 1:7).

To receive power and wealth and wisdom (Rev. 5:12).

Clearly we are to receive gifts, and there is a way to receive them (humbly) that makes us more a part of God's gracious gift-giving exercise than we could possibly be if we did not see ourselves as the receiver of gifts as well as the giver of them. Another metaphor cluster emphasizes that giving and receiving are part of the same package of gospel grace:

One man gives freely, yet gains even more; another withholds unduly, but comes to poverty (Prov. 11:24).

He who gives to the poor will lack nothing, but he who closes his eyes to them receives many curses (Prov. 28:27).

Freely you have received, freely give (Matt. 10:8).

And you will receive the gift of the Holy Spirit (Acts 2:38).

It is more blessed to give than to receive (Acts 20:35).

Each one should use whatever gift he has received (1 Pet. 4:10).

Obviously there is much in the biblical metaphor of gift and grace that relates directly to the distinctives of the cultures we come in contact with, be they indigenous, Western, or Eastern cultures. The biblical language, for example, is no stranger to the ideas of gift-giving obligations, which we find

SIDEBAR 24.2
THE BIBLE AND GIFTIVE MISSION

- We give to our own people, our own "tribe" (Neh. 8:8; Esther 9:19).
- We give to those in need:
    A cup of cold water (Matt. 10:42).
- We give in humility (James 4:6 and 1 Pet. 5:5).
- We receive in giving:
    A man finds joy in giving an apt reply (Prov. 15:23).
    A righteous man will receive a righteous man's reward (Matt. 10:41).
    Whatever you have asked for in prayer, believe you have received it, and it will be
    yours (Mark 11:24).
    Receive the Holy Spirit (John 20:22).
    But eagerly desire the greater gifts (1 Cor. 12:31).
    The man [who doubts] should not think he will receive anything from the Lord
    (James 1:7).
    To receive power and wealth and wisdom (Rev. 5:12).
- Giving and receiving are both a part of grace:
    One man gives freely, yet gains even more, another withholds unduly, but comes
    to poverty (Prov. 11:24).
    He who gives to the poor will lack nothing, but he who closes his eyes to them
    receives many curses (Prov. 28:27).
    Freely you have received, freely give (Matt. 10:8).
    And you will receive the gift of the Holy Spirit (Acts 2:38).
    It is more blessed to give than to receive (Acts 20:35).
    Each one should use whatever gift he has received (1 Pet. 4:10).

in indigenous cultures. This is not surprising; the culture of the Bible is more indigenous in its human cultural makeup than it is Western or Eastern. But that is not to say that the distinctives of biblical culture are totally foreign to the ideas of gift giving found in Western or Eastern culture. Both can be teased out of the texts we have been examining.

What is very possible, even likely, however, is that some biblical examples of mission and gift giving are more appropriate to some cultures than others. Choosing which to use is the real art of mission. Perhaps identifying some possible applications of the gift-giving metaphor to our three ideal-type cultures will help illustrate the process of giving the gospel in appropriate ways to any culture. Note two qualifiers: *possible applications* and *appropriate ways*.

All applications we suggest here are merely possibilities, since every culture is unique: not all indigenous cultures are the same; not all Western cultures are the same; not all Eastern cultures are the same. Although we have given some family-resemblance type similarities in our descriptions above, we have emphasized that these three cultures as we described them—indigenous,

Western, and Eastern—are ideal types, rarely occurring in pure form in any of the cultures we may confront. Most cultures today, because of globalizing forces, are combinations of indigenous, Western, and Eastern cultural forces. This adds to the need to make applications context specific.

Similarly, the way we give the gift of the gospel needs to be appropriate to the context in which we find ourselves. The gospel story can be told in many ways with many different metaphors and emphases. What is appropriate in one setting may repel people in another setting. Paul's admonition that he was willing to become all things to all people in order to save some is not Paul's way of admitting to a relative gospel but rather an acknowledgment that there are both appropriate and inappropriate ways to present the gospel to the different peoples of the world.

With those caveats in mind, however, let's consider possible ways the gospel may be appropriately given to indigenous, Western, and Eastern cultures, that is, ways that mesh with rather than confront the gift-giving practices of those cultures. How might participants in each of those cultures receive the incomparable gift of the gospel of Jesus Christ that we offer? What tropes does the culture provide for talking about the gift of the gospel, and what might the positive implications of using the gift trope be in general terms for each of these three categories?

Indigenous Giving

The indigenous gift-giving metaphorical cluster, as we have seen, can be summarized ethically with the word *obligation*, economically by the word *reciprocity*, and theologically with the word *community* (*ecclesia*).

The importance of life-giving obligations that create community was not foreign to people in the Bible. One thinks, especially, of course, of the Jewish requirement that in order to be part of the community, one needs to be circumcised. Circumcision (and other lifestyle issues, such as kosher eating) were signs that one belonged to the community of God's people. Infant sons were circumcised as a matter of course, and adult men who wanted to join the community (proselytes) were circumcised as a sign of their membership intentions. Lack of circumcision raised questions about one's commitment to the community (Josh. 5:3).

These kinds of passages referring to rituals that signal membership in a community resonate especially well with members of indigenous communities. Even when the apostle Paul later called some of these practices into question, he did not question the idea of having community-building practices as much as their nature as salvation helpers. Paul was opposed not to community building but to works righteousness. For Paul, community (*ecclesia*) was not a requirement for salvation but a fruit of the Spirit. If you have accepted God's gift of salvation, then you will begin to behave in ways that build community by being loving and patient and long-suffering—and by giving gifts.

Paul argued this position several times in his letters. His basic argument was that becoming a Christian by grace does not free one of obligations. He maintained that it changes the directions of one's obligations, from allegiance to human-made gods, or human communities, or human ideologies, to total obligation to God. By shifting allegiances and a sense of obligation from human-made things to God, one often continues to carry out the obligations toward others that one had before, but for a different reason: to honor God. By shifting allegiances and a sense of obligation from human-made things to God, community still results, but it comes from a sense of everyone together being obligated to God and behaving in loving ways toward one another because of that obligation, not obligation to people and systems.

The practices of indigenous gift giving can continue, but the focus and rationale shift. It is not unusual for indigenous groups to read these texts and digest this teaching in a different way than those who have moved from subsistence economies and social organizations to managed economies or market-oriented ones. Whereas for managed and market economies, community and talk about community building are seen as nice ways to discuss physical well-being, for indigenous groups community is all there is. In reading these texts, we will appreciate Paul's radical reorientation of allegiances not as doing away with community-building practices (as Westerners might) but as showing a better way for producing community: if we put allegiance to God first, everything else will be added to it, community included.

Western Giving

The Western gift-giving metaphorical cluster can be summarized ethically with the word *freedom*, economically with the word *value*, and theologically with the word *personhood* (*imago Dei*).

Perhaps no culture in the world has greater difficulty understanding the idea of free gift than Western, market-oriented cultures. Whereas indigenous groups see free gift as a wonderful thing, freeing people from the obligations of their gift-giving practices, and many Eastern cultures immediately recognize the concept as one familiar to their religious cultures and want to relate to it, Westerners think they understand it fully but because of their underlying market orientation can hardly grasp it.

This is so because Westerners think that by understanding the individual freedom inherent in a democratic political process, they also grasp the idea of a free gift. Nothing could be further from the truth. Free gift is more foreign to market economies than almost any other type of culture. Gift giving for people living in market economies is inextricably tied to the language of giving and getting, of quid pro quo, of giving value in the expectation of getting value. One reason for Western Christians' propensity to emphasize grace as the signature teaching of the faith is that they never cease to be amazed that such a thing can exist. It certainly doesn't exist in an economic system built on the concept of the careful balancing of individual desires.

This is not to say we should discourage the idea of using grace as an entrée to Western secularists. The fact that they find it so appealing and mistakenly think that it is already a part of their worldview means that it can be used as a good entrée into their thinking. The key, however, is that even while introducing it, we locate it not in the usual economic sphere reserved for gift giving but in the frustrations that arise from wanting to give free, unself-interested gifts but realizing that we are unable to do so. Locate it in the theological area staked out by Romans 7:14–15: "I am unspiritual, sold as a slave to sin. I do not understand what I do. For what I want to do I do not do, but what I hate I do." Thus the thinking goes, *I want to give the gift of the gospel as a free gift, free of my self-interest and grasping, but I cannot do so without the help of God, who first gave the gift to me.*

The practices of Western gift giving can continue, but as with the indigenous practices, the focus and the rationale shift. We are talking not about gift as understood in the same spiritual marketplace sphere but about an understanding of gift so free of self-interest that it can only be of God. In terms of religious gift giving the forms most natural to the Western mind-set are sacrifice and ritual remembrance.

Indian (Eastern) Giving

The Indian (Eastern) gift-giving metaphorical cluster can be summarized ethically with the word *altruism*, economically by the word *determined*, and theologically with the word *selflessness (kenosis)*.

Altruism resonates strongly with people from the cultures of India. The value of altruism, intentionless giving, is ingrained in their way of life. Since caste makes the seeking and getting of material things a well-established path of occupation and lifestyle, gift giving does not run the danger of being confused with amassing goods. And since caste establishes a lifelong community that cannot be changed, gift giving does not fall into the category of maintaining community membership. *Dana*, or gift giving, then, falls into two categories of the mental architecture of Indian cultures. It can be a sign of the quality of one's observance of caste membership (since elaborate texts define how and what and when to give gifts); one will always be a member of one's caste, but one can be a good member or a bad member in terms of caste observance. Or it can be part of one's personal spiritual exercise, a growth-producing observance that both signals progress and, in an indirect way, results in spiritual progress. Since one of the irreducible elements of a gift well given is that it be given without any expectation of a return gift, talk about selfless behavior is natural for Indians.

SIDEBAR 24.3

YES . . . THE BIBLE AND GIFTIVE MISSION IN CONTEMPORARY CULTURES

Giftive mission can redirect the positive values of each culture's use of the metaphor of gift.

Indigenous cultures:	• Obligation
Gift giving creates community.	• Reciprocity
	• Community
Western cultures:	• Freedom
The free gift of God's grace amazes us.	• Value
	• Personhood
Eastern cultures:	• Altruism
The best gift is one given without expectation of a return.	• Determinism
	• Selflessness

Such talk is common to the Bible. Consider, for example, James 3:14, 16–18:

> If you harbor bitter envy and selfish ambition in your hearts, do not boast about it or deny the truth. . . . For where you have envy and selfish ambition, there you find disorder and every evil practice.
>
> But the wisdom that comes from heaven is first of all pure; then peace-loving, considerate, submissive, full of mercy and good fruit, impartial and sincere. Peacemakers who sow in peace raise a harvest of righteousness.

The apostle Paul often spoke of selflessness as a sign that one was properly acknowledging the greatness of God. These "less of me, more of Thee" passages have a natural resonance with Asian peoples in general.

A prominent Japanese Zen Buddhist scholar, Masao Abe, often said that the strongest connection he felt with Christianity came when he read the kenosis passages of the second chapter of Philippians. The model of Christ, an all-powerful being, emptying himself of rightful prerogatives of power in order to serve human beings better, personifies the ultimate gift, the gift of one's own life in service to others.

When Buddhist groups especially read about gift giving in the form of selfless action, these texts do not seem odd or out of place but central. In fact, they resonate so well that the danger lies in Western Christians presenting these as startling new truths, whereas they have been part of the Indian civilizational ethos for millennia. That, of course, does not mean we should not present this truth about God's grace, but we should present it as a point of contact, a similarity we can build on rather than as a remarkable new idea.

361

In terms of religious gift giving, the forms most natural to the Eastern mind-set are alms and devotional gift giving, with self-sacrifice, specially understood, also playing an important role.

BUT . . .

As we can see, resonances between cultural expressions of gift giving and biblical teachings on gift giving are not hard to tease out of these three ideal-type cultures. All, in their own way, see gift giving as important, if not central, to their ways of looking at the world. Using the concept of gift giving as a way of communicating the Christian mission effort has great missiological power today.

But inherent in all expressions of the gospel is an element of critique of prevailing cultures, whether indigenous, Western, or Eastern. Gift giving in whatever human, cultural form simply cannot measure up to the Christian free gift, to grace. Thus, the "but . . ." of our metaphorical method.

Before we consider what might be the specific "buts . . ." of indigenous, Western, and Eastern cultures, it would be worthwhile to comment on how the "but . . . ," the reservations about culture, should be expressed. We offer three suggestions.

Guidelines for Critique

1. *The critique is best if it is internal.* Self-criticism is always more effective than that which comes from outsiders. The "yes" part of our method is more readily accepted from outsiders, because "yes" is filled with respect and agreement and mutual appreciation and innovation. "But," on the other hand, no matter how sensitively expressed, cannot help but seem at least a bit judgmental, a bit holier than thou, a bit triumphalistic. And as anyone involved with mission work on any level learns, indicating that I have it and you don't does not lead to good long-term relationships. It more often leads to envy, mistrust, and enmity.

Our gift is not doctrine. Our gift is not judgment. Our gift is not about us but about Jesus. Our gift is the story of Jesus. We do best if we present this gift from the outside with a big "yes." The story alone, without any interpretation or commentary, has enormous power, more power, in fact, when presented as unembellished story. The task is to suggest that the story of a people's culture fits into the Jesus story.

Once we tell the story, with passion and commitment and love, however, it is up to the people themselves to see how their culture's story fits into this bigger, more comprehensive story. And it is in the fitting together of the stories, the meshing, that the questions and inconsistencies arise. This is the "but . . ." part of our method, and it is best done internally, in the culture. Since people know their own stories far better than outsiders can ever learn them, they know best where the pinch points will be. Will the problem involve the part of the story that tells us Jesus is the Son of God? Will the problem arise from the fact that God let Jesus die on a cross? Will the problem come from understanding human lack as rebellion against a personal God? Outsiders can guess at these difficulties; insiders live them.

Further, insiders will know how the problems might best be resolved. Cultures have different ways of critiquing their own cultural forms. Sometimes the critique takes the form of discussions involving the entire community. Sometimes it is done by an elite leadership core. Sometimes it is almost entirely implicit: change and adjustment take place without conscious reflection on the part of the people. However the process occurs, it follows clear, almost invariable patterns, patterns that only an insider can appreciate and implement.

2. *The critique runs off the rails of effectiveness if it ceases being specific and local and becomes a universal condemnation of the whole culture.* Perhaps the biggest mistake antimissionaries have made is to confuse the gift of the gospel story with the gift of their own culture. Mistaking Western culture for the gospel, for example, has led to the excesses of colonialism and imperialism, the attempt to replace so-called foreign cultures with Western cultures. Even if, as some claim, this has most often been done with positive intentions, the effects have still debilitated the subject cultures. Much of their uniqueness and value have been discarded with the elements incompatible with the gospel.

And if that is not a serious enough loss, the effect on the gospel story itself has been even worse. The story either becomes associated with cultural forms with which its essential elements are incompatible, or it takes on nuances, sometimes even changes, that make it less than the gospel. Instead of the peaceful Savior of the world, for example, Jesus sometimes becomes a warmonger, a capitalist, a communist—the list is as long as the list of human ideologies.

An important theological truth is at stake here. Since all human beings have been created by God, and since the *imago Dei* means that much good resides in the works produced by those human beings, including the work that produces human cultures of all sorts, then it stands to theological reason that cultures are good things. They are necessary to the functioning of human communities. No culture is entirely good. All are mixtures of good and bad. It is sorting out the good and the bad that becomes the challenge.

One evaluates cultures with the gospel story. Many, if not most, enduring human cultures will be found compatible with that story. Because of the fall, however, there will be elements in every culture, sometimes important elements, that are not compatible with the gospel story and must be regarded differently. Usually, however, the basic elements of successful human cultures will stand. The entire culture does not need to be jettisoned for it to be seen as a carrier of gospel truth. Less change, rather than more change, is the rule.

Why is the "but . . ." part of the process so often short-circuited with wholesale condemnation of the culture in question? Perhaps because it is easier. Perhaps because it appeals more to the human chauvinistic impulse that is forever tempting us to privilege our way of looking at things as the best and most effective one. It is more difficult to pick out the antigospel nuance than to demolish the whole structure and start over with what one has found to work.

3. *The critique only works if it is clear that the standard is not another, better human culture but the world of the gospel story.* It is easy sometimes to see the gospel story as simply an alternative culture. When this is the understanding, the task simply becomes one of replacing the one culture with the other. This is a mistake rooted in the failure to recognize that *story* and *culture* mean different things.

Culture means many things to many people, but our use of the term corresponds roughly to French historian Fernand Braudel's definition (1995). Our definition is that *culture is a set of normative principles, values, and ideals that shape the life of a specific group of people.* These normative principles, values, and ideals are often explicit, stated or implied in the way people talk to one another, the rules they teach children, the modes of behavior they favor, even the laws they enact and follow. But even if the principles, values, and ideals are only implicit, they are never far below the surface of consciousness. People "know" what they are because they are a part of the culture that favors them. People "know" what they are and live accordingly.

Story, on the other hand, is something different. A people's story is not unrelated to its culture, but it is much deeper than cultural affects. It differs in form. A story is a narrative with a beginning, a middle, and an end. Often the beginning, the middle, and the end of a culture roughly correspond to a culture's view of its past, present, and future. *A story is a narrative—historical, nonhistorical, or ahistorical—out of which a culture derives its creative, sustaining, and redemptive meanings.* Stories of this sort provide meanings, not in a didactic, discursive way, but by furnishing the occasion for members of a culture to personalize more universal meanings. The members of a culture share general meanings; the members of a culture each personalize the story in unique ways that relate the idiosyncrasies of their particular lives to the larger story.

Stories vary in their scope. Some cultures' stories are intentionally limited to that group. Others claim more universal intent that includes other cultural groups in some way. When we capitalize the word *Story,* we usually mean that this story is meant to be comprehensive of all other particular stories. (Sometimes such stories are called metanarratives.) The Christian Story is meant this way. It is a story in the sense that it describes the events of a particular group of people. But it is a Story because even when it refers just to the chosen people, it is intended to describe divine events with implications for everyone. And at a certain point, the Story explicitly embraces all humanity as its audience.

364

In the Christian's eyes, all the world's cultures have the capacity to make the Christian Story their own. Some have gone a long way toward doing so already. Others have not. One way to view Christian mission is to see it as the endeavor to tell the Story so that all the world's cultures can see where their stories fit in the larger one. Mission workers are storytellers, in the first instance. They bring the gospel story as a gift.

But at a certain point they become tailors, when they realize that the fit between the gospel Story and the culture's story are not perfect. Some tailoring is required. A shortening here. Taking in a waistline there. A tuck. A new buttonhole. Mission workers can often see the general outline of the tailoring that is required. But the tailoring itself is best done by members of the culture themselves.

What critique does the biblical understanding of the gift of the gospel bring to the cultural understanding of gift? Of course, the tailoring required would differ for every culture one encounters. But to give an idea of the work involved, let's explore some possibilities in the case of our three ideal-type cultures—indigenous, Western, and Eastern.

Critique of Indigenous Cultures

The offer of the free gift of the gospel in cultures that emphasize obligation and reciprocity has much that fits between story and Story, but it is also the occasion for tailoring. As a cultural system, obligation and reciprocity can continue to work within the more encompassing story of the gospel. Obligation and reciprocity mesh well with, for example, the ethical teachings of the Sermon on the Mount. But the gospel relativizes this story in two ways. First, it clearly states that the story of Jesus extends the positive obligations such as kindness and gentleness and patience and caring for the poor and the needy not just to a clan, a tribe, and a certain geographical area but to all people everywhere. Paul said that he was "obligated both to Greeks and non-Greeks, both to the wise and the foolish" (Rom. 1:14). The second nuance involves the source of the obligation. The obligation is not to human systems and human ideologies but to the Spirit of God: "Therefore, brothers, we have an obligation—but it is not to the sinful nature, to live according to it," but to the Spirit of God because "those who are led by the Spirit of God are sons of God" (Rom. 8:12, 14). Obligation goes beyond the immediate tribe to all humanity because that is the nature of God.

Another interesting instance of the "but . . ." when it comes to indigenous groups concerns the power of evil. Most indigenous groups have an understanding of evil and evil spirits that is powerful and determinative. Evil powers must be accounted for, reckoned with, kowtowed to. This is a distasteful, burdensome fact of life. This part of indigenous cultures' stories is changed in a positive way by the introduction of the gospel Story, which tells us that the most powerful spirit, the Spirit of God, has dominion over all spirits, evil and otherwise. The gospel Story says not that the evil spirits are unreal but that they have been, are, and will be defeated by the most powerful spirit, the Holy Spirit of God. The indigenous story has much in common with parts of the Bible that describe evil spirits. But the story becomes part of the larger Story when the most powerful Spirit masters all other spirits on the ground.

Critique of Western Cultures

The freedom of market economies and democratic political systems compares favorably with the idea of the free gift of the gospel. Unfortunately, it doesn't take a great deal of profound thought to discern the unintended riders accompanying this natural contextualization of the gift of the gospel.

One of the riders is license, a danger Paul recognized in the way that the early church was often tempted to misuse the free gift of grace. Too often the freedom of the free gift goes to our heads. When political and economic conditions are such that free choice becomes possible, some of us "change the grace of our God into a license for immorality" (Jude 4). This is perhaps the greatest danger of democratic stories in the modern world.

The danger of freedom is not just material, however, but also spiritual. Freedom is an essential element of the Christian understanding of the ways and reasons of God working in the world. God created us as freely deciding beings because God desired freely chosen relationships with each of us. Such freedom is dangerous, however. We don't always make the correct choices. Part of the "but . . ." that must be addressed in Western stories by the Story is that we need help in making God-honoring choices: help from friends, help from societal structures, help from the church, help from God.

Another of the riders that must be checked is greed. Market economies usually operate according to what might be called the balancing of individual greed, just as democratic religious pluralisms operate according to a balancing of religious interests. One of the elements of most Western cultures' stories is the chance for economic improvement and the chance to succeed financially. This is a good feature of the story, but because of fallen human nature, just succeeding does not seem to satisfy us. The material freedom of Western stories needs to be governed by the command of the gospel Story to help the poor and needy.

Critique of Eastern Cultures

We have seen that the metaphor of gift giving is ideal for relating the gospel gift of grace to Eastern cultures, with their emphasis on reciprocal relationships and intentionless giving. In a way, though, the match is almost too good. In the non-Eastern cultures of the world, the good news of free gift is startling. It comes across as eye-opening. Release from age-old, oppressive obligations suddenly seems possible. The chance for exercising natural gifts in the pursuit of wealth and happiness overwhelms us.

Yet in Eastern cultures this is not a new idea. In these cultures, one of the signs of an acceptable, successful gift is that it was given with no expectation of return, at least from the recipient. In these cultures, receiving a gift does not place one under the burden of overwhelming responsibility to return with an even more valuable gift. In fact, to receive such a gift is an affirmation of one's worthiness to receive the gift. All of this comports very well with the gospel ideal of free gift.

The danger here, the "but . . . ," is that we present this idea as the essence of the gospel Story and risk being met with a ho-hum, been-there-done-that

---

SIDEBAR 24.4
BUT . . . CULTURES AND GIFTIVE MISSION

Human gift giving cannot measure up to the free gift of God's grace presented in the gospel.

Critique: How can we handle critiques of cultural forms of gift giving?
- Critique is best if it is internal.
- Critique becomes ineffective if it moves away from the specific and local and becomes a universal condemnation of a whole culture.
- Critique only works if it is clear that the standard is not a human culture but the gospel story itself.

Some ideas for tailoring the gospel to cultures:

For indigenous cultures:
- The gospel expands obligation to all (Rom. 1:14).
- The source of obligation becomes the Spirit of God (Rom. 8:12).
- God's Spirit has dominion over the powers of evil.

For Western cultures:
- Valued freedoms compare well with the idea of the free gift of the gospel.
- But we need to beware of confusing freedom with license (Jude 4).
- But we need help in making wise choices.
- But we need to be careful not to become greedy.
- But we need to temper our freedom to receive and remember to give gifts to the poor.

For Eastern cultures:
- The intentionless giving of Eastern cultures meshes well with the idea of free gift.
- But the ordinariness of this idea may get a cool response.
- But we can emphasize the nature of the gift, a personal relationship with God.
- We can emphasize the relationships of commitment with others that develop through accepting God's gift of grace.

367

attitude. Of course, that is what gift giving is all about, a member of that culture might think. Our sages have taught that for centuries. Do you have anything else for us? Anything really new?

Perhaps in such cultures the "new" thing we need to present is the relational end of gift giving. The importance of gift giving is the nature of the gift, not the gift itself, not the social cost of the gift. The gospel gift is a gift of personal relationship, first with God, the most powerful spirit, and then with other human beings who have also been given—and accepted—the gift of grace. Can such a gift be imagined? In Eastern, particularly Indian cultures, this kind of personal relationship and commitment is rare. Relationship in Indian cultures is not something that lasts and leads anywhere but rather something to be used and then overcome in one's march toward enlightenment. Yes, but. . . .

AND STILL . . .

Once the metaphor of gift giving has been used to introduce the gospel, and the gospel itself has become an occasion for a culture to evaluate itself and its capacity to fit into the larger Story of Jesus, the work is barely begun.

Mission workers may indeed be the ones who introduce the Story to a culture that has not heard it. Storytelling is important, but it is the work of an instant.

And indigenous community leaders, together with mission representatives of the global church, may begin the work of evaluating the culture with the Story, their story with the Story. This is an ongoing task, one that is never finished.

After a while, however, evaluation needs to be complemented by another task, the task of creating theological approaches to the gospel that have meaning in the context of the gospel Story and the cultural story together.

The dual role of mission metaphors mandates that when we discuss them we are not just talking about ways to use indigenous, Western, and Eastern thought forms to communicate gospel truth, but we also must be aware that indigenous metaphors of gift giving can become centerpieces in the theologies developed in different countries and cultures. Metaphorical constructs are not one-way. Each culture impacted by the gospel develops its own theologies, appropriate to its thought forms. And those theologies will become teachers to other cultures in the future. Those of us in the West will learn as much about the gospel from the forms it takes in indigenous and Eastern cultures as we learn about the gospel from our Western theologies.

The Christian theologies of the twenty-first century will be, to our eyes at least, curious mixtures of biblical, Middle Eastern thought forms, Western cultural forms (probably as mediated by traditional Western theologies: Augustine, Aquinas, Luther, Calvin, Wesley, Barth), civilizational religious forms (whether Hindu, Buddhist, Muslim, or indigenous), and the new language of globalized, urban culture. Some of these theologies have already begun to emerge, and we have alluded to them throughout this book: Kōsuke Koyama in Southeast Asia, Watchman Nee in China, Mercy Amba Oduyoye in Africa. But scores more are being developed as we write, and future generations will all, of course, write their own, doing the ongoing work of the church begun by the Latin and Greek fathers, Augustine, Aquinas, Wesley, and all the others in an attempt to make the gospel Story come alive to everyone.

New metaphors for this work will continue to develop. The developing globalized culture will put special pressures on the metaphors to be used in new theologies. We think one of the metaphors that satisfies those globalized pressures will be the exchange of gifts, but others may equally well satisfy the needs of the twenty-first-century world. But using gift giving as a sample metaphor, what is it about the current world conditions that makes this a particularly appropriate metaphor?

Frequency of Cross-Cultural Interchange

Cross-cultural exchange used to be the province of the power elites of any culture, used to be one-way in its direction (or at most two-way), and was a relatively rare, specialized occurrence. All of that has changed. International travel has exploded in scope. Whereas as recently as 1990 world travelers spent $270 billion traveling to foreign countries, in 2000 they spent $475 billion traveling in the pursuit of both pleasure and business. Today the direction of intercultural exchange can only be described as multidirectional. It is not just Western tourists going to Europe and Asia. The largest national travel groups are Japanese and Chinese, going to all parts of the world, including the United States. And "travel" is by no means just physical. The Internet has revolutionized cross-cultural interactions. Armchair tourists can with a keystroke access any culture in the world and make firsthand contacts with people from that culture. Chat rooms, blogs, and personal Web pages make intercultural contact a universal possibility for everyone who has access to computers (over half of US households own computers, but millions more can access public computers). Computers are changing the meaning of restricted-access countries. The value of limiting physical access to a country is diminishing rapidly given the near-ubiquitous nature of computer access.

What are some terms that might describe this state of affairs? *Global neighborhood* comes to mind. Today the interactions among people of different cultures resemble the interactions, good and bad, that used to take place only in physical neighborhoods. *Informal* also comes to mind. Contacts tend to be random and spontaneous. *Personal* is another word we might use to describe this state of affairs. Informal, neighborhood, personal interactions do not develop well using the methods of formal, statist contacts. The old metaphors no longer work: "East meets West" smacks of confrontations; "reaping the harvest" is one-way, objectifying, and manipulative; "spiritual warfare" can too easily become confused with physical warfare. What does one do in informal, neighborhood settings? Well, one thing one does is exchange gifts. And it is becoming increasingly common to include in these gift exchanges the telling of one's spiritual stories and experiences.

It is not unusual for business travelers to Asia, for example, to take courses in cultural interactions—forms of greetings, ways to dress, and so on—and the frequency of exchanging gifts is always addressed in those courses. Using metaphors from these kinds of common, everyday interactions makes a great deal of sense in a world that is indeed becoming one large neighborhood.

Need for a Spiritual Alternative to Materialized Globalization

Historically, the contacts between cultures tended to begin with either military or merchant interactions, and only after either warfare or trade had established the base did Christian mission workers arrive on the scene. This protocol has not changed significantly. The dominant interaction with other cultural groups continues to be mercantile. The trading of goods and services is far and away the most frequent reason for intercultural contact, where wholesale trade, retail sales, or tourist purchases are the occasion for the exchange. So powerful are these reasons for contact that it is extremely easy for any other basis for interaction to be pushed to the background or ignored altogether.

To be sure, the rewards for such material interactions are exciting. Despite the obvious profit motive of multinational corporations, the overall, long-term effect of globalization (or perhaps we should say the promise of globalization) is a contribution to human well-being: raising the world's health quotient; encouraging worldwide, universal education; fostering higher standards of living. Sound familiar? "For I was hungry and you gave me something to eat, I was thirsty and you gave me something to drink, I was a stranger and you invited me in, I needed clothes and you clothed me, I was sick and you looked after me, I was in prison and you came to visit me" (Matt. 25:35–36).

Still, "man does not live on bread alone" (Matt. 4:4). Our cross-cultural engagements become one-sided if they remain on the material level alone. To ensure that the gospel does not become totally identified with material exchanges of one sort or another, we need to develop a language for spiritual exchanges. Initially that language should be focused on a common experience that all cultures recognize to be something other than strictly material. All cultures, as we have seen in some detail, consider gift giving to be such an experience. Borrowing the language of gift giving, especially since it is so compatible with the gospel of grace, seems a good way to enter into discussions that rise above the material.

This is a particularly helpful language because in general it avoids the association more traditional mission languages have tended to use, the languages of civilizing, colonizing, defeating, even saving. Gift-giving language matches the real-life experience of people as they encounter those of other cultures these days. Such encounters are relational, mutual, reciprocal. They recognize that both sides in the encounter have something to offer. Few other facets of cultural existence are as compatible with what preaching the gospel actually means given the cultural conditions of the twenty-first century.

Shift from Coercive Power to a Meeting-Needs Model

Even a cursory reading of Christian mission history, let alone human history, reveals the ubiquitous presence of coercive power as the modus operandi of choice in human interactions. Christian mission workers, sad to say, have too often fallen prey to coercive power's alluring capacity to get things done. Examples? Following up on military conquests to present the gospel in the ensuing power vacuums. Using the power of satisfying economic need to entice unbelievers. Even maintaining order in the church itself through the use of coercive power. Is it fair to say that even though these mission tactics have produced short-term gains, the long-term effects have been to encourage other civilizational religions to use the same coercive-power tactics against Christians, not to mention that they have weakened a central message of the gospel, namely, that the story of Jesus is a story of peace, not war?

This gospel truth is being buttressed these days by a social development that it would have been difficult to predict. There is some evidence that the effectiveness of coercive power is losing its ability to control people.

Throughout much of history, the use of coercive power has produced the desired result: total control over the people against whom it is used. Whatever the power mechanism used—warfare, law, guilt—the people in control of the power mechanisms of society have by and large been able to control, for various lengths of time, the people in their charge. We might summarize this common historical dynamic thus: the use of coercive power creates control.

Two historical developments have changed this invariable result of the use of coercive power. One is the nature of power itself. The means of power have become themselves so extreme that they are losing their effectiveness at controlling people. We are thinking particularly of nuclear power, of course. The nuclear threat is no longer an effective threat against others because it is such a powerful tool that its use threatens not just "them" but "us." That is, the users of this kind of power might very well destroy themselves in the process of attempting to control others. The true meaning of the proverb "biting off one's nose to spite one's face" becomes increasingly true in the twenty-first-century political climate.

The second development is the growing capacity of people to resist the use of power. Physical boundaries, such as nation-state borders, are now less effective at controlling people's ability to organize resistance against the powerful. The physical capacity of police and the military to control a group of people is diminishing as people find themselves able to communicate across borders meant to stop communication. The use of the Internet enables resisters of power not only to find comrades in resistance but to mobilize world opinion in championing their cause. So important is this development that it is fair to say that the old maxim "The use of coercive power creates control" is being replaced by a new one: "The use of coercive power creates resistance." Not just any resistance, mind you, but *effective* resistance.

This development means a great deal to the Christian mission effort. It means that more than ever we must avoid becoming associated with those who would use coercive power to further their aims. Coercive power—whatever the theological implications—did indeed once produce "positive" effects. Nowadays it produces resistance, effective resistance. The more we use it in the Christian mission effort, the more resistance to the gospel it will produce.

All the more reason for us to search for metaphors for Christian mission that eschew power and emphasize the relational, such as gift giving.

Religious Competition

Perhaps we have written more than we should about the competition Christianity is encountering with the other civilizational religions of the world these days, particularly Hinduism, Buddhism, and Islam. They are growing religions, increasingly using the same methods as Christians in their work of self-advocacy. That is, they are mission minded and growth focused. This has created, in our minds at least, a tendency to rely too much on the marketplace metaphor as the primary one to describe interreligious interactions. To be sure, to be faithful to the world scene as it is, describing it as a marketplace of religious ideas, needs to be part of the mix. It does describe what is happening in a certain sense.

If it is the only metaphor we use, however, we will miss the boat in presenting the gospel fully and faithfully to non-Christians. The problems with the marketplace competition metaphor, if it is the only one used, are several. For one, it is based on fear—or perhaps a better twenty-first-century word is *anxiety*. Anxiety about losing ground in building God's kingdom. Anxiety that the unsaved will be forever lost. Anxiety about the spiritual opportunities that our children, and their children, will have. Anxiety is not the best basis for preaching. If anxiety is our motivation, then it becomes part of our message. And more anxiety is not needed in the world today. The real need is the opposite of anxiety: hope. And hope is a much more biblical motivation for witness (1 Pet. 3:15).

SIDEBAR 24.5
STILL . . . THE METAPHOR OF GIFT IS APPROPRIATE BECAUSE . . .

SIDEBAR 24.5
STILL . . . THE METAPHOR OF GIFT IS APPROPRIATE BECAUSE . . .

- of the frequency of cross-cultural interchange, both physical and electronic;
- of the crying need for a spiritual alternative to materialized globalization;
- of a shift from coercive power as the most effective human social glue to a meeting-needs model;
- of religious competition;
- gift giving as a metaphor replaces fear with hope;
- gift giving puts relationships ahead of making a sale;
- gift giving is two-way rather than one-way; and
- gift giving reflects how God acts toward us—with grace and free gift.

The marketplace metaphor also risks betraying an overestimation of human means for communicating the gospel, although it is true enough that we must use any and all gospel-compatible means for witness. Put another way, the marketplace metaphor risks betraying a lack of faith about what God is doing in the world. The biblical message is that God will prevail, that God's purposes will be done. If the salvation of humanity is God's desire and purpose, then it will be done, whether we engage in a salesmanship competition with other religions or not.

Gift giving as a metaphor avoids some of these more obvious shortcomings of the marketplace metaphor. It replaces fear with hope. It puts a desire for relationships ahead of making a sale. It is two-way rather than one-way. And it is more compatible with the way God acts toward us—with grace or free gift—than the business model allows. For our time, mission works better with this metaphor than any other.

GIFTIVE MISSION IN PRACTICE

How does giftive mission express itself in terms of mission practices? Once giftive mission's bona fides (as biblically based and theologically viable) have been established, does it work? Put another way, would Paul, Patrick, Cyril and Methodius, Aquinas, Las Casas, Ricci, Carey, Booth, Sheppard, Mother Teresa, and Graham (and other model mission workers) recognize it as a useful and effective way to speak of God's mission? How might it relate to each of the eleven practices we have chosen to highlight in this book?

Universality: Reaching out to all, including Christians. The apostle Paul emphasized the universality of the gospel story. He was the focal figure in taking Jesus's insistence that his gracious gift was for all people (he called them Gentiles), not just the Jewish people. This is compatible with the giftive mission metaphor. All cultures, all people, have an understanding of gift giving and receiving. Most have an explicit understanding of free gift, regardless of how successfully their cultures model this ideal. In encouraging the Corinthian church members, Paul insisted that they excel in gift giving, specifically giving the gift of grace. For Paul, giving God's grace to others was an indispensable sign of Christian maturity (2 Cor. 8).

Fellowship: Belonging precedes believing. Patrick's whole life was a gift to others. From the day he was kidnapped and taken to Ireland, he determined to spend the rest of his life as a gift to the very people (the Celts) who had torn him from home and family. His gift to the Irish, however, was even more specific. He determined to embrace a mission principle that is universally useful. Creating the conditions of fellowship for everyone, regardless of their spiritual status, enabled him to gain a foothold in a difficult culture and eventually witness to the gospel by his very presence—actually the presence of the monasteries he established throughout Ireland. Patrick's idea of free gift was that there are no strings attached to fellowship and Christian love, not even the crucial strings of orthodoxy.

Localization: Focusing on questions and concerns of the local community. As we have seen, the great contribution of Methodius and Cyril was a gift. Recognizing that the gospel is for everyone, they went about making it understandable to all (at least all the people they encountered, the Slavs). Their gift was to give the gospel in the language of the indigenous church. They had to fight to give this gift because not everyone agreed that the common person should be able to read the Scriptures and understand the liturgy. The Slavs must surely have perceived this to be a gift of huge proportions. Before Methodius and Cyril, the gospel story was rehearsed in a foreign tongue. After Methodius and Cyril, the Slavs heard it in their own language every Sunday.

Commitment: Holding ideas with conviction; acting decisively on those ideas; not letting those ideas be divisive. Thomas Aquinas's gift was to show Christians how to think about the faith, yet in the context of other people's way of looking at things. He believed that non-Christian stories were not all wrong but simply not big enough to include the gospel story. He demonstrated how to include without abandoning commitments. He wrote a six-volume compendium on mission practice to Muslims (*Summa Contra Gentiles*). He would have related well to the idea of mission seen as an exercise in gift giving. He would have focused on his gift to mission as the gift he gave to the church in the form of mission theology and strategy.

Freedom: Honoring the principle of religious choice. In championing the cause of mission to the populations of Latin America who followed animistic religions, Las Casas found himself defending a principle that one would not think a Christian mission worker would have to defend. The principle that all human beings are equally able to love and glorify God was under attack. One might say that Las Casas had to argue that the Native populations of Latin America were capable of receiving the gift of the gospel. Underlying this argument, of course, were the ideas that Native Americans needed the gift, and that by giving it to them, the Europeans were doing their Christian duty.

Effectiveness: Allowing the context to determine the form of witness. Matteo Ricci gave the gift of the gospel to the Chinese. At first he thought that talking about the gospel in terms Chinese Buddhists would understand would be the best approach, but that method proved ineffective. So Ricci resorted to talking about the gospel in Confucian terms and was successful in giving this gift, until his superiors in the church thought he had gone too far. A gift for Ricci was not a good gift unless it satisfied an important need in the recipients, in language they could understand. We might say that Ricci focused on the nature of the gift more than others, who may have focused more on the giver, the receiver, the motivation, or the result.

Consistency: Striving for consistency between methods and goals. In William Carey's day, the church's position regarding missions as a gift might be summarized this way: The church does not need to spend too much time giving the gift of the gospel, because God has already given the all-important gift of his Son, Jesus. The gift has been given by an all-powerful gift giver. What more needs to be done? William Carey thought much more needed to be done, primarily in the area of informing the people of the world that God's gift was available to everyone, everywhere, at all times. Any method used to communicate this message that was consistent with the principle of gospel love should be used. He himself followed this practice with the Hindus of India.

Variety: Communicating the gospel in many forms. Catherine Booth cared for the poor. She spent her mission convincing other Christians that giving to the poor, providing medicine for the sick, helping the disadvantaged gain some advantage was as much a part of the gospel as was preaching hellfire and damnation. She could do—and did—both. But she wanted to make sure she lived her life committed to giving all the gifts of the gospel, not just a select few that some group had decided were the most important.

Respect: Not disparaging others in order to champion your own; not disparaging your own in order to respect others. William Sheppard did effective ministry by focusing on the importance of mission to African traditional religionists. For Sheppard the importance of this mission superseded all the difficulties of being an African American attempting to gain support in a mission that had traditionally been all white. He had a gift to give, and he gave it with respect—even if he did not receive the gift of respect in return from those who "supported" him. For Sheppard, how one gave the gift was as important as the gift itself, and this translated into all the mission practices he used in Africa.

Charity: Loving the people to whom we witness. Mother Teresa was certainly not a quid pro quo gifter. She measured her gift to the Hindus of India not by how many came for help but by how well those who came to the Sisters of Charity were treated. She once said that she did mathematics

---

SIDEBAR 24.6
PERSON AS WITNESS

The missioner is a witness to God's grace and to the wonderful gift of salvation in Jesus Christ. In developing the giftive mission metaphor, we have emphasized the appropriateness of gift giving and receiving as part of that witness.

The following chart contrasts four models of God's mission and our role in it: the missioner as maker, the missioner as citizen, the missioner as answerer, and the missioner as witness. Each model can be used productively for good ends. Notice the comparisons and contrasts of witness as a giftive metaphor with the other models of personhood.

	GREAT COMMISSION MISSIONS	GREAT COMMANDMENT MISSIONS	RESPONSIVE MISSIONS	GIFTIVE MISSIONS
Primary Task	Maker	Citizen	Answerer	Witness
Highest Good	Good	Right	Fitting	Graceful
Ethical System	Teleological	Deontological	Cathekontic	Charisological
First Virtue	Creative	Obedient	Responsible	Loving
Regulatory Mechanism	Ideas	Laws	Cultures	God's Will
Interaction Ideal	Competition	Cooperation	Compatibility	Concern
First Divine Role	Creator	Redeemer	Sustainer	Friend
Primary Question	What shall I do?	How shall we obey?	How shall I respond?	What is God doing?
Illustrative Hymn	"Bringing in the Sheaves"	"Holy, Holy, Holy"	"In Christ There Is No East nor West"	"In the Garden"
Locus Classicus	Matthew 28:19	John 20:21	1 Peter 3:15	Luke 10:27

---

differently than most people. She didn't worry about the incredibly small percentages of Indian Hindus she and her colleagues were able to treat medically. Her mathematics considered the one she was loving right now as the total of God's universe at that moment. That kind of care can only come with gospel love.

Missional Ecumenicity: Practicing mission as the joint project of the church. As we said, Billy Graham's ironic gift to the church, as a twentieth-century evangelical evangelist, was the gift of ecumenism. He insisted that all churches everywhere should not only be involved in the exercise of evangelism, but they should partner together to do it. The metaphor of gift giving illumines his insistence. Ideally when people give gifts, they should not be trying to outdo one another like some modern-day Pharisee but should be doing so with loving, open, and humble hearts. At one point, churches did work together on mission. Somehow mission has become no longer an ecumenical exercise. We must reduce the fragmentation and work together to avoid overlapping in our efforts.

Biblical Interreligious Encounters

I n the Bible the people of God (the Israelites, the followers of Jesus) had frequent contact with people who did not know the biblical God. The following 239 biblical citations are examples of either those contacts or teachings about such contacts:

OLD TESTAMENT

1. Genesis 3:1–24—Adam and Eve and Serpent
2. Genesis 6:1–22—Noah and Nephilim
3. Genesis 11:1–9—Tower of Babel
4. Genesis 12:1–3—Abraham and Move to Israel
5. Genesis 12:10–20—Abraham and Egyptians
6. Genesis 14—Abraham and Melchizedek
7. Genesis 15:12–21—Abraham and God's Covenant
8. Genesis 16:1–16; 21:8–20—Abraham/Sarah and Hagar
9. Genesis 17—Abraham and Promised Land
10. Genesis 18—Abraham and Sodom and Gomorrah
11. Genesis 19—Lot and Sodom
12. Genesis 20; 21:22–34—Abraham and Abimelech, King of Gerar
13. Genesis 23—Abraham and Hittites
14. Genesis 24:3–4; 28:1—Abraham and Intermarriage of Sons
15. Genesis 26—Isaac and Abimelech

16. Genesis 24, 29–31—Isaac and Laban
17. Genesis 34—Dinah and Shechem
18. Genesis 38—Judah and Shua/Tamar
19. Genesis 39–41; 47—Joseph and Egyptians
20. Genesis 50:1–3—Joseph and Jacob's Death in Egypt
21. Exodus 1:8–22; 2:1–10—Israelites and Egyptians
22. Exodus 17:8–15—Israelites and Amalekites
23. Exodus 22:18, 20, 21—Israelites and Sorceresses, Idols, Aliens
24. Exodus 23:4–9; Leviticus 19:33; Deuteronomy 5:15—Israelites and Aliens
25. Exodus 23:20–33; 34:10–35; Deuteronomy 7:1–11—Israelites and Amorites, Hittites, Perizzites, Canaanites, Hivites, Jebusites
26. Exodus 32; Deuteronomy 9:7–29—Israelites and Golden Calf
27. Leviticus 24:10–23—Israelites and Blasphemers
28. Numbers 20:14–21—Israelites and Edom
29. Numbers 21:1–3—Israelites and Canaanites
30. Numbers 21:21–35—Israelites and Amorites
31. Numbers 22–24—Israelites and Moabites
32. Numbers 25, 31—Israelites and Moabites, Midianites
33. Deuteronomy 4:15–31; 6:13—Israel and Idolatry
34. Deuteronomy 13; 16:21—Israelites and Asherah Poles
35. Deuteronomy 20—Israel and Wars
36. Deuteronomy 21:21; 22:21; 22:23, 24—Israel and Purity
37. Joshua 2—Israel and Rahab
38. Joshua 5:13–6:27—Israel and Jericho
39. Joshua 7, 8—Israel and Ai
40. Joshua 9—Israel and Gibeonites, Hivites
41. Joshua 10:1–28—Israelites and Amorites
42. Joshua 10:29–43—Israel and Southern Cities
43. Joshua 11—Israel and Northern Cities
44. Judges 1:1–36—Israelites (Judah and Simeon) and Canaanites, Perizzites
45. Judges 2:1–5—Israelites and Canaanite Failure
46. Judges 2:6–3:5—Israelites and Philistines, Canaanites, Sidonians, Hittites, Amorites, Perizzites, Hivites, and Jebusites
47. Judges 3:7–11—Othniel and Aramites
48. Judges 3:12–31—Ehud and Moab
49. Judges 4:1–24—Deborah and Jabin
50. Judges 6–8:32—Gideon and Midian
51. Judges 8:33–35—Israel and Baal Worship
52. Judges 10:6–12:7—Jephthah and Philistines, Ammonites
53. Judges 13–16—Samson and Philistines
54. Judges 17, 18—Micah and Laish

55. Ruth 1:1–22—Naomi and Ruth
56. 1 Samuel 4–7:1—Israelites and Philistines
57. 1 Samuel 7:2–17—Israel and Philistines, Amorites
58. 1 Samuel 11:1–12—Saul and Nahash
59. 1 Samuel 12:1–25—Samuel and Israelites
60. 1 Samuel 13:1–14:52—Saul/Jonathan and Philistines
61. 1 Samuel 15:1–35—Saul and Amalekites
62. 1 Samuel 17—David and Goliath
63. 1 Samuel 23:1–6—David and Philistines
64. 1 Samuel 27:1–12—David and Geshurites, Girzites, and Amalekites
65. 1 Samuel 28:1–25; 31:1–13; 1 Chronicles 10:1–13—Saul and Medium of Endor
66. 1 Samuel 29, 30—David and Amalekites
67. 2 Samuel 1:1–16—David and Amalekite Messenger
68. 2 Samuel 5:6–10; 1 Chronicles 11:4–9—David and Jebusites
69. 2 Samuel 5:11–12; 1 Chronicles 14:1–2—David and Hiram
70. 2 Samuel 5:17–25; 8:1; 1 Chronicles 14:8–17—David and Philistines at Baal Perazim
71. 2 Samuel 8:2–14; 1 Chronicles 18:1–13—David and Philistines, Moabites, Arameans, and Edomites
72. 2 Samuel 10:6–19; 1 Chronicles 19:1–19—David and Ammonites, Arameans
73. 2 Samuel 12:26–31; 2 Chronicles 20:1–3—Joab, David, and Rabbah
74. 2 Samuel 15:19–22—David and Ittai the Gittite
75. 2 Samuel 21:1–14—David and Gibeonites
76. 2 Samuel 21:15–22; 1 Chronicles 20:4–8—Israel and Philistines at Gob and Gath
77. 1 Kings 2:2–4—David and Solomon
78. 1 Kings 5:1–16; 2 Chronicles 2:1–18—Solomon and Hiram
79. 1 Kings 8:41–51; 2 Chronicles 6:32–39—Solomon, Israelites, and Aliens
80. 1 Kings 9:6–9; 2 Chronicles 7:19–22—God and Solomon and Idols
81. 1 Kings 9:10–28; 2 Chronicles 8:1–18—Solomon and Hiram and Aliens
82. 1 Kings 10:1–13; 2 Chronicles 9:1–12—Solomon and Queen of Sheba
83. 1 Kings 11:1–13—Solomon and His Foreign Wives
84. 1 Kings 11:14—Solomon and Hadad
85. 1 Kings 14:21–28; 2 Chronicles 12:1–16—Rehoboam and Shishak
86. 1 Kings 15:1–22; 2 Chronicles 14:2–3; 15:16–16:6—Asa and Ben-Hadad
87. 1 Kings 16:19–34; 18:4; 21:17–28; 22:37–38—Ahab and Jezebel
88. 1 Kings 17:7–24—Elijah and Widow at Zarephath
89. 1 Kings 18:16–45—Elijah and Prophets of Baal

90. 1 Kings 20:1–43—Ahab and Ben-Hadad
91. 1 Kings 22:29–38; 2 Chronicles 18:28–34—Ahab, Jehoshaphat, and King of Aram
92. 1 Kings 22:46; 2 Chronicles 20:31–32—Jehoshaphat and Prostitutes
93. 1 Kings 22:52–53—Ahaziah and Baal
94. 2 Kings 1:1–18—Ahaziah and Elijah
95. 2 Kings 3—Joram, Jehoshaphat, and Moabites
96. 2 Kings 5:1–18—Elisha and Naaman
97. 2 Kings 6:8–23—Elisha and Aram
98. 2 Kings 6:24–7:20; 8:7–15—Elisha and Ben-Hadad
99. 2 Kings 8:20–22; 2 Chronicles 21:5–11, 20—Jehoram and Edom, Libnah
100. 2 Kings 8:25–29; 2 Chronicles 22:1–6—Joram and Hazael
101. 2 Kings 10:18–35—Jehu and Prophets of Baal
102. 2 Kings 12:17–21; 2 Chronicles 24:23–27—Joash and Hazael
103. 2 Kings 13:1–8, 22–25—Jehoahaz and Hazael
104. 2 Kings 14:7; 2 Chronicles 25:11–12—Amaziah and Edomites
105. 2 Kings 15:19–20—Menahem and Pul
106. 2 Kings 15:29—Pekah and Tiglath-Pileser
107. 2 Kings 16:1–18—Ahaz, Tiglath-Pileser and Rezin, Pekah
108. 2 Kings 17:1–23; 18:9–12—Hoshea and Shalmaneser
109. 2 Kings 18:1–19:37—Hezekiah and Sennacherib
110. 2 Kings 19:21–34—Israel and Assyria
111. 2 Kings 20:12–21—Hezekiah, Isaiah, and Merodach-Baladan
112. 2 Kings 21:1–16—Manasseh and Baal
113. 2 Kings 22:1–23:28—Josiah and Book of Law
114. 2 Kings 23:28–30; 2 Chronicles 35:20–36:1—Josiah and Neco
115. 2 Kings 23:31–35—Jehoahaz and Neco
116. 2 Kings 23:36–24:6—Jehoiakim and Nebuchadnezzar
117. 2 Kings 24:8–17; 25:27–30—Jehoiachin and Nebuchadnezzar
118. 2 Kings 25:1–26—Zedekiah and Nebuchadnezzar
119. 2 Chronicles 14:8–15—Asa and Zerah
120. 2 Chronicles 20:1–30—Jehoshaphat and Moabites, Ammonites
121. 2 Chronicles 21:16–17—Jehoram and Philistines
122. 2 Chronicles 25:14–15—Amaziah and Idols
123. 2 Chronicles 26:6–8—Uzziah and Philistines
124. 2 Chronicles 27:5—Jotham and Ammonites
125. 2 Chronicles 36:22–23; Ezra 1:1–3, 7–11—Israelites and Cyrus
126. Ezra 3:7—Returned Exiles and People of Sidon and Tyre
127. Ezra 4:1–5—Returned Exiles and Enemies of Judah and Benjamin
128. Ezra 4:6–24—People of Judah/Jerusalem and Men of Trans-Euphrates
129. Ezra 5:1–6:15—Judah/Jerusalem and Trans-Euphrates/Shethar-Bozenai
130. Ezra 7:1–28—Ezra and Artaxerxes
131. Ezra 9, 10—Ezra and Israel

132. Nehemiah 2, 4, 6—Nehemiah/Artaxerxes and Sanballat the Horonite, Tobiah the Ammonite and Geshem the Arab
133. Nehemiah 5:1–13; 13:1–9, 15–18, 23–28—Nehemiah and Judah
134. Esther—Esther and Haman
135. Psalm 9:2–6, 13–16—David and Nations
136. Psalm 18:34–48—David and His Enemies
137. Psalm 44—Sons of Korah and Enemies
138. Psalm 60:4–12—David and Edomites
139. Psalm 74:4–8—Asaph and His People
140. Psalm 83—Israel and Enemies
141. Psalm 115—Levites and Foreign Gods
142. Psalm 135—Levites and Idols
143. Isaiah 8:19–20—Isaiah and Spiritists
144. Isaiah 10:20–34—Remnant of Israel and Nations
145. Isaiah 13:1–14:23—Babylonia/Assyria/Others and God
146. Isaiah 30:1–5; 31:1–9—Israelites and Egypt
147. Isaiah 44:6–23; 57:5–13—Isaiah and Israel
148. Isaiah 56:3–8—Foreigners and Israel
149. Jeremiah 1:11–19; 19:1–5—Jeremiah and Idolatry
150. Jeremiah 22:1–9—Jeremiah and Evil Kings
151. Jeremiah 25:15–38; 27:1–22—God's Wrath
152. Jeremiah 29:1–23—Jeremiah and Nebuchadnezzar
153. Jeremiah 38:7–13; 39:15–18—Jeremiah and Ebed-Melech
154. Jeremiah 40:1–6—Jeremiah and Nebuzaradan
155. Jeremiah 40:7–41:15—Gedaliah and Ishmael
156. Jeremiah 41:16–44:30—Jeremiah and Egypt
157. Jeremiah 46–51—Jeremiah and Prophecies about Nations
158. Lamentations 1:3, 5, 7–10, 17—Judah in Exile
159. Lamentations 2:7, 15–18; 4:12–13—Destruction of Jerusalem
160. Lamentations 5:6—Israel and Egypt/Assyria
161. Ezekiel 11:16–25; 20:30–44—Restoration of Israel and Judgment on Nations
162. Ezekiel 21:28–32—Prophecy about Nations
163. Daniel 1:1–21; 2; 4—Daniel and Nebuchadnezzar
164. Daniel 3—Shadrach/Meshach/Abednego and Nebuchadnezzar
165. Daniel 5—Daniel and Belshazzar
166. Daniel 6—Daniel and Darius
167. Hosea 8:8–10; 10:5–8; 11:5; 13:1–2—Israel and Assyria
168. Joel 3—Israel and Nations
169. Amos 1:3–2:5—Amos and Israel's Neighbors
170. Obadiah—Obadiah and Edom
171. Jonah 1:1–16—Jonah and Sailors
172. Jonah 3, 4—Jonah and Nineveh

173. Micah 4:2–5—Israel and Nations
174. Nahum—Nineveh Prophecies
175. Zephaniah 1:4–6—Idolatry
176. Zephaniah 2—Philistia, Moab, Cush, Assyria
177. Zechariah 9:1–8; 12:1–9; 14:2–21—Judgment on Israel's Enemies
178. Malachi 2:11–12—Intermarriage and Idolatry

NEW TESTAMENT

179. Matthew 2—Jesus and Wise Men
180. Matthew 5:43–48—Jesus and Religious Teachers
181. Matthew 6:5–6—Jesus and Prayer
182. Matthew 6:7–8—Jesus and Foreign Religious Practice
183. Matthew 7:1–5—Jesus and Judgmental Attitude
184. Matthew 7:6—Jesus and Hostile Audiences
185. Matthew 7:15–20—Jesus and Spiritual Fruit
186. Matthew 8:5–13—Jesus and Roman Centurion
187. Matthew 10:5–42—Jesus and Disciples
188. Matthew 13:24–30—Jesus and Wheat and Tares
189. Matthew 15:3–20—Jesus and False Teaching
190. Matthew 18:1–14—Jesus and Modeling Behavior
191. Matthew 22:36–40—Jesus and Great Commandment
192. Matthew 24—Jesus and False Teachers
193. Matthew 25:14–30—Jesus and Parable of Talents
194. Matthew 26:59–64; 27:11–14—Jesus and Sanhedrin
195. Matthew 28:18–20—Great Commission
196. Mark 3:24–27—Jesus and Knowing Our Own Witness
197. Mark 9:50—Jesus and Christians as Salt
198. Luke 2:44–50—Jesus and Engaging the Powers
199. Luke 10:25–37—Jesus and Good Samaritans
200. Luke 12:49–53—Jesus and Necessity of Taking Stand
201. Luke 18:9–14—Jesus and Self-Righteousness
202. Luke 24:46–49—Jesus and Holy Spirit
203. John 2:12–23—Jesus and Clearing Temple
204. John 14:6; 15:1–17—Jesus and Vine and Branches
205. John 15:18–16:4—Jesus and Persecution
206. Acts 2:1–12—Christians and Godly Jews
207. Acts 8:1–25—Paul and Simon the Sorcerer
208. Acts 8:26–40—Philip and Ethiopian
209. Acts 10:9–23—Peter's Vision
210. Acts 15—Peter, Paul, and Jerusalem Council
211. Acts 17—Paul in Athens
212. Acts 19:23–20:38—Paul and Artemis

213. Acts 27—Paul and Shipwreck
214. Acts 28—Paul in Prison in Rome
215. Romans 1, 2—Paul, Sin, Conscience, Image of God
216. Romans 3—Paul and Righteousness
217. Romans 12—Paul and Christian Love
218. Romans 13—Paul and Politics
219. Romans 14—Paul and Weak and Strong
220. 1 Corinthians 2:1–5—Paul and Humility
221. 1 Corinthians 8:1–13—Paul and Love and Knowledge
222. 1 Corinthians 10:1–22—Paul and Evil Things
223. 1 Corinthians 10:23–33—Paul and Food Offered to Idols
224. 1 Corinthians 13—Paul and Love
225. 1 Corinthians 16:13—Paul and Commitment
226. 2 Corinthians 4—Paul and Witnessing
227. 2 Corinthians 6:14–18—Paul and Separatism
228. Galatians 5:16–26—Paul and Fruits of Spirit
229. Philippians 2:1–11—Paul and Imitating Christ's Humility
230. Colossians 2:16—How Not to Argue with Others
231. 2 Thessalonians 2:5–12—Contend for Gospel
232. Titus 3:9–11—Paul and Foolish Controversies
233. 1 Peter 4:8—Love Each Other
234. 2 Peter 2:1–22—False Teachers
235. 1 John 2:18—Antichrists
236. 1 John 3:11–24—Love One Another
237. 1 John 4—Testing the Spirits
238. Jude—Godless Men among You
239. Jude—How to Love Neighbors

Bibliography

Abbott, Walter, ed. 1966. *The Documents of Vatican II.* Piscataway, NJ: New Century.

Acharya, Kala. 1993. *The Puranic Concept of Dana.* Delhi: Nag.

Adeney, Frances. 2003a. *Christian Women in Indonesia.* Syracuse: Syracuse University.

———. 2003b. "What I Have Learned from Buddhist Meditation." In *Christians Talk about Buddhist Meditation, Buddhists Talk about Christian Prayer,* edited by Terry C. Muck and Rita M. Gross, 15–19. New York: Continuum.

Adeney, Frances, and Arvind Sharma, eds. 2007. *Christianity and Human Rights: Influences and Issues.* Albany: State University of New York Press.

Allen, Roland. 1962. *Missionary Methods: St. Paul's or Ours?* Grand Rapids: Eerdmans. (Orig. pub. 1912.)

Anderson, Gerald, ed. 1998. *Biographical Dictionary of Christian Missions.* New York: Macmillan.

Aragon, Lorraine V. 1996. "Twisting the Gift: Translating Pre-Colonial into Colonial Exchanges in Central Sulawesi, Indonesia." *American Ethnologist* 23 (February): 43–60.

Ariarajah, S. Wesley. 1993. *The Bible and People of Other Faiths.* Geneva: WCC.

Arias, Mortimer, and Alan Johnson. 1992. *The Great Commission: Biblical Models for Evangelism.* Nashville: Abingdon.

Banks, Robert. 1994. *Paul's Idea of Community.* Rev. ed. Peabody, MA: Hendrickson.

Barrett, David. 2000. "Missiometrics." In *Evangelical Dictionary of World Missions,* general editor A. Scott Moreau, 445. Grand Rapids: Baker Academic.

Barrett, David, and Todd Johnson. 2001. *World Christian Trends AD 30–AD 2200: Interpreting the Annual Christian Megacensus.* Pasadena, CA: William Carey.

Barrett, David, George Kurian, and Todd Johnson. 2001. *World Christian Encyclopedia: A Comparative Survey of Churches and Religions in the Modern World*. 2nd ed. Oxford: Oxford University Press.

Bavinck, Johan Herman. 1948. *The Impact of Christianity on the Non-Christian World*. Grand Rapids: Eerdmans.

Beaver, R. Pierce. 1962. *Ecumenical Beginnings in Protestant World Mission: A History of Comity*. New York: Thomas Nelson.

Bede. 1994. *The Ecclesiastical History of the English People*. Translated and edited by Judith McClure. Oxford: Oxford University Press.

Bediako, Kwame. 1995. *Christianity in Africa: The Renewal of a Non-Western Religion*. Maryknoll, NY: Orbis.

Benenate, Becky, ed. 1997. *In the Heart of the World*. New York: Barnes and Noble.

Benenate, Becky, and Joseph Durepos, eds. 1997. *Mother Teresa: No Greater Love*. New York: Barnes and Noble.

Berger, Peter. 1990. *The Sacred Canopy: Elements of a Sociological Theory of Religion*. New York: Anchor. (Orig. pub. 1967.)

Bertodano, Teresa de, ed. 1993. *Daily Readings with Mother Teresa*. London: HarperCollins Fount Paperbacks.

Bevans, Stephen. 1992. *Models of Contextual Theology*. Maryknoll, NY: Orbis.

Beyerhaus, Peter. 1971. *Missions: Which Way? Humanization or Redemption*. Translated by Margaret Clarkson. Grand Rapids: Zondervan.

Boba, I. 1971. *Moravia's History Reconsidered: A Reinterpretation of Medieval Sources*. The Hague: Springer. (Orig. pub. 1899.)

Boethius, Ancius. 2000. *The Consolation of Philosophy*. New York: Penguin.

Bonk, Jonathan. 2007. *Missions and Money: Affluence as a Western Missionary Problem*. Maryknoll, NY: Orbis.

Booth, Catherine. 1993. *Aggressive Christianity*. Wheaton: Worldwide.

Borgen, Peder, Vernon K. Robbins, and David B. Bowler, eds. 1998. *Recruitment, Conquest, Conflict: Strategies in Judaism, Early Christianity, and the Greco-Roman World*. Atlanta: Scholars Press.

Bosch, David. 1991. *Transforming Mission: Paradigm Shifts in Theology of Mission*. Maryknoll, NY: Orbis.

Bowie, Katherine. 1998. "The Alchemy of Charity: Of Class and Buddhism in Northern Thailand." *American Anthropologist* 100 (June): 469–81.

Braaten, Carl. 1992. *No Other Gospel: Christianity Among the World's Religions*. Minneapolis: Fortress.

Braudel, Fernand. 1995. *A History of Civilizations*. New York: Penguin. (Orig. pub. 1963.)

Brekke, Torkel. 1998. "Contradiction and the Merit of Giving in Indian Religions." *Numen* 46: 1–33.

Burnett, David. 1988. *Unearthly Powers: A Christian Perspective on Primal and Folk Religions*. Eastbourne, England: MARC.

Burrows, William, ed. 1994. *Redemption and Dialogue: Reading "Redemptoris Missio" and "Dialogue and Proclamation."* Maryknoll, NY: Orbis.

Bury, John. 1998. *The Life of St. Patrick and His Place in History*. New York: Dover. (Orig. pub. 1905.)

Camenisch, Paul. 1981. "Gift and Gratitude in Ethics." *Journal of Religious Ethics* 9 (1): 1–34.

Cannon, Dale. 1996. *Six Ways of Being Religious*. Belmont, CA: Wadsworth.

Carey, Eustace. 1837. *Memoir of William Carey, D.D.* Hartford, CT: Canfield and Robins.

Carey, S. Pearce. 1923. *William Carey*. New York: George H. Doran.

Carey, William. 1988. *An Enquiry into the Obligations to Use Means for the Conversion of the Heathens*. Dallas: Criswell. (Orig. pub. 1792.)

Carmichael, Alexander. 1992. *Garmina Gadelica*. Edinburgh: Floris.

Carrier, James. 1995. *Gifts and Commodities: Exchange and Western Capitalism since 1700*. London: Routledge.

Chang, Curtis. 2000. *Engaging Unbelief: A Captivating Strategy from Augustine to Aquinas*. Downers Grove, IL: InterVarsity.

Chenu, Marie-Dominique. 2002. *Aquinas and His Role in Theology*. Collegeville, MN: Liturgical Press. (Orig. pub. 1959.)

Chesterton, G. K. 1956. *Saint Thomas Aquinas*. Garden City, NY: Doubleday. (Orig. pub. 1933.)

Chia, Roland. 2002. "Pragmatism, Progress, and Paradox: A Tale of Two Cities in Modern Singapore." Seminar paper, Trinity Theological College, Singapore.

Chilton, Bruce. 2004. *Rabbi Paul: An Intellectual Biography*. New York: Doubleday.

Conrad, Joseph. 1967. *Heart of Darkness*. New York: Harcourt, Brace and World. (Orig. pub. 1899.)

Covell, Ralph. 1986. *Confucius, the Buddha, and Christ: A History of the Gospel in Chinese*. Maryknoll, NY: Orbis.

Cracknell, Kenneth. 1995. *Justice, Courtesy and Love: Theologians and Missionaries Encountering World Religions, 1846–1914*. London: Epworth.

Dafei, Gong, and Feng Yu, eds. 1998. *Chinese Maxims: Golden Sayings of Chinese Thinkers*. Singapore: Asia Pacific.

Dale, Douglas. 1997. *Light to the Isles: Missionary Theology in Celtic and Anglo-Saxon Britain*. Cambridge: Lutterworth.

D'Costa, Gavin, ed. 1990. *Christian Uniqueness Reconsidered: The Myth of a Pluralistic Theology of Religions*. Maryknoll, NY: Orbis.

De Bary, William Theodore, Wing-tsit Chan, and Burton Watson, eds. 1960. *Sources of the Chinese Tradition*. New York: Columbia University Press.

De Paor, Liam. 1993. *Saint Patrick's World*. Notre Dame, IN: University of Notre Dame Press.

De Paor, Máire. 1998. *Patrick: The Pilgrim Apostle of Ireland*. New York: HarperCollins.

Derrida, Jacques. 1995. *The Gift of Death*. Chicago: University of Chicago Press.

DeWaal, Esther. 1997. *Celtic Light: A Tradition Rediscovered*. London: HarperCollins.

Donovan, Vincent. 2000. *Christianity Rediscovered*. Maryknoll, NY: Orbis.

Douglas, J. D., ed. 1975. *Let the Earth Hear His Voice*. Minneapolis: World Wide.

Drewery, Mary. 1979. *William Carey: A Biography*. Grand Rapids: Zondervan.

Dries, Angelyn. 1998. *The Missionary Movement in American Catholic History*. Maryknoll, NY: Orbis.

Drummond, Lewis. 2001. *The Evangelist*. Dallas: Word.

DuBose, Francis, ed. 1979. *Classics of Christian Missions*. Nashville: Broadman.

Duff, Mildred. 2004. *Catherine Booth: A Sketch*. Whitefish, MT: Kessinger.

Duffy, Joseph. 2000. *Patrick in His Own Words*. (*The Confession* and the *Letter to the Soldiers of Coroticus*). Dublin: Veritas.

Duichev, Ivan, ed. 1985. *Kiril and Methodius: Founders of Slavonic Writing*. New York: Columbia University Press.

Dupuis, Jacques. 1991. *Jesus Christ at the Encounter of World Religions*. Maryknoll, NY: Orbis.

———. 1997. *Toward a Christian Theology of Religious Pluralism*. Maryknoll, NY: Orbis.

Dvornik, F. 1970. *Byzantine Missions among the Slavs*. New Brunswick, NJ: Rutgers University Press.

Dyrness, William. 1983. *Let the Earth Rejoice! A Biblical Theology of Holistic Mission*. Westchester, IL: Crossway.

Eason, Andrew Mark. 2003. *Women in God's Army: Gender and Equality in the Early Salvation Army*. Ontario: Wilfrid Laurier University Press.

Elmer, Duane. 2002. *Cross-Cultural Connections: Stepping Out and Fitting in Around the World*. Downers Grove, IL: InterVarsity.

Engel, James, and William Dyrness. 2000. *Changing the Mind of Missions: Where Have We Gone Wrong?* Downers Grove, IL: InterVarsity.

Everson, William. 1981. "A Remembrance." *Radix Magazine* 12 (1): 3.

Farrugia, Edward G., Robert F. Taft, and Gino K. Piovesana, with the editorial committee. 1988. *Christianity among the Slavs: The Heritage of Saints Cyril and Methodius; Acts of the International Congress Held on the Eleventh Centenary of the Death of St. Methodius, Rome, October 8–11, 1985, under the direction of the Pontifical Oriental Institute*. Orientalia

Christiana Analecta 231. Rome: Pontifical Institutum Studiorum Orientalium.

Fernando, Ajith. 2001. *Sharing the Truth in Love: How to Relate to People of Other Faiths.* Grand Rapids: Discovery House.

Findly, Ellison Banks. 2003. *Dāna: Giving and Getting in Pali Buddhism.* Delhi: Motilal Banarsidass.

Finney, John. 1996. *Recovering the Past: Celtic and Roman Mission.* London: Darton, Longman and Todd.

Fowler, James. 1995. *Stages of Faith: The Psychology of Human Development.* San Francisco: HarperOne. (Orig. pub. 1976.)

Fromm, Eric. 1998. *The Essential Fromm.* Edited by Ranier Funk. New York: Continuum.

Furfey, Paul Hanly. 1978. *Love and the Urban Ghetto.* Maryknoll, NY: Orbis.

Gadamer, Hans Georg. 1983. *Reason in the Age of Science.* Cambridge, MA: MIT Press.

———. 2005. *Truth and Method.* Rev. ed. New York: Continuum.

Gaustad, Edwin, ed. 1999. *Memoirs of the Spirit.* Grand Rapids: Eerdmans.

George, Timothy. 1991. *Faithful Witness: The Life and Mission of William Carey.* Birmingham, AL: New Hope.

Georgi, Dieter. 1986. *The Opponents of Paul in Second Corinthians.* Philadelphia: Fortress. (Orig. pub. 1964.)

Gilligan, Carol. 1993. *In a Different Voice: Psychological Theory and Women's Development.* Cambridge, MA: Harvard University Press.

Gilliland, Dean. 1983. *Pauline Theology and Mission Practice.* Grand Rapids: Baker Academic.

Gittens, Anthony. 1989. *Gifts and Strangers: Meeting the Challenge of Inculturation.* Mahwah, NJ: Paulist Press.

———. 1993. *Bread for the Journey: The Mission of Transformation and the Transformation of Mission.* Maryknoll, NY: Orbis.

Glasser, Arthur, and Donald McGavran. 1983. *Contemporary Theologies of Mission.* Grand Rapids: Baker Academic.

Goethe, Johann Wolfgang Von. 1901. "Wilhelm Meister's Apprenticeship." In *Goethe's Works.* Translated by Thomas Carlyle. New York: International.

González-Balado, José Luis, and Janet N. Playfoot, eds. 1985. *My Life for the Poor: Mother Teresa of Calcutta.* New York: Ballantine.

Goodman, Martin. 1996. *Mission and Conversion: Proselytizing in the Religious History of the Roman Empire.* New York: Oxford University Press.

Graham, Billy. 1984a. *Peace with God.* Dallas: Word. (Orig. pub. 1953.)

———. 1984b. *A Biblical Standard for Evangelists.* Minneapolis: World Wide.

———. 1985. *The Secret of Happiness.* Dallas: Word. (Orig. pub. 1955.)

———. 1997. *Just As I Am.* San Francisco: HarperCollins/Zondervan.

Green, Michael. 2004. *Evangelism and the Early Church.* Rev. ed. Grand Rapids: Eerdmans.

Griffiths, Paul. 1989. *Christianity through Non-Christian Eyes.* Maryknoll, NY: Orbis.

Guder, Darrell, ed. 1998. *Missional Church: A Vision for the Sending of the Church in North America.* Grand Rapids: Eerdmans.

Gunton, Colin. 1988. *The Actuality of Atonement: A Study of Metaphor, Rationality, and the Christian Tradition.* Edinburgh: T&T Clark.

Gurevitch, Zali. 1988. "The Power of Not Understanding: The Meeting of Conflicting Identities." *Journal of Applied Behavioral Science* 25 (March): 1179–99.

Habermas, Jürgen. 1985. *A Theory of Communicative Action.* Vol. 1, *Reason and the Rationalization of Society.* Boston: Beacon.

Hahn, Norma, Robert Bellah, and William Sullivan, eds. 1983. *Social Science as Moral Inquiry.* New York: Columbia University Press.

Hanke, Lewis. 1974. *All Mankind Is One: A Study of the Disputation between Bartolomé de Las Casas and Juan Ginés de Sepúlveda on the Religious and Intellectual Capacity of the American Indians.* DeKalb: Northern Illinois University Press.

Harris, Elizabeth J. 2006. *Theravada Buddhism and the British Encounter: Religious, Missionary and Colonial Experience in Nineteenth-Century Sri Lanka.* New York: Routledge.

Hastings, Adrian. 1995. *The Church in Africa, 1450–1950*. Oxford: Clarendon.

———, ed. 1999. *A World History of Christianity*. Grand Rapids: Eerdmans.

Hattersley, Roy. 2000. *Blood and Fire: The Story of William and Catherine Booth and the Salvation Army*. New York: Doubleday.

Hefner, Robert, ed. 1993. *Conversion to Christianity: Historical and Anthropological Perspectives on a Great Transformation*. Berkeley: University of California Press.

Heim, Maria. 2004. *Theories of the Gift in South Asia: Hindu, Buddhist, and Jain Reflections on Dana*. New York: Routledge.

Hengel, Martin. 1989. "Messianische Hoffnung und politischer 'Radikalismus' in der 'judisch-hellenistischen Diaspora.'" In *Apocalypticism in the Ancient Near East and the Hellenistic World*, edited by David Hellholm, 2nd ed., 35–76. Tübingen: J. C. B. Mohr.

Hesselgrave, David. 1991. *Communicating Christ Cross-Culturally*. 2nd ed. Grand Rapids: Zondervan.

Hiebert, Paul. 1985. *Anthropological Insights for Missionaries*. Grand Rapids: Baker Academic.

Hiebert, Paul, Daniel Shaw, and Tite Tienou. 1999. *Understanding Folk Religions*. Grand Rapids: Baker Academic.

Hochschild, Adam. 1999. *King Leopold's Ghost: A Story of Greed, Terror, and Heroism in Colonial Africa*. New York: Houghton Mifflin.

Hogg, William Richey. 1952. *Ecumenical Foundations: A History of the International Missionary Council and Its Nineteenth Century Background*. New York: Harper and Brothers.

Hopewell, James. 1987. *Congregation: Stories and Structures*. Philadelphia: Fortress.

Hunter, George. 1992. *How to Reach Secular People*. Nashville: Abingdon.

———. 2000. *The Celtic Way of Evangelism*. Nashville: Abingdon.

Hunter, Jane. 1984. *The Gospel of Gentility: American Women Missionaries in Turn-of-the-Century China*. New Haven: Yale University Press.

Hutchison, William. 1987. *Errand to the World: American Protestant Thought and Foreign Missions*. Chicago: University of Chicago Press.

Hu Wenzhong and Cornelius L. Grove. 1999. *Encountering the Chinese: A Guide for Americans*. 2nd ed. Yarmouth, ME: Intercultural.

Irvin, Dale, and Scott Sundquist. 2001. *History of the World Christian Movement*. Vol. 1, *Earliest Christianity to 1453*. Maryknoll, NY: Orbis.

John Paul II. 1990. *Redemptoris Missio*. Vatican City: Libreria Editrice Vaticana.

Johnstone, Patrick. 2001. *Operation World*. Carlisle: Paternoster.

Jones, E. Stanley. 1928. *Christ at the Round Table*. London: Hodder and Stoughton.

Jongeneel, Jan, ed. 1997. *The Philosophy, Science, and Theology of Mission in the 19th and 20th Centuries: A Missiological Encyclopedia, Part I, The Philosophy and Science of Mission, Part II, Missionary Theology*. Frankfurt: Peter Lang.

Kane, P. V. 1968. *History of Dharmasastra*. 5 vols. Poona: Bhandarkar Oriental.

Kennedy, Pagan. 2002. *Black Livingstone: A True Tale of Adventure in the Nineteenth-Century Congo*. New York: Viking Penguin.

Kirk, Andrew. 1999. *What Is Mission? Theological Explorations*. London: Darton, Longman, and Todd.

Kliment Ohridski. 1985a. "Life and Acts of Our Blessed Teacher Konstantin the Philosopher." In Duichev 1985, 49–80. (Orig. pub. 869.)

———. 1985b. "Memory and Life of Our Blessed Father and Teacher Methodius." In Duichev 1985, 81–92. (Orig. pub. 885.)

Knitter, Paul. 1986. *No Other Name: A Critical Survey of Christian Attitudes Toward World Religions*. Maryknoll, NY: Orbis.

———. 2002. *Introducing Theologies of Religions*. Maryknoll, NY: Orbis.

Kohlberg, Lawrence. 1981. *The Philosophy of Moral Development*. San Francisco: HarperCollins.

———. 1984. *The Psychology of Moral Development*. San Francisco: HarperCollins.

Kolb, David. 1993. *Learning Style Inventory*. New York: McBer.

Kolodiejchuk, Brian, ed. 2007. *Mother Teresa: Come Be My Light*. New York: Doubleday.

Komter, Aafke, ed. 1996. *The Gift: An Interdisciplinary Perspective*. Amsterdam: Amsterdam University Press.

Kostenberger, Andreas, and Peter O'Brien. 2001. *Salvation to the Ends of the Earth: A Biblical Theology of Mission*. Downers Grove, IL: InterVarsity.

Koyama, Kōsuke. 1999. *Water Buffalo Theology*. Maryknoll, NY: Orbis.

Kraemer, Hendrick. 1938. *The Christian Message in a Non-Christian World*. New York: Harper and Brothers.

Kraft, Charles. 1996. *Anthropology for Christian Witness*. Maryknoll, NY: Orbis.

Küng, Hans, and Karl-Joseph Kuschel. 1994. *A Global Ethic: The Declaration of the Parliament of the World's Religions*. New York: Continuum.

Lacko, Michael. 1969. *Saints Cyril and Methodius*. Rome: Slovak.

LaGrand, James. 1995. *The Earliest Christian Mission to "All Nations" in the Light of Matthew's Gospel*. Grand Rapids: Eerdmans.

Lakoff, George, and Mark Johnson. 1980. *Metaphors We Live By*. Chicago: University of Chicago Press.

Las Casas, Bartolomé de. 1971a. *Bartolome de Las Casas: A Selection of His Writings*. Edited and translated by George Sanderlin. New York: Knopf.

———. 1971b. *Witness: Writings of Bartolomé de Las Casas*. Translated by George Sanderlin. Maryknoll, NY: Orbis.

———. 1992a. *In Defense of the Indians*. Translated by Stafford Poole. DeKalb: Northern Illinois University Press. (Orig. pub. 1550.)

———. 1992b. *The Devastation of the Indies: A Brief Account*. Translated by Herma Briffault. Baltimore: Johns Hopkins University Press. (Orig. pub. 1552.)

———. 1992c. *The Only Way*. Translated by Francis Sullivan. New York: Paulist Press.

———. 1992d. *A Short Account of the Destruction of the Indies*. Translated by Nigel Griffin. New York: Penguin Putnam. (Orig. pub. 1542.)

Latourette, Kenneth Scott. 1929. *A History of Christian Missions in China*. New York: Macmillan.

———. 1941. *A History of the Expansion of Christianity*. Vol. 4, *The Great Century: In Europe and the United States of America, AD 1800–AD 1914*. Grand Rapids: Zondervan.

Lausanne Committee for World Evangelization. 1982. *Evangelism and Social Responsibility: An Evangelical Commitment*. Wheaton: Lausanne Committee for World Evangelization.

Le, Joly, and Jaya Chaliha, eds. 2002. *Mother Teresa's Reaching Out in Love*. New York: Barnes and Noble.

Levin, David Michael. 1989. *The Listening Self: Personal Growth, Social Change and the Closure of Metaphysics*. New York: Routledge.

Lietaert Peerbolte, L. J. 2003. *Paul the Missionary*. Leuven: Peeters.

Lingenfelter, Sherwood. 1996. *Agents of Transformation: A Guide to Effective Cross-Cultural Ministry*. Grand Rapids: Baker Academic.

Little, Paul. 1966. *How to Give Away Your Faith*. Downers Grove, IL: InterVarsity.

Longenecker, Richard. 1971. *The Ministry and Message of Paul*. Grand Rapids: Zondervan.

Macmullen, Ramsey. 1984. *Christianizing the Roman Empire (A.D. 100–400)*. New Haven: Yale University Press.

Malinowski, Bronislaw. 1953. *Argonauts of the Western Pacific*. New York: E. P. Dutton. (Orig. pub. 1922.)

Mann, David. 1990. "Toward Understanding Gift-Giving in Relationships." *Missiology: An International Review* 18 (January): 49–60.

Maritain, Jacques. 1958. *St. Thomas Aquinas*. New York: Meridian.

Marsden, George. 2006. *Fundamentalism and American Culture*. New York: Oxford.

Marshman, John C. 1859. *Life and Times of Carey, Marshman and Ward: Embracing the History of the Serampore Mission*. London: Longmans.

Martin, David. 1990. *Tongues of Fire: The Explosion of Protestantism in Latin America*. Oxford: Basil Blackwell.

Martin, William. 1991. *A Prophet with Honor.* New York: William Morrow.

Martinson, Paul Varo, ed. 1999. *Mission at the Dawn of the Twenty-first Century: A Vision for the Church.* Minneapolis: Kirk House.

Maslow, Abraham. 1994. *Religions, Values, and Peak Experiences.* New York: Penguin.

Matthews, Victor. 2001. "The Unwanted Gift: Implications of Obligatory Gift-giving in Ancient Israel." *Semeia* 87: 91–104.

Mauss, Marcel. 1990. *The Gift: The Form and Reason for Exchange in Archaic Societies.* New York: J. J. Norton. (Orig. pub. 1925.)

McClendon, James. 2002. *Biography as Theology: How Life Stories Can Remake Today's Theology.* Eugene, OR: Wipf and Stock.

McGavran, Donald. 1970. *Understanding Church Growth.* Grand Rapids: Eerdmans.

McInerny, Ralph. 1977. *St. Thomas Aquinas.* Notre Dame, IN: University of Notre Dame Press.

McKnight, Scot. 1991. *A Light among the Gentiles: Jewish Missionary Activity in the Second Temple Period.* Minneapolis: Fortress.

McLoughlin, William. 1960. *Billy Graham: Revivalist in a Secular Age.* New York: Ronald.

McQuilkin, Robertson. 1984. *The Great Omission: A Biblical Basis for World Evangelism.* Grand Rapids: Baker Academic.

Mead, George Herbert. 1934. *Mind, Self, and Society.* Chicago: University of Chicago Press.

Meeks, Wayne. 2003. *The First Urban Christians: The Social World of the Apostle Paul.* 2nd ed. New Haven: Yale University Press.

Michaels, Axel. 1997. "Gift and Return Gift, Greeting and Return in India: On a Consequential Footnote by Marcel Mauss." *Numen* 44: 242–69.

Mitchell, Curtis. 1966. *Billy Graham: The Making of a Crusader.* New York: Chilton.

Moffett, Samuel. 1992. *A History of Christianity in Asia.* Vol. 1. San Francisco: HarperCollins.

Moreau, Scott, gen. ed. 2000. *Evangelical Dictionary of World Missions.* Grand Rapids: Baker Academic.

Moreau, Scott, Gary Corwin, and Gary McGee. 2004. *Introducing World Missions: A Biblical, Historical, and Practical Survey.* Grand Rapids: Baker Academic.

Mott, John R. 1910. *The Decisive Hour of Christian Missions.* New York: Student Volunteer Movement for Foreign Missions.

Moule, C. F. D. 1959. *Idiom Book of the New Testament.* 2nd ed. Cambridge: Cambridge University Press.

Muck, Terry. 1992. *Those Other Religions in Your Neighborhood.* Grand Rapids: Zondervan.

———. 2006. *How to Study Religion.* Wilmore, KY: Wood Hill.

Mugambe, Jesse. 1989. *The Biblical Basis for World Evangelization: Theological Reflections on an African Experience.* Nairobi: Oxford University Press.

Muggeridge, Malcolm. 1971. *Something Beautiful for God: Mother Teresa of Calcutta.* New York: Harper and Row.

Muller, Karl, et al., eds. 1997. *Dictionary of Mission: Theology, History, Perspectives.* Maryknoll, NY: Orbis.

Munck, Johannes. 1959. *Paul and the Salvation of Mankind.* Richmond: John Knox.

Murdoch, Norman. 1995. "The 'Army Mother.'" *Cross Point* 8 (Fall): 36–39.

Myers, Bryant. 1993. *The New Context of World Mission.* Monrovia, CA: MARC.

———. 2003. *Exploring World Mission: Context and Challenges.* Monrovia, CA: World Vision.

Neely, Alan. 1999. *Christian Mission: A Case Study Approach.* Maryknoll, NY: Orbis.

Neill, Stephen. 1970. *Christian Faith and Other Faiths: The Christian Dialogue with Other Religions.* 2nd ed. London: Oxford University Press.

———. 1986. *A History of Christian Missions.* 2nd ed. New York: Penguin.

Netland, Harold. 1991. *Dissonant Voices: Religious Pluralism and the Question of Truth.* Grand Rapids: Eerdmans.

Newbigin, Lesslie. 1995. *The Open Secret: An Introduction to the Theology of Mission.* Rev. ed. Grand Rapids: Eerdmans.

Nichols, Alan, ed. 1989. *The Whole Gospel for the Whole World: The Story of Lausanne II Congress on World Evangelization, Manila, 1989.* Charlotte: Lausanne Committee for World Evangelization.

Niebuhr, H. Richard. 1965. *The Social Sources of Denominationalism.* New York: Meridian. (Orig. pub. 1929.)

———. 1967. *The Meaning of Revelation.* New York: Macmillan.

———. 1993. *Radical Monotheism and Western Culture.* Louisville: Westminster John Knox. (Orig. pub. 1943.)

———. 1999. *The Responsible Self.* Louisville: Westminster John Knox. (Orig. pub. 1963.)

Niles, D. T. 1967. *Buddhism and the Claims of Christ.* Richmond: John Knox.

Olson, Bruce. 1978. *Bruchko.* Alamonte Springs, FL: Creation House.

Palmer, Phoebe. 1859. *Promise of the Father, or, A Neglected Specialty of the Last Days.* Boston: Henry V. Degen.

Panetta, Glayann Gilliam, ed. 2001. *Contrastive Rhetoric Revisited and Redefined.* Mahwah, NJ: Lawrence Erlbaum.

Papasogli, George. 1959. *Saint Ignatius Loyola.* New York: Society of St. Paul.

Pargament, K., et al. 1988. "Religion and the Problem-Solving Process: Three Styles of Coping." *Journal for the Scientific Study of Religion* 27: 90–104.

Parry, Jonathan. 1986. "The Gift, the Indian Gift, and the 'Indian Gift.'" *Man* 21 (3): 453–73.

Perez, Joseph. 2005. *The Spanish Inquisition: A History.* New Haven: Yale University Press.

Phan, Peter. 2004. *Being Religious Interreligiously: Asian Perspectives.* Maryknoll, NY: Orbis.

Phillips, James, and Robert Coote, eds. 1993. *Toward the 21st Century in Christian Missions: Essays in Honor of Gerald H. Anderson.* Grand Rapids: Eerdmans.

Phipps, William. 1991. *The Sheppards and Lapsley: Pioneer Presbyterians in the Congo.* Louisville: Presbyterian Church USA.

———. 2002. *William Sheppard: Congo's African American Livingstone.* Louisville: Geneva.

Pieper, Josef. 1962. *Guide to Thomas Aquinas.* New York: Random House.

Piper, John. 1993. *Let the Nations Be Glad! The Supremacy of God in Missions.* Grand Rapids: Baker Academic.

Plantinga, Richard, ed. 1999. *Christianity and Plurality: Classic and Contemporary Readings.* Oxford: Blackwell.

Plato. 2006. *Protagoras and Meno.* Edited by Lesley Brown and Adam Beversford. New York: Penguin Classics.

Pobee, John, and Gabriel Ositelu. 1998. *African Initiatives in Christianity: The Growth, Gifts, and Diversities of Indigenous African Churches.* Geneva: WCC.

Pocock, Michael, Gailyn Van Rheenen, and Douglas McConnell. 2005. *The Changing Face of World Missions: Engaging Contemporary Issues and Trends.* Grand Rapids: Baker Academic.

Pohl, Christine. 1999. *Making Room: Recovering Hospitality as a Christian Tradition.* Grand Rapids: Eerdmans.

Polanyi, Michael. 1964. *Personal Knowledge.* New York: Harper Torchbooks.

Pollock, John C. 1966. *Billy Graham: The Authorized Biography.* New York: McGraw-Hill.

Pollock, Sheldon. 1985. "The Theory of Practice and the Practice of Theory in Indian Intellectual History." *Journal of the American Oriental Society* 105 (3): 499–519.

———. 1993. "Deep Orientalism?" In *Orientalism and the Postcolonial Predicament,* edited by Caroll Breckenridge and Peter van der Meer, 76–133. Philadelphia: University of Pennsylvania Press.

Priest, Robert. 1994. "Missionary Elenctics: Conscience and Culture." *Missiology: An International Review* 22 (July): 291–315.

Rabinow, Paul. 1983. "Humanism as Nihilism." In *Social Science as Moral Inquiry,* edited by N. Hahn, R. N. Bellah, and W. M. Sullivan, 45–63. New York: Columbia University Press.

Radcliff-Brown, Alfred. 1922. *The Andamen Islanders.* Cambridge: Cambridge University Press.

Ramachandra, Vinoth. 1996. *The Recovery of Mission: Beyond the Pluralist Paradigm.* Grand Rapids: Eerdmans.

Ricci, Matteo. 1953. *China in the Sixteenth Century: The Journals of Matteo Ricci, 1583–1610.* Translated by Louis Gallagher. New York: Random House.

————. 1985. *The True Meaning of the Lord of Heaven*. Translated and with introduction and notes by Douglas Lancashire and Peter Hu Kuo-chen. Edited by Edward J. Malatesta. St. Louis: Institute of Jesuit Sources. (Orig. pub. 1601.)

Richardson, Don. 1981. *Eternity in Their Hearts*. Ventura, CA: Regal.

Robert, Dana. 1996. *American Women in Mission: A Social History of Their Thought and Practice*. Macon, GA: Mercer University Press.

Rogers, Everett. 1983. *Diffusion of Innovations*. 3rd ed. New York: Free Press.

Rommen, Edward, and Harold Netland, eds. 1995. *Christianity and the Religions: A Biblical Theology of World Religions*. Pasadena, CA: William Carey.

Rousseau, Jean-Jacques. 1959. "Les reveries du promeneur solitaire." In *Oeuvres completes*, edited by Marcel Raymond and Bernard Gagnebin, 1:1092–93. Paris: Gallimard.

Rowbotham, Arnold. 1942. *Missionary and Mandarin: The Jesuits at the Court of China*. Berkeley: University of California Press.

Rowley, Harold. 1945. *The Missionary Message of the Old Testament*. London: Carey.

Runciman, Steven. 1987. *A History of the Crusades*. Cambridge: Cambridge University Press.

Sanneh, Lamin. 1983. *West African Christianity: The Missionary Impact*. Maryknoll, NY: Orbis.

Scherer, James. 1987. *Gospel, Church, and Kingdom: Comparative Studies in World Mission Theology*. Minneapolis: Augsburg.

Schmidlin, Josef. 1933. *Catholic Mission History*. Translated by Matthias Braun. Techny, IL: Mission Press, SVD.

Schreiter, Robert. 1985. *Constructing Local Theologies*. Maryknoll, NY: Orbis.

Schrift, Alan, ed. 1997. *The Logic of the Gift: Toward an Ethic of Generosity*. New York: Routledge.

Seamands, J. T. 1981. *Tell It Well: Communicating the Gospel Across Culture*. Kansas City: Beacon Hill.

Shenk, Calvin. 1997. *Who Do You Say That I Am? Christians Encounter Other Religions*. Scottdale, PA: Herald Press.

Shenk, Wilbert. 1999. *Changing Frontiers of Mission*. Maryknoll, NY: Orbis.

Sheppard, William. 2006. *Pioneers in Congo*. Wilmore, KY: Wood Hill. (Orig. pub. 1921.)

Shorter, Aylward. 1972. *Theology of Mission*. Notre Dame, IN: Fides.

Sider, Ron. 1990. *Rich Christians in an Age of Hunger*. Dallas: Word.

Simpson, A. B. 1915. *The Gospel of Healing*. Harrisburg, PA: Christian Publications.

Skreslet, Stanley. 2006. *Picturing Christian Witness: New Testament Images of Disciples in Mission*. Grand Rapids: Eerdmans.

Smith, Archie. 1982. *The Relational Self: Therapy and the Black Church*. Nashville: Abingdon.

Smith, Dinitia. 2002. "A Black Adventurer in the Heart of Darkness." *New York Times*, January 8.

Smith, George. 1885. *The Life of William Carey*. London: John Murray.

Snook, Lee. 2000. *What in the World Is God Doing?* Minneapolis: Augsburg.

Snyder, Howard. 2001. *Models of the Kingdom*. Eugene, OR: Wipf and Stock.

Soni, D. L. 2001. *Significance of Dana*. Kuala Lumpur: Alatulis Dan Pencetak Capital Sdn Bhd.

Spalatin, Christopher. 1975. *Matteo Ricci's Use of Epictetus*. Taegu, Korea: Waegwan.

Spence, Jonathan. 1984. *The Memory Palace of Matteo Ricci*. New York: Penguin.

Spink, Kathryn. 1997. *Mother Teresa: A Complete Authorized Biography*. San Francisco: HarperCollins.

Stamoolis, James. 1986. *Eastern Orthodox Mission Theology Today*. Maryknoll, NY: Orbis.

Stanley, Brian. 1992. *The History of the Baptist Missionary Society, 1792–1992*. Edinburgh: T&T Clark.

Stark, Rodney. 1997. *The Rise of Christianity: How the Obscure, Marginal Jesus Movement Became the Dominant Religious Force in the Western World in a Few Centuries*. San Francisco: HarperOne.

Starke, Linda, ed. 2002. *State of the World 2002*. New York: W. W. Norton.

Starobinski, Jean. 1997. *Largesse*. Chicago: University of Chicago Press.

Stewart, Pamela, and Andrew Strathern. 2000. "Returns of the Gift, Returns from the Gift." *Journal of Ritual Studies* 14 (1): 52–59.

Storti, Craig. 1999. *Figuring Foreigners Out: A Practical Guide*. Yarmouth, ME: Intercultural.

Stott, John. 1975. *Christian Mission in the Modern World*. Downers Grove, IL: InterVarsity.

Strabo. 1930. *Geography*. Loeb Classical Library, vols. 15, 16, 17. Cambridge, MA: Harvard University Press.

Strong, John. 1978. "The Transforming Gift: An Analysis of Devotional Acts of Offering in Buddhist Avadana Literature." *History of Religion* 18: 221–37.

Tachiaos, Anthony-Emil N. 2001. *Cyril and Methodius of Thessalonica: The Acculturation of the Slavs*. Crestwood, NJ: St. Vladimir's Seminary.

Taylor, Charles. 1989. *Sources of the Self: The Making of Modern Identity*. Cambridge, MA: Harvard University Press.

Telford, Thomas. 1998. *Missions in the 21st Century*. Wheaton: Harold Shaw.

Thapar, Romila. 1994. "Sacrifice, Surplus, and the Soul." *History of Religions* 33: 305–24.

Thomas, Norman, ed. 1995. *Classic Texts in Mission and World Christianity*. Maryknoll, NY: Orbis.

———. 2004. "The Church at Antioch: Crossing Racial, Cultural, and Class Barriers." In *Mission in Acts: Ancient Narratives in Contemporary Context*, edited by Robert L. Gallagher and Paul Hertig, 144–56. Maryknoll, NY: Orbis.

Thomas Aquinas. 1975. *Summa Contra Gentiles*. Translated by Anton C. Pegis. Notre Dame, IN: University of Notre Dame Press. (Orig. pub. 1260.)

Tippett, Alan. 1987. *Introduction to Missiology*. Pasadena, CA: William Carey.

Tournier, Paul. 1963. *The Meaning of Gifts*. Richmond: John Knox.

Toynbee, Arnold. 1946. *A Study of History*. Oxford: Oxford University Press.

Travis, John. 1998. "The C1 to C6 Spectrum." *Evangelical Missions Quarterly* 34 (October): 407–8.

Tucker, Ruth. 1983. *From Jerusalem to Irian Jaya: A Biographical History of Christian Missions*. Grand Rapids: Zondervan.

———. 1988. *Guardians of the Great Commission: The Story of Women in Modern Missions*. Grand Rapids: Zondervan.

Van Engen, Charles, Dean Gilliland, and Paul Pierson, eds. 1993. *The Good News of the Kingdom: Mission Theology for the Third Millennium*. Maryknoll, NY: Orbis.

Verkuyl, Johannes. 1978. *Contemporary Missiology*. Translated by Dale Cooper. Grand Rapids: Eerdmans.

Vicedom, Georg. 1965. *The Mission of God: An Introduction to the Theology of Mission*. Translated by Gilbert Thiele and Dennis Hilgendorf. St. Louis: Concordia.

Vickery, Paul. 2006. *Bartolomé de Las Casas: Great Prophet of the Americas*. New York: Paulist Press.

Vlasto, A. D. 1970. *The Entry of the Slavs into Christendom*. Cambridge: Cambridge University Press.

Von Balthasar, Hans Urs. 1995. *Grains of Wheat: Aphorisms*. San Francisco: Ignatius.

Wacker, Grant. 2001. *Heaven Below: Early Pentecostals and American Culture*. Cambridge, MA: Harvard University Press.

Wagner, C. Peter. 2000. *Apostles and Prophets: The Foundation of the Church*. Ventura, CA: Regal.

Walls, Andrew. 1996. *The Missionary Movement in Christian History: Studies in the Transmission of the Faith*. Maryknoll, NY: Orbis.

———. 2002. *The Cross-Cultural Process in Christian History*. Maryknoll, NY: Orbis.

Ward, Ted. 1984. *Living Overseas: A Book of Preparations*. New York: Free Press.

Ware, Timothy. 1963. *The Orthodox Church*. New York: Penguin.

Weatherford, Jack. 2005. *Genghis Khan and the Making of the Modern World*. New York: Three Rivers.

Welliver, Dotsey, and Minnette Smith, eds. 2002. *Handbook of Schools and Professors of Missions and Evangelism*. Wheaton: EMIS.

Wink, Walter. 1992. *Engaging the Powers: Discernment and Resistance in a World of Domination*. Philadelphia: Fortress.

Winston, Diane. 1999. *Red Hot and Righteous: The Urban Religion of the Salvation Army*. Cambridge, MA: Harvard University Press.

Winter, Ralph, and Steven Hawthorne, eds. 1999. *Perspectives on the World Christian Movement: A Reader*. Pasadena, CA: William Carey.

Woodberry, J. Dudley, Charles Van Engen, and Edgar J. Elliston, eds. 1996. *Missiological Education for the Twenty-First Century*. Maryknoll, NY: Orbis.

Wyschogrod, Edith, et al., eds. 2002. *The Enigma of the Gift and Sacrifice*. New York: Fordham.

Yamamori, Tetsunao, Bryant Myers, and David Conner, eds. 1995. *Serving with the Poor in Asia*. Monrovia, CA: MARC.

Yang, C. K. 1961. *Religion in Chinese Society*. Berkeley: University of California Press.

Yates, Timothy. 1994. *Christian Mission in the Twentieth Century*. Cambridge: Cambridge University Press.

Yeoman, Barry. 2002. "The Stealth Crusade." *Mother Jones* (June): 42–49.

Yung, Hwa. 2002. *Mangoes or Bananas? The Quest for an Authentic Asian Christian Theology*. New York: Paternoster.

Zahniser, A. H. Matthias. 1997. *Symbol and Ceremony: Making Disciples Across Cultures*. Monrovia, CA: MARC.

Zwemer, Samuel. 1902. *Raymund Lull: First Missionary to the Moslems*. New York: Funk and Wagnalls.

Index

abandonment, 90
Abe, Masao, 361
Abraham, 82
accommodationism, 112, 146, 147
accommodators, 72
acculturation, 112
achievement, 236–37
action, 193
adaptation, 112, 142–43
Addai, 56
Adorno, Theodor, 265
Africa, 9, 66–68, 175, 177–78, 179–82, 257, 297–98
African Americans, 176–77
African Initiated Church movement, 66–67
"aggressive evangelism," 165, 169
agreements (disputation), 120, 122
agricultural metaphors, 303–4, 310, 311–12, 317
alcoholics, 169–70
Alexander (coppersmith), 89
Alexander the Great, 82
aliens, 212
Allen, Roland, 58
alms, 348–51, 362
Alopen, 56, 65
altruism, 360–61
American Board of Commissioners for Foreign Missions, 60
"American method," of evangelism, 165
Ananda, 343
anatta, 183

Anglican missions, 57–58
answer (disputation), 120–21, 122
anticonversionist model, 29
anticonversion laws, 209
Antioch, 88
anxiety, 372
Aquinas. *See* Thomas Aquinas
architectural metaphors, 310, 313
Aristotle, 38, 103, 117, 123, 130, 132–33, 135, 218, 242, 244, 264, 265
ascription, 236–37
Asia Missions Association, 66
Asian Christianity, 65–66, 139–40
asking questions, 258, 267
Assemblies of God, 61
assimilators, 72, 74
Association of International Missions Agencies, 62
atheism, 203
athletic metaphors, 310, 313–14
audience, 284
Augustine, 52, 95, 103, 121, 132, 368, 369
authority, 240–41, 278
autonomy, 236

backsliders, 90
Ballalasena, King, 343
bapakism, 235
baptism, 45
Baptist Missionary Society, 60, 153–54
Baptists, 59, 60

Bar-Jesus (Elymas), 89
Barrett, David, 8
Barth, Karl, 52, 286, 288, 289, 368
base gifts, 345
Basil the Great, 112
behaving, 69–70, 73–74, 100
beliefs, 231
believing, 101–3
Bellah, Robert, 199
belonging, 94, 95, 236, 237
    precedes believing, 100–103, 103, 374
Berger, Peter, 251, 253
bhikkhus, 183, 292
Bible
    authority of, 132–33, 241
    interpretation of, 35–50
    interreligious encounters in, 33–34, 379–85
    missional intent, 33
    norms in, 278
    on religious freedom, 18
    sufficiency of, 42
    as text, 13–14, 32–50
    translation of, 112
biblical criticism, 62
Billy Graham Evangelistic Association, 201
Blaikie, Ann, 194
Bob Jones College, 200, 204
Boethius, 339
Book of Common Prayer, 58
Booth, Catherine, 162–73, 210, 214, 375
Booth, William, 162–73
Boris the Great, 110
Braudel, Fernand, 364
Brazil, 228
Brethren, 60
"Bringing in the Sheaves" (hymn), 303, 312
Britain, 57, 98, 247–48
Buddhism, 15, 66, 123, 125, 139, 141–43, 146,
    183, 285–88
    on emptiness, 273–74
    in Europe and North America, 8
    gift-giving in, 343
    growth of, 27, 65
    understanding, 264–65
Buddhists
    love for, 212
    mission to, 8–10
    as neighbors, 16, 25
Bunyan, John, 316–17
Burma, 66
"but" phase, 354, 362–68

Calcutta, 187, 188–95, 245
Calvin, John, 52, 58, 59, 120, 252, 368
Calvinism, 52, 53, 152, 157, 172
Cannon, Dale, 71–72
canon law, 100
Carey, William, 28, 60, 61, 62, 150–61, 172,
    210, 375
caste system, 341
Celtic Christianity, 97
Celtic evangelism, 99, 101–2
Celtic faith, 15
Chang, Curtis, 117, 118
changes, 87, 290–91
character, 244, 278
charismatic missions, 61–62
charity, 185–97, 375–76
Charles V, 103
Chia, Roland, 234
China, 19, 65, 66, 138–47, 235, 239, 295–97, 375
Chinese language, 143–44
Chisholm, Robert, 36
Cho, David Yonggi, 62
Christ for the Nations, 62
Christianity
    among other world religions, 15, 27
    growth of, 27
    stagnation and decline of, 8
Christianity and Plurality (Plantinga), 37–39
Christianity and the Religions (Rommen and
    Netland), 35–37, 39
Christian Mission. See Salvation Army
Christian missions, failure of, 8–10
Christians and politics, 45
Christology, 37
Chrysostom, John, 112
church
    global and local expressions, 112–13
    purity of, 95
    Roman Catholics on, 54
    serves the gospel, 200
Church Missionary Society (CMS), 57
Church of England, 153
Church of God Cleveland, 61
circumcision, 87, 358
civil rights movement, 205
clarity, 122–23
Clement XI, 147
Codrington, Robert, 58
coercive power, 371–72
cognitive vs. relational development, 234
Coke, Thomas, 61
collaborative approach (problem-solving), 70, 73

collectivism, 239
colonialism, 30, 54, 64, 151, 182
Columbus, 128, 131, 132, 133
comfort zone, 233, 247
comic outlook, 70, 73
commitment, 115–26, 374
commodification, of gift-giving, 339
common loyalty, 275
communalism, 235–36, 237, 316, 332
communication, 251, 264, 372
    and bracketing of convictions, 261
    and gift-giving, 332
    theology as, 53
communications, 17
communicative reason, 264, 265
community, 52, 87, 94, 97, 99, 102, 358
compassion, 241
compatibility, 168
competition, 28, 29–30, 372
    among world religions, 10, 16
    in church-state sphere, 23–25
    in missions and evangelism, 26
complexity, 168
conceiving the world, theology as, 53
Confucianism, 16, 139, 141–45, 235
Congo, 175–76, 177–78, 179, 180–82
Congregationalists, 59, 60
Congregation for the Propagation of the Faith, 55
conquest, 134, 264
Conrad, Joseph, 178
consistency, 150–61, 375
constructive, theology as, 52
contemplation, 193
context, 13–14, 77, 243, 271, 278, 283
contextualization, 53, 73, 112, 147, 149, 251, 262
contextual knowledge, 69
continuum, of identity theories, 235–38
control, 371
convergers, 72
conversation, 122
conversion, 28–29, 45
converts, Paul on, 84–85
convictions, 238–40
    bracketing of, 225–26, 229, 240, 249–62, 278, 289, 298
    reengagement of, 226–27, 229, 277, 283
cooperation, 28–29, 44, 331–32
    among world religions, 16, 47
Cornelius, 47, 81, 87
creation, 38, 123

cross-cultural exchange, 369–70
cross-cultural mission, 60
Crusades, 136, 196, 204
crusades (Billy Graham rallies), 201, 204, 313
cultural anthropology, 232
cultural carriers, 22, 23
cultural relativism, 41
cultural sensitivity, 10
culture
    changes in, 44
    complexity of, 199
    evaluated by gospel story, 363–68
    transformation of, 45
Cunningham, Loren, 62
cursing stone, 270–71
customs, 231
Cyril, 104–14, 199, 210, 214, 374
Cyrillic alphabet, 110, 111

Dalai Lama, 241
dana, 343, 344, 360
Darjeeling, 186, 188
Darwinism, 62
de Decker, Jacqueline, 194
deferring approach (problem-solving), 70, 74
Demetrius, 89
de Nobili, Roberto, 55
De Paor, Máire B., 93
desertion, 90
de Silva, David, 183
De Smet, Pierre-Jean, 148
determinism, 360–61
devotion, 71
devotional gift giving, 348–51, 362
Dewey, John, 275
dharmasastra, 344, 351
dialogue, 39, 218
    as pre-evangelical, 145
    vs. evangelism, 44, 47–48
disagreements (disputation), 120, 122
disciple-making, 50
dispositions, 68
disputatio, 117–23
dissonance, 259, 270–71
divergers, 72, 74
Dominicans, 116, 118, 135
Donatists, 95
"do-nothing" approach to mission, 7, 159, 244
Donovan, Vincent, 257, 273, 274–75, 281–82, 297–98
DuPlessis, David, 62

Eastern gift-giving, 331, 341–46, 347, 356–58, 360–62, 366–67
economism, 17, 21–23
ecumenism. *See* missional ecumenism
Edwards, Jonathan, 52
effectiveness, 138–49, 375
Eliot, T. S., 305
Elizabeth I, 57
Elliot, Jim, 63
emptiness, 273–74
encomienda system, 103, 128–29, 132, 133, 217
encountering, 229, 263–76, 289, 298
enculturation, 147
Enlightenment, 37, 135, 255, 265
Enquiry into the Obligations to Use Means for the Conversion of the Heathens (Carey), 153, 155–60
Epicureans, 89
equality, 239, 241, 242
eschatological hope, 65
eschatology, 50
essentialist vs. social self, 234
ethnocentrism, 113
evaluation, 277–89, 298
evangelical missions, 62–64
exclusions, in missions, 199
exclusivism, 37
experience, 132, 218–19, 225, 230–48, 289, 298
  directs learning, 252–53
  externalization, 253

fairness, 241
faithfulness, 9–10
Falwell, Jerry, 71
fear, 373
fearlessness, gifts of, 346
feeling/valuing, 71–72
fellowship, 71, 92–102, 374
Ferdinand, 132, 133, 135
festivals, 201, 204
field, 283–84
Finney, Charles, 165, 176
Finney, John, 99
First Amendment, 24
foreign missions, 8
foremeanings, 255, 257–59
Fort William College, 154
Franciscans, 135
Francis of Assisi, 287
Free Churches of England, 172
free church missions, 59–61
freedom, 127–37, 359, 366, 374

freedom of religion, 18–20, 22, 24, 25, 28
freedom of speech, 241
free gift, 329–30, 334–36, 340, 346
Fromm, Eric, 70
fruits of the Spirit, 100
Fuller, Andrew, 154, 172
fundamentalist-modernist controversy, 62–63

Gadamer, Hans-Georg, 255, 258, 259
Gallagher, Louis J., 140
Ganin, Siddhasena, 343
gender equality, 241
General Missionary Convention of the Baptist Denomination, 60
generosity, 339
  in New Testament, 324, 325
  in Old Testament, 321, 322
Gentiles, 81–83, 87, 88, 207
German mission, 109–10
getting the message, 267, 273–75
gift, metaphor of, 10, 301, 320–25, 328, 354
gift-giving, 362–65, 370–71, 372
giftive mission, 7, 10–11, 51, 221–23, 245–46, 301, 353–77
gifts, 191
  in New Testament, 323, 325
  in Old Testament, 320, 322
gift theory and practice, 330
Gill, Robin, 99
Gilligan, Carol, 236
giving
  in New Testament, 322–23, 325
  in Old Testament, 320, 322
globalization, 17–18, 19, 22, 28, 65, 203, 235, 369, 370–71
Gnanakan, Ken, 65
gnosticism, 14, 15
goals, 242–43, 244, 278
God
  as God of all religions, 44, 48
  as personal, 281–82
  sovereignty of, 59, 157
  suffering of, 289
  transcendence and immanence of, 38
Goethe, 339
Golden Rule, 50
good gifts, 345
Good Samaritan, 247
Gordon, A. J., 62
gospel story, evaluates cultures, 363–68
government resources, 195
grace, 10, 83, 326–28, 359, 360, 366

Graham, Billy, 63, 198–206, 210, 214, 312–13, 376
Graham, Franklin, 201, 204
Graham, Ned, 201
Graham, Ruth, 200
gratitude
  in New Testament, 324–25
  in Old Testament, 321, 322
Great Awakening, 176
Great Commandment, 50, 376
Great Commission, 50, 152, 153, 155
Great Commission missions, 63–64, 376
Great Model, 50
Great Schism of 1054, 56
Great Transformation, 50
greed, 31, 366
Greek language, 110
Greek philosophy, 38
Gregory the Theologian, 112
Grotius, 137
Grove, Cornelius, 239
Gurevitch, Zali, 260–61, 274, 276

Habermas, Jürgen, 264, 265
Ham, Mordecai, 200
happiness, in God, 124, 126
Harris, Elizabeth, 183
harvesting image. See agricultural metaphors
healing metaphor clusters, 315
hearing well, 257
Hearst, Randolph, 201
heathen, 28
Hegel, G. W. F., 259
Heidegger, Martin, 270
Heim, Maria, 342, 344, 345
Hellenists, 86, 87
Hemacandra, 343
Hemadri, 343
Henry, Carl, 63
Henry VIII, 57
heresy, 125
hermeneutical circle, 28
Hinduism, 66, 123, 139, 292
  gift-giving in, 342–43
  growth of, 27, 65
Hindus
  love for, 212
  and Mother Teresa, 195, 196
  as neighbors, 15–16, 25
history, 349
holiness, 165
holistic, metaphor clusters as, 316

"holy pagans," 47
Holy Spirit, 43, 280–81
  and missions, 61–62, 67–68, 158, 223–24
  power of, 355
  presence in all things, 281, 282
  and work of Paul, 89
honor/respect, and gift-giving, 333
hope, 373
Hopewell, James, 70
horizon of meaning, 227–29, 289, 290–99
Horkeimer, Max, 265
hospitality, for the stranger, 27, 30, 268
Howell, Don, 37
human nature, 22
human rights, 18, 239
humility, of giving, 355–56
Hunter, George, 99

idealists, 38
identity, 234–38
idolatry, 37
Ignatius Loyola, 55, 140
image of God, 22, 48, 120, 180, 359, 363
immigration, 67
imperialism, 30, 64, 151
incidental nature, of African missions, 67
inclusion, in missions, 199
inclusivism, 37
independence, 236, 237
India, 66, 154, 159, 160, 186
Indian gift-giving, 341–42, 360–62
Indians, American, 129–35
indigenization, 56, 57–58, 66, 67
indigenous gift-giving, 331–36, 347, 356–59, 365–66
individualism, 135, 235–36, 237
Indonesia, 225, 235, 243
Industrial Revolution, 163, 164
informal contacts, 369
inner city, 164
Innocent IV, Pope, 125
Inquisition, 125, 161
Institute for Theological Education of Bahia, 228
integrating horizon of meaning, 227–29, 289, 290–99
intentions, of gift-giving, 344
internalization, 253
internal warnings, bracketing of, 259–60
Internet, 369, 372
interreligious encounters, 75, 205, 208
  in the Bible, 379–85

intra-Christian interactions, 204, 207
intra-group harmony, 239
Ireland, 93, 98, 100
ironic outlook, 71
irony, of gift-giving, 329
Isabella, 128, 131, 132, 133, 135
Islam, 15, 66, 123, 125
    growth of, 8, 27, 65
    religious freedom in, 19
Israel, 38

Jains, 343–44
Japan, 287
jargon, 122
Javanese, 243
Jerusalem council, 87
Jesuits, 140, 141, 143, 145
Jesus
    incarnation of, 38
    invitation to fellowship, 99–100
    as mission innovator, 210–15
Jewish-Christian interactions, 207–8
Jewish evangelism (Paul), 101–2
Jewish proselytizers, 85, 86
Jews
    Billy Graham on, 202, 204–5
    expelled from France, 136
    and Gentiles, 81–83, 207
    and Palestinians, 274, 276
Jim Crow laws, 176
John Paul II, Pope, 55
Johnson, Mark, 307–8
Johnson, Todd, 8
Jonah, 91, 269
journeying metaphor, 316–17
Judaism, 15
judgment, 50, 53, 327
Judson, Adoniram, 60, 61, 66
justice, 30–31, 239, 288

kairos moment, 232, 246
Kant, Immanuel, 265
Khan, Güyük, 125
King, Martin Luther, Jr., 42, 205, 288
kingdom of God, 50, 65
Kitamore, Kazoh, 65
knowing, 72, 73–74
knowledge, and exegesis, 69
Kohlberg, Lawrence, 236
Kolb, David A., 72
Korea, 9, 139
Köstenberger, Andreas, 37

Koyama, Kōsuke, 65, 284–89, 294, 369
kula system, 332

Lakoff, George, 307–8
Laksmidhara, Bhatta, 343
Lancashire, Douglas, 145–46
language, learning, 156
Lapsley, Samuel, 177–78, 179
Larkin, William, 36
Las Casas, Bartolomé de, 55, 103, 127–37, 210,
    214, 217, 374
Latin, 106, 109
lawful means, 152, 155, 158, 159, 160
learning, 224, 346
Learning Style Inventory, 72
Legge, James, 58
Leopold, King, 177
Leo XIII, Pope, 117
Levin, David Michael, 270
liberation theologies, 65, 66
lifestyle, 101
listening, 266–67, 269–72
little children, 253–54
lived methodology, 285
Livingstone, David, 67
local church, 114
localization, 104–14, 374
London, East End, 163, 164, 166–69
London Missionary Society, 60
Lotz, Anne Graham, 201
Louis IX, 136
love, 190–91, 193, 279–80, 282
    for enemies, 27, 30, 41, 212
    for God, 214, 215
    for neighbor, 27–28, 30, 31, 41, 50, 211–15
    and understanding, 264
Luke, 88
Luther, Martin, 52, 58, 289, 368
Lutheran missions, 58–59

Mahayana Buddhism, 141, 142
mainline church missions, 58–59
Malaysia, 226
Malinowski, Bronislaw, 332, 351
Manifest Destiny, 177
manipulation, 11
Manitowish Community Church (Wisconsin),
    170–71
market economy, 235, 366
    and gift-giving, 336–41
market metaphors, 10, 310, 314–16, 317, 319,
    372–73

marketplace
  and conversion, 29
  evangelism in, 23–25
  of religious ideas, 16–23
Marshman, Joshua, 154
Martyn, Henry, 58
Marxism, 62
Masai culture, 281–82, 297–98
mass-marketing approaches to missions, 26
material gifts, 346
Mathews, Ed, 36
Mauss, Marcel, 329–31, 332, 333, 335, 343, 347
McClendon, James, 42, 288
Mead, George Herbert, 236, 275
meaning, 258
  as socially constructed, 251–52, 253
means, of missions. *See* lawful means
measuring instrument, 278–79, 280
meditation, 44, 48
megachurches, 114
Melchizedek, 47
Mennonites, 60
mercy, 53, 327
messengers, 221–22
metaphor clusters, 310–11, 315–17
metaphors, 282, 303–28, 354
  as changing, 317, 318
  as communal, 318
  as complex, 307, 308, 311, 318
  as everything, 306–7, 308
  as human constructs, 317
  as literary device, 305–7, 308
  as provisional, 318–19
Methodism, 59, 163, 176
Methodius, 104–14, 199, 210, 214, 374
methods, of ministry, 173
migration, 67
military chaplains, religious diversity among, 24
military metaphors, 310, 312–13, 319
Mills, Samuel, 61
mind of Christ, 43
Minjung theologians, 65
miracles, 61
missio Dei, 64–65
missio externa, 87, 88, 147, 206, 211
missio interna, 87, 99, 147, 206, 211
missiometrics, 159
mission
  centrality of, 152, 158, 159
  and establishment of churches, 45
  as God's mission, 64
  grows out of experience, 222–23

  as Spirit-directed, 223–24
  as two-directional, 223
missional ecumenism, 64–65, 198–209, 376–77
Missionaries of Charity, 189, 192, 194
mission boards, 176
mission metaphors, 368–69
mission societies, 159
modernity, 39
monasticism, 100, 102
Mongols, 125
Montesinos, Antonio, 129, 133, 135
Moravia, 107–10
Morrison, William, 179, 180
Mother Teresa, 185–97, 199–200, 209, 214, 217, 241, 245, 375–76
Muggeridge, Malcolm, 192
Muslims, 130
  in Indonesia, 292
  love for, 212
  as neighbors, 16, 25
  on prayer, 228
  and Qur'an, 240
  Thomas Aquinas on, 117–18, 121, 124, 126, 374
mutuality, 191
mystery religions, 85, 86–87
mystical quest, 72, 74

national churches, 57, 112–13, 114
nation-states, 30–31, 372
natural law, 137
need, of missionaries, 222
needs, hierarchies of, 236
Nee, Watchman, 66, 369
negative tolerance, 19–20, 28
neighborhood, 369–70
  ethics, 25–26
  as global, 369
neighbors, 211–15, 247
Neill, Stephen, 44, 45, 57
neo-Confucianists, 146–47
Nestorian missionaries, 141, 142
Netland, Harold, 35–37, 39
Newbigin, Lesslie, 65
new religious movements, 19
New Testament
  gift metaphor in, 322–25
  interreligious encounters in, 384–85
Niebuhr, H. Richard, 199, 243, 275
Nineveh, 91, 269
Nixon, Richard, 202
non-Christian religions, origin of, 44, 49

norm, 278–79, 280
Northwestern Bible College, 201
nuclear weapons, 209
numerical success, 10

objectivation, 253
"objective" truth, 255
obligation, 354, 358
    of gift-giving, 333–34, 344
obvious differences, bracketing of, 259
Oceania, 9
Oduyoye, Mercy Amba, 369
Old Testament
    gift metaphor in, 320–22
    interreligious encounters in, 379–84
Olson, Bruce, 63
"Only Method of Converting the Indians"
    (Las Casas), 134
"Onward Christian Soldiers" (hymn), 312
openness, 218, 226, 261
opponent's answers (disputation), 119–20, 122
Orthodox missions, 55–57, 114
Orthodox theology, 112
Osirian mystery religions, 14, 85

pagan belief systems, 15
pain of God theology, 65
Pakistan, 236
Palestinians and Jews, 274, 276
Panikkar, Raymundo, 65
parachurch, 63
Parākramabāji I, 343
Pargament, Kenneth, 69
Particular Baptists, 153, 157, 158, 172
partnership concept, 59
passionate gifts, 345
Patrick, 92–102, 199, 210, 214, 217, 374
patronato real, 54
Paul
    in Athens, 46, 48, 73–74, 89, 218, 227
    contextual theology of, 36
    evangelism of, 100–102
    on gift-giving, 358–59
    as idealist and pragmatist, 89
    on the marketplace, 21
    on mind of Christ, 43
    on rewards to messengers and receivers,
        221–22
    universality of, 79–92, 199, 210, 373
    use of metaphors, 319
    on world religions, 36, 37
Paul III, Pope, 135, 140

Peirce, C. S., 275
Pelagian heresy, 98
Pentateuch, 36
Pentecostal missions, 61–62
personal interactions, 369
personality, 51, 68–72, 73, 233
personal knowledge, 69
personhood, 359
perspective, 41
Pharisees, 48
Phillip, Prince, 135
philosophy, 22, 38
Pieper, Josef, 119–22
Pieris, Aloysius, 65
pietism, 176
Plantinga, Richard, 37–39
Plato, 38, 272
pluralism, 37, 39. See also religious pluralism
Pocock, Michael, 36
poor, 50, 164, 167, 190–97
Portugal, 54
Portuguese missions, 141–42
positive tolerance, 20
potlatch ceremony, 332
power, 11, 19, 239, 355, 371–72
practices, 77–78
pragmatism, 165, 166
prayer, 156, 187
predestination, 60
pre-evangelistic dialogue, 145–46, 147
prejudices, 253, 254–57, 258, 271
Presbyterians, 175–76, 178–81, 228
presuppositions. See pre-texts
pre-texts, 14, 51–52
    blinding by, 252
Primitive Methodists, 164, 166
principles, 241–42, 278
problem solving, 69
process, of ministry, 173
proof texting, 41
prophets, 36
Protestant Christian hegemony, 23–24
providence, 194
provincialism, 151
psychotherapy, religion as, 22
public respect, 181

question (disputation), 119, 122
questions, 272–73
Qur'an, 240, 261

Rabinow, Paul, 232, 293
racial identity, 205–6, 208

racism, 182
Rastislav, 109
rationalism, 172
realists, 38
realpolitik, 18, 31
reason, 117, 123–24, 265
reasoned inquiry, 72, 74
reassessment, 258
receivers, 221–22, 245
receiving
    in New Testament, 323–24, 325
    in Old Testament, 321, 322
reciprocation, of gift-giving, 334, 346, 358
reconciliation, 208
redistribution, 332–33, 342
reflexive evangelism, 16, 23–28
Reformation, 37, 58–59
Reformed missions, 59
rejection
    of beliefs, 292–93
    of Paul, 89–90
relationships, 251
    and bracketing of convictions, 261–62
relativism, 20, 293
relevance, 71
religion
    in general, devalued as commodity, 22–23
    as generic category, 17–18
    and political power, 19
    Thomas Aquinas's definition, 126
religious differences, bracketing of, 260
religious freedom. See freedom of religion
religious gift giving, 346–51
religious homogeneity, 30
religious pluralism, 15, 18, 30–31, 36, 37–39,
    205, 366
Religious Problem-Solving Scale, 69–70
religious relativism, 41
remembering, 247
replacement outcome, 293
rescue metaphor clusters, 315
researcher, 284
respect, 174–84, 375
    in community, 181
    for self, 181
responsibility ethics, 275
responsive missions, 376
retribution, 241, 272
revelation, 69, 123
revival meetings, 165, 166, 168, 200, 201
Ricci, Matteo, 138–49, 210, 304, 375
Richard, Timothy, 295–97

Richard the Lion-Hearted, 196
rich young ruler, 49
right action, 71
Rites Controversy, 145–49
ritual, of gift-giving, 345
ritual remembrance, 348–51
Roberts, Oral, 70
Rogers, June and Jack, 228
Roman Catholic missions, 54–55
Roman Catholics, Billy Graham on, 204
Roman Empire, 81–82, 95, 97, 98, 109–10
Roman evangelism, 101–2
Romanticism, 70, 172
Rommen, Edward, 35–37, 39
Roosevelt, Theodore, 180
Rousseau, Jean-Jacques, 338, 339
Royce, Josiah, 275
Ruggieri, Michele, 141
Runciman, Steven, 196
Russia, 110
Russian Orthodox Church, 112
Ryland, John, 154, 172
Ryland, John, Jr., 172

sacred rite, 71
sacrifice, 165, 348–51
Saladin, 196
salvation, of adherents of non-Christian reli-
    gions, 44, 46–47
Salvation Army, 163–73
Samaritan woman, 47, 252
Samartha, Stanley, 65
Samoa, 333
Samuel, Vinay, 65, 66
Sanford, Henry Shelton, 177
Schmidlin, Josef, 55
scholasticism, 41, 119
Schuller, Robert, 70
scientism, 65
Scripture. See Bible
second wave (Pentecostal missions), 61
secularism, 203
secularization, 22, 65
self, 233–34, 238
self-criticism, 362–63
self-directing approach (problem-solving), 70
self-giving, 348–51
selflessness (kenosis), 360–61
self-reliance, 240
self-sacrifice, 362
selling spiritual products, 26
sending and receiving churches, 59

seniority, 237
sensationalism, 122
sensus divinitatus, 120
separation, in mission, 232
separation of church and state, 19, 22, 60
separatism, 47, 60, 206
Sepúlveda, Juan Ginés de, 103, 131, 132, 264
Serampore College, 154
Sergius Paulus, 88
Sermon on the Mount, 42
Serra, Junípero, 55
Seville, 131
Seward, Rick, 62
shamanic meditation, 72
shang-ti, 144, 147
sheep and goats parable, 42
sheep-stealing, 125
Shembe, Isaiah, 67
Sheppard, Lucy, 179, 182
Sheppard, William, 174–84, 210, 214, 375
Siddhārtha Gautama Buddha, 264
signs and wonders movement, 61
Simons, Menno, 52
simplicity, of Paul's universality, 83
Simpson, A. B., 62
Singapore, 234
Sisters of Charity, 195, 245, 375
Sitting Bull, 148
Sixtus IV, Pope, 161
Six Ways of Being Religious (Cannon), 71–72
Skreslet, Stanley, 310–11, 315
slavery, 130, 132–33, 137, 176–77, 178, 180, 182
Slavs, 105–6, 107, 108, 110, 111–12, 374
Smith, Archie, 236
Snook, Lee, 281, 282
socialization, 256, 283
social justice, 45, 180
social self, 275
Society for Promoting Christian Knowledge
    (SPCK), 57
Society for the Propagation of the Faith, 55
Society for the Propagation of the Gospel in
    Foreign Parts, 57
Society of Friends, 242
sociology, religion as, 22
Soka Gakkai Buddhism, 241
Somadeva, 345
South Africa, 205
Southern Baptists, 60, 200
Spain, 54
    conquest of New World, 103, 128–32, 133
spheres, of biblical interpretation, 35–50

Spink, Kathryn, 194
spiral of knowledge, 219, 224–29, 293–94, 298
Spirit baptism, 61
spiritual practices, of other religions, 44, 48
spiritual warfare, 50, 370
Sri Lanka, 183, 270–72, 292
stage theories of development, 236
standard, 278, 280, 282
statistics, use of, 159–60
Stillman, Charles, 179
Stillman College, 178, 182
"still" phase, 354, 368–73
Stoics, 89
story, 117–18, 247, 364–65
storytelling metaphor clusters, 315
Strabo, 82
"subjective" knowledge, 255, 307
success, 9–10
suffering, 222, 245, 289
Sumatra, 243
Sung, John, 66
Suracarya, 344
Suri, Devendra, 343
Sutcliff, John, 154, 172
Svetopolk, 109
syncretism, 37, 67

Tachiaos, Anthony-Emil N., 108
talents, parable of, 293
talismans, gifts as, 334
Taoism, 141–43, 146
Taylor, Charles, 233–34, 239, 287
technical reason, 265
10/40 window, 8
Ten Commandments, 100
terrorism, 209
text, Bible as, 13–14, 32–50
Thailand, 284–89, 294
theologizing, 70–71
theology, 51
    of giving, 222
    integration with culture, 287
    as interpretive grid, 52–68
    of ministry, 173
Theology I, 53
Theology II, 54
Theravada, 292
thinking, 73–74
third wave (Pentecostal missions), 61
Thomas, John, 154
Thomas, M. M., 65

Thomas Aquinas, 52, 115–26, 145, 210, 218, 286, 288, 289, 368, 369
 on Muslims, 117–18, 121, 124, 126, 374
 on witnessing, 124
Tierra Firma (Venezuela), 132
Tillich, Paul, 52
time, 349
Tinker, George, 148
tolerance, 20, 293
Torquemada, Juan de, 161
Torquemada, Tomás de, 161
tracts, of La Casas, 131
tradition, 53
traditional mission efforts, 8
tragic outlook, 70–71, 74
transformation, in Anglican missions, 57
travel, 369–70
trialability, 83, 169
tribalization, 203
trilingualism, 106, 113
Trinity, Patrick on, 95–97
triumphalism, 11
truth, in non-Christian religions, 44, 45, 46

Ulfilas, 56
unbelief, 203
understanding, 251, 263–64, 283
 and bracketing of convictions, 260–61
 reordering of, 272
United Methodists, 59
United Nations Declaration of Human Rights, 18, 137
United States Constitution, 18, 19
universal, meanings of, 82
universal and particular, 38–39
universality, 37, 58, 79–92
urbanization, 67

Valignano, Alessandro, 141, 143
values, 14, 73–74, 238–44, 248, 359
Van Exem, Celeste, 192, 193
variety, 162–73, 375
vernacular, missions in, 57
Verner, S. Phillips, 179
violence, 287–88, 312
virtue, 126
Vitoria, Francisco de, 137
Vladimir, 110
voluntary agencies, 63

walking together, 275–76
walking with the other, 267
Walls, Andrew, 295
war, 287
Ward, William, 154
warfare metaphor, 157–58, 204
Warnack, Gustav, 58
Washington, Booker T., 178
water buffalo theology, 65, 284–89, 294
way of measuring, 278–79
"way of the strange," 274–75
weak, 191
Weatherford, Jack, 125
Wenzhong, Hu, 239
Wesley, John, 52, 58, 59, 120, 164, 368, 369
Wesleyanism, 53, 163
Western civilization, 139–40, 149, 177, 224
Western gift-giving, 331, 336–41, 347, 356–58, 359–60, 366
Western philosophy, 38
Wheaton College, 200
Whitefield, George, 60
Wiching, Bishop, 113
"wipe them out" response, 7, 244
wisdom literature, 36
witnessing, 51, 101, 124
women
 in leadership, 164, 166
 in Malaysian Islamic culture, 226
 and relationships, 236
World Council of Churches, 64–65, 67
world culture. See globalization
worldview, 251
World Vision, 241
worship, 252, 271, 272

Xavier, Francis, 55, 65–66, 141, 143

"yes" phase, 354, 355–61
yoga, 44, 48
Youth for Christ, 201
Youth with a Mission (YWAM), 62

Zechariah, 268
Ziegenbalg, Bartholomaeus, 59, 159
Zinzendorf, Nikolaus Ludwig von, 59